CROWN JEWEL
WILDERNESS

CROWN JEWEL WILDERNESS

CREATING NORTH CASCADES NATIONAL PARK

LAUREN DANNER

WSU
PRESS

Washington State University
Pullman, Washington

WSU PRESS
WASHINGTON STATE UNIVERSITY

Washington State University Press
PO Box 645910
Pullman, Washington 99164-5910
Phone: 800-354-7360
Fax: 509-335-8568
Email: wsupress@wsu.edu
Website: wsupress.wsu.edu

Library of Congress Cataloging-in-Publication Data

Names: Danner, Lauren, 1967-
Title: Crown Jewel Wilderness : Creating North Cascades National Park /
    Lauren Danner.
Description: Pullman, Washington : Washington State University Press, 2017. |
    Includes bibliographical references and index.
Identifiers: LCCN 2017022063 | ISBN 9780874223521 (alk. paper)
Subjects: LCSH: North Cascades National Park (Wash.)--History.
Classification: LCC F897.C3 D26 2017 | DDC 979.7/73--dc23 LC record available at
    https://lccn.loc.gov/2017022063

On the cover: Sahale Glacier Camp, North Cascades National Park. Andy Porter Images,
www.andyporterimages.com

Maps by Chelsea Feeney, www.cmcfeeney.com

Contents

Illustrations

Maps

Tables

Introduction

A "Stupendous, Primitive Wilderness"

In September 1939, Bob Marshall stood on the crest of the Cascade Range and reveled in the view. Extravagantly forested valleys below gave way to broad alpine meadows awaiting autumn's first snow flurries. More than a dozen eponymous glaciers carved the flanks of nearby Glacier Peak, the most isolated of the range's five major volcanoes. A sea of white-capped mountains dissolved into the blue horizon.

The mountains captivated Marshall, America's foremost wilderness advocate and co-founder of the Wilderness Society.[1] Writing anonymously in the organization's inaugural newsletter in 1935, Marshall urged the preservation of the North Cascades, the "second largest potential forest wilderness remaining in the United States," located just two hours from Seattle.[2] Four years later, Marshall stood deep in those wild mountains at one of the most scenic spots in the country. On government business in his role as the United States Forest Service's Director of Recreation and Lands, he surveyed the national forests, seeking areas whose aesthetic qualities and potential for backcountry recreation merited reservation from logging, grazing, and other uses allowed by the agency.

An indefatigable hiker who considered thirty miles a minimum daily walk, Marshall backpacked through some of the wildest places in the United States wearing high-top sneakers, a denim shirt, and jeans.[3] With a doctorate in plant physiology from Johns Hopkins University, he was a trained forester who felt "a great need to use every available hour to absorb raw Nature."[4] In his career with the Forest Service, Marshall consistently urged more national forest land be set aside for wilderness and drafted stronger wilderness preservation policies.

When Marshall trekked through the North Cascades in 1939, the region was relatively unknown. Indigenous peoples used the mountains as travel and trade corridors and for subsistence and shelter for millennia, but Euro-American explorers and settlers did little more than nibble at the edges, daunted by "immensity beyond the scope of description or imagination."[5] Since the mid-nineteenth century, the mountains' rugged

1

beauty has inspired comparison with the Swiss Alps. Even in the middle of the twentieth century, writers intimate with the Cascades observed much of the northern range was "largely wilderness, with vast areas still unexplored, inaccessible."[6]

The Cascade Range is the Pacific Northwest's defining geographic feature. Rising to more than fourteen thousand feet at Mount Rainier, the highest peak in the range, the mountains run north-south from British Columbia to northern California. The North Cascades, a tumult of precipitous, glaciated peaks partitioned by narrow valleys and usually considered a subregion of the larger range, extend northward about one hundred miles from Stevens Pass to Canada's Fraser River. Formed primarily by geologic uplift, Mount Baker and Glacier Peak are volcanic punctuation marks at roughly opposite corners of the range. At one hundred miles across from east to west, the northern Cascades is "one of the great ranges of North America—an overwhelming confusion of high ridges, glaciers, sharp peaks, and deep, wild valleys."[7]

Dizzying vertical relief, a measure of mountain steepness, distinguishes the North Cascades from the rest of the range. Mountains soar imposingly from low valleys to high summits, creating breathtakingly jagged vistas and strenuous hiking. Mount Baker, the westernmost big peak in the region and the third-tallest mountain in Washington, attains 10,775 feet barely thirty miles from Puget Sound. Glacier Peak, the tallest southernmost summit in the North Cascades, reaches 10,541 feet only sixty miles from salt water. Less well-known peaks are equally impressive. Though only ten peaks exceed nine thousand feet in elevation, the North Cascades' vertical relief is unmatched in the contiguous United States.[8]

Such towering heights forge an intimidating landscape of alpine majesty, where mountain monikers leave little doubt of the exertion required to get closer than a roadside pullout. Mount Fury, Sinister Peak, Mount Terror, Damnation Peak, Mount Challenger, Desolation Peak, Mount Formidable, Mount Despair, Forbidden Peak, and Mount Redoubt announce the region's rugged remoteness and suggest the hardships early explorers faced and contemporary mountaineers relish. The North Cascades' desolately spectacular high terrain contains nearly half of all glaciers found in the lower forty-eight states.

Marshall's 1939 journey to the North Cascades was a repeat visit. As part of a Forest Service effort to address increasing recreational use, he inspected vast, roadless areas of the national forests in 1937 and 1938, including much of the North Cascades. Back at camp, he drew rough boundaries on maps suggesting proposed wilderness areas. Marshall believed these highly scenic portions of the national forests should be set aside to protect their aesthetic qualities and to offer unmechanized recreation for those hardy souls who sought it. For Marshall, wilderness was a use to which land could be put, like timber, water, or grazing.[9]

Well before Marshall's trip, the Forest Service had set aside more than a million acres in the North Cascades for wilderness recreation or scenery, largely to stave off National Park Service attempts to transfer those lands to national park status. In 1931, the Forest Service reserved nearly a quarter-million acres around Glacier Peak and another 172,800 acres near the Canadian border north of Mount Baker for scenic and recreation values. Pressured by wilderness advocates, the Forest Service in 1935 expanded the smaller, northern unit to 801,000 acres and renamed it the North Cascade Primitive Area.[10] Under agency rules adopted in 1929, both areas were set aside to preserve their primitive conditions, but the designations could be undone with the stroke of an administrator's pen, potentially reopening the region to logging and mining.

The North Cascades should be a Forest Service priority, Marshall believed, and nearly all the land between Glacier Peak and the North Cascade Primitive Area, some 795,000 acres, should be classified as wilderness. "I don't know of any country that surpasses in beauty the Northern Cascades," he wrote.[11] The September 1939 trip rekindled Marshall's enthusiasm: "No part of the whole United States is so well adapted for a wilderness as the country between Stevens Pass and Harts Pass," a distance of about fifty air miles that encompasses much of the North Cascades.[12]

Marshall exhorted the Forest Service to protect the area permanently as wilderness, partly out of concern it would otherwise be made a national park.[13] To the Forest Service's chagrin, much of the Olympic Peninsula became a national park in 1938, permanently transferring nearly a million acres to the Park Service and quashing any hopes of logging some of the richest forests on the planet. Empowered by an influx of Depression-era funding, the Park Service was making noises about expanding its dominion by putting much of the Cascade crest into a giant national park, and the Forest Service was determined to avoid a repeat of what it viewed as the Olympic disaster.

Marshall believed Forest Service wilderness areas were superior to national parks. The National Park Service favored building roads deep into the heart of the scenic lands it managed to accommodate visitors. In contrast, the Forest Service's mission of resource conservation meant areas reserved as wilderness remained road-free and truly wild. Marshall knew the Park Service wanted a new national park along the crest of the Cascades. He entreated C. J. Buck, the North Cascades' regional forester, "If we don't recognize the wishes of the folks who are eager for a superb wilderness in the Northern Cascades...they will turn to the Park Service for (what they think will be) help. The Forest Service has never lost an area to the Park Service because it did too much for those interested in the preservation of primitive conditions."[14]

Writing again in November 1939, this time to new regional forester Lyle Watts, Marshall again warned that the Forest Service should prove its commitment to recreation in the national forests by preserving the North Cascades, thereby preempting a potential Park Service takeover of the region.[15]

Five days after writing the letter and only six weeks after his trip, Marshall died of heart failure, just thirty-eight years old.[16] He never knew the fate of the North Cascades. The controversy, however, was just beginning. Marshall's trips to the North Cascades and his advocacy of a great wilderness area were early sorties that presaged a decades-long conflict over land use there.

The dispute began in earnest in the 1950s when the Forest Service reassessed wilderness designation at Glacier Peak, the fourth-tallest mountain in Washington State. The plan caught the attention of local outdoors enthusiasts, many of them white-collar professionals who poured into Seattle during the wave of wartime and postwar economic diversification. Engineers, scientists, doctors, and professors, many with connections to the Sierra Club and the Mountaineers, a Seattle-based mountain climbing club, hiked and camped in the North Cascades. Dismayed by Forest Service plans to restrict wilderness around Glacier Peak to rocky ridgetops and permit logging in timbered valleys leading to the mountain, these local conservationists[17] tried to work with the agency to develop a plan amenable to midcentury concerns about unrestricted resource exploitation at the expense of non-extractive uses like wilderness recreation.

The Forest Service, attempting to balance pressure from private timber interests to log the national forests to meet escalating housing demand against increasing recreational use in those same forests, was structurally unable to oblige. Since its inception, the agency had managed the national forests for multiple uses: timber production, water supply, wildlife habitat, livestock grazing, and recreation. It was able to do this for many years because the demand for these uses stayed relatively low. However, the introduction of new technologies from the chainsaw to the automobile, and postwar economic conditions that raised Americans' purchasing power and standard of living, led to increased demand for forest resources. The agency tried to please all of its diverse constituencies but gave preference to timber interests.

Conservationists vigorously challenged this approach at Glacier Peak, arguing wilderness was the highest and best use of the area. "There are few parts of the United States in so completely a wild state," wrote political scientist Grant McConnell.[18] Like Marshall, midcentury conservationists believed wilderness had tangible social benefits. It was a place for recreation, aesthetic appreciation, and spiritual rejuvenation. Significantly, though, they also believed wilderness should include economically valuable areas, like forested river valleys, because they were important as recreation corridors. In their view, hiking through clearcuts to get to wilderness was not a wilderness experience.

Frustrated by Forest Service proposals limiting the proposed Glacier Peak wilderness to treeless alpine high country, conservationists considered pursuing national park designation. Like Marshall two decades earlier, they had serious concerns about the National Park Service's proclivity toward intensively developing the lands it managed—its establishing act mandates the agency provide access and preserve scenery—but perceived no feasible alternative with the Forest Service. Alienated from the Forest Service, which had had a wilderness system since the 1920s but which was focused on maximizing timber yield in the postwar years, and wary of the Park Service, which had just commenced a ten-year initiative to develop more facilities to meet skyrocketing visitor demand, conservationists debated but finally decided a national park offered more permanent protection and began advocating for that goal. The Sierra Club, flexing newfound political muscle after stopping dam construction in a national monument in the Southwest, influenced strategy from afar, while local activists worked to bring attention to the region's national park qualities.

The North Cascades fit the conventional notion of what a national park should be: a "crown jewel" with monumental scenery, a fitting example of the nation's magnificent natural heritage. At the same time, changing national consciousness about wild lands and the creation of a statutory wilderness system under the Wilderness Act of 1964 made possible a vision of the North Cascades as a wilderness national park that retained traditional national park characteristics. Historical impracticality of access left most of the region untouched, a quality that pleased wilderness advocates. Crown jewel park proponents viewed the construction of a highway across the North Cascades, already underway, as a means to concentrate most visitor impact along the highway corridor, where travelers would be able to enjoy spectacular roadside views from their cars. When a national park became the conservationists' goal, their principal claim was that the North Cascades was a vast, scenic wilderness equal to any of the great crown jewel national parks of the American West. Most land worthy of the designation had long since been placed into a national park or monument. The North Cascades was an opportunity to add a stunning but little-known treasure to the national park system. Conservationists leveraged the national pro-wilderness mood to influence the National Park Service, the Forest Service, and Congress to achieve their goal.

Buttressed by the postwar era's remarkable economic boom, an executive branch receptive to expanding the amount of public land available for recreation, and powerful Western legislators overseeing public lands issues, park proponents capitalized on the difficulties both the Forest Service and National Park Service experienced as they tried to serve diversifying constituencies. Conservationists successfully conceptualized the North Cascades as a wilderness crown jewel national park and embraced politics as the means to achieve their objective. The result was an entirely new land designation: a park complex comprising national park, national recreation areas, and wilderness areas, with the component parts managed by the rival agencies. The designation forced the Park Service and the Forest Service to confront directly the issue of wilderness protection, something each had tried to deflect. Thus North Cascades National Park is a natural and political landscape, a scenic window into midcentury environmental activism and postwar pressures on the federal agencies that managed public lands.

The North Cascades eventually involved two presidents, two federal agencies, numerous members of Congress, Washington's governor and state officials, resource industry leaders, the state legislature, and citizens within and beyond the state's borders. All were divided over persistent questions about our relationship to the land. How should that relationship be defined? Whose interests are paramount, and why? These questions were fiercely debated in the middle of the twentieth century, as conservationism evolved into environmentalism, as the pressures of industrialization and urbanization led increasing numbers of people to seek renewal and recreation in wild places, and as those wild places felt the impact of increasing use.

The answers in the North Cascades are deceptively straightforward: in 1968, more than a million acres was set aside as a vast national park and wilderness area complex. On contemporary maps, the North Cascades are a patchwork quilt of land-use designations in discrete green hues, each boundary line the result of political negotiation and compromise. How the park became a reality is a compelling story of political maneuvering and shifting consciousness about the human-environment relationship. This book tells that story by tracing the history of the park's creation, arguing that intensifying calls for wilderness protection, embodied in the Wilderness Act, and the magnificent scenery of the North Cascades, one of the wildest, most pristine landscapes in the continental United States, ultimately tilted the balance in favor of what became a wilderness crown jewel national park.

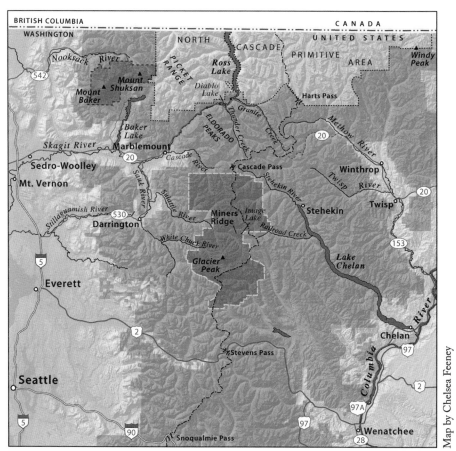

Map 1. The North Cascades, 1955

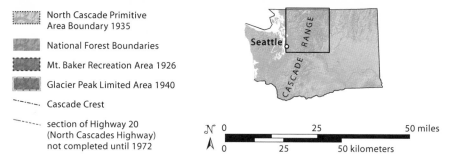

North Cascade Primitive
Area Boundary 1935

National Forest Boundaries

Mt. Baker Recreation Area 1926

Glacier Peak Limited Area 1940

Cascade Crest

section of Highway 20
(North Cascades Highway)
not completed until 1972

Map by Chelsea Feeney

N

0   25   50 miles

0   25   50 kilometers

Map labels

BRITISH COLUMBIA
CANADA
WASHINGTON
UNITED STATES

NORTH CASCADE PRIMITIVE AREA

Windy Peak

Nooksack River
542
PICKET RANGE
Ross Lake
Mount Shuksan
Mount Baker
Diablo Lake
Granite Creek
Thunder Creek
Harts Pass
Methow River
20
Baker Lake
ELDORADO PEAKS
Skagit River
Marblemount
20
Cascade River
Cascade Pass
Winthrop
Sedro-Woolley
Stehekin River
Twisp River
20
Mt. Vernon
Sauk River
Twisp
Stillaguamish River
530
Suiattle River
Miners Ridge
Image Lake
Stehekin
153
Darrington
White Chuck River
Railroad Creek
5
Glacier Peak
Lake Chelan
Everett
Columbia River
2
Chelan
97
Stevens Pass
2
Seattle
97A
5
97
90
Wenatchee
Snoqualmie Pass
28

Seattle
CASCADE RANGE

CHAPTER 1

The Federal Government in the North Cascades, 1892–1940

After Bob Marshall visited the North Cascades in 1939, he urged the United States Forest Service to nearly double national forest wilderness there to 1.8 million acres. In his capacity as the agency's Director of Recreation and Lands and as a passionate advocate for wilderness, Marshall feared the North Cascades could be transferred to the National Park Service unless the Forest Service reserved more of it for wilderness recreation. The New Deal increased both funding and the number of national parks, and made the National Park Service "expansive, confident, vigorous, and effective."[1] Marshall was concerned because the Park Service, a keen competitor with the Forest Service on conservation issues, was jockeying for position, studying thousands of square miles of the Cascade Range for national park potential.

The Park Service's inquiry transpired under the auspices of a New Deal initiative for long-range land planning. The agency saw potential for a possible new park in the North Cascades, but an insider warned it would be the "most bitterly opposed for park status of any area that is being considered."[2] The Forest Service would not willingly cede lands it managed, and most of the area had been national forest land for forty years.

In reality, the Park Service study was the latest in nearly fifty years of land management proposals in the North Cascades. These early schemes underscore the competition between the Forest Service and National Park Service, agencies with distinctive and sometimes conflicting approaches to public lands management, and illuminate why the controversy that erupted in the late 1950s, and the potential Park Service takeover Marshall dreaded, was so contentious.

From its inception, the Forest Service played a central role in managing the North Cascades. For most of its history, the federal government's efforts focused on getting rid of the public domain through homestead and land grant laws. The 1878 Timber and Stone Act offered land not suitable for farming to private individuals who wanted to log or mine it. Timber companies, relishing the prospect of increasing their holdings at low cost, offered a fee to individuals willing to claim the land, make nominal improvements, and sell it to the companies. While not technically illegal, this interpretation of the law put thousands of acres of timberland into industrial ownership.

Yet when logging reached the Pacific coast in the mid-1800s, it quickly became obvious that forests were not infinite. Instead of giving away the public domain, some argued it should be reserved, particularly forested areas that protected watersheds. This represented a new way of valuing public lands that emphasized wise use and scientifically sound conservation of existing resources. It prioritized certain uses such as forests, water supplies, and grazing land over others, such as settlement or mining. Responding to these shifting views, Congress in 1891 empowered the president to proclaim forest reserves. Over the next two years, President Benjamin Harrison created sixteen reserves totaling seventeen million acres in the West, including the nine-hundred-thousand-acre Pacific Forest Reserve around Mount Rainier.[3]

Although the reserves were legally closed to homesteading and other private entry, Congress made no provision for their administration, leaving timber poachers and trespassers essentially uncontrolled.[4] Pressure for systematic management led to an 1896 federal study commission recommending thirteen new reserves and a new oversight structure. The Department of the Interior, which managed all federal public lands, maintained control of the reserves and split their administration rather inefficiently between the General Land Office, which managed the paperwork, and the Division of Forestry, which provided rangers.

President Grover Cleveland created the new reserves on George Washington's birthday, February 22, 1897, including three in Washington State. Nearly half of the state's eight million acres of new reserves became the Washington Forest Reserve, encompassing more than 3.5 million acres from the Canadian border to just south of Glacier Peak—virtually all of the North Cascades.[5]

Nearly 20 percent of the state's land was now under explicit federal control, and many in the state saw the move as limiting private enterprise. In particular, miners predicted the devastation of their embryonic industry, although mining in the North Cascades never really achieved the success prospectors imagined.[6] The steep, glacier-draped mountains that made the region so picturesque also made getting ore out of the mountains too costly.[7] Washington miners' complaints faded when the new reserves were suspended for nine months in 1897 to allow claims to be filed on them. By the peak of the mining bubble in the late 1890s, tens of thousands of claims had been filed in the North Cascades. Only a few mines ever achieved sustained production, notably the Lone Jack and Boundary Red Mountain mines near Mount Baker, the Monte Cristo mine east of Everett, and the Holden Mine west of Lake Chelan.[8]

Unhappiness over the boundaries of the Washington Reserve resurfaced in 1899 when logging reached its western edge, where "green gold"—valuable Douglas-fir and hemlock—grew straight, tall, and dense in the river valleys draining the mountains.[9] Large lumber companies often supported the reserves because federal timber, set aside for long-term conservation, kept private timber prices high. But when the reserves encroached on forests the timber companies wanted to cut, they protested, often underhandedly.[10] For example, when timber interests wanted to shrink reserve boundaries along the Stillaguamish and Skagit Rivers, timber speculators paid people to file homestead claims, even going so far as to build and minimally furnish primitive cabins to prove someone lived there. The claimants would then relinquish their claims to a local timber company for a modest sum. Recognizing this attempt at land-law abuse, the government declined to change the reserve boundaries.[11]

Although the Washington Reserve included much of the ponderosa pine forests around Lake Chelan, the climate on the drier east side of the Cascades meant forests were sparser and trees did not reach the same gigantic size as those on the wet west side. In the first decades of the twentieth century, mining was more important to the east side economy than timber, though a few mills operated on the eastern slopes of the mountains. But whether timber or mining, natural resources were the lifeblood of thinly populated settlements there, and locals did not look kindly on what they perceived as federal government interference. This resentment played a role in the failure of the first, short-lived proposal for a national park in the North Cascades.

———————————◆———————————

In 1892, the community of Chelan, with a population of a few hundred, tried to attract settlers by promoting the area's mineral potential and tourist attractions, including hunting. However, "wanton slaughter of the abundant game" on the slopes above the lake worried some, who suggested preserving the "hunter's paradise" as Lake Chelan National Park before the mountain goat, deer, and elk that made such good sport were extinguished.[12] Reflecting national concern about declining wildlife populations caused by overhunting and loss of habitat (a concern that was the impetus for the Boone and Crockett Club, a hunter-conservation organization founded by Theodore Roosevelt in 1887, and the Audubon Society, among other organizations), the proposal suggested a park incorporating the upper two-thirds of the lake and extending several miles on each side. Scenery was an ancillary consideration, although one recent arrival to the area mused, "Strange as it may seem, I have also been thinking that some steps should be taken to protect the scenery. Generally when business and poetry go into competition poetry gets the worst of it, and unless something is done at once the lake will suffer in consequence."[13]

Such sentiments reflected broader debates over what values should predominate on public lands. Until the late nineteenth century, a straightforward utilitarian zeitgeist prevailed. The efficient extraction of abundant natural resources served the needs of the rapidly expanding nation. Yet as industrialization and urbanization inexorably transformed society, some called for a more conservative approach to manage natural resources for the benefit of future generations. This conservation movement held two main streams of thought, seen at the time as complementary if not congruent.

Utilitarian conservation was championed by Gifford Pinchot, the founding father of the Forest Service, whose philosophy of wise use indelibly shaped the national forests. Pinchot believed resources existed for the people's benefit, and government should regulate their use to ensure long-term supply. Central to this viewpoint is the conviction that a highest or best use can be identified and land managed to that end, preferably by a government agency with scientific expertise. The Organic Act of 1897 creating the Bureau of Forestry, the predecessor to the Forest

Service, embodied these principles. National forests could be established by the president to protect forests and watersheds, and to "furnish a continuous supply of timber for the…citizens of the United States."[14]

In contrast, the philosophy of preservation was embodied by eminent naturalist and writer John Muir, a "hairy wood sprite" who called for setting aside public land so people might reinvigorate their city-worn souls by soaking in the scenic natural splendors of America.[15] Nature was Muir's cathedral, and he believed God was closest in scenic places, which therefore merited protection. "Going to the mountains is going home," he wrote. "Wildness is a necessity…mountain parks and reservations are useful not only as fountains of timber and water and irrigating rivers, but as fountains of life."[16] National parks were fitting venues to pursue this renewal, and Muir was an early and effective advocate. Though their means were different, both Pinchot conservationists and Muir preservationists were concerned about the sustainability of public lands. Both viewed nature through an instrumental lens, believing it should be regulated by government in the people's interest.[17]

At the time, the national parks were few and the national park concept was malleable. Yet early parks shared certain commonalities. Congress established them in exceptionally scenic lands deemed to have no commercial value except that derivable from public enjoyment through tourism. Yellowstone National Park, created in 1872, preserved magnificent scenery and geological curiosities and provided the Northern Pacific Railway, which backed its establishment, the opportunity to develop the area for tourists and bring them to the park.[18] Yellowstone was a harbinger of things to come, "a resounding declaration that tourism was to be important in the economy of the American West."[19] Thanks to efforts by Muir and other preservationists, Yosemite, Sequoia, and General Grant (now a part of Kings Canyon) were added in 1890. The handful of national parks extant in 1892 had been created largely to preserve scenery and promote tourism.

Beyond preserving "natural conditions" for desirable and rare species like bison, protecting wildlife was not yet an explicit rationale for national parks.[20] The Lake Chelan idea was clearly less a park proposal than a casting about for a way to maintain game stocks for hunters. But the timing was bad. Perhaps seven hundred miners had poured into the area in summer 1892, lured by reports of profitable veins of silver-lead galena ore in Horseshoe Basin at the head of the lake.[21] Opposition appeared quickly from those who asserted a park would "shut Lake Chelan out from the commercial world" by prohibiting mining "in a district prospectively second to none in the United States."[22] Form a rod and gun club instead, one resident suggested. The park idea was effectively dead.

While local sentiment opposed a national park on grounds it would inhibit resource development, Chelan boosters recognized the economic potential of scenery and promoted the area as "the tourists' Elysium."[23] Completion of the Great Northern Railway route across the Cascades in 1893 opened the region to more visitors, although the trip still required considerable effort. Debarking at Wenatchee, tourists took a boat forty miles up the Columbia River to Chelan Falls. A short stage ride brought them to Chelan, where the *Belle of Chelan* and other steamboats plied the fifty-mile-long lake to Stehekin at the head of the lake. Destination finally attained, visitors could revive in a comfortable hotel and marvel at three-hundred-foot Rainbow Falls, Horseshoe Basin, and other scenic wonders.[24]

They could also climb mountains. By the turn of the century, many visitors were enthusiastic members of outdoors clubs seeking alpine recreation in the high Cascades. Members of the Portland-based climbing club Mazamas journeyed to Horseshoe Basin, the headwaters of the Stehekin River, for their annual outing in 1899. Climbing and naming Sahale Peak, they reflected, "Some of the most extraordinary of all Nature's achievements in our New West are not generally known to the traveling public...Most notable among these neglected wonders is Lake Chelan." Mazamas founder William Gladstone Steel, the force behind what became Crater Lake National Park in 1902, wrote about the Lake Chelan region in a manner his friend John Muir surely would have approved, rhapsodizing of "beauty unsurpassed and grandeur beyond conception" in this "unutterably glorious" realm.[25]

More publicity followed in the early nineteen hundreds, favorably comparing the Lake Chelan region to European counterparts and suggesting it was only a matter of time until the region was the "Yosemite of Washington." As one newspaper told readers, "There is no need of going to Switzerland or anywhere else to find sublime scenery. We have it right here."[26] The North Cascades were America's Alps, a metaphor that dates from at least 1879, when Jules Verne compared the mountains to their

European counterparts.[27] Indeed, mid-nineteenth century Americans were soul-searching for an identity separate from the Old World. They looked to the dramatic geographic features of their homeland, namely, the spectacular scenery of the American West. This was America's landed heritage, "sanctioned by God and inscribed across the natural landscape," and it more than compensated for the lack of an ancient past.[28]

By the end of the nineteenth century, heritage tourism, "the marketing of the historic, scenic, and mythic past," was well established in the West. Lake Chelan was emerging as the tourist destination it is today, though it appealed mostly to hardy outdoor types willing to rough it for a glimpse of "bewildering splendor." Traveling around the American West was not as easy as traveling in Europe, with its efficient systems of trains, boats, and coaches.[29] "See America First," a national tourism initiative, tried to address this problem. Its rise coincided with the first noteworthy proposal for a national park in the North Cascades.

✦

In January 1906, more than one hundred politicians, boosters, and businesspeople gathered in Salt Lake City to discuss Western tourism. The brainchild of Fisher Sanford Harris, the secretary of the Salt Lake City Commercial Club, the See America First campaign urged boosters to sell the West as a tourist destination, especially to Easterners, for the simple reason that American spending on European travel, about $150 million in 1904–1905, created a financial loss for their homeland. "Scenery is a valuable asset," and by spending their hard-earned dollars to see the natural wonders that made their country great, Americans fulfilled a patriotic duty and enhanced national identity. The group's motto was "See Europe if you will, but See America First."[30]

By accident or design, See America First gained momentum at the same time a Canadian artist proposed a national park around Lake Chelan. Polite and quiet, Julian Itter came to the Pacific Northwest via British Columbia, where in 1897 he had worked with his brother at a photography studio in Rossland. He was living part-time in Seattle in 1903, lauded as "one of the most noted landscape artists in the country," when he was selected to exhibit his landscape paintings in Washington state's pavilion at the 1904 St. Louis World's Fair. Itter had spent six months in the Lake Chelan region and thought it the "finest scenery in the world...the superior of anything that can be found in Switzerland." The state's World's Fair Commission hoped a lavish exhibit of Washington landscape paintings would enchant visitors and motivate them to include the state in future travel plans.[31] Whether the exhibit was successful is unclear, but Itter's popularity as a landscape artist appears to have continued. In summer 1905, Itter returned to the North Cascades to paint scenes around Lake Chelan and Stehekin. He showed the landscapes the following January in Seattle and sold every painting after a flattering write-up appeared in the *Seattle Times*.[32] Opportunely, the See America First campaign commenced a few weeks later, and Itter applied its tenets to his idea that the area around Lake Chelan should be a national park, perhaps seeing a way to garner more publicity for his paintings.

In early March 1906, Itter picked up endorsements for the park idea from Seattle to Spokane, referencing the See America First movement with his assertion that Lake Chelan had "the cream of all the scenery of the world." The Mazamas, which had held outings in the region since at least 1899, passed a resolution endorsing the park idea. In Spokane, Itter sought backing from See America First spokesman Fisher Sanford Harris, in town on a lecture tour. Heading to the East Coast, Itter hoped to gain the support of the state's congressional delegation and possibly President Theodore Roosevelt. By mid-March, the local Chelan newspaper claimed, "There is more bread and butter in scenery than in anything else."[33]

Not everyone agreed, and the *Chelan Leader* mirrored different viewpoints: "As between the mining industry and a national park—if the choice had to be made between them—the mining interest would without question be the greater." Many still clung to the hope that the North Cascades concealed rich mineral deposits, awaiting only technological innovation to render them profitable. Judging by local headlines, public opinion around Lake Chelan solidified rapidly, and by early April 1906, the *Leader* barked, "Unanimous Opposition: No One on Lake Chelan Wants a National Park." Without mining, "most of us would have to move out." The newspaper reflected local sentiment: "To kill our chief industry [mining] and ruin hundreds of people whose hopes for many years have been centered upon it, is too much to ask of any community."[34]

A national park, moreover, would mean more government rules and regulations, a chilling prospect for prospectors and loggers. Only a year earlier, management of the forest reserves had been transferred to the Department of Agriculture under the newly renamed United States Forest Service. In Washington, the reserves meant nearly 20 percent of the state's land was closed to private acquisition. Few favored more government interference.[35]

By the end of the month, the proposal was dead. Washington's congressional delegation had considered introducing park legislation but quickly dropped the matter in the face of vociferous local opposition.[36] Itter equivocated, saying those who feared the park would preempt mining did not understand the proposal. In his thinking, logging and fishing would not be affected, and the government could be influenced insofar as mining was concerned. Considered from a contemporary point of view, his response seems naive. Even in 1906, a decade before the National Park Service was established, resource extraction was generally prohibited in national parks, and it would be years before park advocates could convincingly demonstrate park tourism could be equally lucrative.[37] Despite its failure, Itter believed the attention boded well for future discussions about a national park in the North Cascades.[38]

The debate during the artist's brief stint as park champion hinted at some of the factions that would form five decades later when the North Cascades controversy ignited: preservationists versus utilitarian resource interests, proponents of local versus federal control. Few in 1906 perceived any value in preserving wilderness as such, but the Lake Chelan national park proposal firmly cemented the idea of North Cascades tourism into local consciousness. Ten years later, the popular mystery writer Mary Roberts Rinehart traveled to Lake Chelan on a Great Northern Railway-sponsored trip. An excellent booster, her account was first published serially in *Cosmopolitan* magazine and later in book form as *Tenting To-Night*. Crossing Cascade Pass from Stehekin, Rinehart predicted the region would someday become a national park, putting "this roof of the world within reach of anyone who can sit a horse."[39]

No park proposals emerged for several years after Itter's failed campaign, although alpine tourism continued to grow throughout the North Cascades. At Mount Baker, in the northwest corner of the range, the Forest Service found itself in the largely unfamiliar position of recreation provider.

The agency had evolved since the protests over new reserves at the end of the nineteenth century. With the 1898 appointment of Gifford Pinchot as director of the Bureau of Forestry and the 1901 installation of Theodore Roosevelt as president, forest conservation had influential champions. In 1905, Pinchot successfully lobbied to move the forestry bureau from the General Land Office in the Interior Department to the Department of Agriculture, where it was renamed the Forest Service. The reserves were renamed "national forests" shortly thereafter. As implemented by Pinchot, the guiding philosophy of the Forest Service was "the greatest good for the greatest number in the long run." Trees were a precious resource to be utilized sustainably under careful government regulation. To implement this philosophy, Pinchot reorganized the Forest Service to give more control to local offices.[40]

He divided the national forests into six essentially autonomous districts (later renamed regions), each with a district forester who had "practically full authority." The Pacific Northwest's national forests were divided into twenty-six smaller forests to facilitate efficient management.[41] The Washington Forest Reserve was split into the Washington, Wenatchee, Chelan, and Snoqualmie National Forests. The Washington National Forest was renamed Mt. Baker National Forest in 1924 and the Chelan National Forest was renamed the Okanogan National Forest in 1955.[42] Each forest had a supervisor and a team of rangers, often recruited from the surrounding area. One-quarter of the gross receipts earned by the national forests was returned to the counties in which the forest was located, to compensate for property tax losses. Washington State law still requires counties to split federal forest receipts between roads and schools. Counties with significant land reserved in national forests naturally wanted to maximize income from that land, promoting close ties with forest administrators. This administrative paradigm helped the Forest Service develop friendly relationships with local lumbermen, miners, ranchers, and residents, including those seeking recreation in the national forests.[43]

Mount Baker, the state's third-highest peak, had become a popular destination for mountaineers, hikers, and skiing enthusiasts. After the first recorded ascent in 1868, most of the activity in the area centered on mining and road-building, neither of which was particularly successful. But beginning in 1891, a "mountaineering epidemic" began on Mount Baker and nearby peaks, aided by improved access to the mountain.[44] In the space of two years, six parties summited Mount Baker and another made the first ascent of the nearby Twin Sisters. By 1897, when the Washington Forest Reserve was created with Mount Baker inside its boundaries, climbing groups developed close ties with local forest rangers and worked with them to improve access to the alpine country through road- and trail-building.[45]

The Northwest's principal mountain climbing clubs were the Portland-based Mazamas and the Mountaineers; the latter had separated from the Mazamas in 1906 to accommodate Seattle-based members. Following the California-based Sierra Club's model of outings to the high country to attract new members and publicize potential parks, the Mountaineers and Mazamas each sponsored several trips to Mount Baker.[46] The outings were considerably larger than what might be considered appropriate today. A 1906 Mazamas trip included 118 people, a typical size for the time. To accommodate them the Forest Service built a better pack trail on the mountain. When the clubs visited Mount Baker again in 1908 and 1909, the agency built another trail for them. The Forest Service's helpfulness in creating better access to the wild country fostered friendly relations with club members, sowing the seeds of deep loyalty to the agency.[47]

In 1911, some Bellingham citizens formed the Mount Baker Club to promote the mountain as a destination. Inspired by a 1909 Mazamas resolution proposing a Mount Baker National Park, the club over the next several years worked to attract the federal government's interest. The Forest Service, hoping to bolster efforts to have management of the national parks transferred to it instead of creating a new parks bureau in the Interior Department, cautioned district offices to preserve "as nearly as possible in their natural condition" areas that abutted existing national parks or might become national parks.[48] With that in mind, the district office in 1913 proposed a 50,000-acre park around Mount Baker and nearby Mount Shuksan. The mostly alpine proposal reflected the agency's utilitarian conservation philosophy, which dictated parks should consist of otherwise unusable areas.

As the number of national parks increased nationwide, pressure to consolidate their management intensified. In 1906, the Antiquities Act empowered the president to create national monuments for the preservation of archaeological and historical artifacts. Through the end of his term in 1909, President Theodore Roosevelt designated eighteen such sites, including Devils Tower (Wyoming) and Grand Canyon (now a national park). All parks and most monuments were administered by the Department of the Interior, but operated as individual entities competing for meager federal funding.[49] Centralized management and uniform standards for determining the appropriateness of proposed parks were desperately needed.

In 1915, the Mount Baker Club met with Interior Department officials who were building support for a national parks bureau and scouting potential park sites. These officials also liked Mount Baker.[50] The same year, Congressman Lindley H. Hadley (R-WA) became a supporter after an outing to Baker during which he had a small peak on a ridge northwest of the mountain named for him.[51] The following January, Hadley and his Senate counterparts, Republicans Miles Poindexter and Wesley L. Jones, introduced bills for a Mount Baker National Park. The Department of Agriculture was quick to point out that by allowing prospecting and mining, the bills would create "a national park in name only." Ultimately, the larger debate over the creation of the National Park Service, established later that year, precluded serious consideration of the legislation.[52]

The Park Service's enabling act stipulated the agency was to "conserve the scenery and the natural and historic objects and the wild life therein, and to provide for the enjoyment of the same in such manner and by such means as will leave them unimpaired for the enjoyment of future generations."[53] This "tangled mouthful of majestic instruction"[54] neatly captures the paradox that has bedeviled the Park Service ever since, namely, how to provide sustainable access for enjoyment without jeopardizing the scenery people come to see. The Park Service was an agency designed to promote recreational tourism through scenery. Contrast this with the Forest Service's enabling legislation, which directed the agency to protect wood and water in the national forests and sustainably manage them for timber production. The roots of the agencies' philosophical differences are apparent. At a fundamental level, both provided social benefits: the Forest Service provided natural resources; the Park Service, scenic inspiration.

Debates over which social benefit should predominate energized the conservation movement, wrote historian Char Miller, and illustrated the schism between Pinchot conservationism and Muir preservationism that developed in the early twentieth century. While both philosophies espoused use, their proponents differed over what type of use best served the public. Muir had come to see wilderness preservation as offering the highest public benefit, and believed the national parks were the best place to provide it. For Pinchot, national forests ensured resources would be used for the greatest good for the greatest number of people. These differences crystallized in the early twentieth century during the battle over damming Hetch Hetchy valley, part of Yosemite National Park that was impounded to provide drinking water to San Francisco. Pinchot and Muir, good friends for many years, irrevocably split over the issue. Yet as Miller notes, "It was out of the tradition of brawling over environmental policies and politics that the national forest and national park systems were born."[55]

The Park Service's first director, Stephen Mather, and his assistant and successor, Horace Albright, were savvy operators who understood the only way to keep Congressional appropriations coming was to get more parks established and convince people to visit them. They took politicians on comfortably-appointed excursions of the most scenic parks, built parkways to whisk the rapidly increasing number of automobile tourists past famous sights, and worked with local interests and railroads to promote tourism.[56] To build political support for the young agency, they emphasized use over preservation, conceptualizing the parks as a wellspring of national identity that could be commodified as a uniquely American experience.[57]

As director of the fledgling Park Service, Mather's enthusiasm for a Mount Baker park waned. In 1916 alone, members of Congress introduced sixteen bills for new parks. Only two received Mather's blessing. In charge of a small, weak agency, Mather needed to pick his battles with the Forest Service carefully. The Park Service's 1916 creation codified interagency competition already underway. Well before the agency's birth, national parks had been carved from national forests in Washington (Mount Rainier, 1899), Oregon (Crater Lake, 1902), Montana (Glacier, 1910), and Colorado (Rocky Mountain, 1915).[58] Mather focused on potential parks containing features not found elsewhere, and dismissed many proposals because they "merely approximated already established national parks near-by—as Mt. Baker, Mt. St. Helens, Mt. Adams and Mt. Hood approximated Mt. Rainier [established in 1899]."[59] Between 1916 and 1922, national parks were proposed for Mount Baker, Lake Chelan, and the Cascade summit, to no avail.[60] Lake Chelan, almost wholly surrounded by national forest, was "just not good enough," Mather declared.[61] Without Park Service support, there would be no new park anywhere in the North Cascades.[62]

World War I quashed travel to Europe, and the postwar emergence of a leisure-seeking, mobile middle class enamored of the automobile meant more recreationists visited national parks and forests to enjoy outdoor pursuits. In 1917, the year after the Park Service was created, some three million recreation visits were recorded in the national forests and nearly a half-million in the handful of national parks. This trend forced the agencies to consider differences between recreation in national parks and national forests and how each agency's policies should address recreation.

From its inception the Forest Service was primarily a custodial agency, planning for the day when national forest timber would be in high demand. In part to distinguish recreation in national forests from that in national parks, the agency in 1917 commissioned a study of Forest Service recreation facilities with an eye toward quantifying their value and developing efficient management policies. Recreation might not be as important as other forest uses, the report concluded, but it was "certainly a paying investment" for Americans.[63] In 1919, the Rocky Mountain District hired landscape architect Arthur Carhart as the agency's first recreation engineer. Carhart recognized that "recreational use of a National Forest was highly varied and complex."[64] He believed the wilderness experience should be considered a type of national forest recreation, and wrote a recreation plan for the White River National Forest in Colorado opposing development of an area on the shores of scenic Trapper's Lake even as other areas in the forest were slated for campgrounds, summer homes, and picnic areas.

Carhart left the agency in 1922, in part due to frustration over lack of funding for recreation, but he and fellow forester Aldo Leopold corresponded about the idea of wilderness reserves for recreation. In 1921, Leopold proposed a wilderness area within New Mexico's Gila National Forest.[65] A keen hunter, Leopold believed the Forest Service had the ability and space to provide for different types of forest recreation. He conceived wilderness as "preservation *from* certain forms of recreational development," especially roads and summer homes and resorts.[66] Wilderness was a place for primitive recreation like hunting, where users depended on themselves for survival.[67]

Responding to the rise in automobile use and corresponding demand for recreation in the years after World War I, Congress appropriated nearly $14 million for forest road development in 1921 (about $170 million today). Leopold saw a way to distinguish the types of recreation offered by each agency, suggesting "wilderness preservation might be more akin to traditional Forest Service stewardship than would more aggressive recreational development,"[68] such as that practiced by the Park Service. Some preservationists were dismayed by roads slicing through the most scenic regions of the national parks, evidence of the Park Service's inclination to preference visitor access over preservation of scenery. Leopold foresaw that remaining roadless areas in the national forests were at risk, and argued the Forest Service had a responsibility to the minority of users seeking a wilderness recreation experience.[69] Bob Marshall made a similar argument in 1930, likening wilderness to art museums. While only a small group of people made use of art museums or wilderness, he said, the right to do so was explicitly protected (and often government-funded) under democratic principles. Tempting though it might be to give preference to the majority by constructing roads and campgrounds throughout the national forests, doing so would be fundamentally un-American. Some large spaces suitable for wilderness recreation should be left undeveloped.[70]

Politically, this minority rights argument for wilderness was a hard sell. As professional foresters, many in the Forest Service espoused the philosophy that forests were for cutting. Setting some areas aside, they argued, removed them from economic development and human benefit.

Moreover, wilderness areas shut out many potential users because they lacked recreational facilities like campgrounds and boat docks. Nevertheless, in 1924 the Forest Service set aside nearly 700,000 acres of the Gila National Forest under the aegis of recreational planning.[71] Within a few years, it similarly reserved five other roadless areas in other forests, although there was no overarching agency policy for such areas. For the time being, they were "temporarily restricted" for primitive recreational use, but if at any time demand for resources warranted development their status would change.[72] The Forest Service continued to grapple with recreation and wilderness as forest uses.

The National Conference on Outdoor Recreation, convened in 1924 and 1926 at the behest of President Calvin Coolidge, attempted to address the issue. Representatives from more than one hundred organizations and agencies met in Washington, DC, and debated the federal government's role in recreation and a national recreation policy at a time when the Park Service and Forest Service found themselves increasingly at odds. By the mid-1920s, thanks to an aggressive campaign of selectively adding new parks (including Denali, Grand Canyon, Zion, Acadia, and Shenandoah) and assiduously cultivating allies, the Park Service was the "political equal" of the Forest Service.[73] Any gain by one meant a loss for the other, contributing to a "territoriality rivaled only by medieval despots."[74] The National Conference on Outdoor Recreation's report highlighted strengths and weaknesses in the two agencies. It questioned both the Park Service's tendency to emphasize road-building and recreational construction and the Forest Service's tentative embrace of the wilderness recreation reserve concept.

A 1926 Forest Service inventory found that even after construction of planned national forest roads, fully 20 percent of the forests would remain roadless. These were mostly treeless, alpine, rocky, and steep areas with limited potential for economic development. Armed with this information, agency director William B. Greeley drafted a wilderness policy that gave district foresters broad discretion to create national forest wilderness areas and discouraged roads and term permits (a kind of long-term lease for resort and summer home sites). This proved to be a "rather effective deterrent" to carving more national parks out of the forests, even if there was a risk such areas would be seen as the equivalent of national parks and vulnerable to transfer.[75]

In 1929, Greeley's wilderness policy draft became regulation L-20, allowing districts to create Primitive Areas for recreation, education, and preservation of natural values. However, regional foresters could stipulate other uses, such as logging or grazing, and could change the boundaries or eliminate the areas at will. In fact, primitive area designations were highly differentiated across Western forests, with some allowing more uses than others.[76] Still, primitive areas placated some recreation and wilderness advocates and gave the Forest Service another tool to thwart Park Service expansion into the national forests.

Table 1. Selected National Forest Land-Use Classifications, 1929–1963

Primitive Area: Protected "to maintain primitive conditions…to the fullest degree compatible with their highest public use." The L-20 regulation adopted in 1929 allowed designation by regional foresters, who could also undo such areas.

Limited Area: Unique to Region 6, an area reserved for "stop, look, and listen," pending study of its recreation potential. Could be eliminated by regional forester.

Wilderness (pre-Wilderness Act): Established under U-regulations (adopted 1939) for areas of more than 100,000 acres. No roads, logging, or special use permits were allowed. Required Secretary of Agriculture approval and public notice of intent to establish area. If warranted, the regional forester conducted public hearings and submitted the testimony to the Chief or the Agriculture Secretary for final decision.

Forest Service Region 6, encompassing Washington and Oregon, was the first to have primitive areas approved. Regional forester C. M. Granger stated, perhaps optimistically, "It is our intention to supply a sufficient number of large high mountain primitive areas to satisfy the public need for all time."[77] A 1928 federal report, one result of the National Conferences on Outdoor Recreation earlier in the decade, recommended twenty-one national forest wilderness areas, the largest of which was two million acres in the North Cascades.[78] In response, the district forester designated the Whatcom Primitive Area in 1931, circumscribing 172,800 acres of the Picket Range, the most remote and formidable peaks in the North Cascades. It fit like a puzzle piece next to the 75,000-acre Mount Baker Recreation Area (established in 1926 as Mount Baker Park Division) around Mount Baker and Mount Shuksan.[79] The same year, the regional office designated 233,600 acres around Glacier Peak as a "recreation unit," a label designed to signify its highest use but having no other apparent legal significance.

Even as the Depression slowed forest recreational use and therefore any sense of urgency for uniformly applied wilderness standards, the primitive area concept provoked debate within the Forest Service. Although the agency operated under the Progressive utilitarian conservationism instituted by Pinchot, increased recreational demand and a few vocal activists goaded the Forest Service in the 1920s to take small steps toward preserving wilderness for recreation.[80]

The Forest Service has managed Mount Baker for recreation since at least 1926. Note the "stringer stands" of timber climbing the ridge in the foreground. *North Cascades National Park Service Complex Museum Collection, NOCA 11931cc*

By the early 1930s, the Forest Service managed 7.7 million acres of national forests in Washington State and had decades of experience with recreation-seeking visitors. Increased recreation demand compelled the agency to give attention to uses other than resource extraction. It built access roads and trails for recreational users, offered term permits for summer home and resort sites, and developed facilities for popular activities such as fishing, hunting, picnicking, boating, and camping. This brought the agency squarely into conflict with the Park Service, which felt recreation was its exclusive domain and federal recreation funding should be channeled to the parks.[81] The Forest Service recognized the demand for recreation. In most cases, getting to a national forest to camp, fish, hunt, or hike was easier than getting to a national park because forests were larger and closer to population centers. But the agency found it challenging to reconcile recreation with the utilitarian conservation philosophy, which gave precedence to logging, grazing, and mining—uses that had patent economic benefits. The Forest Service viewed recreation as a legitimate but incidental use of the national forests.

The agency had another opportunity to consider wilderness recreation in 1932, when New York Sen. Royal Copeland requested a comprehensive survey of American forests and forestry to inform future planning and generate support for more Forest Service oversight of privately held forestlands.[82] The Forest Service asked Bob Marshall to write the sections on forest recreation, a task he enthusiastically accepted. Authoring three chapters of what became known as the Copeland Report, Marshall asserted recreation was a valid use of the national forests and should be given the same weight as other uses such as timber production. The key, he felt, was finding a balance so that forests could provide all of the social benefits within their potential.

To that end, Marshall proposed forty-five million acres of forests (the report looked at all commercial forestland in the United States, not just the national forests) be dedicated to seven types of recreational areas. Three of these emphasized wilderness and hands-off management, while four focused on recreational development and facilities. Managing recreational areas for different purposes met the needs of different types of users, Marshall wrote, and would help minimize recreational overuse. At the same time, the remaining forestland needed to be better managed to provide sustainable resources. The Copeland Report allowed Marshall to spell out his plan for wilderness preservation. He proposed at least ten million more acres of forest wilderness, including more than a million acres around the Whatcom Primitive Area east of Mount Baker.[83] C. J. Buck, the forester in charge of Region 6, resisted the idea.[84]

Many western regional foresters felt there were enough primitive areas already, but the New Deal expansion of the Park Service added military battlefields, cemeteries, national monuments, and other historic sites to the agency's portfolio, cementing its position as recreational administrator for a wide variety of inspirational and educational sites.[85] Moreover, increasing demand for recreation on all public lands prompted some in the Forest Service to reconsider.[86] A 1934 Region 6 recreation report urged, "The Pacific Northwest needs at least one extremely large Primitive Area, which must be of sufficient scope and remoteness to satisfy the most rigid wilderness qualifications...There is growing sentiment among a considerable portion of the general public which demands the setting aside of primitive areas at all possible points."[87] The next year, Region 6 expanded the Whatcom Primitive Area to 801,000 acres and renamed it the North Cascade Primitive Area. Finally, the Forest Service was "giving much belated, vigorous attention to forest recreation."[88]

As part of the New Deal reorganization of government, a 1933 executive order transferred all national monuments managed by other agencies to the Park Service.[89] The national park system instantly doubled in size (the transfer also included historical, military, memorial, and cemetery parks) and the agency's mission expanded to include interpretation and education about the new sites.[90] Pragmatically, the transfer had the desired effect of making the Park Service immune to any potential merger with the Forest Service or any other land management agency.[91] At the time of the executive order, the Forest Service managed fifteen monuments, including the three-hundred-thousand-acre Mount Olympus National Monument in Washington State. Now the foresters watched in horror as the monument transferred to Park Service control, permanently removing some of the finest forests in the world from potential harvest.[92] As one historian remarked, it did not "improve relations between the two bureaus."[93]

The transfer was part of a larger scheme by the notoriously cantankerous Interior Secretary Harold L. Ickes to consolidate land-planning offices in the Department of the Interior. The proposed Department of Conservation would make the Park Service the unquestionable leader of federal recreation planning and diminish the Forest Service's burgeoning engagement in that area. The Forest Service found itself fighting to maintain the Pinchot tradition of utilitarian conservation while also trying to establish itself as a trustworthy manager of recreation lands. Trying to reconcile these conflicting objectives while fending off Ickes's expansionism consumed significant agency energy during the New Deal.[94]

One of Secretary Ickes's first tactics was to assign to the Park Service a major recreation study. President Franklin Roosevelt appointed Ickes chair of the National Resources Board, a New Deal national land planning program. Seeing an opportunity for the Park Service to strengthen its claim as the federal recreation authority, Ickes commissioned a report that recommended studying twenty-two areas for national park potential, including the Cascade Range in Washington and Oregon.[95] Published in 1934, the report gave the Park Service latitude to select the juiciest opportunities for expanding its reach, which it did almost immediately.

In 1935, Mount Rainier National Park superintendent Owen A. Tomlinson urged his superiors to study the "outstanding snow peaks and certain rugged wilderness" in the Washington Cascades for a "Five Ice Peaks National Park."[96] In 1937, the agency studied about 5,000 square miles (an area the size of Connecticut) of the Cascade Range in Washington, from Mount Baker to Mount Adams.[97] It concluded that an Ice Peaks national park stretching from the Columbia River to the Canadian border, linking Mount Baker, Glacier Peak, Mount Rainier (a national park since 1899), Mount St. Helens, and Mount Adams would "outrank in its scenic, recreational, and wildlife values any existing national park and any other possibility for such a park within the United States."[98] The proposed park, carved almost entirely from existing Forest Service land, would have excluded almost everything below timberline, a transparent attempt to forestall objections on economic grounds.[99] At the time, the state led the nation in log production, harvesting more than six billion board feet of timber in 1937.[100]

Some Forest Service staff thought the idea of a Cascade summit park "manifestly absurd," suspecting the Park Service of trying to stimulate public interest so smaller parks could be proposed later with greater chance of success.[101] Others felt perhaps some other portion of the region could be offered as a national park, throwing a bone to the Park Service without giving up valuable Forest Service land: "Consider the creation of a National Park out of the Lake Chelan Watershed…There is very little timber or other utility value."[102] While ostensibly cooperating with the Park Service study team, local Forest Service staff operated under orders from Washington, DC, to fight the proposal by emphasizing the potential economic losses.[103]

But Bob Marshall thought the best way to preempt the Park Service was to strengthen Forest Service rules protecting the wilderness values of national forest land. The possibility of a national park in the northern Cascades worried Marshall, because parks meant roads, roads meant cars, and cars meant people who would love the wilderness to death. He had cofounded the Wilderness Society in 1935 largely to fend off the invasion of automobiles on public lands.[104] Marshall fretted about what would happen if the Park Service took over the North Cascades, writing to Seattle conservationist Irving Clark: "I know and you know perfectly well that if this area should be made a park, it would have roads extended into its heart."[105] This concern would reemerge in the 1950s as conservationists debated whether to pursue a national park.

Through the 1930s, Marshall repeatedly pushed for the North Cascades to be made a wilderness, but his was a lonely voice in an agency founded on principles of utilitarian conservation.[106] As a trained forester, he ascribed to the principles of sustainable forestry and believed trees should be harvested for human benefit. At the same time, though, he thought some of the national forests should be reserved in their natural state to provide places for primitive recreation. For Marshall, timber and wilderness recreation were both social benefits the national forests should provide. Back in the North Cascades in 1939, he implored the Forest Service to double the size of the North Cascade Primitive Area by adding 795,000 acres to the south, between Harts Pass and Stevens Pass.[107] He asked a friend in Seattle to start a letter-writing campaign supporting the expansion.[108] Marshall's efforts bore fruit posthumously in 1940 as the agency approved setting aside 350,000 acres around Glacier Peak as a Limited Area, a designation unique to the Pacific Northwest that reserved national forest land pending study of its recreation potential, but the new status was not made official for another six years.[109]

In the meantime, the National Resources Board released its report on recreation, and in 1939 the Park and Forest services appointed an Interdepartmental Committee of agency staff to study the Cascades.[110]

Locally, the Ice Peaks idea did not sit well with the Washington State Planning Council, a group created by the state legislature in 1934 and charged with making recommendations on appropriate use of the state's natural resources. Responding to the New Deal philosophy of planning as a government function, many states had formed such groups by the mid-1930s. The governor-appointed group, dominated by business and resource industry leaders, provided information on the state's planning activities and resources to the National Resources Board.[111] In April 1937, the Planning Council voted to study the Cascades proposal "with a view to safeguarding the right to develop natural resources within the boundaries of such a park, if established."[112]

Of more immediate concern was the Olympic Peninsula's fecund timber stands. When the Ice Peaks idea was broached, the council was losing a desperate fight to keep hundreds of thousands of acres of Olympic forests under Forest Service management.[113] The creation of Olympic National Park in 1938 permanently removed nearly 700,000 acres from potential utilization.[114] The Planning Council viewed the Ice Peaks proposal with grim resolve that no one was going to deprive the state of yet more forestland. Many in Washington State resented the heavy-handed tactics of Secretary Ickes, whose attempt to get the Forest Service transferred to the proposed Department of Conservation was a chilling prospect in a timber-dependent state.[115] In point of fact, 1938 was the last year Washington led the nation in timber production (Oregon surpassed it in 1939) but the industry remained the foundation of the state's economy.

The Planning Council studied all the lands within the five national forests that would be affected by the Ice Peaks proposal, an area more than double that studied by the Park Service.[116] Irving Clark, a key local player in the Olympic fight, told Marshall the council had appointed "loggers and lumber men and Forest Service officials and University of Washington Forestry School professors."[117] Defeated in the Olympic park controversy, where it had fought for the Forest Service to retain control of public lands on the peninsula, the Planning Council came out swinging. At public hearings in timber towns on both sides of the Cascades, witness after witness bitterly complained about the imposition of a national park on the Olympic Peninsula by Eastern nature lovers over the wishes of the state's citizens.[118] They warned of disastrous economic consequences,[119] and opposed transferring more land to federal management (conveniently overlooking the fact that the study area was already under Forest Service jurisdiction), particularly Park Service management.[120] After the Olympic debacle, the state had "all the parks, state and national, that its population will ever require."[121] The response illustrates the warm feelings many had toward the Forest Service, which prioritized local economic interests.

Battered by widespread animosity over the creation of Olympic National Park, the Park Service backed away from the Ice Peaks proposal, saying it was "merely a land-use study…to determine what areas in the Cascades are the most scenic." Agency officials hedged, saying they were "not just sure" where the park idea originated. No one in the Park Service, it seemed, wanted to even acknowledge the proposal.[122]

Yet in 1940 the Park Service released yet another report, this time suggesting 1.7 million acres managed by the Forest Service, plus Mount St. Helens, Mount Stuart, and Mount Adams, be considered for national park status.[123] A far cry from the original suggestion of the range's summit along the length of the state, this proposal too was dead on arrival, but it ironically put the Forest Service in the awkward position of having to reject some of the original assessments of areas under its jurisdiction.

Although the Forest Service had set aside several areas to preserve scenic and recreation values, particularly in the northern Cascades, it now contended that except for the volcanoes, "the summit country is scenically dull, uninteresting and reputedly much inferior" to similar areas in the West. The proposed park lands contained valuable timber and mineral resources that would become accessible as technology became more sophisticated. Most potential visitors would not be able to get there easily, because it was "extremely remote" compared to other large Western national parks. Finally, creating new national park areas in the high Cascades would simply cause unnecessary agency overlap since the Forest Service was already managing the areas appropriately.[124] This argument would reappear during the North Cascades controversy less than twenty years later.

The Forest Service had a staunch ally in the Planning Council, whose 1940 report left no doubt of its position: "The importance of [the Cascades] to the economic well-being of the state is self-evident." That the Olympic controversy had embittered the council on the prospect of increased Park Service presence in Washington was crystal clear. The people of Washington appreciated the Forest Service's thirty-plus years of "broad and careful supervision," which precluded the need for a national park.[125] A grateful Forest Service leader wrote to the Planning Council, "Any type of relationship other than the friendly and cooperative one which now exists would be quite unthinkable."[126] The council reserved its harshest critique for Secretary Ickes, whom it viewed as the manipulative force behind Olympic National Park and the Ice Peaks proposal.[127] Determined to kill Ice Peaks, the Planning Council blanketed the state with its report and sent a fourteen-minute radio script to local stations.[128] Hundreds of supportive letters poured into the council's office.

Despite the Park Service's purported ambivalence about the Ice Peaks proposal, the report's vitriolic tone stung, and the agency reproached the council.[129] But it was a timid rebuke, because Ickes rather duplicitously disavowed any knowledge of a proposed national park in the Cascades, conceding only that the area was under study. In reality, the Secretary had received Ice Peaks updates at least since 1938 and a draft park bill was floated in early 1939.[130] Demoralized by public opposition, unsupported by its own leader, and trying to resolve administration issues in Olympic National Park, the Park Service backed down. The agency acknowledged the contentious establishment of Olympic National Park in 1938 inflamed opposition to Ice Peaks.[131]

Soon after, Mount Rainier National Park superintendent O. A. Tomlinson, who had first suggested a Cascade crest national park in 1935, wrote, "My guess is that some time there will be more of the Cascades given national park status. Comparatively small areas which, of course, have always been the aim. ...It will probably require a few years [sic] time to soften the blow for 'the interests'."[132] The Ice Peaks proposal may have been a red herring, a way to discombobulate the Forest Service while Ickes maneuvered to get Olympic National Park and his Department of Conservation, the latter unsuccessfully. Ickes made no secret that the creation of Olympic and Kings Canyon National Parks were his top park priorities, and he promised to manage both by emphasizing their wilderness qualities. This won support from wilderness preservationists, who viewed scenic roads as equally distasteful as logging, and helped Ickes achieve both parks.[133]

The Forest Service retained control of the North Cascades, but would find itself on the defensive when public attention again turned to the region in the 1950s. Schemes for national parks in the North Cascades regularly materialized during the first decades of the twentieth century. These recognized the area's scenic magnificence, the increasing importance of alpine recreation, the growth of automobile tourism, and the young state's interest in economic development. But at every turn, proponents were not able to argue convincingly that a national park would achieve something that national forest management did not provide. Not until after World War II would the balance start to shift slowly in favor of the idea of a national park.

CHAPTER 2

Conservationists Coalesce around Glacier Peak

It all started with Glacier Peak. This "somber king on throne of granite"[1] is not granite at all, but a volcano composed of layers of pumice and dacite. Its last known eruption was 1,100 years ago, but modern geologists believe that when Glacier Peak erupts again it will be especially destructive.[2] One observer wrote, "Much of the fun in walking around Glacier Peak comes from looking at the comparatively recent violence—layers of tuff sliced deep by the Suiattle and White Chuck Rivers, bits of pumice littering summits many miles [away,] which 12,000 years ago cast ashes at least as far as Montana."[3] Famously remote, Washington's fourth-tallest mountain requires miles of hiking through difficult terrain just to reach the base. It did not even appear on a map until 1898, though it was long known to Native Americans, who called it Tda-ko-buh-ba or Dakobed ("Great Parent").[4] The peak's glaciers create views that "resemble Arctic landscapes—a sea of ice through which loom isolated peaks and ridges."[5] Dazzlingly beautiful as it floats above surrounding peaks, Glacier Peak "bestows familiarity only to those willing to strive for it."[6]

A group of Wenatchee citizens in 1926 proposed that Glacier Peak—a favorite destination of outdoors clubs like the Mazamas and Mountaineers—be set aside for recreation under Forest Service supervision.[7] Five years later, the Forest Service approved a 233,600-acre Glacier Peak-Cascade Recreation Unit. Little more than a name change for the mountain's alpine high country, the new category satisfied locals who wanted to see Glacier Peak reserved.[8] The Depression forestalled further action until 1938, when the Forest Service approved a new land classification order that expanded the area to 275,000 acres and renamed it the Glacier Peak Recreation Unit.

The label was a Forest Service attempt at systematic land use classification. In 1929, the Forest Service implemented regulation

L-20, which allowed the creation of Primitive Areas for national forest recreation; however, regional foresters were instructed that "no hard and fast rules" or standards could be universally applied to the use of such areas.[9] Over the next decade, Bob Marshall and others who wanted stronger protection for forest wilderness worked to create clearer and more systematic policies for land use classification. In 1938, the same year the Glacier Peak Recreation Unit was created, the Forest Service proposed the U-regulations, new rules written by Marshall for reclassifying primitive areas as wilderness. Under these rules, areas of more than one hundred thousand acres would be renamed Wilderness Areas and require the approval of the Secretary of Agriculture. Those between five thousand and one hundred thousand acres would be called Wild Areas and could be established by the regional forester. No roads, logging, or special use permits were allowed in either. Both designations required public notice. If public opposition to proposed boundaries emerged, the regional forester had to conduct public hearings and submit the testimony to the Chief or the Agriculture Secretary for a final decision.[10] If the Forest Service were to reclassify Glacier Peak as a Wilderness Area, a process requiring boundary studies, public notice, and possibly hearings, the area would enjoy stricter protection.

Citing the forest recreation study and his own trips through the North Cascades backcountry, Marshall in 1939 called for expanding the Glacier Peak unit to 795,000 acres and designating it a Forest Service wilderness area under the U-regulations. In response, Chief Forester Ferdinand Silcox, who supported Marshall's views, placed a hold over the entire area. That autumn, the Forest Service published the U-regulations, but required that existing primitive areas be reviewed before they could be reclassified. Marshall died in November and Silcox died unexpectedly the following month, leaving the Forest Service without a prominent wilderness champion (Aldo Leopold had left the agency in 1933).[11] In 1940, acting Chief C. M. Granger released more than half the land around Glacier Peak, citing mineral values and a proposed highway over the mountains. This left 347,525 acres held for possible reclassification.

Then World War II began, and reclassifying primitive areas fell down the Forest Service's list of priorities. It focused instead on fulfilling its founding mission of utilizing the nation's timber, and logging on the national forests increased accordingly. Federal timber sales nearly doubled during the war, although the national forests supplied only 10 percent of the wartime timber needed. Most timber still came from private forest lands.[12] Forest Service historian Gerald Williams writes that near the end of World War II, the agency "told Congress that the national forests, especially in the Pacific Northwest, could take more of the national timber burden."[13] Congress allocated more funds for road-building and timber planning, and the Forest Service responded by increasing the amount of timber harvested from the national forests.

A truck carrying sixty-foot logs and Forest Service vehicle on the upper Skagit, 1947. The agency tried to accommodate the timber industry's voracious appetite for national forest timber. *North Cascades National Park Service Complex Museum Collection, NOCA 11269*

The postwar housing boom shifted demand for national forest timber into high gear. When the war ended, the Forest Service ordered all regions to create timber plans for all "working circles" containing marketable timber. A working circle was an area, typically one hundred thousand to five hundred thousand acres in size, used to calculate how much timber an area could produce.[14] This informed the "allowable cut," the maximum quantity that could be harvested while maintaining a sustainable forest. After the war, many regions increased the allowable cut on their forests, citing better timber data, better access, and more efficient equipment.[15] Further, the move toward intensive management and ever-higher yields expressed the national belief that maximizing natural resource utilization was a moral imperative. Prosperity was writ large in the tracts of suburban housing that were the right of every hardworking American. In this context, the Forest Service's reasoning that its "overriding purpose was not so much to protect the national forests but rather to develop their resources," as historian Paul Hirt wrote, makes sense.[16]

The timber industry also found itself in a wholly different situation than before the war. Three years before Pearl Harbor, Washington State relinquished its standing as the nation's number-one timber producer as big companies moved southward into Oregon and California. Nevertheless, the timber industry accounted for nearly half the state's workforce in 1939, evidence of lumbering's continued dominance.

With its vast hydroelectric resources, Washington was ideally positioned to take on defense manufacturing needs when the nation entered the war. Aluminum and chemical production, shipbuilding, and aircraft construction quickly pushed the timber industry from the forefront of the state's economy. Labor statistics bear this out. In 1939, 46 percent of the state's workforce was employed in the lumber industry, while only 1 percent worked in shipyards. By 1944, lumber employment had dropped to 17 percent, while shipyard workers made up 32 percent.[17] Those trends continued into the 1950s. From 1947 to 1953, employment in lumbering fell 8 percent while employment in the aircraft industry skyrocketed 154 percent.[18]

Still, the development of new technologies helped the timber industry utilize the bark, chips, and debris that had previously been left on the forest or mill floor, and by the 1940s, pulp, paper, and plywood manufacturing became as important as logging to the state's economy.[19]

As private lands were cut over, and with few sustained yield replanting programs, many timber companies turned to the national forests. During the 1950s, timber production from the national forests nearly tripled, from 3.5 billion to 9.3 billion board feet; the total cut in the Pacific Northwest, while smaller, mirrored the dramatic increase.[20] The

Forest Service's philosophy of multiple-use, wherein the many uses of the forests were balanced for maximum public benefit, devolved into the pursuit of one dominant objective: maximizing timber harvest.[21]

The Forest Service's eagerness to promote logging led it to undervalue the demand for recreation. As historian Samuel Hays suggested, the agency "seemed to be trapped by its own internal value commitments" to timber harvest, and unable to acknowledge or respond to increasing public interest in wilderness.[22]

That public interest grew proportionately with Washington's population. Wartime economic diversification meant Washington gained more people during the war than any other state but California.[23] Between 1940 and 1950, Washington's population grew by more than one-third. During the 1950s, it grew another 20 percent.[24] Most of the impact was felt in urban areas such as Seattle, where the new industries were located. The city's population increased by more than half between 1940 and 1960, to well over a half-million people. The population of King County, where suburbs sprang up like weeds, grew a whopping 85 percent during the same time period to nearly one million people. As the manufacturing industries grew, so did professions that supported the new residents, including health care and education. Between 1940 and 1948, personal income in Washington tripled, and per capita income more than doubled.[25]

Flush with postwar prosperity and plentiful leisure time, Washington's growing urban middle class took off for forests and parks in unprecedented numbers. They geared up with surplus military equipment or new, lightweight equipment from companies like REI, and set out to hike, backpack, climb, ski, snowshoe, fish, boat, and more. In the three years from 1952 to 1955, recreational visits to the Region 6 national forests increased by more than one-third, and membership in the Mountaineers grew at precisely the same rate.[26] Indeed, during the 1950s, membership in the Mountaineers doubled to more than four thousand. When outdoor enthusiasts arrived in their national forests, many found cutover slopes, muddy rivers, and slash piles. Recreation groups, historical allies of the Forest Service, began to pressure the agency to set aside more unspoiled land.

Increasing population and growing demands for recreational resources steered conservationists and the Forest Service on a collision course. Internal Forest Service documents from the time show the agency purposely emphasized multiple-use to mollify recreation and conservation groups, but in reality logging was always given precedence. The Forest Service reconceptualized Pinchot's concept of utilitarian conservationism to benefit timber interests. The primacy given logging on national forest lands led many to believe multiple-use, the idea that the national forests could be managed to serve many purposes simultaneously, was not a viable operational paradigm.[27]

Indeed, in the years after World War II, the Forest Service reconsidered recreation use at Glacier Peak only in fits and starts. In 1946, the Glacier Peak Recreation Unit was renamed Glacier Peak Limited Area. The Limited Area designation, unique to Region 6, prohibited road-building and resource extraction until further studies could be undertaken, and could be undone at will by the regional forester.[28]

In 1950, the agency began another study of the area, this time to consider reclassification from Limited to Wilderness Area.[29] By November, supervisors from the affected forests recommended a nominal decrease from the existing limited area acreage. Before the recommendations could be implemented, Silcox, the regional forester, died in a car accident, bringing that effort to a halt. In late 1951, the agency admitted it had not devoted enough time to the reclassification study but noted that outdoors groups had generally agreed on boundaries earlier that year. Two years later, the Forest Service was still saying it planned to proceed with reclassifying Glacier Peak, but nothing happened.[30]

In June 1955, University of California, Berkeley political science professor Grant McConnell was enjoying the summer break at his cabin in Stehekin. A longtime North Cascades enthusiast, McConnell climbed around Lake Chelan in the late 1930s and early 1940s with the Wyeasters, a Portland mountaineering club.[31] During World War II, he was rescued from the Pacific Ocean when the destroyer on which he was stationed sank in combat. McConnell spent a month recuperating in a cabin under Si Si Ridge, west of Stehekin. Captivated by the area's beauty and tranquility, he and his wife Jane bought a cabin on the banks of Company Creek, a tributary of the Stehekin River, and moved there after the war ended. In 1948, the McConnells moved to Berkeley, where Grant earned his doctorate, then joined Berkeley's faculty and began a prolific and prominent career as a political scientist with an abiding passion for conservation.[32]

The McConnells returned to Stehekin each summer, and it was while there in 1955 they heard rumors of a Forest Service timber sale in the valley. Stehekin, accessible only by foot, boat, or plane, had remained virtually unchanged since the 1930s. But after World War II, people returning from the war, like McConnell, moved there, and the tiny Stehekin school reopened for the first time since the early 1940s. The tourist trade picked up again. With gas rationing over, people began vacationing, and remote Stehekin was an ideal escape from the bulging Seattle suburbs and other urban areas. Stehekin appealed anew to land developers, who began buying old homesteads and subdividing them. Predictably, the timber industry became interested in the mostly untouched valleys along the Stehekin River. Specifically, the Stehekin watershed interested the Chelan Box Manufacturing Company, which foresaw that logs cut there could be floated downriver to Lake Chelan, chained into rafts, and towed to the company's mill near Chelan. Talk of logging the Agnes Creek valley, a major tributary of the Stehekin River that drains a large geographic area from Dome Peak to Suiattle Pass, was especially widespread. Much of the valley was part of the existing Glacier Peak Limited Area, and McConnell felt much of this secluded, isolated haven should be part of any new wilderness area.[33]

McConnell was not the only conservationist interested in the fate of Glacier Peak. Later that summer of 1955, three backpackers were camped in the snow near Suiattle Pass when they saw a helicopter overhead, bringing equipment to a proposed mining operation on nearby Miners Ridge. About halfway through a forty-mile trek that included Railroad Creek, Lyman Lake, Suiattle and Cloudy passes, and Agnes Creek, the trio felt this "very upsetting" incident made their objective all the more imperative.[34] They were there on assignment to get an idea of what the Glacier Peak country looked like and report back to their organization, the Mountaineers.

As one of the oldest and most respected outdoors clubs in Washington, the Mountaineers had followed Forest Service activities at Glacier Peak for decades, in part because the mountain was a popular destination for club outings. The Forest Service had delayed the reclassification study that was supposed to have begun in 1950, citing mounting Cold War tension, the unexpected death of the regional forester, and a lack of time.[35] In 1953, the Mountaineers Conservation Committee noted preserving wilderness values at Glacier Peak was "a tremendous project, but a very vital one."[36] The group's monthly newsletter hinted at its apprehension about the Forest Service's ability to apply multiple-use principles to Glacier Peak. Time and again, proposed Forest Service wilderness "tragically eliminates most of the river areas which contain the virgin forests." The Mountaineers urged members to backpack into the remote, difficult-to-reach area, taking pictures and writing reports to help develop boundary recommendations. Agnes Creek was called out as one of several areas of concern.[37]

Logging the Stehekin valley, 1955. This photo may show a Chelan Box Manufacturing Co. logging operation. The company sought to log valley timber to build fruit boxes. *North Cascades National Park Service Complex Museum Collection, NOCA 11912*

The Mountaineers had reason to fear the possibility of eliminating valley floors and forests from the wilderness area. In an effort to demonstrate its commitment to the principle of multiple-use, the Forest Service habitually omitted merchantable timber found in river valleys. In this scenario, recreationists got the high mountain vistas and timber companies got the lowland trees. Conservationists dubbed the result a "wilderness on the rocks" or "starfish wilderness," since such wilderness areas hugged barren ridges and steep slopes. To raise awareness about what such a wilderness would look like, the Mountaineers sponsored more trips into the Glacier Peak region in 1953 and 1954. Member Dick Brooks, the president of a Seattle chemical manufacturing company who had climbed in the North Cascades for years, took the lead on Glacier Peak. He had become involved in conservation as a Boy Scout when he testified in 1943 against reducing the size of Olympic National Park to allow wartime logging.[38] In 1954, he accompanied the Forest Service on field trips to the Suiattle, Sauk, and White Chuck Rivers as part of the agency's reclassification study, and he kept after the Mountaineers Conservation Committee to monitor Glacier Peak.[39]

That year, the Mountaineers and others interested in wilderness preservation gained valuable insight into the Forest Service's priorities. A few hundred miles south of Glacier Peak loom the Three Sisters, a cluster of mountains that includes three of Oregon's five tallest peaks (Mount Hood and Mount Jefferson are taller). The Forest Service had set aside nearly two hundred thousand acres surrounding the Three Sisters as a Primitive Area in 1937, adding another fifty-five thousand acres the following year. In 1954, the Forest Service proposed reclassifying the Primitive Area into Three Sisters Wilderness Area, much as it was doing with Glacier Peak. The proposal eliminated fifty-three thousand acres of low-elevation forests and offered instead two new, high-elevation Wild Areas at nearby Diamond Peak and Mount Washington. Local conservationists were outraged by this quid pro quo, which they viewed as trading irreplaceable old-growth forest for wind-scoured alpine ridges with little harvestable timber. A "loose-knit collection of hikers, scientists, and social liberals" gelled into a unified opposition group, Friends of the Three Sisters. They would spend the next three years fighting the Forest Service proposal, and the Mountaineers closely tracked their work.[40]

Back in Washington, the Mountaineers appointed Polly Dyer chair of the Conservation Committee in January 1955.[41] Dyer had moved to Seattle from California in 1950, joining the Mountaineers and becoming a prominent member of the Olympic Park Associates, a watchdog group formed to protect Olympic National Park.[42] Polly took several trips to the Glacier Peak area in 1955, including one with representatives from the Forest Service and the Federation of Western Outdoor Clubs, a regional umbrella organization dedicated to keeping its member clubs informed of conservation issues. That trip left from Darrington, on the west side of the mountains, and followed the Suiattle River and Sulphur Creek to Meadow Mountain, familiarizing club members with the "Shangri-La of the Cascades."[43] But Dyer's Railroad Creek-to-Agnes Creek journey with two other Mountaineers, Phil and Laura Zalesky, was by far the more significant trip for future activism in the North Cascades.

The Zaleskys had been hiking in Glacier Peak country for several years by the time they invited Polly Dyer to see the eastern side of the range in July 1955. Phil Zalesky taught in the Everett School District, and he and Laura were members of the Everett Mountaineers. After reading an influential *Harper's* magazine article by Bernard DeVoto about the effects of overuse on the national parks, Phil had written to his congressman, Rep. Jack Westland (R-WA), expressing his concern.[44] Receiving an unsympathetic reply from Westland's office, Phil contacted the Seattle Mountaineers Conservation Committee, where he met Polly Dyer. She had not seen the Glacier Peak country before—most Seattle Mountaineers hiked in the closer-to-home Interstate 90 corridor around Snoqualmie Pass—and the Zaleskys asked her to come on a backpacking trip.[45]

Sitting in a Stehekin café after their trek while waiting for the downlake ferry, the trio probably looked a bit bedraggled. But their ice axes caught the eye of a resident who had come to the dock to collect her mail. Jane McConnell wandered over and asked what they had climbed. Agnes Creek, Railroad Creek, Miners Ridge, Cloudy Pass, they responded, adding they were members of the Mountaineers conducting a study trip. You need to meet Grant, Jane insisted, because he was concerned about proposed logging in the Stehekin valley.[46] Thus the McConnells and the nascent Seattle conservation movement, all of them professionals enjoying the fruits of the midcentury economic boom, first connected. The importance of this chance meeting would become increasingly clear over the next decade.

In fall 1955, Polly and John Dyer visited the McConnells at their home in Berkeley, and Polly and Grant began talking about ways to protect Glacier Peak and the Stehekin valley.[47] As Conservation Committee chair, Polly kept a close eye on the Three Sisters controversy, and she saw how the local group enlisted help from national conservation organizations such as the Wilderness Society and the Sierra Club. When the Dyers lived in California, Polly's husband had climbed with Sierra Club executive director David Brower, and they maintained the friendship after the Dyers moved north.

McConnell's interest was both personal and professional. In a 1954 article in *Western Political Quarterly*, he argued the conservation movement had become "small, divided and frequently uncertain." Pinchot's utilitarian philosophy emphasized material uses of natural resources for "the greatest good for the greatest number in the long run." Humans were at the center of this argument: their needs were paramount. This starkly conflicted with the approach recently expressed by Aldo Leopold, whose wilderness thinking had evolved toward an ecological perspective.[48] Leopold asserted that humans were part of larger ecological systems and could not be elevated among other elements. Natural resources had values that could not be expressed in economic terms, and those should be considered equally in land use decisions.[49] McConnell realized that Glacier Peak could be a flash point for this conflict and, possibly, a means to create common cause among conservation groups.

In this spirit, McConnell invited Brower to speak to his political science class about the role of interest groups in conservation.[50] Brower grew up wandering the hills around Berkeley and joined the Sierra Club in 1933. A prolific climber, he recorded seventy first ascents during the 1930s, but found time to edit the Sierra Club *Bulletin* beginning in 1937. In 1939, he made a Sierra Club film about Kings Canyon that helped win support for its creation as a national park. After serving in the ski troops of the Tenth Mountain Division during World War II, he returned to the Sierra Club, accepting an appointment to the board of directors and leading high trips. In 1952, Brower became the seven-thousand-member club's first executive director and led its transformation to a national organization dedicated to wilderness preservation.[51] Rangy and charming, with vivid blue eyes and a wave of white hair, Brower proved an effective leader of the growing movement.

Beginning with the first Biennial Wilderness Conference in 1949, the Sierra Club in the 1950s became a major proponent of wilderness preservation and national park activism.[52] The Dinosaur National Monument campaign exemplified this new approach. A proposed dam on Colorado's Green River that would have flooded parts of the exceptionally scenic monument was defeated under the leadership of Brower and the Sierra Club, resulting in what many view as the first victory of modern environmentalism.[53]

McConnell believed the North Cascades, like Dinosaur, warranted national attention because the wilderness there was largely unknown, scenically magnificent, and one of the largest such tracts remaining in the continental United States. The Sierra Club could bring national credibility to the issue, and Brower was the key. Brower accepted the invitation to speak to his Berkeley class, and McConnell used the opportunity to show him slides of the North Cascades, hoping to pique his interest. It worked. McConnell re-upped his lapsed Sierra Club membership, Brower installed him on the club's Conservation Committee, and they began strategizing how the Sierra Club could become involved in Glacier Peak.[54]

To Brower's way of thinking, the North Cascades was a natural issue for the Sierra Club to tackle, in part because it was a wilderness issue and potentially a national park issue. His strategy was four-pronged: 1) act locally and activate the grassroots; 2) influence the broader conservation community through meetings and private contacts; 3) get national publicity; and 4) lobby policymakers in Washington, DC.[55]

Step one was connecting with McConnell and, by extension, local conservationists. Brower utilized his connections in the Northwest to build a grassroots base of support. In addition to the Dyers and now the McConnells, he had a good friend in Seattle who became the lodestone of the regional effort to preserve the North Cascades. Irish-born Patrick Goldsworthy had been a Sierra Club member since 1940. He had worked as a "horse," carrying equipment for photographer Cedric Wright in California, who first introduced him to the Sierra Club. After serving in World War II, Goldsworthy was an assistant trip leader under Brower, taking over when Brower's efforts in national conservation became a full-time enterprise. Like Grant McConnell, Goldsworthy held a doctorate from Berkeley, his in biochemistry. Appointed to the University of Washington Medical School's research faculty in 1952, Goldsworthy and his wife, Jane, moved north.[56] Goldsworthy wanted to see the Cascade Range up close, and on a colleague's recommendation, hiked to Cascade Pass. Deeply impressed, he decided to join the Mountaineers to learn more, and in 1953 the Goldsworthys completed the club's climbing course.[57]

Late in 1953, Brower flew to Seattle to discuss forming a Pacific Northwest chapter of the Sierra Club with the Goldsworthys and Dyers. The foursome sent letters to every Sierra Club member in Washington, Oregon, Idaho, Montana, and Alaska, inviting them to join the new chapter. The Pacific Northwest chapter allowed the club to claim a national presence while helping local groups adopt Sierra Club techniques for involving members in conservation issues.[58] For example, instead of relying on committee members to spread the word, as the Mountaineers did, the Sierra Club sent mailings to each member urging them to take the initiative. The Pacific Northwest chapter's sole objective was to work on conservation issues, starting with Glacier Peak.[59]

With the enlistment of Brower and the Sierra Club in California, and the ongoing activities of the Mountaineers in Washington, Glacier Peak was poised to become a nucleus of conservation activism. Longtime Northwest conservationist Harvey Manning described the California-Washington connection as a tipping point, comparing it to the nineteenth-century alliance between followers of New England's Henry David Thoreau and California's John Muir: "The San Francisco-Puget Sound [alignment]...produced a significant explosion."[60] The Glacier Peak issue attracted local and national attention, and many saw it as an important test of the Forest Service's commitment to wilderness.

———————◆———————

At his cabin in summer 1956, McConnell received a phone call from a downlake orchardist, who said the Forest Service had posted notice of a timber sale in Stehekin.[61] Alarmed, McConnell contacted Wenatchee National Forest supervisor Ken Blair's office, where staff denied any such sale was planned. Rather, they said, a small area near the mouth of Company Creek was to be logged for construction of an airstrip for firefighting planes. But a neighbor in Stehekin, Ray Courtney, insisted he had seen the same sale notice.[62] Increasingly skeptical, McConnell decided to compel Blair to tell him what was really going on.

During late 1955 and early 1956, McConnell had corresponded with Blair, stating his concerns about logging in the Stehekin valley. Blair assured him no timber sales were planned and that great care would be taken when they were. In March 1956, Blair wrote McConnell to say work on the Glacier Peak reclassification study was proceeding and the Forest Service hoped to have it completed within a year.[63] Then news of the timber sale notice spread up the valley.

In June 1956, McConnell wrote to Mountaineers president Chet Powell to say he had followed up on the rumors of timber sales and had been assured that the only logging planned was for an airstrip. Blair was not in the office, McConnell continued, but "I did try to learn the source of the story which we got on other large scale logging," he wrote. "It relates apparently to a notice of prospective sales in this forest which included an item about some two million feet in this area. I have not yet seen this notice....Until I actually see it, I am inclined to be skeptical about the story since it does not at all accord with which I heard in Wenatchee."[64] Then he copied the letter and enclosed it with a note to Blair asking for confirmation. Faced with the contradiction between what the Wenatchee National Forest office had told McConnell and the alleged notice of a much larger sale, Blair admitted 2.2 million board feet of timber near Company Creek had been included in the forest's cutting budget, but insisted that "such a sale will be held in abeyance until...the final boundaries of the proposed Glacier Peak Wilderness area, are determined."[65]

For McConnell, "It was one of those moments that come occasionally in every lifetime; instants not of revelation but of realization, when a series of long-known facts suddenly arrange themselves in a pattern of certainty which a moment before would have been unbelievable."[66] The rumors, the vanishing timber sale notice, the evasiveness of the Wenatchee Forest supervisor—everything fell into place. The Forest Service was going to sell Stehekin valley timber.

McConnell thanked Blair in a friendly note, but within days reported to Brower that the Forest Service had probably tried to downplay the sale because of growing conservationist interest in Glacier Peak. Brower had written to Forest Service Chief Richard McArdle earlier in the year, asking about the issue.[67] At the end of July, McConnell received a copy of a letter to Washington Sen. Henry "Scoop" Jackson in which the Forest Service said no timber sales were planned in Stehekin and the only cutting would be for the airstrip.[68]

Still waiting for the Forest Service's report on reclassifying Glacier Peak, McConnell was not placated. He knew that once the Forest Service started selling national forest timber in the Stehekin valley, there would be no foreseeable end to the logging: "Once a policy of systematic logging was begun in the area, there would be no point at which it could be expected to stop, other than the availability of trees and the limits imposed by cost."[69] Most of the valley was national forest land, with just a few private inholdings scattered along the lower Stehekin River. McConnell's sanctuary was in danger of being lost forever, and he was determined to do what he could to save it. He called everyone he knew in Seattle.

The Mountaineers, through Polly Dyer, the Zaleskys, and club president Chet Powell, knew about the Stehekin timber situation. To solidify strategy, Dyer hosted a meeting at her Auburn home in June 1956 attended by McConnell, the Zaleskys, Goldsworthy, Powell, and a dozen other Mountaineers. Dyer recalled that McConnell, the political scientist, tried to persuade the group that "if we *really* wanted to save this area we needed a single-purpose organization."[70] But the larger group was not convinced, in part because they felt the Mountaineers, backed by the Sierra Club, were effectively leading the effort on Glacier Peak. A year earlier the club spent $500 to publish 6,500 copies of a Conservation Committee-designed brochure to publicize Glacier Peak.[71] In December 1955, the club's magazine, *The Mountaineer*, featured a two-page spread on the history of Glacier Peak, asking members to submit photos and information that could help with the preservation effort.

Just about when McConnell was pushing for a single-purpose group to lead the Glacier Peak effort, the Mountaineers published its proposal for a Glacier Peak Wilderness Area. Now the Mountaineers' 3,500-plus members, Federation of Western Outdoor Clubs members, the Forest Service, and anybody interested could see on one crisp map the existing boundaries of the Limited Area, the 1939 proposal by Bob Marshall, and the Mountaineers' recommendation.[72]

The half-million-acre proposal represented a 45 percent increase in size but was still far smaller than Marshall's 795,000-acre recommendation, with what the group termed "very minimum" boundaries. Although not included in its proposal, the club believed the area between the North Cascade Primitive Area and Glacier Peak was "the missing link needed to complete the wilderness area" and should be protected, either within the final wilderness area boundaries or separately. For now, the club suggested that natural features should be used to delineate the Wilderness Area, and that "variety" should be the watchword for the determining its boundaries. Accordingly, "rain forest and open, dry pine forests, giant trees and stunted timberline growth, growing glaciers and ice fields, alpine meadows and spectacular concentrations of rugged peaks" were all represented. The entire Agnes Creek watershed was included, and existing Limited Area borders were expanded in every direction but southwest, where the boundary was reduced to eliminate Sloan Creek, a tributary of the Sauk River. One of the largest outdoor clubs in the country was now on record in favor of placing most of the North Cascades under wilderness area protection.[73]

The Mountaineers' proposal drew on traditional arguments for wilderness preservation, warning that without it "man's loss of the sense of relationship between himself and nature would be disastrous."[74] This argument is rooted in the Romantic primitivist concept of wilderness espoused by John Muir, who believed wilderness was an antidote to the rapidly increasing pressures of civilization, a way to rejuvenate one's spirit through exposure to the natural handiwork of a divine creator. For historian Donald Worster, this "aesthetic spiritualism" is the most important value underlying modern environmentalism, and it was frequently cited in support of wilderness preservation.[75] But the plan also contains hints of the more confrontational posture conservationists adopted in wilderness debates during the 1950s and early 1960s, arguing that "lasting wilderness enjoyment is more important to America than timber utilization." In other words, wilderness was a social benefit more important than timber harvest, at least at Glacier Peak. Furthermore, the increasing mechanization of society meant "more people with more leisure will want to see samples of nature unspoiled."[76]

This argument has special resonance in the Pacific Northwest, especially in the Cascade Range. Nationally, battles over dam construction in scenic wonders like Dinosaur National Monument and the Grand Canyon galvanized conservationists. In the Pacific Northwest it was timber harvest in the national forests that inspired action.[77] The Forest Service's ramped-up sales of national forest timber affected backcountry recreationists' views of wilderness. Increasingly, many thought wilderness should be set aside before it was all clearcut, because it provided long-term benefits that short-term timber harvest could not. Wilderness was a "release valve" for the pressures of midcentury population growth.[78] Structured as it was to maximize harvests on the national forests, the Forest Service could not or would not incorporate this view into its operations. The challenge for conservationists was to assign an instrumental value to wilderness, an economic value the Forest Service could understand.

To emphasize the gravity of the Glacier Peak issue, the Mountain-eers planned their 1956 summer outing to the mountain, opening it to nonmembers. Conservation groups commonly used such outings to raise awareness. With climbs scheduled for eight peaks not in the existing Limited Area, plus the imposing peak itself, the trip was designed to inspire interest and action.

———————◆———————

The Mountaineers were not the only group interested in Glacier Peak. Starting in 1954, the Federation of Western Outdoor Clubs passed res-olutions about Glacier Peak at each of its annual conventions. Initially, the group simply resolved to cooperate with the Forest Service in its study. But over the next few years, the resolutions became more strongly worded, supporting a larger wilderness area using either the Mountain-eers' 1956 or Bob Marshall's 1939 recommendations. Such resolutions were important because member groups then voted on whether to adopt them; for example, the Washington State Sportsmen's Council adopted the Federation of Western Outdoor Clubs' 1956 resolution in favor of Marshall's proposed boundaries, thereby disseminating information about Glacier Peak among its own members.[79] In this manner, conser-vationists throughout the West learned about the issue. Similarly, when a Washington, DC, resident went on a Mountaineers-sponsored Glacier Peak trip in 1955, he wrote about it for the Mazamas' journal and the *Washington Post*, helping to spread the word further.[80]

The Sierra Club continued monitoring the Glacier Peak issue.[81] Its Conservation Committee started digging up resource information on Glacier Peak, knowing that mineral and timber values would play a role in the final recommendation.[82] Brower urged the Pacific Northwest chapter to work with other regional outdoors groups for unity on Glacier Peak; he knew that all the conservation organizations speaking with one voice would improve the chances of getting an adequate wilderness.[83]

As 1956 wound down, other national groups publicized Glacier Peak. Following Brower's philosophy of engaging national groups, McConnell had asked for support from Wilderness Society executive director Howard Zahniser.[84] From his friendships with Polly Dyer and others, McConnell knew that Zahniser and the Wilderness Society had been involved in the controversy over the proposed Three Sisters Wilderness Area virtually since its beginning, publishing several articles about it in its journal *The Living Wilderness*.[85] Zahniser wrote an editorial supporting the Mountaineers and Sierra Club positions on Glacier Peak and urging a large wilderness be established.[86] *National Parks* magazine expressed concern about the Forest Service's focus on short-term economic profit versus long-term recreational and spiritual benefits, arguing, "It would be one of America's greatest tragedies if, out of the former wilderness, nothing ultimately remains but the land nobody can turn into dollars." Public support was needed to "solve intelligently what may well prove to be one of the greatest wilderness preservation issues of our time."[87]

A January 1957 article by McConnell in the *Sierra Club Bulletin* gave a final heads-up to conservationists. The Forest Service's reclassification study of Glacier Peak was due any day. McConnell criticized the method the Forest Service used in conducting the study. Maps showing different kinds of land use in the Glacier Peak region had been laid one on top of another to show where conflicts might be.[88] This overlay method reflected the Forest Service's ongoing effort to incorporate the multiple-use concept into national forest planning. But there was no map indicating wilderness or scenery as a land use; only recreational visits were included. For an area as remote, difficult to access, and little-known as Glacier Peak, the number of visits was unsurprisingly low. But those who had traveled the area "categorically assert[ed] that the region's scenic resources constitute its highest value."[89]

Moreover, McConnell wrote, the reclassification study area was itself simply too small. Marshall's original 1939 boundaries encompassing

795,000 acres, and also the 801,000-acre North Cascade Primitive Area, should be studied as a whole instead of relying on "piecemeal planning." The Sierra Club echoed the sentiment, urging the Forest Service to conduct a comprehensive study of the entire North Cascades, from Stevens Pass to the Canadian border, before making any land use decisions.[90]

With the activities of the Mountaineers and the Sierra Club in the Pacific Northwest, plus the ongoing work of Grant McConnell to raise awareness outside the region, the conservation movement centered in the Puget Sound basin coalesced around Glacier Peak. They were ready to act when, in February 1957, the Forest Service released its long-delayed Glacier Peak Limited Area reclassification study.

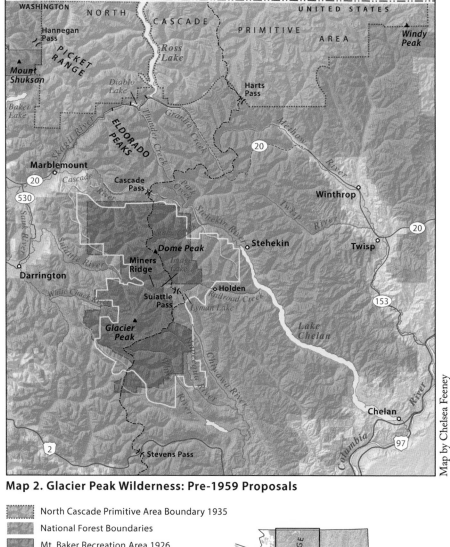

Map 2. Glacier Peak Wilderness: Pre-1959 Proposals

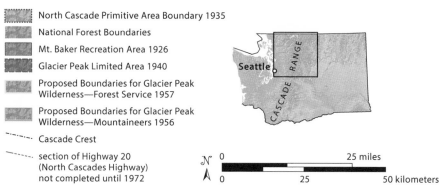

North Cascade Primitive Area Boundary 1935

National Forest Boundaries

Mt. Baker Recreation Area 1926

Glacier Peak Limited Area 1940

Proposed Boundaries for Glacier Peak
Wilderness—Forest Service 1957

Proposed Boundaries for Glacier Peak
Wilderness—Mountaineers 1956

Cascade Crest

section of Highway 20
(North Cascades Highway)
not completed until 1972

Map by Chelsea Feeney

Seattle

CASCADE RANGE

N

0   25 miles

0   25   50 kilometers

CHAPTER 3

The Forest Service Stumbles, and Conservationists Debate

The Forest Service's Glacier Peak Limited Area reclassification study, released in February 1957, initially seemed promising. It called for a Glacier Peak Wilderness Area of 434,310 acres, almost 25 percent larger than the Limited Area's 347,525 acres. The study defined wilderness as "a special type of recreation area catering to special classes of recreationists who possess the physical energy to hike or climb over rugged terrain, or who are financially able to hire pack and saddle animals to travel in the area."[1] This definition was partly informed by Bob Marshall's description nearly three decades earlier. Free of permanent settlements, roads, and mechanized conveyances like cars, and large enough to require "sleeping out," wilderness demanded self-sufficiency from those who used it and preserved "as nearly as possible the primitive environment."[2] Devoted to the multiple-use paradigm that characterized national forest management, the Forest Service could not set aside so much land for a single, noneconomic purpose that served so few people. Therefore, the Glacier Peak boundaries were drawn to provide "recreation opportunities for all classes of outdoor recreationists."[3]

This required roads to be built to place "the scenic beauty of Glacier Peak within the enjoyment of the roadside recreationists" and open the same areas to logging. Accordingly, densely forested river valleys leading into the Glacier Peak region were excluded from the wilderness. Nine thousand acres of commercial timber that had been inside the Limited Area would now be available for harvest. To get to the backcountry, hikers would be walking along logging roads and through clearcuts, particularly on the west side of the proposed wilderness.[4]

For example, much of the White Chuck River was left outside the wilderness area to facilitate access to Kennedy Hot Springs, a tiny natural

55

pool where the Forest Service wanted camping, picnicking, and perhaps a resort.[5] By skirting the springs, the boundaries opened to logging the lower White Chuck valley. The agency also proposed extending the road along the Suiattle River by six miles to shorten western access to Miners Ridge and Image Lake, considered by many to be the scenic climax of the region. At places like Illabot Creek, a tributary of the Cascade River in the northwest corner of the Limited Area, "timber harvesting is considered the preference use," but roads built to facilitate logging would create easier access for other uses, like fishing at Illabot Lakes, which remained inside the boundaries.[6]

Glacier Peak and White Chuck River valley from Lake Byrne. A Forest Service wilderness reclassification study of Glacier Peak in the mid-1950s piqued the interest of conservationists, who valued heavily timbered river valleys on the western slopes of the Cascades as access corridors to alpine areas. The Forest Service valued these valleys for their merchantable timber. *North Cascades National Park Service Complex Museum Collection, NOCA 11751*

The Forest Service asserted the proposed roads and recreational developments would make the region more accessible and substantially increase use. Fewer than three thousand people visited Glacier Peak in 1956. At Kennedy Hot Springs alone, the agency predicted twenty thousand visitors per year, with the added benefit of more tourist traffic through Darrington, a nearby logging town just outside the national forest that could potentially lose harvestable timber to a wilderness area designation.[7]

Grant McConnell was particularly distressed by the Forest Service's proposal to log five miles of lower Agnes Creek, a tributary of the Stehekin River. Not part of the existing Limited Area, rumors of a timber sale had swirled around this area since 1955 and prompted McConnell's involvement in the Glacier Peak reclassification process. For recreationists, Agnes Creek was a primary route to Suiattle Pass, Dome Peak, and the Cascade Crest Trail (later the Pacific Crest Trail). The study stated that "orderly harvesting of good quality timber stands in the valley floor" would promote roadside recreation.[8]

On the ground, "orderly harvesting" meant clearcutting, the removal of all trees in a given area. By the mid-1950s, clearcutting was the favored logging practice in Region 6 of the Forest Service, comprising Washington and Oregon. The Forest Service believed logging was necessary to make recreational opportunities available to more people, because logging roads were also used by recreationists. Clearcutting was the most efficient, economically expedient type of logging. Even as clearcutting accelerated, helped by advances in logging technology that allowed trees to be cut and taken out of the forest faster than ever, "there was a growing concern that the Forest Service was clearcutting too many areas and building roads in areas that were also used for recreation."[9]

From the agency's point of view, recreation and logging could coexist. Both were legitimate uses of the national forests. Wilderness by itself was not considered a use except insofar as it enhanced recreation.[10] In other words, wilderness recreation was one use to which the national forests might be put, much as watershed protection, timber production, and soil conservation were legitimate uses. The Forest Service's multiple-use philosophy, on which the agency predicated its land-use decisions, did not allow forests to be viewed as more than commodity production plantations for human benefit. Trees and recreation were forest products. The agency's Progressive roots obliged it to serve as many people as possible, and its founding doctrine of "the greatest good for the greatest number" stood in opposition to its definition of wilderness as areas available only to "special classes" of people (i.e., those fit or wealthy enough to enjoy it). This meant areas deemed useful for mass recreation (and thus logging) were excluded from the Glacier Peak boundaries.

Yet these were the very areas conservationists argued were integral to the wilderness experience. A few small "representative stands of virgin timber low down along the numerous water courses" were included in the boundaries, but wilderness was given precedence only in areas so remote or steep that no other uses could be contrived. One of these was on the east side of the Cascades. Lyman Lake and Lyman Glacier were originally excluded from the Limited Area because mineral values were deemed dominant in the Railroad Creek basin, where a copper mine was located. Now, however, "recreation values are so important in this zone, and the possibility of making these values available to roadside recreationists is so limited" that wilderness was the logical option. The same rationale applied to Panther Creek and the upper Napeequa River on the southeast side, where "the character of the soil and topography makes logging unfeasible." The Forest Service preferred wilderness in these two areas because other uses were not practical.[11]

The Forest Service released its final decision on Oregon's Three Sisters wilderness simultaneously with the Glacier Peak study report. To the dismay of conservationists and despite opposition from five of Oregon's six-member Congressional delegation, the agency permanently deleted fifty-three thousand acres of old-growth forest from the new Three Sisters wilderness, opening the area to logging and reducing the size of the wilderness by 20 percent.[12] This was, perhaps coincidentally, the same percentage by which the proposed Glacier Peak wilderness had been enlarged. The timing of the Three Sisters decision and the Glacier Peak study seemed suspicious to some, who felt the Forest Service was trying to distract attention from the hotly debated Three Sisters controversy by proposing a larger Glacier Peak wilderness area.[13] For conservationists, larger did not necessarily mean better, as the forested valleys leading to Glacier Peak were still omitted.

Motives notwithstanding, the Three Sisters decision and the ongoing debate over Glacier Peak helped crystallize support for a national wilderness system.

With rising postwar demand for timber and recreation in the national forests and the passing of agency wilderness advocates like Bob Marshall and Aldo Leopold, wilderness seemed like an afterthought, a leftover designation from the custodial era. In truth, Forest Service wilderness policy "was not the result of a 'grass roots' movement but was sponsored chiefly by a few Forest Service officials in Washington [DC]…and forced on various western forest supervisors."[14] By and large, the agency looked at forests as storehouses of natural resources to be used, and wilderness did not fit easily into that paradigm.

In contrast, conservationists increasingly framed national forest recreation in a wilderness context. Two years of working on the Glacier Peak issue convinced them that economic values were not a viable model for making land use decisions about wilderness. Wild places had intrinsic, aesthetic, and noneconomic value, many believed, and should be preserved in part because a rich nation ought to be able to afford to preserve some wild remnants of its past before they disappeared forever. One conservationist wrote to Regional Forester Herb Stone, "The value of an area for wilderness is directly based on its aesthetic quality, rather than the quantity of visitors to it, the number of square miles of snow and ice it contains, or any other quantitative measurement of it."[15] As utilization, visitation, and plans for development grew, sentiment for preserving some land in its untouched state grew concurrently. Four days after the Glacier Peak reclassification study was issued, Sen. Hubert Humphrey of Minnesota again introduced legislation for a statutory wilderness system. Sen. Richard Neuberger (D-OR) cosponsored it, in part because he was angered by the Three Sisters decision.[16] While the Wilderness Act would ultimately take eight years to pass, the campaign transformed conservationists' tactics in the North Cascades.

Grant McConnell and the Sierra Club's David Brower had been pondering the best approach for months before the Forest Service published the Glacier Peak study in February 1957. The previous November, McConnell wrote, "The time has come, it seems to me, for the formation of a fairly flexible organization directed to the problems of conserving the splendid wilderness and scenic areas of the northern Cascades." The group should be small and stay small, he added, and consist of individuals, not representatives of other outdoors organizations. Its sole purpose should be to "preserve the scenic wilderness of the northern Cascades…for its highest uses as wilderness and scenic enjoyment."[17] Polly Dyer wrote to a friend, "Perhaps it's a la Olympic Park Associates," a group formed in 1948 as a watchdog for Olympic National Park, which had barely escaped logging during the war and was still vulnerable to boundary revision proposals, mostly from timber companies.[18]

Others were unconvinced. Patrick Goldsworthy, for one, felt a separate group would duplicate efforts. The Mountaineers Glacier Peak Subcommittee had already taken the lead, he noted, with the Sierra Club providing additional help and publicity. Instead of a new group, Goldsworthy suggested the ongoing informal correspondence among interested parties be expanded, ensuring those who wanted to be informed would be.[19]

Less than two weeks after Goldsworthy's response, though, the Forest Service released its Glacier Peak report and Three Sisters decision. Keeping commercial grade timber available for the lumber industry was demonstrably the agency's top priority. Any wilderness would be created from the least valuable land and only as a token gesture to conservationists. Dismayed by the Glacier Peak proposal and incensed by the Forest Service's final boundaries at Three Sisters, more than two dozen Northwest conservationists convened at the Mazamas clubrooms in Portland in late March 1957 for an emergency meeting. The Glacier Peak reclassification study was the first step in the wilderness designation process, and conservationists did not want a repeat of Three Sisters. The big questions were how to proceed and what course of action to pursue.[20]

Despite their frustration, conservationists on the whole liked the Forest Service. The agency was the primary custodian of backcountry in the Pacific Northwest, and since the early years of the century had devoted much time and effort toward developing good relationships with local residents. At the same time, it was apparent the Forest Service of 1957 had enthusiastically embraced its utilitarian mission. Multiple-use might be the catchphrase, but logging was always given primacy.[21] Conservationists did not want to alienate the Forest Service, but were skeptical the agency truly sympathized with their concerns. The Three Sisters decision and Glacier Peak proposal exacerbated this unease.

The Forest Service was aware of these tensions. Recreation visits to the national forests increased nearly 400 percent from the mid-1930s to

the mid-1950s, but existing facilities could not accommodate the growing crowds.[22] Nationally, the strain became pronounced enough by 1956
that some outdoors groups lobbied for a national recreation resources
and needs assessment, an idea introduced by Brower and others. In 1957
the Forest Service implemented Operation Outdoors, a five-year plan
to improve national forest recreation facilities.[23] From this point of view,
wilderness was considered only insofar as it might boost recreational use.
The agency's approach was out of sync with the agenda of wilderness
advocates, who increasingly saw wilderness as an end in itself.

Cognizant of the philosophical gap between their views of wilderness and those of the Forest Service, the conservationists debated possible strategies all morning in Portland, then met with Regional Forester
Stone and agency staff to talk about the bureau's process for determining the proposed Glacier Peak wilderness boundaries. After seeing their
concept of wilderness values was largely absent and recreation was only
considered in terms of the number of visits an area received (more visits
equaled more use and therefore more people served), the conservationists reconvened in the afternoon and voted overwhelmingly to create a
single-purpose organization to work on wilderness issues in the North
Cascades, including trying to convince the Forest Service of the importance of wilderness areas.[24] The original working name for the group was
Conservationists for the North Cascades, but by the time preliminary
by-laws were proposed it had become the North Cascades Conservation
Council, which most immediately shortened to N3C.[25]

The N3C modeled itself on the Friends of the Three Sisters Wilderness, the Eugene, Oregon-based group that had campaigned unsuccessfully for the retention of low-elevation forests in that wilderness area.
Like the Friends, the N3C had one purpose: to fight to preserve the
wilderness of the North Cascades. By choosing to identify itself with
the entire North Cascades region, the group gave notice its aspirations
extended beyond Glacier Peak.

The N3C's organizational structure offers insight into how conservationists became professionalized during the 1950s. An executive committee led the organization, appointing a nominating committee to submit names for the board of directors. In turn, board members elected the
executive committee.[26] Theoretically, new members joined because they
already supported N3C positions. This circular arrangement potentially
meant the general membership had no say in who represented them in

the organization's leadership and carried the risk of insularity. Conversely, this structure reduced the possibility of internal strife and ensured leaders would be wholly committed to N3C objectives.

Newly elected president Phil Zalesky wrote to McConnell in Berkeley, announcing the creation of the group McConnell had pushed for and inviting him to join the board.[27] McConnell accepted, but his involvement would be from a distance; he moved to the University of Chicago later that year. Still summering in Stehekin, McConnell played a key role from the family cabin on Company Creek. Other founding board members included Goldsworthy and Dyer; Brower was added at the next meeting.[28] Virtually every conservationist who had been following the Glacier Peak issue since 1955 or 1956 was on the board.

The N3C spent much of the rest of 1957 developing relationships with other conservation groups, an effort facilitated by the fact that many board members concurrently served on like-minded organizations. The Mountaineers continued their activism, sponsoring a July 1957 outing to Glacier Peak and publishing in September a brochure, "Glacier Peak—Today a Wilderness Intact." Each of the Mountaineers' 3,600-plus members received a copy. The Federation of Western Outdoor Clubs and the Wilderness Society supported the Mountaineers' proposed boundaries for Glacier Peak. Major conservation groups in the Pacific Northwest and beyond were speaking with one voice, urging more thoughtful consideration for the North Cascades. By October 1957, the N3C had more than one hundred members, many drawn by the monthly *NCCC News.*

While conservationists organized, opposition to the proposed Glacier Peak wilderness focused on the timber standing inside its boundaries. Chelan County responded decisively when lifelong resident and Chelan Box Manufacturing Company president George Wall appeared before the county commission in late February 1957.[29] The firm's privately held timber would be depleted within five to seven years, he said. It was then logging more than two million board feet of timber in the Stehekin Valley on a tract it had purchased in 1956, and had unsuccessfully pushed for a national forest timber sale in Stehekin a few years earlier. "It's a battle" for the company's existence, Wall said. Chelan Box Manufacturing had been in business since 1931, employing dozens of workers who built fruit boxes for the area's commercial orchards.

"The head of Lake Chelan area is the only forest area near enough to be practical financially for logging," Wall said. Closing the area to timber harvest would have a devastating economic impact, he argued. Because a portion of national forest timber sale revenues were used for funding schools and roads in the counties where forests were located, Chelan County stood to lose money if any merchantable timber remained inside the proposed wilderness.[30] The prior year, more than two-thirds of the county's timber came from national forest lands, representing 20 percent of Washington's national forest harvest east of the Cascade Crest.[31] "We aren't asking [the Forest Service] to drop the entire wilderness idea," Wall said, "but to exclude from the boundaries the deep canyons that have no scenic value and today are such thick forests that if you leave the trail you can't ride through them."[32]

Convinced, the commissioners passed a resolution protesting the inclusion of the upper Agnes Creek, Park Creek, and Stehekin River drainages in the proposed wilderness; the fact that only the upper Agnes was actually inside the boundaries did not seem to matter. "We feel that the boundaries...can be meandered around all of these timbered areas," the commission wrote to Wenatchee National Forest supervisor Ken Blair. "We do not feel that these deep canyons where there is standing timber is of any particular value from a scenic standpoint. One must get to the high areas to really enjoy the finer scenery."[33]

Less than a week after the county commission registered its opposition, the Lake Chelan Chamber of Commerce voted unanimously to oppose any boundary below four thousand feet in elevation, thus excluding most timbered valleys. Chamber president Rev. Riley Johnson predicted the wilderness would cause "a local depression...We're asking school boards, PTA's, service clubs, community groups, merchants, and just plain individuals to protest this area vigorously in letters to our senators, representatives and legislators in Olympia. We're enlisting support to fight like we've never fought before—for our bread and butter."[34] Other regional groups rapidly followed suit. By year's end, the Omak and Spokane Chambers of Commerce had voted to oppose the wilderness area, as had the Manson Grange and Chelan County Development Council.[35] Republican congressman Walt Horan, who represented the eastern part of the Glacier Peak area, warned, "Personally, I am opposed to tying up, for all time, valuable blocks of commercial timber."[36]

Lumber companies also followed the Glacier Peak controversy. An executive from Weyerhaeuser, one of the country's largest timber companies with millions of acres of private holdings in Washington State, told one conservationist, "there no doubt would be a big battle over the eventual boundaries" because of the timber they contained.[37] The Forest Service's 1957 Glacier Peak study report concluded only 17 percent of the proposed wilderness contained commercial timber, down from one-quarter of the acreage in the existing Limited Area. Most of the commercial timber stood in the Mt. Baker National Forest portion of the proposed wilderness, because the wetter climate on the west slopes of the Cascades produced denser forests. Chelan County was worried about the potential loss of income from federal timber sale receipts, but in the Wenatchee National Forest, only 8 percent of the acreage proposed for wilderness was commercial timber.[38] There simply was not very much commercial timber included in the proposal, but the prospective loss of timber receipts deeply worried local residents.

For wilderness opponents, the amount of timber was not the point. At stake were not simply a few million board feet of commercial timber, but the livelihoods of residents in timber-dependent communities, the importance of the state's entrenched, powerful lumber industry, and decades of responsible Forest Service management. Setting aside Glacier Peak as a wilderness flew in the face of deeply held beliefs that timber was a crop, that it existed for human benefit, and that not harvesting it was wasteful. To reserve more than four hundred thousand acres for wilderness was literally locking it up for a single use that could be enjoyed only by a privileged few. This was antithetical to the multiple-use principles espoused by the Forest Service and lumber companies. A July 1957 article in *American Forests*, the journal of the American Forestry Association, echoed Gifford Pinchot's approach: "Idealists" would reserve nearly a million acres around Glacier Peak, but "realists say, 'Timber is a crop as well as a thing of beauty. Salvage mature trees before they die, but provide for other uses also.'"[39] Such powerful rhetoric reinforced conservationists' belief that for the Forest Service, multiple-use meant logging was given preeminence.

Wilderness supporters and opponents had their first public debate in December 1957, when the Society of American Foresters Puget

Sound section hosted a panel on Glacier Peak that included Phil Zalesky, Regional Forester Herb Stone, who had approved the Forest Service reclassification study, and Rev. Riley Johnson, who in addition to being Chamber of Commerce president was vicar of Chelan's St. Andrew's Episcopal Church, a stunning log edifice built in 1898 with logs towed from about ten miles uplake.[40] An energetic and prolific wilderness opponent, he spoke before some seventy groups and wrote countless letters soliciting support for his position. By at least one account, Johnson dominated the panel, arguing that wilderness boundaries below the timberline spelled economic doom for the already stagnant Chelan County. In July 1957, the Holden Mine had shut down after two decades in operation. The largest copper-mining business in Washington, Holden was an important producer during World War II and employed several hundred people. Falling prices and increasingly difficult access to the ore had prompted the closure. Take away lumbering, Johnson warned in his booming preacher's voice, and "you take the groceries off the shelf."[41]

Johnson presented what would become the opposition's main arguments against wilderness. It was undemocratic, as only relatively few people had the means and strength to use it; decisions about local timber should be made locally, not by people "far from the scene" in Washington, DC; and any wilderness designation posed economic hardship for local residents. Stone presented "token defense" for the Forest Service proposal, saying it was merely preliminary and that changes could be made. Zalesky tried to play to the audience, arguing the national forests could accommodate both sustained yield forestry and wilderness, while skyrocketing recreation use actually indicated the need for more wilderness. The Glacier Peak wilderness, he said, should be bigger, not smaller. For the audience of about 175 professional foresters and timber industry representatives, Johnson's rhetoric carried the day.[42]

The debate can be seen as a microcosm of viewpoints about wilderness in the postwar era that would repeatedly arise during the North Cascades controversy. Opponents generally argued wilderness was elitist, supported by those who did not depend on the land for their livelihoods, and it "locked up" resources that by rights should be the province of local people who depended on them for economic sustenance. Proponents countered that increasing recreation demands merited a more balanced approach to multiple-use in the national forests, that wilderness recreation attracted tourists and was more economically sustainable than logging or mining, and that the pressures of modern life required places untouched by humans.

In January 1958, Johnson wrote and circulated a seven-page brochure titled *Have You Been Told? Do You Know the Facts? on the Proposed Glacier Peak Wilderness Area.* Johnson represented the rather grandiose-sounding National Forest Multiple Use Association, Washington State Chapter, a local group formed specifically to fight the Glacier Peak proposal. The pamphlet asked readers, "Do you know the effect [the wilderness] will have upon you as a wage earner, as a business man and a taxpayer and how it will have a bearing upon the education of your children?" Because one-quarter of national forest timber sale receipts were directed back into the local community to fund schools and roads, any reduction in the amount of harvestable timber would result in fewer funds. Locking up the timber contained in the proposed wilderness, Johnson contended, could increase local residents' "heavy tax burden" by imposing new property or other taxes to replace reduced national forest receipts.[43]

Johnson's polemic drew on the class distinctions often employed by wilderness opponents: because wilderness was so remote, the only people who could afford to enjoy it were those in superb physical condition or who had the means to buy equipment and hire guides and pack trains. The implication was that wilderness was undemocratic. In contrast, if the forested valleys were kept outside the wilderness boundaries, roads could be constructed to "make the area accessible to *all classes* of people." He urged readers to write state and federal legislators in support of the Forest Service's multiple-use approach to Glacier Peak.[44]

Within two months, the North Cascades Conservation Council published its own brochure. The eleven-page *Are You Aware? Comments Concerning the Glacier Peak Wilderness Area* appeared in March 1958, charging that the National Forest Multiple Use Association, "sponsored and financed by members of the pulp industry in Bellingham," stirred up a "frenzy" and "grossly confused the facts" through "statistical manipulating." The N3C painstakingly refuted Johnson's arguments, citing timber industry representatives and the Forest Service to support its claims the proposed wilderness would not cause a timber shortage or significantly affect local economies. The president of Weyerhaeuser, the chief of the Forest Service, and a national forest products industry association all agreed there was no foreseeable shortage of timber.

Moreover, the revenue projections Johnson used were woefully out-of-date, representing timber bid prices a third or more higher than 1957 prices. Timber in the proposed wilderness often grew in "stringer strands," smaller clumps of trees separated by meadows, glaciers, and other alpine features. Such strands were more expensive to get to, and therefore would cost more to log, but Johnson had treated the entire wilderness as if the timber it contained grew in low-elevation valley floors.[45]

The N3C tackled the multiple-use concept, arguing wilderness exemplified its highest form. Wilderness areas provided recreation, watershed and soil conservation, mining (previous claims were allowed to be developed), grazing (permits were sometimes allowed), habitat protection that benefited wildlife and sportsmen alike, a place for scientific study and education, and a possible "reserve of commodity resources for future generations." Attempting to redefine wilderness to fit the paradigm of resource use, conservationists argued it was necessary for recreation: "Forests dedicated for recreation will, in the long run, serve as many people, and thus be as valuable, as forests reserved for logging."[46]

The N3C concluded the opposition to a Glacier Peak wilderness revealed the perpetuation of the "myth of inexhaustibility" and the industry's unwillingness to adopt more responsible forestry methods. Replanting private timberland lagged behind logging, with only seventy-five thousand acres planted for every three hundred thousand acres logged each year: "One can only suspect that [opposition to wilderness areas] is part of a propaganda offensive to camouflage [industry's] own failings." As Johnson had done, the N3C ended by urging readers to write their legislators and the Forest Service in support of the proposed Glacier Peak wilderness.[47]

In March 1958, the Sierra Club and N3C unveiled a major strategem in the fight for Glacier Peak, a half-hour film titled *Wilderness Alps of Stehekin*. The movie was inspired by *This is Dinosaur*, the Sierra Club film many credit with helping to prevent construction of a dam in the threatened national monument.[48] McConnell had seen the film, tracked down the filmmaker, and asked about a similar project for the North Cascades, believing it could do much to raise awareness of the still little-known region. Brower came up with part of the funds and the Sierra Club started production. Abigail Avery, a Sierra Club member who was Jane McConnell's friend and former college roommate, gave a $2,500 grant to the Sierra Club to help complete the film.[49] When Brower unveiled the film at a Yakima-area N3C meeting, though, Seattle conservationists were disappointed that most footage was of the Stehekin area.[50] Nonetheless, with its spectacular footage and compelling commentary—the opening sequence described the North Cascades as "an amazing wilderness of rugged Alps built in grand scale, unique, unsurpassed anywhere in the United States, a crown jewel of America's scenic grandeur"[51]—the film won many converts to the conservationists' cause. It was "something that you could take out and talk about and show people, and it really made a great impression on everybody who saw it," Zalesky recalled.[52] The N3C and other groups began showing it all over the Northwest.[53]

By the time *Wilderness Alps of Stehekin* was released, the major conservation groups involved in the Glacier Peak fight agreed the Forest Service proposal was inadequate. The vexing question was how to oppose it. Until mid-1958, the focus had been on ensuring adequate wilderness was protected at Glacier Peak. Despite the stricter regulations protecting wilderness developed by Bob Marshall and adopted by the Forest Service in 1939, wilderness areas could still be undone administratively.

Some conservationists thought a national park might offer better, permanent long-term protection for the area. Under Brower's leadership, the Sierra Club became increasingly skeptical of the utilitarian conservation approach emphasizing timber harvest, mass recreation, and other quantifiable uses that characterized wild lands policy in the postwar era, especially when it was applied to the vulnerable areas under Forest Service management.[54] As early as 1940, a Seattle conservationist suggested that "either a national park or a national recreation area offers the best method of protection for this region."[55] In November 1955 Brower told McConnell that pursuing a national park might "wake up the boys in the Forest Service."[56] At the time, McConnell thought the national park idea intriguing; some Stehekin visitors had mentioned it the previous year.[57]

In April 1957, McConnell floated the idea of pursuing national park status for the Agnes Creek and Stehekin River valleys to journalist friends in New York and California.[58] The North Cascades Conservation Council, however, was established to focus on preserving *wilderness*, and many conservationists felt the National Park Service was not the best guarantor of wilderness protection. In fact, in their view, the Park Service seemed bent on developing the parks to better accommodate the millions of visitors streaming into them every year.

Postwar prosperity severely strained the national parks and the Park Service. During the height of war in 1943, the parks received fewer than seven million visits. By 1951, visitation increased to more than thirty-seven million. In 1956, the parks recorded nearly sixty-five million visits, with no slowdown in sight.[59] Many facilities built in the early days of the Park Service and during the heyday of the New Deal by the Civilian Conservation Corps and Public Works Administration were dilapidated and dangerous. Overcrowding was common. Options included adding more parks, which would presumably disperse the tourists, or closing some parks altogether until funding matched demand, as famously suggested by historian Bernard DeVoto in a 1953 *Harper's* article. In a theme that has since become an annual refrain bemoaning the paucity of park funding by Congress, he wrote, "So much of the priceless heritage which the [Park] Service must safeguard for the United States is beginning to go to hell." Close Yellowstone, Yosemite, Grand Canyon, and Rocky Mountain National Parks until proper funding is allocated and they can be safely operated, he opined, not entirely tongue-in-cheek.[60]

National Park Service Director Conrad Wirth chose a different approach, a long-term plan to improve the parks by adding more visitor facilities. Thus the Park Service developed Mission 66, a ten-year plan to "expand the entire carrying capacity of the parks" at a cost of $1 billion, beginning in 1956 and ending in 1966, the golden anniversary of the agency's creation.[61] Mission 66's goal was to improve park facilities throughout the national park system: pave the roads and make them safer, upgrade lodging, build or renovate visitor centers. The program was predicated on the idea that "national park development would control where the public went and prevent misuse through…the 'paradox of prevention by development.'"[62] Congress agreed, appropriating $273 million to the Park Service between 1956 and 1959. More than two thousand miles of roads were constructed under Mission 66, including Hurricane Ridge Road in Olympic National Park and Stevens Canyon Road in Mount Rainier National Park.[63]

While Mission 66 was popular with Congress, conservation organizations were less enthusiastic. They feared Mission 66's development
focus would attract even more people to the parks, further endangering the wild places the Park Service was supposed to protect. Here the
preservationist stance supporting national parks came full circle. The
founding mandate of the National Park Service, to preserve monumental
nature while providing means for people to experience it, had generally
been interpreted in favor of use. Early in the twentieth century, preservationists aligned with the first director of the National Park Service, Stephen Mather, who believed the long-term viability of the national parks
depended on getting people to them. At first, the means of visitation
were the railroads, which collaborated with the federal government and
the tourism movement to bring people to the parks.[64] But as the number
of automobiles grew, so too did the number of car tourists to the parks
and the number of roads built to accommodate them. After World War
II, 98 percent of national park visitors came by automobile.[65]

As national parks historian Alfred Runte noted, "The dilemma for
preservationists…was that the automobile was needed to protect natural
wonders, let alone wilderness."[66] It was the same concern that led some,
perhaps most notably Bob Marshall, to focus on wilderness preservation as an antidote to rampant roadbuilding and auto tourism.[67] This was
"not unlike the decision facing preservationists throughout the national
park system. Although a prerequisite for public support, development
invariably compromised the values they had struggled to save."[68] In the
mid-1950s, conservationists looked around and saw more people, more
cars, and more roads in the national parks and forests, and many worried
about what it meant for wilderness.

Mission 66 gave lip service to wilderness preservation, but in reality
any protection afforded wilderness within national parks was by default.
Since the Park Service for decades regarded wilderness as "everything
not developed," it did not view wilderness as a quality of the national
parks that needed management or planning.[69] In this sense, Mission 66
continued the management approach instituted by Stephen Mather of
increasing public support for the national parks by "accommodating as
wide a range of public tastes as possible" with desperately needed facilities.[70] Conservation groups' criticism of Mission 66 worried Park Service
director Wirth, who feared in 1958 the bureau was "losing ground with

that important and vocal part of its constituency."[71] Likewise, the Sierra Club feared "a manager like Conrad Wirth saw a national park as the sum of facilities, roads, and buildings built for visitors…a different reality from those engaged in the wilderness movement." Brower in particular felt the Club had not been given adequate time to develop an informed position on Mission 66.[72] The Park Service's predilection for development meant the agency was "at odds with the rising tide of conservation," which, with its focus on protecting wilderness, had more in common with nineteenth-century preservationists.[73]

Indeed, conservationists faced a difficult decision. The wilderness bill introduced in 1957, which eventually became the Wilderness Act of 1964, looked far from certain to conservationists in 1958. Like most conservation groups, the N3C supported the wilderness bill and urged members to do the same. If the N3C were to pursue a national park, the fate of wilderness in the North Cascades might be jeopardized because Mission 66 did not appear to bode well for wilderness preservation. On the other hand, since Forest Service wilderness areas could be unmade by administrative directive, a national park offered the protection of Congressional statute. It was not an easy decision, but the N3C realized it had to choose a course and pursue it single-mindedly.

In May 1958, McConnell wrote Brower about the dilemma. The basic question, he said, was whether continued Forest Service administration or National Park Service management would best serve the North Cascades. Employing the full force of his political science and conservation expertise, McConnell summarized the arguments for and against both agencies.

Forest Service management, he wrote, offered existing wilderness protection policies adequate for the areas of concern and additional protection under the wilderness bill when it passed; further, any change in management would inflame long-simmering bureaucratic rivalries. On the other hand, the Forest Service had no real means to protect wilderness beyond Wild and Wilderness Area designations. It did not prioritize scenic or wilderness values. Its main focus was logging. The agency was subject to changing political whims, which could undo existing wilderness areas, and as of yet had not designated any Glacier Peak Wilderness Area.

In contrast, the Park Service offered more permanent protection by statute, as parks were theoretically inviolable once created. The agency had the ability to protect areas that would not qualify as wilderness under the Forest Service, such as the primitive road from Stehekin to Horseshoe Basin used by McConnell to reach his cabin, and it could create a zoned protection area for wilderness. It could purchase mining claims. Park Service roads, should they be built, would prioritize scenic values, not commerce. However, tourist access was often emphasized to the detriment of wilderness, and Mission 66 clearly promoted construction. Still, the Park Service's founding philosophy emphasized the protection of spectacular natural areas.[74]

Given these arguments, McConnell continued, the problem was essentially defining the area to be protected. As of May 1958, there was no indication that any kind of long-range planning for Glacier Peak, much less the larger North Cascades region, was in the works. Moreover, the current Forest Service proposal was barely half the size of the original wilderness proposed by Bob Marshall in 1939. McConnell urged Brower to consider that the local economy, based largely on natural resources, was susceptible to boom-and-bust cycles. In contrast, scenery could be managed as a renewable resource. Finally, he wrote, grassroots support could be better mobilized for a national park than for a Forest Service wilderness area. A national park, McConnell concluded, was the best, and really the only possible, solution.[75]

McConnell had an ally in Brower protégé and Berkeley student David Simons, a Eugene native who worked on the Three Sisters Wilderness fight. As a high school student, Simons had won a photography contest that included a trip to Washington, DC, where he met the Wilderness Society's Howard Zahniser and other prominent conservationists. The experience inspired him to work on conservation causes, and he joined the Sierra Club in 1955 after taking an outdoor photography workshop with Ansel Adams. In early 1956, Simons knocked on McConnell's office door and asked what he could do to help with Glacier Peak. McConnell invited Simons to use his cabin as a base for exploring and photographing the North Cascades. Brower scrounged funding for food and equipment from the Sierra Club, and Simons spent two summers gathering data for a report that convinced him, and eventually thousands more, the North Cascades should be a national park.[76]

Clearcut areas such as this below Mount Shuksan convinced conservationists they needed to pursue protected status for the entire North Cascades. *1963 photo, North Cascades National Park Service Complex Museum Collection, NOCA 17271*

The Sierra Club published Simons's North Cascades report for internal use in mid-1958. It analyzed different kinds of protection, whittling the options down to wilderness, wild, or recreation areas managed by the Forest Service and national parks or monuments run by the Park Service. Forest Service areas were created and could be undone administratively. Park Service areas were created by an act of Congress, in the case of national parks, or executive order, in the case of national monuments. Forest Service wilderness might seem better at first glance, Simons wrote, but the bureau was "under almost irresistible pressures to eliminate lands of supposed economic value…The plain fact is that it is becoming extremely difficult under the Forest Service to protect any wilderness or scenic resource containing trees or minerals."

On the other hand, the Park Service would undoubtedly develop parts of the wilderness to meet its mandate of preserving scenery while making it readily accessible. In sum, "It is a choice between a few too-small wilderness areas which do not protect against mining, dams, or private development, nor protect vital forested gateways, and a large national park which protects against all forms of resource exploitation, but which may be subject to a certain degree of development in some places." His conclusion: go for a national park of about 1.3 million acres, stretching from the North Cascade Primitive Area to Stevens Pass, in essence the area Bob Marshall had suggested preserving.[77] This was a far larger area than Glacier Peak alone, but Simons believed the Sierra Club had to work to preserve the entire region.[78]

The report was effective. "Dave Simons had Dave Brower's ear," Goldsworthy recalled.[79] Brower thought the twenty-two-year-old Simons "extraordinary" and relied heavily on him for perspectives on the North Cascades.[80] Brower wrote, "We don't want to meet our opposition on their terms and allow them to choose the battlefield. Arguing only over a GLAPWA [Glacier Peak Wilderness Area] would be disastrous. While we battle over minutiae, the Cascades will be riddled."[81] Brower wanted the N3C and local conservationists to think bigger; to think, in fact, about the whole of the North Cascades as a wilderness battle in a national context.

With Simons and McConnell both pressing for a national park, Brower brought McConnell's letter to the executive committee of the N3C in July 1958, now headed by Goldsworthy. After a year at the helm, Zalesky had stepped down, satisfied the group was well-organized.[82] Brower told the group the Park Service was not a perfect solution, but "at least it wasn't in the business of promoting logging."[83] Goldsworthy initially was not sure a national park was the best option, but the possibility of mining at Glacier Peak (which the Zaleskys and Dyer had seen on their 1955 backpacking trip) convinced him. Months earlier, he told Brower, "Ply me with more propaganda and I will discuss your point of view with the Board members up here."[84]

In Patrick Goldsworthy, the N3C had a leader for whom the North Cascades became a lifelong passion. His single-minded dedication was heavily influenced by his friendship with Brower. While working as an assistant trip leader on Sierra Club high trips in the 1940s, Goldsworthy recalled that Brower would make a short speech to participants gathered around the campfire. "'If you go into the wonderful country like Yellow-

stone or various national parks,' Brower would say, 'you have an obliga-
tion to spend some time saving them. They're not going to stay the way
they are.'" That philosophy embedded itself in Goldsworthy's psyche, and
when he moved to Seattle and became involved in the Glacier Peak issue,
he knew he'd found a way to put the Brower ethic to work.[85]

But that view was hardly universal. Now the soft-spoken Goldsworthy needed to bring all his leadership skills to bear on the contentious
question before the executive committee. Zalesky "fought it like mad,"
futilely using arcane parliamentary procedures to try to stop the vote.
He felt it undermined the N3C's position adopted a year earlier, namely,
to work for wilderness area protection for Glacier Peak and wait for the
final Forest Service proposal.[86] If that proposal did not make "gener-
ous improvements" to the February 1957 draft, the N3C would back a
park. Moreover, he was concerned about the Park Service's propensity for
development and feared any park bill would have wilderness protection
compromised out of it. Finally, he thought the timing was bad. Better
to wait for the Forest Service's final proposal on Glacier Peak and then
decide how to proceed.[87]

After heated deliberation, the executive committee narrowly voted
to recommend to the board of directors that it approve a study aimed at
creating a national park in the North Cascades.[88] The three-to-two vote
showed the N3C's deep internal division over the best plan for wilderness protection and indicated conservationists' mixed feelings about the
Forest Service and the Park Service.

The vote also reflected the beginnings of a shift in conservation
activism. Through the 1950s, most conservationists worked to defend
existing wilderness areas and national parks from intrusion by developers or resource industries. Glacier Peak and Three Sisters both began as
defensive reactions, where local conservationists tried to forestall drastic
shrinkage of existing wilderness areas. But the national victory prevent-
ing a dam at Dinosaur National Monument and the ongoing fight to
pass a wilderness bill helped conservationists see they could successfully
take the offensive.[89] In this sense, the N3C's decision to pursue national
park status for the North Cascades may be seen as one early example of
this tactical shift.

Still, it was not an easy sell. Many shared Zalesky's misgivings and
bad feelings lingered. One officer resigned over the issue.[90] By choosing

to put all its eggs in the Park Service basket, the N3C ran the real risk of ending up with no national park and a much-reduced wilderness area lacking statutory protection. Bearing in mind these perils, two weeks after the executive committee vote, the board of directors voted to ask the Secretaries of Interior and Agriculture to conduct a joint study of the North Cascades from Stevens Pass to the North Cascade Primitive Area, the area David Simons envisioned as a giant national park and that Bob Marshall recommended for Forest Service wilderness status more than twenty years earlier.[91]

The decision to ask the two agencies to conduct a joint study can be seen as the best available option at the time. In 1958, recreation demand on public lands was higher than ever, but the federal bureaus with the most oversight were focused on logging (the Forest Service) and building visitor facilities (the Park Service). Pressure to get a handle on recreation demand led Congress in June 1958 to establish the Outdoor Recreation Resources Review Commission (ORRRC), charged with surveying recreation needs on all public lands.[92] Interest in a national wilderness system was rising, but until a statutory wilderness system was enacted, there was no guarantee either the Park Service or the Forest Service would or could offer strong wilderness protection.

Having taken a stand, the N3C initially found itself ahead of some local conservation groups, who felt waiting for the ORRRC study and the Forest Service's final proposal at Glacier Peak was a better option. Brower and the Sierra Club were pushing hard for unanimity, trying to get conservation groups on the same page, and found that some were more circumspect. For example, although the Mountaineers' Glacier Peak brochure published in September 1957 suggested the area was "of scenic caliber worthy of National Park status," the organization vacillated until 1960 over whether to formally support a national park.[93] The Mazamas preferred to wait for the Forest Service's final proposal and took no position. Like the Forest Service and the Park Service, conservation groups grappled with the idea of wilderness and how to protect it.

The Wilderness Society, for one, continued to follow the debate in the pages of *Living Wilderness*, publishing several articles throughout this period, including an entire issue devoted to the Glacier Peak controversy in autumn 1958.[94] The society's council held its 1958 meeting at the Golden West Lodge in Stehekin. More than ninety prominent conservationists descended upon the tiny community to discuss, among other issues, the fate of Glacier Peak. Organizations including the N3C, National Parks Association, Federation of Western Outdoor Clubs, National Wildlife Federation, Olympic Park Associates, Sierra Club, Mountaineers, Forest Service, and Park Service sent representatives.[95] National Park Service director Wirth, speaking in a panel presentation, admitted, "I will say, which perhaps I shouldn't say, that I am very much interested in [Glacier Peak]."[96] It was not much of a secret that the Park Service considered the region "one of the most magnificent primitive areas in the country."[97]

Olaus Murie, immediate past president of the Wilderness Society and a respected conservationist, summarized the group's ambivalence about the North Cascades: "[W]e must decide to work for the best that can be attained at this time. If national park status seems best, than [sic] we must try for that...From facts that have come to my attention, the Forest Service proposal for wilderness appears much too small, and perhaps... National Park status should be considered. This question must be examined very carefully."[98]

After the meeting, Wilderness Society executive director George Marshall (Bob's brother) summarized the dilemma in a letter to Polly Dyer: "Here is the last chance for the preservation of a really great wilderness in the Continental United States. The choice however, between the lumbering plans of the Forest Service and the roadbuilding and development frame of mind of the Park Service...is not a happy one."[99] This mirrored the sentiments expressed by his late brother two decades earlier, who fretted that roads would be punched into the wilderness if it were made a national park.[100]

Other organizations were inclined to push toward a park. The Federation of Western Outdoor Clubs resolved in September 1958 in favor of a joint study. *Sunset* published a comprehensive travel article about the North Cascades in August 1958 describing Glacier Peak as the "rallying symbol for the growing sentiment to establish here a national park," and reprinted a May 1958 National Parks Association resolution supporting a park.[101] *National Parks* magazine suggested a national park to protect the Stehekin valley in 1957 and reiterated its position the following autumn.[102]

Led by Brower, the Sierra Club continued to press the park issue, publishing a brochure titled *What is Your Stake in the Northern Cascades?*

that urged readers to ask Congress and the president to delay any decision on Glacier Peak until a joint study was completed. The group also sponsored three more trips to the North Cascades in summer 1958, sending Simons and photographers Ansel Adams and Philip Hyde there to study and photograph the area.[103] In January 1959, the Club published another brochure, this one in cooperation with the N3C. *Our Greatest National Park?* implored readers to contact their federal representatives in favor of a national park: "Creation of a great National Park here can protect the dramatic gateways, the primeval forests…guard the heart of wilderness…[and] provide for public enjoyment now and in generations to come." A map showed the area needing protection between Stevens Pass and the North Cascade Primitive Area, highlighting the 1957 Forest Service Glacier Peak proposal boundaries.[104] Thus, several conservation groups with a stake in the outcome were on record favoring a national park or a park study even before the Forest Service released its final Glacier Peak proposal.

CHAPTER 4

Glacier Peak Redux

Wile conservationists deliberated the best course to ensure wilderness protection in the North Cascades, the Forest Service revised its Glacier Peak proposal. An internal confidential draft circulated in March 1958 suggested that local and industry opposition, combined with the agency's ingrained proclivity toward timber harvest, had some effect. The revised wilderness boundaries were eleven thousand acres smaller than the 1957 proposal, though still larger than the Limited Area. The biggest change was the amount of commercial timber acreage included, which dropped from more than seventy-eight thousand acres to just over sixty-four thousand acres, just 15 percent of the proposed wilderness.[1] With each revision of the proposed wilderness boundaries, the amount of commercial timber included decreased.

The Forest Service defined commercial timber as including both operable and inoperable stands. Operable stands can be logged given current technology. Inoperable stands are unavailable for logging, typically because they are too expensive, too perilous, or too isolated to reach.[2] The 1957 proposal did not distinguish between operable and inoperable timber, but the 1958 draft did. Delving into the draft's details helps illuminate the Forest Service's thinking about how national forests should be used. About two-thirds of the commercial timber inside the proposed wilderness, slightly less than 10 percent of the total acreage, was considered operable. Any potential loss of operable timber was particularly important to communities that depended on timber revenues from the national forests.

The amount of operable timber in the 1958 draft plan shows the Forest Service's keenness to accommodate the timber industry and its internal struggle with wilderness preservation. Glacier Peak straddles two national forests, the Mt. Baker and the Wenatchee, and the proposed wilderness acreage was fairly evenly divided between them. But

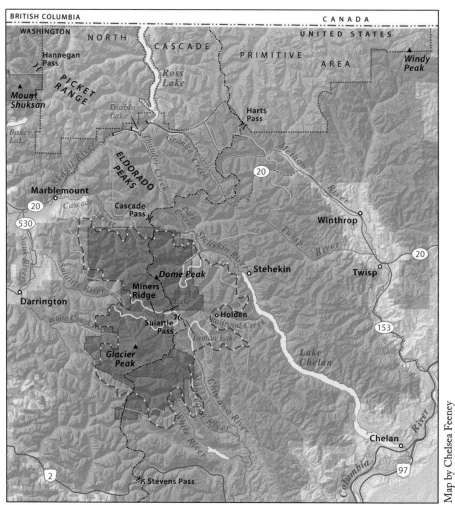

Map 3. Glacier Peak Wilderness: 1959 Proposals and 1960 Final Boundaries

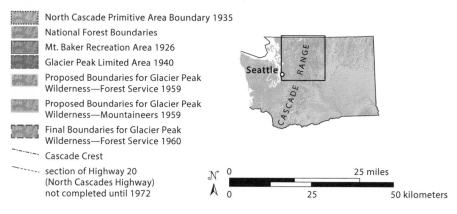

North Cascade Primitive Area Boundary 1935

National Forest Boundaries

Mt. Baker Recreation Area 1926

Glacier Peak Limited Area 1940

Proposed Boundaries for Glacier Peak
Wilderness—Forest Service 1959

Proposed Boundaries for Glacier Peak
Wilderness—Mountaineers 1959

Final Boundaries for Glacier Peak
Wilderness—Forest Service 1960

Cascade Crest

section of Highway 20
(North Cascades Highway)
not completed until 1972

Seattle

0   25 miles

0   25   50 kilometers

the amount of commercial timber available in each forest, and especially the amount of operable timber, was different.

Under the 1958 draft plan, the Wenatchee National Forest stood to lose 6,400 acres of operable timber to the Glacier Peak wilderness area. This was less than 3 percent of the Wenatchee's portion of the wilderness overall. Mt. Baker National Forest would lose thirty-five thousand acres of operable timber, or 18 percent of its portion of the wilderness. This disparity between the forests' operable timber may suggest wilderness opposition in the Chelan area was effective. It could also simply be that the west side, with denser forests and higher timber volumes, had more timber and therefore a higher proportion to be included.[3]

Taken as a whole, however, not even 10 percent of the total wilderness acreage in the 1958 draft was operable timber. Buoyed by the rising tide of postwar timber demand, the Forest Service remained loyal to what it saw as its primary constituency, the timber industry. The draft proposal included "representative stands of virgin timber" in the Agnes Creek, Suiattle River, and White Chuck River valleys, but most low-elevation forests were left out.[4]

The agency worked on the proposal throughout 1958, while elsewhere conservationists debated various options for wilderness preservation. In mid-February 1959, the Forest Service released a final Glacier Peak Wilderness Area proposal virtually identical to the 1958 draft, but much less detailed. Only four pages long, and one of those a map, it recommended a 422,925-acre wilderness based on a "sound multiple-use management program for the area, which would maintain a balance between the different types of developed and undeveloped outdoor recreational opportunities." The final proposal simply noted that 10 percent of the wilderness was operable timber, most of it on the west side of the Cascades.[5]

To get to that timber and provide opportunities for recreational development, the Forest Service proposed "deep indentations" up river valleys on both sides of the Cascades.[6] At its narrowest point, the wilderness would be barely four miles across from east to west. It was a "starfish wilderness" or "wilderness on the rocks," phrases likely coined by Sierra Club activist David Simons to denote the shape made by the boundary lines when mostly treeless alpine areas were included and forested valleys were omitted.[7] According to the Forest Service, roads in those corridors would improve access to the wilderness area, add more opportunities for roadside recreation, and allow entry to mineral patents.[8]

On the west side, the boundary sliced up the Suiattle River all the way to Suiattle Pass at the Cascade crest, excluding most of the river's tributary creeks and their sheltering stands of valuable Douglas-fir, Western redcedar, and Western hemlock. This eliminated from the wilderness Image Lake and Miners Ridge, renowned for glorious vistas of Glacier Peak and deemed by many to be one of the finest scenic spots in the Pacific Northwest. The Forest Service wrote that access to patented mineral claims justified the boundary. The deletion horrified conservationists, some of whom were reminded of the mine-company helicopter spotted by Phil and Laura Zalesky and Polly Dyer four years earlier. The possibility of an open pit and tailings piles on the flanks of Glacier Peak was almost inconceivable.[9]

On the east side, Railroad Creek and the Chiwawa River received similar treatment, with boundaries at the latter again stretching to the Cascade crest to allow access to minerals. The boundary at Agnes Creek, long the concern of Grant McConnell and other Stehekinites, ran alongside the creek for nearly nine miles instead of the five proposed in 1957. Although the final proposal suggested this would allow more campgrounds and picnic areas to be built, as well as easier access to the wilderness area, the 1958 internal draft noted that the Agnes Creek valley would add sixty-eight million board feet of operable timber to the Chelan working circle.[10] The Chelan Box Manufacturing Company would almost certainly benefit from the new boundaries. At the time, one scholar noted that Forest Service administration "mainly concerned local or regional demands and needs rather than retention of wilderness areas for possible future national use. Regional foresters still have dominant influence and jurisdiction over these areas."[11] Wenatchee National Forest supervisor Ken Blair had warned Grant McConnell in 1955, "The trees of the [Stehekin] valley would be cut…The coming sales were necessary, and they would take place."[12] The proposed boundaries clearly left the Agnes Creek corridor vulnerable to logging.

Nonetheless, with the publication of the final Glacier Peak Wilderness Area proposal, Region 6 was at last in compliance with Forest Service policy. The service's U-regulations, requiring primitive areas be studied for reclassification to wilderness, had been conceptualized by Bob Marshall and adopted in 1939. In the Pacific Northwest, this was extended to include the Region 6-specific limited area designation and hence Glacier Peak, though many regions opposed the stricter rules and "nullified the intent of the new regulations by refusing to reclassify" most areas.[13] Two decades earlier, Marshall himself had complained of Region 6, "They just say 'no' to all new wilderness areas, even those they recommended."[14] U-1, which required wilderness areas of more than one hundred thousand acres be approved by the Secretary of Agriculture, governed the Glacier Peak reclassification study, which was finally complete. Knowing there would be significant public reaction, Region 6 scheduled hearings on the proposal for October in Bellingham and Wenatchee.

———————◆———————

Taken aback by what they perceived as a blatant betrayal by the Forest Service, the North Cascades Conservation Council members dug in their heels. Negotiating with the Forest Service was no longer an option. The agency had shown its true colors. The proposal was "completely unacceptable," N3C president Pat Goldsworthy said in a statement. "It is impossible for wilderness conservationists to give serious consideration to this Glacier Peak proposal. Obviously, the Forest Service has little inclination for properly managing wilderness areas...[and] should permit a change in status of the area so as to allow the Department of Interior, which does care, to manage it."[15] Phil Zalesky, who had been initially opposed to a national park, was "shocked" by the new Forest Service plan and declared wholehearted support for a park.[16]

In April 1959, Goldsworthy recounted the evolution of the N3C position in the *NCCC News*: "At first a Forest Service Wilderness Area was recognized as the best type of land dedication. While our faith in the Forest Service's wilderness policy was shaken after the decision on the Three Sisters Wilderness Area and their preliminary proposal for a Glacier Peak Wilderness Area it was completely removed with the publication of their final proposal for a grossly inadequate Glacier Peak Wilderness Area."[17] The N3C wanted the Park Service to study the North Cascades. By this time, the newsletters were reaching more than five hundred members.

Other groups, too, kept their members abreast of the latest developments, primarily by publishing articles skewering the 1959 proposal and urging members to send comments or testify in person at the hearings in October. For example, the *Sierra Club Bulletin* published in February "The Missing Million," a five-page indictment by David Brower of the Forest Service and its wilderness policy. The "missing million" was the acreage outside the 1959 Forest Service proposal that needed protection, Brower wrote, including everything from Cascade Pass to the North Cascade Primitive Area and more acreage around Glacier Peak, that is, the area surveyed by Bob Marshall in the 1930s and recommended for wilderness status. "The most tragically dismal part of the whole proposal," Brower lamented, "is what it omits entirely—the magnificent terrain that remains beyond its purview, in spite of the pleadings of almost every conservation organization."[18] The next month, the Sierra Club launched a new fundraising effort to support Glacier Peak advocacy, selling post-cards and notecards of North Cascades scenes featuring photos by David Simons, Grant McConnell, Philip Hyde, and others.[19]

The Wilderness Society ran a long article brimming with enthusiasm for Glacier Peak and dismissing the Forest Service's rationale for the exclusion of important access valleys and scenic highlights: "We found ourselves comparing each falls, each peak, each glacier, and each forested valley that we knew in this area with its counterpart in the national park system [and] concluded that here was grandeur, more dramatic, more unique, and more varied!"[20] The magazine of the National Parks Association, *National Parks*, printed the Forest Service proposal in April and published an article extolling the virtues of the North Cascades in October, just before the hearings.[21]

The Pacific Northwest's largest conservation groups, the Mountaineers and Mazamas, both wanted wilderness but differed in their respective responses. In May 1959, the Mountaineers updated their 1956 proposal to include far more land north of the Cascade and Stehekin rivers. Originally excluded because it was not well known to the group, the organization had made field studies and confidently suggested a wilderness that essentially mirrored Bob Marshall's 1939 plan, criticizing the Forest Service because "incisions are made into virtually all wilderness pockets where trees are to be found." Although troubled by the Forest Service's "substantial backtracking" from the already inadequate 1957 plan, the Mountaineers tried to thread the needle: "It is our sincere hope that the area comprised in this proposal be eventually established as a wilderness irrespective of whatever federal agency administers it…We believe that the surpassing worth of the country within our proposed boundaries qualifies it for protection as a wilderness for either a national forest or a national park."[22]

The Mountaineers kept their options open. They wanted to see the wilderness protected no matter what, and were longtime allies of the Forest Service in recreation. But unless the agency demonstrated a clear commitment to wilderness, the organization might withdraw any remaining support. The Sierra Club's Simons, for one, felt the Mountaineers were "holding back out of timidity."[23] But another way to understand this is as indecision about whether the Forest Service or the Park Service was a better guarantor of wilderness protection. The Forest Service had wilderness as part of its management framework but did not give it the primacy conservationists wanted. The Park Service, deep in Mission 66, had no provision for wilderness protection beyond its "everything not developed is wilderness" default.

The Mazamas stood firmly behind the Forest Service. In July 1959, Mazamas' Conservation Committee chair Martha Ann Platt chided N3C president Goldsworthy that national park status was "illusory" and "will o' the wisp." The Forest Service study was "competent and realistic, and we are not in sympathy with demands for additional studies," she wrote. "Failure to support the establishment of the Glacier Peak Wilderness Area…can only be viewed as a shocking lack of responsibility to our own [Federation of Western Outdoor Clubs] members, to the cause of wilderness conservation and to the general public." Because the Forest Service was the only agency with a record of actually preserving wilderness in the Pacific Northwest, she said, the Mazamas believed it represented the best chance for long-term wilderness protection. Platt, who was the first woman president of the Mazamas in 1953, served on the board of the Friends of Three Sisters Wilderness and was a thoughtful participant in debates over the wilderness bill. She sent her letter on Glacier Peak to the local Forest Service office, with instructions to distribute it widely.[24] The Mazamas steadfastly supported the Forest Service as the primary recreation agency in the Pacific Northwest, a position that reflected the decades-long friendly interactions between the organizations. The Forest Service built roads and trails for recreational access, often working closely with outdoor groups like the Mazamas and Mountaineers.

Yet even inside the Forest Service, the agency's position was not universally accepted. Mt. Baker National Forest supervisor Harold "Chris" Chriswell was particularly concerned. Echoing Bob Marshall's pleas of two decades earlier, in June 1959 Chriswell expressed misgivings to Region 6 Regional Forester Herb Stone about the agency's plans for timbered river valleys not included in the proposed Glacier Peak wilderness. Citing the Suiattle and North Fork Cascade River corridors, Chriswell contended, "The scenic values are as high as for Mt. Rainier or the Rockies in Glacier National Park. They should be adequately protected…and a maximum of recreational opportunity provided." A current timber operation on the Cascade River illustrated this point, because the so-called beauty strip of trees left to camouflage the clearcut "sinks to insignificance in the face of the great vertical topography found in this area."[25]

The Picket Range, one of the wildest places in the lower 48, became the centerpiece of the northern unit of North Cascades National Park. *John Scurlock photo*

Chriswell worried, too, about the plans for the North Cascade Primitive Area, itself due for study and reclassification. Created in 1935 and stretching some seventy-five miles along the Canadian border, it was one of the largest Forest Service primitive areas in the country, "of sufficient scope and remoteness to satisfy the most rigid wilderness qualifications." The 801,000-acre area was divided by Ross Lake, the reservoir created by Ross Dam on the Skagit River. The western half began at Hannegan Pass, including a "territory of tremendously abrupt ridge systems, compensating canyons carved to terrific depths, jagged peaks, awe-inspiring rock slides, falls interspersed with smaller lakes under glaciers and waterfalls."[26] These were the Pickets, so named because the serrated summit line resembled an imposingly tall fence.[27] Twenty mountains higher than 7,500 feet squeezed into about seven miles, "then as now the wildest and most undiscovered country in the whole North Cascades."[28] When National Park Service director Conrad Wirth saw the spiky Pickets in 1958, he blurted, "I want *that!*"[29] From Ross Lake east to the Okanogan highlands the gentler grades and flower-filled meadows were "indescribably picturesque and romantic."[30] The whole North Cascade Primitive Area was remote and seldom visited, with about 2,500 visits recorded in 1959.[31]

Contemplating the Glacier Peak proposal and potential changes in the North Cascade Primitive Area, Chriswell warned:

> We, in the Forest Service, are prone to belittle the scenic beauties in favor of timber production in our multiple-use plans. I have climbed Sahale Mountain in the Cascade Pass and looked at Eldorado and Forbidden Peak...I can see the point of view of the climbers and outdoor people and, although not agreeing with them, can see the need for this kind of value assessment in a few of these isolated valleys of the North Cascades. I would be bold enough to extend my thinking to many small valleys of the Stehekin—yes, even Agnes Creek! *If we do not assess the value of the scenery in these few areas, we will be legislated into doing so under another department.*[32]

As the Forest Service's most senior official in the Bellingham area, Chriswell was privy to the opinions of local residents in a way the Portland-based regional forester likely was not, and may have sensed the agency was going too far with its plan for a scaled-down Glacier Peak wilderness. In this regard, Supervisor Chriswell was the latest Forest

Service employee to follow the path blazed by Aldo Leopold, Arthur Carhart, and Bob Marshall in advocating for wilderness, although he was responding to public pressure instead of personal predisposition.

Regional Forester Stone's reply epitomized the Forest Service's unwillingness to consider scenery as a resource value equal to timber. "It seems to me it is just as bad to go to extremes in protecting natural beauty as it is to go to the other extreme of ignoring it," he responded. He agreed scenic value protection required careful logging, but suggested parts of the Suiattle and other river corridors could be logged because the steep topography would conceal the clearcuts. Stone's conclusion embodies Forest Service philosophy and, in retrospect, shows the agency's disengagement from the growing wilderness movement: "We should preserve natural beauty, but we can't go the full distance that some extremists would like us to go, nor can we accept their extreme view that any disturbance whatsoever by man is unattractive, particularly when the units are reforested. A nice young stand will provide a pleasant variation in the landscape."[33] Stone toed the agency line, but he appreciated the beauty of the North Cascades. In his memoirs, Chriswell recalled the regional forester "dearly loved to ride in the backcountry. He made enough horse trips in the Cascades to become quite familiar with them and their trails."[34] Despite Stone's aesthetic appreciation for the scenery, he was foremost a forester, and duty-bound to implement Forest Service policy.

Nevertheless, the attempt to unify Forest Service staff met a setback even within Stone's own office in Portland. In an attempt to familiarize Region 6 staff with the Glacier Peak issue, and likely in preparation for the hearings, in August 1959 the Forest Service screened *Wilderness Alps of Stehekin*, the Sierra Club film produced to raise awareness of the area's charms. After watching the film, one worker wondered aloud why the Forest Service opposed a national park. Stone advised senior Forest Service officials to educate staff about the agency's position: "It is evident that some of our folks, particularly in the clerical force, still have insufficient background knowledge of the North Cascades issue."[35]

As the October hearings approached, the N3C, Sierra Club, and Mountaineers sent final pleas to their members, urging them to attend the hearings or write to the Forest Service about Glacier Peak.[36] Some felt the Forest Service was trying to sway the outcome by holding the hearings in Bellingham and Wenatchee, traditionally resource-dependent towns, and by scheduling them for a Tuesday and a Friday, weekdays when urban dwellers would probably be unable to attend.[37] The Mountaineers wrote to Forest Service chief Richard McArdle, asking that the Bellingham hearing be moved to Seattle or that an additional hearing be scheduled for Seattle.[38] McArdle declined, saying the hearing sites were chosen because the two towns housed the headquarters for the national forests involved.[39]

In the end, distance and inconvenient timing did not deter the conservationists, who carried the day at both hearings. The Mountaineers, Federation of Western Outdoor Clubs, Mazamas, Wilderness Society, N3C, and Sierra Club sent representatives. The N3C, Sierra Club, and Wilderness Society testified in both Wenatchee and Bellingham. All urged a larger Glacier Peak Wilderness.

Speaking for the Sierra Club, Brower derided the Forest Service's piecemeal approach to the North Cascades as "tragically inadequate," urging a comprehensive study of the region. David Simons, who by now had spent four summers crisscrossing the North Cascades, said the "climax of the exploiters' banquet has been the great wilderness region between the Stehekin and Cascade Rivers, and the North Cascade Primitive Area. This the Forest Service has chosen to ignore completely."[40]

Focusing on the elimination of the forested valleys, John Warth, a veteran of the battles over Olympic National Park, disparaged the proposal as "a wilderness skeleton with the meat picked off."[41] Wilderness Society director Olaus Murie, whose research on the importance of predators to healthy ecosystems broke new ground in wildlife biology, suggested a full appreciation of the "ecological complex" of wilderness offered another way to value wilderness. The forested valleys were a crucial part of wilderness ecosystems.[42] Speaking for the more than seven hundred members of the N3C, Goldsworthy characterized the Forest Service plan as the "final step backward in wilderness preservation...the last straw in a conflict that we do not mean to lose."[43]

Opponents concentrated on the presumed economic disaster a wilderness area would wreak on local communities by taking natural resources out of production. A Washington State Department of Commerce and Economic Development official said that while wilderness areas had scenic appeal, "it is most certainly retrogressive economics to remove from the economy of the State of Washington any of our natural assets on which our past and future welfare are based."[44] Some, including geologists from a mining company that held claims on Miners Ridge, opposed the concept of wilderness areas altogether.[45]

Still others, including the Puget Sound Section of the Society of American Foresters and the Washington State Cattlemen's Association, supported the Forest Service proposal as written. Martha Ann Platt, chair of the Mazamas Conservation Committee, now recommended that Image Lake be included in the boundaries, but felt that "recreation development along the Agnes Gorge would be desirable" so long as logging was minimized to protect recreation values.[46]

Three general positions emerged from the two days of hearings, each attended by about fifty people.[47] Fewer than twenty supported the Forest Service proposal. About twenty-five opposed the proposal as too big. More than fifty opposed it as inadequate.[48] Another 850 sent letters, most supporting a larger wilderness around Glacier Peak. The Forest Service gathered the testimony and began compiling a recommendation for final boundaries, a process that often took up to a year. Under the agency's U-regulations, the Secretary of Agriculture would make the final decision on Glacier Peak, but Region 6 first had to submit its recommendations to the Chief of the Forest Service. What the final wilderness would look like was anybody's guess.[49]

———————◆———————

Even as the Forest Service rewrote its draft proposal throughout 1958, conservationists worked to expand the Glacier Peak wilderness debate into a study of the entire North Cascades. Goldsworthy twice wrote to Seattle's congressmen, Democrat Don Magnuson and Republican Thomas Pelly, trying to convince them to sponsor legislation for a Park Service study of the area before a final decision was made.[50] The N3C also formally asked the Forest Service to delay any decision on Glacier Peak until the Park Service could study the region. Forest Service chief McArdle firmly rebuffed the request, insisting the agency was fully qualified to make decisions regarding land use around Glacier Peak.[51]

Shortly thereafter, the Forest Service released its final proposal in February 1959. Now Goldsworthy tried again with Pelly, this time appealing to the politician's ego: "You would receive national recognition and acquire considerable prestige in the association of your name with the establishment of the nation's next national park," Goldsworthy suggested.[52] First elected in 1952, Pelly was a fiscal conservative who enjoyed the support of labor in his district, which covered much of north Seattle. As a boy, he camped and fished in the Stehekin valley and considered the area "not only unique, but personally almost sacred."[53] Pelly generally sympathized with conservation groups, believing "certainly the Glacier Peak region of the Cascades should have a high priority," but did not promise to take any action.[54]

Then, on March 6, 1959, Pelly met in Washington, DC, with David Brower, who told him a letter requesting a Park Service study of the North Cascades would "get things started." The next day, flying back to San Francisco aboard a TWA jet, Brower drafted a letter that included nineteen detailed questions, and offered it to Pelly to "crumple, rework, or use as you see fit. (I hope you use it.)"[55] Two days later, Pelly sent the letter, under his signature and virtually unchanged, to National Park Service director Conrad Wirth.

"It is my belief that the public values inherent in the Glacier Peak-Lake Chelan unit of the Northern Cascades are of such high order that the public should have available to it, before the October hearings, far more data than now exist...to appraise the opportunities here in fair perspective," the letter said. While Pelly was confident the Forest Service would carefully evaluate the area's timber resources, he wanted more information on other values, such as scenery, wilderness, and recreation—values the Park Service had been created to protect.[56]

To that end, Pelly asked the Park Service to study the North Cascades, using Brower's questions for Wirth to answer. These ranged from inquiries about potential economic benefits of a national park, to possible recreational development, to the most likely boundaries for such a park. "I realize that studies leading to comprehensive answers to these questions will require considerable time and coöperation between the Park Service and other agencies and organizations," Pelly concluded. "It is my hope that by initiating such studies immediately, and by adding to your previous study [the 1937 Park Service study discussed in Chapter 1]...

you will at least be able to produce for public consideration an evaluation of Northern Cascades potential which is now almost totally lacking."[57] By asking the Park Service to take the lead, Pelly could maintain a generally neutral stance while still trying to obtain the study conservationists wanted. And because a congressman requested it, the Park Service could justify getting involved. It was smart politics.

An Assistant Secretary of the Interior told Pelly that while the Park Service had no authority to enter national forest land without Forest Service consent, it would seek permission to do so and hopefully begin a study.[58] Accordingly, the Park Service wrote to McArdle in early April, but received no reply. Another letter was sent in June with the same result.[59] Finally, Pelly himself wrote to McArdle in July 1959.[60] In late August, with no possibility of completing the requested study before the hearings now less than two months away, McArdle finally responded, formal to the point of frostiness.

"After most careful consideration," he wrote, "we have concluded that the proposed field investigation at this time by the National Park Service of national-forest lands in the North Cascades should not be undertaken." The Forest Service was perfectly capable of managing the North Cascades appropriately, as it had done for decades, he said. "We do not feel that the Forest Service gives undue weight to commercial timber values or roadside recreation, nor that our appraisal of national-forest values is biased," he continued. Moreover, with the hearings less than two months away, it would be "inconsistent" for another agency to study the region with an eye toward managing it when the fate of Glacier Peak had not even been determined yet.[61] In a note to his boss, Interior Secretary Fred Seaton, Wirth noted that despite McArdle's protests, the Forest Service chief had derided the Glacier Peak proposal as inconsistent with the agency's multiple-use approach. Seaton promptly wrote to Agriculture Secretary Ezra Benson, saying he saw nothing wrong with pursuing a joint study of the North Cascades.[62]

Pelly had tried a backdoor approach and was rebuffed. Now he determined to pass legislation forcing the Forest Service to allow the Park Service to study the North Cascades. Rep. Don Magnuson, who followed Pelly's attempts to get answers, also thought legislation could force the question. In April 1959, Magnuson "reluctantly" concluded the Forest Service was unable and/or unwilling to preserve wilderness at Glacier

Peak. In a letter to Goldsworthy, he said, "I am prepared to do all I can to have the National Park Service make a study of the area to see if it is suitable for national park status, and if the Park Service's report is favorable, to recommend establishment of a national park."[63]

Pelly asked the Park Service for draft study legislation.[64] The agency quickly complied, and Pelly and Magnuson each introduced a study bill when Congress convened on January 6, 1960.[65] The bills authorized the Secretary of the Interior to study the "scenic, scientific, recreational, educational, wildlife, and wilderness values" of the region from Stevens Pass to the Canadian border, and to report back to Congress within a year.[66] They were referred to the House Committee on Interior and Insular Affairs, where Rep. Jack Westland of Washington State's Second District was a member.

A Republican elected to fill Henry "Scoop" Jackson's seat when the latter moved to the Senate in 1952, Westland was better known as the "old man of golf" than for his politics. His election had been all but assured when, at 47, he became an instant celebrity as the oldest person to win the U.S. amateur golf championship, barely two months before the election.[67] Westland's district stretched north from King and Jefferson counties to the Canadian border, and east to west from the Cascade crest to the Pacific Ocean. It encompassed important timber-producing country, including the Mt. Baker National Forest, the western portion of Glacier Peak, and the northern half of the Olympic Peninsula. Keenly aware of his timber constituency, Westland was disinclined to press for a hearing on a bill that might ultimately result in the removal of some of that rich timberland from production.

Within a month, Sen. Warren Magnuson (D-WA) followed suit in the Senate with a bill identical to that drafted by Pelly and Don Magnusson, which was sent to the Senate Committee on Interior and Insular Affairs.[68] Senator Jackson was a majority member of that committee and would hopefully push the senior senator's bill.

Both the N3C and the Mountaineers urged members to write Westland and the committee chairs, reminding them that passing even one of the bills "will be of greater importance to the Northwest than any other single conservation proposal."[69] The N3C went still further, distributing one thousand petitions supporting the study bill to its members. By March, the group had gathered five thousand signatures; by May, it had ten thousand.[70]

Despite these grassroots efforts, the bills died in committee. Westland was not interested in moving the bills forward, and the committee chair, Rep. Wayne Aspinall (D-CO) was unlikely to act without the consent of the local congressional representative. Moreover, Aspinall, a stubborn wilderness opponent who singlehandedly almost derailed the wilderness bill numerous times, slowed the bill by requesting department reports on it from both Interior and Agriculture. It was a stall tactic, and Rep. Don Magnuson wrote Goldsworthy that both departments were "dragging their feet" well into summer, and well past the time when the bills might have been heard.[71]

The biggest obstacle, however, turned out to be Senator Jackson. Goldsworthy and other conservationists had met with the senator about the North Cascades in December 1958. Jackson said he would be more inclined to support preserving the region if the initiative appeared to be coming from within Washington state; that is, not from the California-based Sierra Club. As a national organization, the Sierra Club had a presence in the capital that smaller groups like the N3C could not afford. Further, some local conservationists felt the Sierra Club was making policy decisions without consulting them. It was not the first time such tensions had surfaced. When Simons released his report on the North Cascades in summer 1958, Goldsworthy wrote to Brower that the Northwest contingent felt the Sierra Club was taking the lead without conferring with the local movement: "I worked hard to sell the people up here in N3C as a result of a talk with you. Don't leave us too far out in your thinking."[72] Later that year, Goldsworthy cautioned Brower, "A lot of influential feathers up here were badly ruffled by the Sierra Club's present policy re Glacier Peak Area coming out without any consultation whatever with the northwest."[73] Jackson would not push for a study until he felt sure it was a genuinely local initiative, not a Sierra Club-imposed idea.

"Senator Jackson is the only person who can initiate the congressional action we want," Goldsworthy wrote. "His support is essential and we must make sure we get it and hold on to it."[74] When Brower wrote the "nineteen questions" letter for Pelly in March 1959, he drafted a similar one for Jackson. Although Jackson's staff seemed "friendly," Brower wrote, he would have to wait and see.[75] In April 1959, Jackson wrote that he wanted to get a wilderness preservation bill passed before going for a national park in the North Cascades.[76]

The idea for a national wilderness system was born of concerns about the pace of resource extraction, the shrinking number and size of roadless areas remaining in the United States, and the need for places a growing population could go to escape the pressures of city life and reconnect with nature. Threats to wild areas increased in the 1940s and 1950s, bringing the wilderness issue to public attention. Airplanes flew frequently and at low altitudes over Minnesota's roadless Boundary Waters region. Timber companies wanted to log old-growth trees inside Olympic National Park for war manufacturing. Oil companies wanted to drill at the foot of the Teton Range in Wyoming. Dams were proposed inside primitive areas, on the edges of national parks, and within national monuments. Every new proposal to develop wilderness made clearer the inadequacy of current protection. The federal agencies charged with managing public lands, which were the main focus of wilderness protection efforts, had other priorities. The Forest Service's wilderness policy did not ensure permanent protection, and the agency's reclassification of existing primitive areas moved at a glacial pace, partly because of its partiality to multiple-use as an operating model. The Park Service was deep into Mission 66 and fixated on improving visitor facilities to accommodate swarms of visitors. It argued everything in the national parks not developed was already wilderness and thus did not need special protection.

Until the 1950s, conservationists mostly responded to these threats reactively. The primary national players were the Wilderness Society and the Sierra Club. While the organizations were founded with different objectives (the Wilderness Society concentrated on protecting road-less areas, the Sierra Club on national parks and scenic lands), by the mid-twentieth century they concurred on wilderness preservation as a primary conservation goal.

It was a controversial dam proposal that provided the impetus for a national wilderness system and transformed the conservation movement into a proactive one. In 1949, the Bureau of Reclamation proposed a dam on the Green River at Echo Park, a gorgeous sunset-hued canyon inside Dinosaur National Monument on the Colorado-Utah border, as part of a ten-dam Colorado River Storage Project. The director of the National Park Service objected but was overridden by the Secretary of the Interior, who approved the project. The Sierra Club's David Brower and the Wilderness Society's Howard Zahniser spearheaded an unprecedented and successful national campaign against the project, arguing that if national monuments were not safe, nothing was. In 1956, Congress rebuffed the Interior Department and approved the multi-dam project without Echo Park.[77] The experience taught Brower and Zahniser that existing protection was not enough.[78] A national wilderness preservation system was the answer, and Zahniser immediately began work on a draft bill.[79]

While the expected opposition from resource industry groups quickly materialized, Zahniser and his allies were surprised when the National Park Service and Forest Service also opposed it. The Park Service worried that heightened status for wilderness might diminish that given to national parks and monuments, and argued its organic act already required the agency to "preserve unimpaired" areas in its jurisdiction. The Forest Service believed existing wilderness protection under the U-regulations was sufficient. Neither agency saw the need or potential benefit of additional legislation. Nonetheless, Zahniser used his formidable powers of persuasion to recruit ten co-sponsors for the first draft of the bill, introduced by Sen. Hubert Humphrey (D-MN) in 1956.[80] That same summer, the Zahniser and Brower families, along with Goldsworthy and others, participated in the first Sierra Club outing to Glacier Peak, one of the wildernesses under Forest Service scrutiny and, in conservationists' eyes, one of the most imperiled.

For wilderness supporters, the Forest Service's 1957 decision on Three Sisters Wilderness in Oregon and its draft Glacier Peak proposal underscored the need for a national wilderness system. While Zahniser worked to solidify support in the late 1950s, steering the bill through numerous rewrites and hearings, opponents found reasons to stall. One reason commonly given for postponing the wilderness bill was the ongoing work of the Outdoor Recreation Resources Review Commission (ORRRC) to survey national recreation needs. Some felt the ORRRC might conclude there was no need for additional wilderness.[81]

Furthermore, in early 1960 the Forest Service awaited final passage of the Multiple Use-Sustained Yield Act (MUSY), a response to growing concern about the weight given timber harvesting compared to other uses of the national forests, including recreation. Enacted in June, MUSY codified national forest functions as timber, range, recreation, watershed protection, and wildlife. According to the law, no one use was more important than any other, and economic return should not be the main factor in deciding use. It defined multiple-use as managing the national forests "so that they are utilized in the combination that will best meet the needs of the American people."[82] This congressional directive forced the Forest Service to change its interpretation of multiple-use. By statute, timber could not be given preference over other uses.

Conservationists had mixed feelings about MUSY. Some worried that in mandating multiple-use, the legislation gave the Forest Service a way to avoid wilderness preservation or, worse, impose multiple-use management on wilderness areas. N3C member and longtime Mountaineer Harvey Manning quipped that for the Forest Service multiple-use meant "no logging will be permitted above timberline," a pithy characterization of the proposed Glacier Peak boundaries.[83] Others felt the bill's stipulation that "establishment and maintenance of areas of wilderness are consistent with the purposes and provisions of this Act," a line added under pressure from conservationists, provided a safeguard.[84]

In one sense, like MUSY and the ORRRC, the wilderness bill was another piece of legislation trying to address the drastic increase in the public's use of public lands in the postwar era. Taken together, they indicate the amount of national attention these issues received and demonstrate the shift in power from the federal land agencies to Congress. MUSY and the ORRRC gave Senator Jackson a plausible, politically astute reason to delay introduction of a bill for a Park Service study of Glacier Peak, although he referred only to the wilderness bill in his response to conservationists. A wilderness system was one of their top priorities, and Jackson knew conservationists had to win his support to achieve anything in the North Cascades.

They were disappointed, but knew the Secretary of Agriculture's decision on Glacier Peak would be forthcoming any day. They did not know that Pelly's pressure, the statements of hundreds of pro-wilderness supporters, the outrage over Three Sisters, and the push for legislation responding to public land use had an effect in the lofty reaches of the Agriculture Department. In late July 1960, Forest Service chief McArdle wrote to Regional Forester Stone, quashing some of the plans for logging the Suiattle River and Agnes Creek valleys. Stone argued potential mining patents provided justification for excluding the Suiattle, Image Lake,

and Miners Ridge, but McArdle responded it was "unnecessary to anticipate such developments to the extent of refusing to dedicate the area as
wilderness." As for the Agnes Creek valley, the area Grant McConnell
had been worried about for at least five years, McArdle replied, "The
limited roadside recreation opportunities up the Agnes are outweighed
by the advantages of having one or two low valley floors on the east side
within the area."[85] Stone was being overridden by his superiors back east.

✦

In early September 1960, the Forest Service announced the final Glacier
Peak decision. The Agriculture Secretary enlarged the 1959 proposal by
nearly thirty-six thousand acres, reinserting much of the Suiattle, Agnes,
and Phelps River corridors, Image Lake and Miners Ridge, and a small
area on the southeast corner. The decision was made according to the
tenets of multiple-use, the Forest Service averred. MUSY provided the
framework within which such decisions were made, which gave the
agency some cover with constituents who opposed wilderness. "In this
case…wilderness is the predominant public value…[and] other resource
utilization not compatible with wilderness enjoyment has to give way,"
the decision stated.[86]

The hearings had generated nearly one thousand responses, a majority favoring wilderness. But many wilderness supporters had expressed
concern about the starfish appearance of the 1959 proposal, their general
opinion being the corridors proposed for exclusion "were too numerous
and too deep." The wilderness value of the Suiattle and Agnes valleys
merited their inclusion. In fact, "normal methods" of timber harvest, that
is, clearcutting, along the Suiattle "would seriously impair the view of
Glacier Peak from such important vista points as Image Lake and Miners
Ridge." In the Agnes corridor, a "beautiful approach to the high country
beyond," logging was not economically viable because of the valley's low
volume and difficult access. But the White Chuck River was still out,
as was Railroad Creek to the former mining town of Holden. In those
places, which already had roads, "resource development and utilization
will not detract materially from the adjoining wilderness."[87]

The Forest Service now managed more than 1.2 million acres of
administratively designated wilderness in the North Cascades: the

458,505-acre Glacier Peak Wilderness and the 801,000-acre North Cascade Primitive Area.

Significantly, the decision included a management directive for the area north of the new Glacier Peak Wilderness, from Cascade Pass to the North Cascade Primitive Area. More than twenty years earlier, Bob Marshall had urged the agency to protect this region. At the fall 1959 hearings, the Mountaineers, Sierra Club, N3C, and others asked the area be included in the Glacier Peak Wilderness or be given some other formal protection. However, the Forest Service said construction of a highway across the mountains, already underway in that area, precluded any wilderness designation. Instead, the Secretary of Agriculture directed that the region be managed "primarily for the preservation of scenic values and to open up and develop it for the use and enjoyment of the large numbers of people who desire other kinds of outdoor recreation and those who are unable to engage in wilderness travel." Recreation was to be considered the primary value, and "roads, vistas, resorts, ski lifts and other developments" would be planned. Limited logging might also be allowed. In declining to include this region in the wilderness area or otherwise protect it, the Forest Service both kept its options open and potentially forestalled a Park Service study by promising to emphasize scenery and recreation over other values.

The Forest Service proposed to manage Cascade Pass and the Eldorado Peaks region for recreation. The area is now in the southern unit of North Cascades National Park. *North Cascades National Park Service Complex Museum Collection, NOCA 11772*

The re-inclusion of the Agnes, Suiattle, and Chiwawa River valleys pleased conservationists, but the exclusion of the White Chuck and White River corridors did not. They wanted all timbered valleys inside the wilderness, believing that they were essential to the wilderness experience. As the Forest Service tried to balance various uses in accordance with MUSY, though, some valleys were left out. The *NCCC News*, for one, was not celebrating overmuch: "A Glacier Peak Wilderness Area, albeit poor and grossly defective in many respects, has been established."[88]

Three more things needed to be done, the N3C argued. First, a North Cascades Wilderness Area had to be established (the North Cascade Primitive Area was undergoing a reclassification study, the same process that started the Glacier Peak controversy). Second, the Park Service needed to study the North Cascades. And third, a North Cascades National Park needed to be created, with established wilderness areas at its core. The game plan for the N3C was clear. It would act as a watchdog to ensure the Forest Service adequately protected existing wilderness and primitive areas, help pass a park study bill, and help pass the wilderness bill.[89] Echoing general conservationist sentiment, Grant McConnell wrote in the *Sierra Club Bulletin* that although parts of the region were now protected, the country north of Cascade Pass was still vulnerable. The Secretary of Agriculture's directive that this area be managed for scenic values "may be the best the Forest Service can do, but it is not enough. The next step is an objective study of the park potential in the total area." Conservationists, he counseled, "must redouble their efforts."[90]

Glacier Peak was a milestone for conservationists. It would be managed under the strongest wilderness protection available at the time, with the arguable exception of national park status. Initial Forest Service plans for Glacier Peak had given conservationists a target for their dismay over the frequently visible scars of logging in areas used for recreation, especially river valleys. They united in a single-purpose organization dedicated to preserving North Cascades wilderness, and understood the strengths and weaknesses of both the Forest Service and the Park Service, playing them off each other in a politically sophisticated way. Conservationists' growing savvy was evolving into a two-pronged approach, with the N3C's

Goldsworthy leading the regional effort and the Sierra Club's Brower spearheading the national campaign.

For the Forest Service, Glacier Peak was a shot across the bow. The days of Bob Marshall were long gone, especially in Region 6. The agency's attention had focused on providing more and more timber for harvest, not on wilderness or recreation. Glacier Peak was "a national test of Forest Service management for values other than timber harvesting,"[91] a test the Service failed. It was the "ultimate showdown that convinced citizen conservationists that the Forest Service could not be trusted to preserve wilderness."[92] Even the Mountaineers, which had supported a wilderness area at Glacier Peak for months after other groups moved toward pursuing a park, were finally and fully disillusioned by the 1959 "starfish" proposal. One member wrote Regional Forester Stone, "You have managed to alienate your last supporter, as far as major groups are concerned."[93] The Forest Service's failure to understand conservationists' concerns cost the agency dearly. Not only did it lose the support of conservationists, it arguably lost some autonomy with the passage of MUSY, a congressional directive establishing agency priorities. Moreover, without any overt action by the Park Service, conservationists decided the rival agency offered a better option for wilderness preservation even with its alarming penchant for development.

From 1960 forward, the fight for the North Cascades would take a wholly different direction. With the involvement of Representative Pelly, the stage began to shift away from the Pacific Northwest and toward the center of political power. Henceforth, most decisions affecting the fate of the magnificent, wild North Cascades would be made more than two thousand miles away from the snow-clad slopes of Glacier Peak, in the marble-lined hallways of Washington, DC.

CHAPTER 5

A Freshening Political Wind

The Glacier Peak Wilderness Area decision in September 1960 created new challenges for conservationists and the Forest Service. Because the new wilderness was larger than the regional Forest Service office had proposed, conservationists could rightly claim to have won the battle. But the battle did not end the war. Some of the most spectacular parts of the North Cascades still lacked wilderness protection. In the Glacier Peak decision, Secretary of Agriculture Ezra Benson stipulated that the Forest Service manage the Cascade Pass-Ruby Creek area—about eight hundred thousand acres stretching between the North Cascade Primitive Area and the new Glacier Peak Wilderness—primarily for scenic and recreation values. Conceivably, the North Cascades Highway through the mountains, finally under construction after years of fits and starts, could snake past ski lifts, scenic overlooks, and resorts.

The possibility of intense recreational development sharply contrasted with conservationists' wilderness preservation goals. It was, in fact, more typical of the Park Service's style, an irony not lost on anyone. Persuaded by the Glacier Peak controversy that they could not trust the Forest Service to protect wilderness protection, conservationists had to closely monitor the agency's actions in the North Cascades while continuing to pursue a Park Service study of the region. These efforts would consume much of the next two years. The Forest Service, on the other hand, had to convince conservationists its management still offered the best chance for wilderness preservation.

As it happened, the winds of political change shifted favorably for conservationists. John F. Kennedy was elected president in November 1960, bringing with him a raft of Democratic cabinet officials and a "level of concern [about conservation] far higher than that displayed by the Eisenhower administration."[1] President Eisenhower had been resolutely uninterested in most issues that resonated with conservationists.

Indeed, his Interior Department initially supported the proposed Echo Park dam inside Dinosaur National Monument, leading some conservationists to conclude that Eisenhower's administration did not see the national parks as inviolable.[2] In 1954, then-Senator Kennedy's questioning of Western water projects subsidized by East Coast taxpayers, such as Echo Park dam, had implied at least a passing interest in federal management of public lands.[3]

In fact, the new president intended to give conservation high priority. During his campaign he supported the wilderness bill, on which Eisenhower had been "all but silent,"[4] and his appointment of Arizona congressman Stewart Udall to be Secretary of the Interior was promising. Dave Brower may have influenced the selection.[5] The new administration, the *NCCC News* exulted, presented "the finest opportunity in over 20 years" for a North Cascades national park.[6]

In Washington State, which narrowly voted for Nixon in the presidential race, the mostly-Republican incumbents kept their seats, including Reps. Tom Pelly, Jack Westland, and Walt Horan. Their districts together constituted the geographic bulk of the North Cascades, and Westland and Horan opposed the idea of a national park there on grounds it would cause economic harm to local communities by locking up resources for a single use. As a member of the House Committee for Interior and Insular Affairs, Westland had helped kill Pelly's first park study bill in 1960 simply by ignoring it.

Despite Westland's intransigence, Pelly was ready to try again. His district covered northern Seattle to the Snohomish County line, Bellevue and environs, and Bainbridge Island. As the highly regarded former president of the Seattle Chamber of Commerce,[7] Pelly had a front-row seat to the enormous changes wrought on the region by World War II. Many of those changes could be traced to the expansion of the Boeing Company, which grew from a "good, but unspectacular business" of four thousand employees and $10 million in sales in 1939 to fifty thousand employees and $600 million in sales in 1944.[8] Boeing suffered when airplane manufacturing declined after the war, and by 1946 it had shed four-fifths of its workers and sales had dropped by 97 percent. During the Cold War, the company successfully mitigated the boom-and-bust cycle of military contracts by reinventing itself as a commercial jet maker, rolling the first 707 off the factory floor in 1959 and creating a more stable market for its products.

In 1957, Boeing employed half of King County's manufacturing workers, proving "it was not defense that would maintain the boom but the houses, cars, highways, refrigerators, television sets, [and] washing machines" purchased by its employees. In Pelly's district, thousands upon thousands of homes were built north and east of the city, areas especially affected by postwar expansion. One observer described Seattle as a place where "everything was modern...Everyone seemed to be middle class and literate, no matter what his trade. We lived on a street lined with picture-window houses that were owned, not rented, by business people, skilled mechanics, and college professors." People came because "Seattle seemed to offer something fresher, newer, less spoiled or jaded than someplace else...The mountains and the water were there, as always, only now such wonders began to seem more valuable, more explorable to more people."[9]

Waterskiing on Baker Lake in Mt. Baker National Forest, 1963. Recreation in national forests exploded in the 1950s and 1960s. *North Cascades National Park Service Complex Museum Collection, NOCA 11706a*

For Pelly's constituents, the national forests offered many recreational opportunities within a short drive. They enjoyed driving for pleasure, breathing in the sharp tang of evergreen forests and admiring the alpine scenery. They hiked, camped, backpacked, fished, hunted, boated, picnicked, swam, mountaineered, birdwatched, skied, rock climbed, picked berries, photographed nature, canoed, gathered firewood, rafted, spelunked, and snowshoed. The national forests of Region 6 recorded nine million recreational visits during 1960, one-quarter of them for overnight camping.[10]

As his district's population swelled, Pelly understood the appeal of preserving some wild places for these new residents to enjoy as an antidote to what John Steinbeck described as Seattle's "frantic...carcinomatous growth."[11] Three days into the 1961 congressional session, Pelly introduced a national park study bill that was again referred to the House Interior Committee, where it again languished.[12]

In June, Pelly spoke on the House floor about the North Cascades, dramatically unveiling "evidence of widespread grassroots support" for a park study collected by the North Cascades Conservation Council over the previous six months. More than twenty-one thousand people, nearly one-third of them from outside the state of Washington, had signed petitions favoring a study. "The spread of interest in the North Cascades seems quite significant to me," he stated. The petitioners represented every state but one, evidence that the North Cascades issue was attracting national attention. Indeed, the petition effort may have gotten a boost from a flattering March 1961 *National Geographic* article.[13] Further, one-fifth of the signatures came from Westland's and Horan's ostensibly anti-wilderness, anti-park districts.[14] Support for the North Cascades was not, as some scoffed, the purview of a few outspoken conservationists in Seattle.

◆

While Pelly tried to build support for his bill in the House, two of the Northwest's powerful U. S. senators, Henry M. "Scoop" Jackson (D-WA) and Wayne Morse (D-OR), became more interested in the Forest Service's management of lands in Washington and Oregon under multiple-use principles. Morse was concerned about the agency's plan for Waldo Lake

Limited Area, a popular outdoor recreation destination seventy-five miles east of Eugene. Eleven regional outdoor groups challenged the Waldo Lake plan in early 1961. Recognizing conservationists had concerns about several other Forest Service sites in the Pacific Northwest, Morse enlisted Senator Jackson's help.[15]

In late April 1961, the senators, along with Supreme Court Justice William O. Douglas, a Washington native and passionate conservationist who had written about Glacier Peak in his most recent book,[16] met with new Agriculture Secretary Orville Freeman. As head of the department that housed the Forest Service, Freeman had final say over the agency's plans for reclassifying these areas. The group suggested the secretary initiate an assessment of conservation priorities for the national forests in both states, including timber, recreation, watershed, range, minerals, and wildlife. The Multiple Use-Sustained Yield Act of 1960 (MUSY) explicated the various uses to which national forests could be put, and the senators reiterated concern about several sites, including Oregon's Waldo Lake and Minam River and Washington's Copper City and North Cascades.[17] They wanted Region 6 to clarify how MUSY would be applied in these high mountain areas, most of which had "marginal commercial value" because they stood above four thousand feet, at higher elevations than had been previously harvested.[18]

Freeman directed Region 6 to begin the study. Noting the process would take several months, he stopped all development in the Cascade Pass-Ruby Creek area except that needed for construction of the new highway across the North Cascades. A management plan would take more than a year to complete, he projected. In the meantime, there would be no logging. The order reflected sensitivity to the uproar over Glacier Peak and the new administration's support of conservation issues.[19]

At Region 6 headquarters in Portland, some wondered what prompted the request. Regional Forester Herb Stone chalked it up to conservationists leveraging the naiveté of the new administration: "[A] strong group of people had reached influencial [sic] men in government, particularly Justice Douglas, who in turn had brought the subject before Senators Morse and Jackson, and they, in turn, had brought it to the attention of the Secretary."[20] Stone's response ignored Region 6's culpability. Resistant to changing values about wilderness, its management plans repeatedly provoked conservationists' outrage because they focused on timber and mass recreation over wilderness preservation. Moreover, Douglas, Jackson, Morse, and Freeman were all seasoned politicians. Though new to the Department of Agriculture post, Freeman had helped shape Minnesota's Democratic-Farmer-Labor Party in the 1940s and served as Minnesota governor in the 1950s. He had nominated Kennedy for president at the 1960 Democratic National Convention, and was a close friend and ally of Sen. Hubert Humphrey (D-MN), a prime sponsor of the wilderness bill.[21] Region 6 officials, however grudgingly, had to concede conservationists had utilized their growing political influence effectively to force a halt to logging on Forest Service land in the North Cascades.

Conservationists also focused on new Secretary of the Interior Stewart Udall. A former Arizona congressman, Udall had served on the House Interior and Insular Affairs Committee and staunchly supported Echo Park and other reclamation projects that would bring water to his constituents in the arid Southwest. At the same time, he was interested in the relationship between humans and nature explored by Henry David Thoreau and Robert Frost, and believed in "esthetic conservation" of scenic lands. Udall wanted Kennedy to be as passionate, proactive, and expansive as Theodore Roosevelt, the "conservation president" who reserved millions of acres of national forests, and created eighteen national monuments and five national parks. He worked to engage the new president in the issues.[22] Conservationists hoped rising momentum for a national wilderness preservation system would influence Secretary Udall to support their objectives.

In July 1961, Udall and Freeman traveled to Utah's Canyonlands country to evaluate its national park potential. Sitting around a campfire along the Green River, in "a place so remote it appears on few maps," the two secretaries vowed to end "once and for all the feud over recreation policies between the U.S. Forest and Park Services." Freeman pledged, "If National Forest land is better suited to National Park purposes I will not oppose its transfer to the Park Service."[23] The promise potentially signified a stunning shift in the long-running rivalry between the two agencies.

The ongoing antagonism between the Park and Forest services had been attracting renewed attention. A pre-election article by the *New York Times'* conservation writer John Oakes (an old friend of Grant McConnell's) noted that the "principal conservation battle of the next few years" would be over preserving the potential park land remaining in the West, including the North Cascades, in spite of the "jealous guardianship" of the Forest Service.[24] "No bureaucratic squabble" should thwart the addition of these lands to the national park system.[25] When Congress passed the Multiple Use-Sustained Yield Act in mid-1960, the *New York Times* warned its passage should not be seen as an alternative to proposed new parks, the "most notable" of which was the North Cascades.[26] MUSY codified recreation as one legitimate use of the national forests, but clarified that it competed with other uses not permitted under Park Service management.

One of Udall's stated priorities was expanding the national park system, and he nurtured President Kennedy's unequivocal support. Barely a month after his inauguration, the new president delivered an unprecedented message to Congress on natural resources, among other initiatives urging passage of a wilderness bill and directing Udall and Freeman to survey potential new national parks and forests.[27] Lauding the new president's words, the *New York Times* opined that Kennedy's speech "showed him to be aware of the intolerable conflicts, duplications and rivalries that have for many years plagued the Federal Government's natural resource activities."[28] It warned, however, that the president's plan was "only the beginning of what must be done about new parks—and done quickly, before it is too late to do anything."[29]

By July, when Udall and Freeman traveled to Utah, it was becoming clear the Secretary of the Interior envisioned a massive land acquisition program. Citing the disparity between population growth and parkland preservation, Udall called the relative lack of open space, and the apparent reluctance of state and federal governments to preserve more of it, the "quiet crisis" of America. "This generation, as we see it, has a 'last chance' opportunity to save perhaps fifteen or twenty million acres for national parks," Udall said.[30] Finding twenty million acres for new national parks would be challenging, though. No major national park had been created since World War II.[31]

To that end, Udall sent a fellow Arizonan, writer Weldon Heald, to the North Cascades in summer 1961 to report to Interior on several land use controversies in the Northwest. While Udall and Freeman hashed out their departments' differences over a Utah campfire, Heald scouted the North Cascades for its park potential. He wrote Patrick Goldsworthy, "My mission isn't exactly secret by any means, but perhaps it's just as well not to shout from the housetops in the vicinity of the U.S.F.S. that someone from Interior is going to be snooping around."[32] When his contract ended in October, Heald concluded the Forest Service was "no longer competent" to manage lands in the region. "I was appalled at the changes wrought by the creeping blight of multiple use," he wrote Justice William O. Douglas.[33]

Goldsworthy, eager to see action on a Park Service study in the North Cascades, worried when Udall had not responded to Heald's report by late October. Heald reassured him the Secretary probably had not even read the report yet.[34] Udall wanted to proceed carefully. In June, a member of the Mountaineers had written to the Secretary and urged the Mountaineers or a similar group be allowed to study the North Cascades in lieu of the Park Service, the logic being a local group could conduct a study with less blowback from the Forest Service and its supporters. Udall counseled patience. He and Freeman were "discussing national forest and national park matters, seeking to resolve differences…in the most cooperative manner possible."[35] In fact, in November 1961 he and Freeman, assisted by some of President Kennedy's advisors, were working on an "ambitious conservation agenda" based on the as-yet-unpublished report of the Outdoor Recreation Resources Review Commission (ORRRC), a Congress-created task force charged with recommending federal policy for recreation lands.[36] The interdepartmental cooperation promised over the summer appeared to be materializing in ways that only a few years earlier would have been unthinkable. The cooperative approach was unprecedented.

Frustrated by lack of action on the Pelly bill and looking for ways to effectively push the park idea with the new administration, the N3C decided it was time for some professional help.

Throughout 1961, it had become glaringly apparent that conservation issues required more than the volunteer time most people could offer.

Conservationists were trying to keep on top of Forest Service activities throughout Region 6 while working to preserve wilderness at Oregon Dunes, Waldo Lake, Cougar Lakes, and Alpine Lakes. With its many local and federal stakeholders, the North Cascades was a complicated issue, and since 1955 the Sierra Club had spent $70,000 on the North Cascades alone, including three brochures, thirteen outings, several study summers, a film, and numerous articles.[37] At the time, the club did not even have full-time paid staff in Washington, DC. In fall 1960, McConnell pressed Brower to "get a good full-time, Sierra Club staffman" to run a "general conservation office" in the Northwest that served different organizations, developing and implementing strategies and acting as liaison among the various groups.[38] In McConnell's view, the variety of volatile regional issues, the Sierra Club's demonstrated commitment, and the determination of conservationists to work for preservation warranted paid staff.

The first problem, of course, was money. Who would pay for staff? Who would supervise the position? Who would want to take on this job? Federation of Western Outdoor Clubs members and other groups pledged varying amounts according to what they could afford, and the Sierra Club matched the total. N3C member Leo Gallagher, an ardent conservationist who owned a Tacoma mattress company, anonymously donated money for much of the position's salary.[39] The clubs formed an advisory board, and as the only group with a business office capable of handling such arrangements, the Sierra Club agreed to act as the contracting agent.[40]

Hired as the first Pacific Northwest Conservation Representative in 1961, Mike McCloskey, shown here circa 1970, brought political expertise to the North Cascades campaign.
Courtesy Michael McCloskey

A search for the right person turned up Michael McCloskey, a *magna cum laude* Harvard man newly graduated from the University of Oregon Law School. With his horn-rimmed glasses and intense manner, McCloskey looked more like a policy wonk than an avid hiker who had chaired the Conservation Committee of his hometown Eugene outdoor club, the Obsidians. Earnest, dedicated, and gracious, he worked on the Three Sisters controversy and had met Brower at a Federation of Western Outdoor Clubs convention in 1959. McCloskey was twenty-seven years old in November 1961 when he set up shop in downtown Eugene. His new title was Pacific Northwest Conservation Representative.

He quickly realized that conservationists wanted to preserve the North Cascades, but had no "battle plan" in place. "People had just made this decision to go for a park, but I found out they didn't have a strategy, they didn't have a plan," he recalled. "I told them, 'Look, we can't sell an idea until it becomes concrete, until we have something specific to promote!'" At the Sierra Club's biennial wilderness conference six months earlier in April 1961, after a keynote speech by Secretary Udall, McCloskey urged the organization to "enter the political process," arguing it was the only way to achieve its conservation objectives.[41]

Hiring McCloskey professionalized conservation in the Northwest, permanently changing the movement. In his first two weeks on the job, McCloskey drafted legislation for a Northern Cascades National Park and circulated it among stakeholders. His draft bill set aside a chunk of the area between Stevens Pass and the North Cascade Primitive Area as a national park, with a Lake Chelan National Recreation Area adjacent. The bill also provided for an oversight board of Washington residents appointed by the governor and the Secretary of the Interior.[42] By the end of November Goldsworthy had given it to Udall, who was visiting Mount Rainier National Park.[43] The draft legislation provided the Interior Secretary with valuable insight into how conservationists believed the area should be managed.

In early December, Brower met with Udall in Washington, DC, about conservation priorities, and followed up with a handwritten note. "There is a crisis in the Northern Cascades," Brower told him. "By next summer the Forest Service will have forever foreclosed on big chunks of scenic climax needed for a great national park." Only the president could prevent this, Brower entreated. "What can we put in your hands to help you convince him—just as soon as you possibly can?"[44]

Apparently, nothing just yet. The draft bill languished on the Secretary's desk. Conservationists were anxious. Pelly said he would sponsor a park bill if the conservation groups could agree on its contents, and Sen. Warren Magnuson said he had no objection, as it could "always be changed if necessary."[45] Moreover, Brower had learned from Goldsworthy that Senator Jackson would follow Magnuson on the North Cascades.[46] Congress would gavel into session in a few weeks, but the silence from the Secretary of the Interior's office felt ominous to McCloskey and Brower.

Justice William O. Douglas, more sanguine, ascribed the Secretary's reserve on the North Cascades to politics. "He wants to get the Washington Senators fully lined up behind him because of the great mineral and logging company pressures," Douglas wrote confidentially to Brower. "He thinks that if he can get by the '62 elections he will then be in a position to get considerable political strength from the State of Washington. He talks, in other words, in terms of political risks, political feasibility, etc. and on that level it is difficult to argue with a man who is an expert."[47]

The N3C considered at this point asking Udall to propose the North Cascades be declared a national monument. The 1906 Antiquities Act empowered the president to preserve areas of historical, cultural, or scientific interest as national monuments without Congressional signoff or even local support. Brower seemed on the verge of making the request in December 1961, even encouraging Udall to write a draft proclamation, but conservationists ultimately decided such a move might be politically rash.[48] Heald, author of the Department of the Interior's report on the North Cascades, warned many "would feel the North Cascades were being jammed down their throats. There's a large group who are being softened up to the idea of a North Cascades park and are willing, at least, to have a park study made." A monument would "greatly antagonize" them.[49] By April 1962, the N3C had dropped the idea.[50]

———————————◆———————————

While conservationists waited for some signal from Udall, they were heartened by growing evidence of the administration's commitment to conservation. The historic bad blood between the Park Service and Forest

Service, which Udall and Freeman had promised to end, was again in the spotlight. In early 1962, the *New York Times* urged more national parks be established, especially the North Cascades, but noted the Forest Service "has shown no inclination to relinquish jurisdiction without a struggle."[51] A *Harper's* article agreed that too often "the head of an agency is much more concerned about building up his empire than about meeting the nation's needs...Certainly some Presidential head-knocking is long overdue."[52]

The publication of the long-awaited report from the Outdoor Recreation Resources Review Commission in January 1962 also gave conservationists reason for optimism. Congress had tasked the ORRRC with getting a handle on the federal government's recreation assets and needs to fashion a response to booming postwar use. Three of its many recommendations had potential consequence in the North Cascades. Those were to pass a wilderness bill, establish a Bureau of Outdoor Recreation to coordinate federal recreation planning and policy, and establish a Recreation Advisory Council to develop and implement a policy for National Recreation Areas.[53]

In March, President Kennedy delivered another conservation message to Congress in which he again expressed strong support for a wilderness bill and ordered implementation of the first two ORRRC recommendations. The new Bureau of Outdoor Recreation would reside in the Department of the Interior and work with a variety of agencies on federal recreation priorities, while the Outdoor Recreation Advisory Council would include several agency heads and focus specifically on national recreation area policy. In addition, Kennedy proposed creation of a Land Conservation Fund to acquire private land to expand the federal recreation system, funded by user fees imposed at certain recreation sites.[54] Although the North Cascades were not mentioned specifically, the president's wish list of new national park sites (Point Reyes, Great Basin, Canyonlands, and more) confirmed new parks remained a high priority for the administration.

In May 1962, the White House hosted the first Conference on Conservation since Theodore Roosevelt's administration. Udall's comments there decisively captured the turning tide in national conservation consciousness. "It is time for the American people to assume the burdens of maturity," he said. "Social values must be equated with economic values; the overriding need of men for an environment that will renew the human spirit and sustain unborn generations requires some sacrifice of short-term profits."[55]

It was music to the ears of Brower, Goldsworthy, and hundreds of others who had been arguing precisely that for nearly a decade. Just one week earlier, the chief of the Forest Service stood with other officials in front of the eight-foot-high electric population clock at the Department of Commerce, watching as the counter ticked to 186,160,311 Americans—exactly the same number as there were acres of national forest land.[56] It seemed an auspicious affirmation of the need for more recreation lands, and to many the soaring, expansive wilderness of the North Cascades was an obvious choice. The area was already in the public domain. The question was management, and management depended on which values were deemed highest. Udall's remarks indicated the administration placed high value on wilderness and recreation in addition to traditional resource use.

Indeed, the administration's conservation agenda reflected the evolving national consciousness about the environment. Cold War fears about nuclear fallout and ongoing threats to forestland sparked concern about water quality. Increasing population in cities and more traffic led to worries about smog. In 1962, marine biologist Rachel Carson addressed these concerns in *Silent Spring*, a bestselling book often credited with laying the foundation of the modern environmental movement.[57] Carson argued the entire environment, not just one species, was endangered, and therefore humans were endangered as well. By challenging humans' "collective right to manipulate nature at will," Carson issued a widely heeded warning. Humans needed to see themselves as part of a larger, complex, and delicate ecological system, she said. Mess with the system, and they risked hurting themselves.

Historian Roderick Nash noted America was not quite becoming a nation of tree-huggers, but "the scales were clearly tipping in the direction of the wild."[58] This was evident in the Sierra Club's membership roster, which increased by more than half between 1962 and 1963, from 16,500 to 25,000 members.[59]

While the N3C watched conservation events unfold nationally and waited for Udall to make a move on the North Cascades, its members also anxiously awaited a long-promised Forest Service report on the reclassification of the North Cascade Primitive Area, the same type of study that had ignited the Glacier Peak controversy in the first place.

In 1931, the Forest Service had set aside 172,800 acres between Mount Shuksan and the Skagit River Valley as a primitive area, to be reserved for recreation, education, and preservation of natural values. An agency memo written three years later criticized the area as too small and poorly designed, an opinion echoed in an internal report: "The Pacific Northwest needs at least one extremely large Primitive Area...of sufficient scope and remoteness to satisfy the most rigid wilderness qualifications."[60] Prodded by Bob Marshall, Forest Service chief Ferdinand Silcox agreed, establishing 801,000 acres along the border with Canada as the North Cascade Primitive Area in July 1935.[61] Ross Lake effectively divided the new primitive area into two sections.[62] The western portion encompassed the rugged Picket Range, long considered to be some of the most inaccessible and challenging mountaineering terrain in North America.[63] The eastern section, while still mountainous, featured "friendly country" with lush wildflower fields, easier grades, and no commercially viable timber.[64]

Following World War II, the North Cascade Primitive Area came up for study as part of the system-wide reclassification required by the 1939 wilderness policy developed by Bob Marshall. A 1950 internal report suggested the Ross Lake division be made permanent, creating two separate wilderness areas. Dividing the area would allow the Forest Service to make other boundary adjustments "in the interests of multiple use." In other words, timber deemed second-rate or too remote in the 1930s was, from the 1950 perspective of the Forest Service's post-war role as timber supplier, now desirable. Timber along the fringes of the area was merchantable, and logging would "not detract from its appeal as a primitive area." The report suggested adding some alpine acreage to offset the timber loss, and "therefore dispel objections to these eliminations which wilderness lovers might have."[65]

It looked like Glacier Peak all over again.

Like the Glacier Peak area, the North Cascades Primitive Area was remote and breathtakingly beautiful. In the mid-1950s, Beat poets Jack

Kerouac and Gary Snyder worked there as fire lookouts, a lonely and often monotonous job. Their experiences flavored their writings. Kerouac's books *The Dharma Bums* and *Desolation Angels* were inspired by his sixty-three-day stint in the North Cascades, which he described as "unbelievable jags and twisted rock and snow-covered immensities, enough to make you gulp."[66] N3C board member Chuck Hessey, who with his wife Marion traveled extensively in the North Cascades, described hiking across the Primitive Area as "drama…Those who accept the lure and the dare—and many do—find beauty beyond compare." Hessey argued the North Cascade Primitive Area deserved wilderness protection as a "living museum" of biology, geology, and climate, in addition to its scenic splendor.[67] The Wilderness Society predicted the North Cascade Primitive Area would ultimately be reclassified as a Wilderness Area with no changes, because it was just too wild, too rugged, and too remote to be anything else.[68]

Nonetheless, the Forest Service delayed any work on the North Cascades Primitive Area reclassification study for ten years, until 1960, after the Glacier Peak hearings were over but before the final decision had been issued. As at Glacier Peak, conservation groups watched closely. Regional Forester Herb Stone had learned some lessons from Glacier Peak. Writing to the supervisors of the Mt. Baker and Okanogan national forests, which would be affected by the North Cascade Primitive Area reclassification study, he suggested, "From experience gained through the Glacier Peak study and hearings, it appears preferable not to make public a preliminary proposal on which we invite public comment and debate." This, of course, was what had attracted conservationists' attention in 1957 and led to the formation of the N3C.

Instead, he wrote, "an attempt should be made to determine in advance views of interested groups and individuals," which would then be considered in the Forest Service's final report. Stone left it to the forest supervisors to identify those groups and individuals, giving them six months to gather the information.[69] The Forest Service published a brochure explaining the reclassification study and requesting comments be sent to the supervisors at Mt. Baker or Okanogan national forests by December 1960.[70] Three thousand copies were sent to state and local governments, schools, chambers of commerce, timber companies, media outlets, outdoors clubs, utility companies, banks, hotels, and conservation groups.[71]

The forest supervisors appeared to recognize the conservationists' impact at Glacier Peak and their potential influence on the North Cascade Primitive Area reclassification. Barely two weeks after Stone issued his instructions, Mt. Baker National Forest supervisor Chris Chriswell, who had unsuccessfully urged Stone to take scenic values into account at Glacier Peak, invited Goldsworthy and representatives from the Mountaineers, Oregon Trails Club, and Mazamas on a five-day pack trip through the area west of Ross Lake in summer 1961.[72] Several directors of the Wilderness Society took a separate three-day pack trip into the Primitive Area as well.[73] Chriswell also sent letters to conservation groups, asking for comments by the end of the year. The N3C responded by suggesting minor boundary changes, mostly adding land on the western edge and eliminating some acreage on the east.[74] The Mountaineers published a similar proposal, cautioning that "in view of the past record, [we] should prepare for a proposal of logging corridors up the Baker River, Bacon Creek, and so on."[75]

Surprisingly, the Forest Service's confidential draft report on the North Cascade Primitive Area, circulated internally in February 1962, generally heeded the recommendations of conservation groups. Although some areas were recommended for exclusion, the total area of the proposed wilderness increased by thirteen thousand acres, and the N3C and Mountaineers endorsed most of the changes.[76] One exception was the exclusion of Windy Peak at the far eastern end of the primitive area, where seven thousand acres of harvestable forest were deemed more important than the area's many waterfalls and alpine meadows. "This timber is accessible to the Okanogan, Tonasket, and [Oroville] communities, where it will help support local industry,"[77] the report said. In the eastern part of the proposed wilderness, nearly half the land was classified as commercial forest, but 90 percent was deemed too expensive to log. Omitting Windy Peak reaffirmed the Forest Service continued to support local timber interests where it could.

Similarly, the Forest Service concluded that about one-fifth of the western portion of the proposed North Cascade Wilderness Area contained commercial timber, of which 80 percent was not harvestable under current standards. The area's major values were recreation and water production from glacier-fed rivers. The region's tumbled geology hampered mineral exploration. Increasing demand for recreational use and its "remoteness, scenery, ruggedness, and natural setting" meant the North Cascade Primitive Area was best suited for wilderness.[78] The Forest Service recorded about 1,400 visits to the Primitive Area in 1950; by 1960, that number increased to nearly 4,000.[79] While the agency's basic values remained unchanged, it clearly was more attuned to political reality than it had been in 1957 when the Glacier Peak controversy started. The Forest Service planned to keep the North Cascade Primitive Area largely intact.

But the agency never made public its recommendations for the North Cascade Primitive Area. Rep. Wayne Aspinall, chair of the House Committee on Interior and Insular Affairs, asked Agriculture Secretary Orville Freeman in April 1962 to suspend the reclassification process while the wilderness bill was being debated. That bill, cosponsored by Senator Jackson, included a provision that would make the North Cascade Primitive Area part of the proposed wilderness system. Conservationists hoped the reclassification would be completed before the wilderness bill passed, but Freeman acceded to Aspinall's request, and the Forest Service again put the North Cascade Primitive Area on hold.[80]

———————◆———————

While Region 6 worked on the North Cascade Primitive Area reclassification, Freeman directed it to prepare the study of high mountain areas in Washington and Oregon requested by senators Jackson, Magnuson, Morse, and Neuberger. Since Freeman assigned the study in July 1961 logging had ground to a virtual halt in the North Cascades. Then, at almost the exact moment when Representative Aspinall requested the North Cascade Primitive Area reclassification study be suspended, the Forest Service released its high mountain policy report.

The new policy covered all the high alpine areas within Washington and Oregon's national forests not already dedicated as wilderness, wild, and primitive areas. Recreational visits to the region's forests were increasing at a dizzying pace, with 9.5 million recorded in 1960 alone. The stated goal of the policy was to ensure people could enjoy wilderness and traditional outdoor recreation such as picnicking and camping in a "near-natural, scenic" landscape.[81] These designated Landscape Management Areas in the national forests were to be managed to promote recreation.

Roads, trails, campgrounds, picnic areas, shelters, scenic overlooks, winter sports, and resorts were all possible recreational developments for such areas. All other uses, including logging, were to be managed to enhance the recreational opportunities within these areas.[82]

The report shows the influence of the 1960 Multiple Use-Sustained Yield Act on Forest Service policy. Logging in high mountain sites was typically cost-prohibitive. There were not enough trees to make it worthwhile and the trees that did exist were usually in small, wind-sculpted "stringer" stands hemming avalanche chutes or perching next to glacial lakes.[83] By allowing some logging in these areas, the Forest Service hewed to its founding philosophy that an orderly, scientifically managed forest was vastly preferable to a jungle-like snarl of old-growth snags. Conservationists might have hoped Region 6 would ban logging altogether in high alpine areas, but the high mountain policy made it clear the region would not readily relinquish potentially harvestable trees.

At the same time, the high mountain policy forced Region 6 to spell out its multiple-use plans for alpine regions, areas of particular interest to conservationists. MUSY codified these uses, and in one sense, all the region did was explain to Washington and Oregon's senators how the law would be applied in certain areas within their states. Significantly for conservationists and timber-dependent communities alike, logging had stopped for the better part of a year. But now that the report was out, and just in time for the summer season, the possibility of continued logging was very real.

Trying to preempt any timber harvest until the future of the North Cascades was settled, Representative Pelly asked Agriculture Secretary Freeman to continue the moratorium on logging at twenty sites covering about two hundred thousand acres in the North Cascades pending completion of a park study of the area. Freeman warned a continued moratorium would probably interfere with multiple-use, sustained-yield management principles, but agreed to ask the regional forester about the plans at each site.[84] Regional Forester Stone, eager to get back on track now that the high mountain study was complete, had already sought permission to forge ahead with some small timber sales in five of the twenty areas affected by Freeman's stop order of mid-1961. The five sales amounted to just under three hundred acres, and Stone argued, "Even a two-year moratorium would have an important effect on our plans to salvage dead and dying timber…and to construct or better important recreation roads and campgrounds." He added the halt had "considerable impact" on the economy of Lake Chelan, a comment that hints at the regional office's longstanding loyalty to resource-dependent communities.[85]

Sen. Warren Magnuson, one of the original quartet of senators who requested the high mountain policy, expressed surprise at Pelly's request. He told Freeman that while he generally agreed with the idea of the moratorium and was "particularly interested" that ten sites be reserved from logging, at least for now, he also understood the practical considerations and suggested the Forest Service move ahead on about half the sites.[86] Accordingly, in early September a senior Agriculture Department official informed Pelly that while half the proposed moratorium sites had no developments planned for the next five years, "it is necessary that the present plans for recreation developments, roads actions and timber management actions proceed" at the remainder, including the upper White Chuck River, which conservationists had unsuccessfully fought to include in the Glacier Peak Wilderness Area, parts of the Stehekin River drainage and other creeks draining into Lake Chelan, and the upper Cascade River drainage.[87]

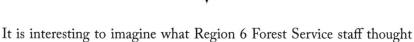

It is interesting to imagine what Region 6 Forest Service staff thought about these developments. At some level, it must have felt like they were being attacked from all sides. Conservationists wanted more land set aside for wilderness and recreation, and far less logging. Timber interests wanted more national forest land available for logging. Congress, caught among competing constituencies, seemed determined to force the agency to account for its activities and had no compunction about involving the Secretary of Agriculture. Certainly the high mountain policy study was politically motivated, a way to force the Forest Service to explain how it would apply MUSY in the alpine regions of the Pacific Northwest and at the same time suspend logging in those regions. The North Cascade Primitive Area turned into a political pawn when Representative Aspinall asked the Forest Service to suspend its reclassification study. Aspinall wanted the national wilderness preservation system constrained to its originally proposed nine million acres, and by stopping the study process he ensured the North Cascade Primitive Area would not be included in the bill.

Developing the high mountain policy and an appropriate response to Pelly's request for a continued moratorium on logging had taken several months. The season is short in the high country, and Region 6 found itself waiting, once again, for warmer weather. Come 1963, the Forest Service would once again find itself unable to act. The president was getting involved in the North Cascades.

CHAPTER 6

The Peace of the Potomac

The North Cascades Conservation Council and Dave Brower had pushed hard to get Interior Secretary Stewart Udall's attention on the North Cascades. Advised to wait until after the 1962 elections, they had complied. On first look, the political landscape had not changed much in Washington State. Only one representative was defeated: Don Magnuson, the Democrat who had introduced the first park study bill. He landed on his feet as special assistant to Udall and would work at the Department of the Interior for the next six years.[1] The House delegation now comprised six Republicans: Jack Westland, Thomas Pelly, Bill Stinson, Catherine May, Walt Horan, and Thor Tollefson; and one Democrat, Julia Butler Hansen. Sen. Warren Magnuson also won re-election to a fourth term.

The most important change, especially for those interested in the North Cascades, befell the one official who was not up for re-election. In January 1963, Sen. Henry "Scoop" Jackson became chair of the Senate Interior and Insular Affairs Committee, a position he would hold for the next eighteen years. Any park bill would come before the Interior Committee. As chair, he had the power to push bills through the committee, if he chose. Jackson and Magnuson each said they would back the other on the North Cascades, which meant only legislation the duo supported would move forward.

When Jackson assumed the committee chairmanship, he had been in Congress for nearly a quarter-century. Elected to the House in 1940 at age twenty-eight, Jackson was the youngest member of Congress. By the time he successfully ran for Senate in 1952, his reputation as a Cold War liberal was entrenched. Jackson supported civil rights and human rights, denounced Communism, and favored a strong American presence abroad backed by ample military spending. A native of Everett, Jackson witnessed firsthand the timber town transform into a manufacturing

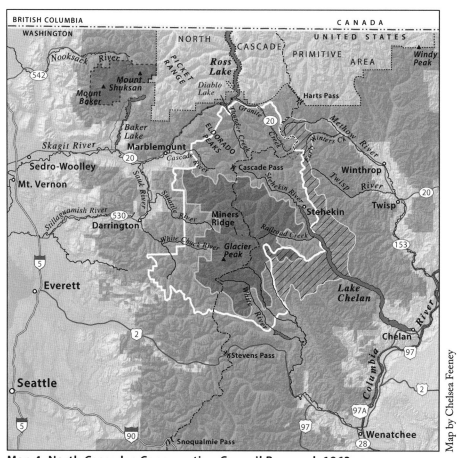

Map 4. North Cascades Conservation Council Proposal, 1963
from *Prospectus for a North Cascades National Park*

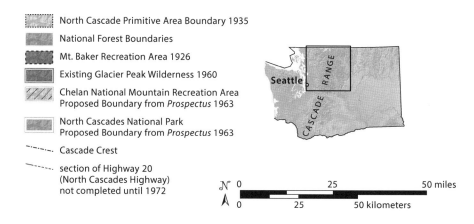

North Cascade Primitive Area Boundary 1935

National Forest Boundaries

Mt. Baker Recreation Area 1926

Existing Glacier Peak Wilderness 1960

Chelan National Mountain Recreation Area
Proposed Boundary from *Prospectus* 1963

North Cascades National Park
Proposed Boundary from *Prospectus* 1963

Cascade Crest

section of Highway 20
(North Cascades Highway)
not completed until 1972

0   25   50 miles

0   25   50 kilometers

Map by Chelsea Feeney

mecca during World War II. He was sometimes called the "senator from Boeing," an unsubtle jab at his efforts, along with those of the state's senior senator, Warren Magnuson, to steer military contracts toward the aerospace company. By 1963, Jackson, whose crinkly-eyed smile belied a razor-sharp political instinct, was one of the most powerful senators in Washington, DC.[2]

Warren Magnuson likewise commanded respect. A member of the Senate Appropriations Committee, he would have influence over funding any new national park in the North Cascades. While his policy expertise and accomplishments lay in consumer protection, health care, and civil rights, living in Seattle fostered a love of Puget Sound that eventually led him to write the Marine Mammal Protection Act of 1972. Well liked on both sides of the political aisle, Magnuson was close to eight presidents, and spent the night before Kennedy's inauguration with the president-elect, the only guest invited to do so.[3] Magnuson worked closely with Jackson in the interest of Washington State citizens. Together the two made a formidable team.

With Washington's senators advantageously positioned, the time was right for the administration to make its move. In late January 1963, Udall and Agriculture Secretary Orville Freeman sent a joint letter to President Kennedy, outlining their plan to resolve some of the most contentious issues between the Forest and Park Services. The so-called Peace of the Potomac proclaimed "a new era in cooperation" for managing lands in five Western states. Among the issues were two new national recreation areas, one in California, the other in Wyoming and Utah, and the creation of the long-debated Oregon Dunes National Seashore. Momentously, Udall and Freeman declared a joint study would be made of the North Cascades "to determine the management and administration of those lands that will best serve the public interest." The secretaries would appoint a committee of representatives from the two departments and select a chair, then make recommendations to the president based on the study team's findings. Within three days President Kennedy gave the green light.[4]

For the North Cascades, the Peace of the Potomac was both a response to conservationists' activism and an acknowledgment of the longstanding feud between the Forest Service and the National Park Service. The future of the North Cascades was now deemed of national interest and would not be decided in a regional Forest Service office. The issue was permanently encamped on the federal stage and would be debated, discussed, and decided there. With the executive branch taking the lead, a situation encouraged by Pacific Northwest Conservation Representative Mike McCloskey, the agreement also meant Senator Jackson could remain above the fray in his home state, a politically expedient consequence.[5]

About a month after the Peace of the Potomac and the announcement of the joint study, Udall and Freeman selected the five-member Joint Study Team. Their choices signified each department's stake in the study's outcome. Each secretary appointed the second-in-command of the pertinent office within his department. Udall tapped George Hartzog Jr., associate director of the National Park Service. Freeman chose Arthur Greeley, deputy chief of the Forest Service and son of the agency's third director, William B. Greeley, who oversaw the bureau's first tentative steps toward wilderness protection in the 1920s, including the 1924 designation of the first Forest Service wilderness in the Gila National Forest. Whether these men could or would overcome their ingrained partiality for their home office's way of thinking remained to be seen. Interior also selected Resources Program Staff assistant director Henry Caulfield. Agriculture's second member was George Selke, consultant to the secretary.[6]

The selection of the chair was fraught with perils. No matter who was chosen, some stakeholders would likely be displeased. When the secretaries selected Bureau of Outdoor Recreation (BOR) director Ed Crafts, reaction was mixed. Crafts, "a tidy looking gentleman with a very tidy mind,"[7] had been appointed head of the BOR in May 1962 after a long career in the Forest Service. Author of the Multiple-Use Sustained Yield Act of 1960, which ensured all national forest uses, including recreation, would be equally considered in management decisions, Crafts called the law "one of the real milestones" of Forest Service policy.[8] He had been passed over for Forest Service Chief when Richard McArdle retired in early 1962. Traditionally, the Agriculture secretary recommended to the president someone who had come up through the ranks of the Forest Service. Freeman's short list was three deputy chiefs: Crafts, Edward Cliff, and Arthur Greeley. Politically savvy, Crafts believed in an expanded role for recreation and wanted the Forest

Service to be more attuned to public opinion. Greeley had been selected as a member of the Joint Study Team. Cliff was a classic Forest Service man: an "enthusiastic exponent of intensive management and a staunch defender of agency prerogative."[9] Freeman chose Cliff, and Crafts left the agency to head BOR.

The BOR was a direct result of the Outdoor Recreation Resources Review Committee (ORRRC) recommendations, and when Crafts' appointment as BOR director was announced in May 1962, the N3C had reacted pessimistically. Crafts was "a competent man, a career man, and no doubt a devoted man," *The Wild Cascades* opined. "However, in view of the aggressive imperialism of the Forest Service, in view of its cold antagonism to its fellow public servants in the Park Service...can we preservationists be blamed if we ask why a Forest Service man was abruptly thrust into the Department of Interior, cheek by jowl with the Park Service he has, as a professional duty, subverted throughout his Forest Service career?"[10]

Now, barely ten months later, Crafts was a senior official in the Interior Department and in charge of a study that conservationists desperately wanted. His long Forest Service career must have caused some suspicion he would uphold that agency's position on the North Cascades, evidenced in part by conservationists' deliberately labeling themselves in *The Wild Cascades* as "preservationists," a term evoking John Muir and suggesting an emphasis on wilderness preservation over recreational use.

The secretaries acknowledged the Joint Study Team had a "complex, difficult and controversial assignment." Although they imposed no specific deadline, they urged the team to apply "due deliberation and haste" in investigating the North Cascades' natural resource potential, determining the region's best use, and making recommendations for how it should be administered.[11] Perhaps anticipating that decades of interagency competition could not be resolved in one fell swoop, Udall and Freeman instructed team members to present their individual viewpoints if they could not agree.[12] They encouraged the team to hold public hearings. They directed the team to invite Washington's governor, Albert Rosellini, to present the state's position.

The team went to work immediately. Instead of focusing only on the parts of the North Cascades that had been the subject of controversy thus far, the Joint Study Team elected to look at seven million acres of mostly federal land, from what is now Highway 12 along the southern border of Mount Rainier National Park to the Canadian border. About the size of Vermont, or nearly one-sixth of the total area of Washington, nearly nine-tenths of the gigantic study area was federal land. It included all of Mount Rainier National Park, the entirety of the Mt. Baker and Wenatchee National Forests, and portions of the Okanogan, Gifford Pinchot, and Snoqualmie National Forests. It encompassed more than half the federal land in the state. Less than 10 percent was privately owned; the state or municipal governments owned about 1 percent. Since conservationists had focused their efforts on about two million acres in the North Cascades, one can speculate that by expanding the study area the team may have had some notion of creating a politically acceptable patchwork of land management that included both the Park Service and Forest Service as land managers. Seven million acres gave the team much more land to work with, so if some were placed into a national park, plenty would still be available for the Forest Service and its supporters.

With the study area settled, the Joint Study Team decided it would meet regularly to review the history of the study area and reports prepared by relevant agencies, conduct on-the-ground examinations of the area, and hold public hearings. By May, individual team members were assigned responsibility for seven resource studies examining recreation, timber, water and power, minerals and geology, fish and wildlife, forage, and socioeconomic resources. The team member in charge of each study worked with Park Service and Forest Service personnel as well as state and local agencies.[13]

The resource studies did not include one on wilderness, which suggests two things. First, despite the ongoing effort to pass the wilderness bill, wilderness was not considered a resource to which economic value could be assigned, a perception conservationists struggled to change.[14] Second, the political debate in the North Cascades was, by this point, less about preserving wilderness as such and more about which agency was better able to provide recreation there. Wilderness would be protected anyway because it was part and parcel of the region's monumental scenery. The question had become, under what land designation?

In mid-August 1963, Caulfield resigned from the Joint Study Team after being promoted within Interior. Owen "Pete" Stratton, a political science professor consulting for Interior while on sabbatical from

Wellesley College, replaced him.[15] Correspondence between Agriculture designees Selke and Greeley about this and other issues makes clear that while the secretaries envisioned the team as friendly and objective, agency competition continued unabated, albeit less visibly.

Selke predicted Stratton could devote all his time to the study because as a consultant, his role was flexible. "This means increased emphasis on the study by Interior," he warned Greeley. "The manpower and financial investment that Interior is making seems to exceed greatly that being made by Agriculture. Interior truly looks upon the study as an opportunity of maximum importance."[16] Despite his fears about lopsided representation, Selke was wrong about the proportion of staff assigned to the Joint Study Team, which actually had about twice as many people from the Forest Service as from the Park Service. The exception was the Recreation Substudy Team, where Park Service personnel outnumbered Forest Service eleven-to-two.

Selke also worried about the conservationists, acknowledging "how well organized the group or groups interested in a million or more acre national park really is…The cohesion of the group and its national contacts in places of influence must not be underestimated." He urged the Forest Service to conclusively demonstrate its longstanding, mutually beneficial relationship with Washington State in pursuing its goal of continued management of the North Cascades. Greeley concurred. "Alas, you are so right about how well organized the Park proponents are on this matter!" he responded. "It is very important that we get copies of this announcement [of public hearings] into the hands of all the people we can think of who are interested in thinking of this area from the non-park point of view."[17] The next day, Greeley sent Regional Forester Herb Stone a list of groups to which he had forwarded the hearings notice. It included loyal Forest Service allies such as the American Mining Congress, National Cattleman's Association, National Lumber Manufacturer's Association, and Society of American Foresters.[18]

Region 6 staff discussed the "likelihood of a minority report" on recreation, which Selke encouraged starting immediately, even outlining the salient points to be made. First, national parks existed to preserve scenery, not provide recreation. Second, harsh North Cascades winters and short summers meant higher costs for operating a national park there relative to the number of potential visitors. Third, BOR and Congress could mandate federal recreation areas and decide who should manage them.[19] Greeley agreed the Forest Service would probably have to submit a separate recreation study.[20] The Forest Service was fully focused on the question of which agency could manage recreation better. Wilderness was no longer the issue. The scenery of the North Cascades guaranteed their preservation. What remained was a bureaucratic turf fight over which agency was better at providing recreation and what other uses of the land should be allowed.

Suspicious of their rival agency's team members and desperate to keep the North Cascades under Forest Service management, the exchange between Selke and Greeley is instructive for what it reveals about the on-the-ground reality in contrast to the Peace of the Potomac's lofty stated ambitions. Overcoming two generations of interagency rivalry would be anything but easy.

For the conservationists, 1962 had been a year of waiting and hoping—waiting for action from the Kennedy administration, hoping for a park study. In Seattle, home base of the North Cascades Conservation Council, many park supporters enjoyed the 1962 World's Fair. Science-oriented and future-focused, the six-months-long Century 21 Exposition gave the city the iconic Space Needle and the monorail that silently zipped visitors on a one-mile, ninety-five-second ride to downtown. Exhibits such as Boeing's Spacearium allowed fairgoers to feel as if they were on a journey into outer space. At the height of the Cold War, when many felt uneasy about nuclear arms, the World's Fair took an optimistic view of the future and the science that would make it possible.[21] Even as it looked toward the twenty-first century, the "City of the Future" wanted wilderness nearby, and conservationists' efforts continued unabated.

The N3C also worked on other wilderness issues in the North Cascades, including proposed reclassifications of Forest Service areas at Cougar Lakes and Alpine Lakes and the North Cascade Primitive Area.[22] But gaining a national park was the top priority. When Interior Secretary Udall visited the World's Fair, conservationist Irving Clark, who had been Bob Marshall's correspondent in the 1930s, invited Patrick Goldsworthy to a party honoring Udall on Bainbridge Island, a short ferry ride from

Seattle. The N3C president showed up "armed with maps" despite Clark's pleas to let Udall enjoy the event in peace. Seattle *Post-Intelligencer* columnist Joel Connelly recalled that Goldsworthy took the secretary "into the study and laid out the case for a park."[23]

The efforts of the N3C, the Sierra Club, and Pacific Northwest Conservation Representative Mike McCloskey demonstrated that both public and political support were essential to achieve a national park in the North Cascades. Much credit for the conservationists' success in securing a study belongs to Goldsworthy. Indefatigable in enlisting support, lobbying officials, and energizing the grassroots, the soft-spoken biochemist held fast to the conservation ethic he learned from David Brower: if you enjoy wild places, you are responsible for helping to preserve them. But credit also belongs to McCloskey, who brought needed expertise in government, law, and conservation issues to aid the N3C and its allies in their campaign for a national park.

The Wild Cascades, journal of the North Cascades Conservation Council, changed to reflect the organization's increasing political sophistication. Left, August 1962. Right, September 1962. *Courtesy North Cascades Conservation Council*

Reaffirming the group's status as regional leader on the North Cascades, the N3C's newsletter changed to reflect this with the appointment of a long-term, professional editorial team. In Harvey Manning, the N3C wielded an incisive and quick-witted pen, equally willing to criticize and praise (though tending toward the former). Manning had been climbing peaks in the North Cascades for more than twenty years, and he was certain that if "we didn't act it was all going to go."[24] In 1961, the Mountaineers published Manning's first book, *Mountaineering: The Freedom of the Hills*, starting a long and profitable enterprise for both author and organization. In May of that year, Harvey and his wife, Betty, became the editors of the N3C newsletter, quickly changing its title from the prosaic *NCCC News* to the more stirring *The Wild Cascades*. Working with Goldsworthy, the Mannings gradually changed the look and feel of the newsletter until, by fall 1962, it was wholly different from the mimeographed, stapled sheets of the Glacier Peak days. Beginning with the September 1962 issue, readers received a smaller, magazine-style newsletter with black-and-white photos on the front cover and a table of contents on the back. It was a slick, professional journal befitting an increasingly sophisticated organization and audience.

The appointment of the Joint Study Team in early 1963 fulfilled one of the N3C's chief objectives. The group now turned its full attention to a proposal for a North Cascades National Park, which McCloskey had drafted in bill form in late 1961. He knew that to win political support, conservationists needed a specific plan and a detailed strategy for promoting it. Thus, in 1962 and early 1963, McCloskey devoted himself to completing a comprehensive park proposal. In a 2003 interview, he reminisced:

> The area was too vast for me to know enough to draw the boundaries. Instead, I picked the brains of the climbers, backpackers, and mountain photographers who had gotten to know the various parts of the area quite well over the years...and got them to sketch out their ideas on maps...Then I searched out every piece of information I could find about competing values. I went to state agencies to learn about mining and minerals and water resources. I got type maps from the Forest Service showing prime timber stands, and I got transportation maps showing projected road extensions. I wanted to know what arguments would be made against putting any area in the park and

how well founded they were. I evaluated these competing values, and put together what I felt was a defensible proposal for a new national park there of 1.3 million acres.[25]

McCloskey's work resulted in a hefty book, *Prospectus for a North Cascades National Park,* which definitively outlined the conservationist position on the North Cascades. The *Prospectus* opened with thirteen pages of black-and-white photographs, many of the classic alpine scenery characteristic of the North Cascades. Here were Image Lake and Glacier Peak, a landscape the N3C worked relentlessly to preserve, and the great glaciers of Dome Peak. These pictures depicted what many associate with national parks: stunning scenery, soaring majesty, a jewel in the crown of our national landscape. But the first picture in the *Prospectus* showed a trail winding through ancient forests near the Sauk River. There were no serrated mountains, no imposing glaciers, no cascading waterfalls, just a quiet trail in a lovely wood of Western redcedar and thimbleberry.

The photos captured what the N3C argued for years: the North Cascades should be a wilderness national park, and wilderness included forests and river valleys, not just alpine heights. The inclusion of the trail photo made clear that wilderness recreation was part of that vision. It was what they had fought hard for at Glacier Peak. To drive home this point, the last page of photos showed clearcut areas, blemishes on the pristine landscape that demonstrated how the Forest Service's multiple-use philosophy endangered both the health and magnificent scenery of the proposed park.[26]

After this moving opening, the *Prospectus* got down to business. Maps showed the proposed million-acre park and adjacent 270,000-acre Chelan National Mountain Recreation Area. Five chapters authored by McCloskey, Goldsworthy, and others covered the scenic qualities of the North Cascades, Forest Service shortcomings, National Park Service potential, proposed legislation, and economic analyses of the impact of the park on the state's timber and tourism industries. These clearly tried to anticipate opposition arguments. For example, the *Prospectus* argued a national park "should prove to be a major tourist attraction in Washington, and increases in tourist revenues should more than offset minor losses from curtailed timber production." Although a national park would remove only 6 percent of the total allowable annual cut from the four national forests involved (Mt. Baker, Wenatchee, Okanogan, and Snoqualmie), the *Prospectus* nonetheless stipulated compensatory payments should be made to adjacent counties which would lose some timber sale revenues.[27]

For the North Cascades Conservation Council, the *Prospectus* culminated years of thought, study, debate, and activism. It represented the position of the N3C and most other conservation groups, including the Sierra Club and the Mountaineers. As such, the *Prospectus* would be what opponents and proponents pointed to when they talked about what conservationists wanted in the North Cascades. The proposed park boundaries stretched south from the North Cascade Primitive Area almost to Lake Wenatchee, and eastward from the upper half of Lake Chelan (including Stehekin) to much of the timbered Sauk, White Chuck, Suiattle, and Cascade River valleys on the west. The park subsumed entirely the Glacier Peak Wilderness within its boundaries. The Chelan National Mountain Recreation Area hugged the eastern side of the park, from Early Winters Creek to the White River, including the east side of Lake Chelan. The 1,308,186-acre proposal mostly closely resembled David Simons' 1958 proposal to the Sierra Club, but was bigger and much more detailed. The question for the N3C was, when to roll out the *Prospectus*?

McCloskey's political instincts kicked in. He pointed out there was no sense lobbying the governor if you needed a congressman—or an Interior Secretary.[28] Although *The Wild Cascades* published drafts of the proposal in the months before the hearings, the N3C decided to wait, partly because the *Prospectus* was not yet finalized and partly to give the Study Team a "fair chance to do its work in an objective atmosphere."[29] The upcoming Joint Study Team hearings would likely attract significant media attention, providing the perfect opportunity for the N3C to release the *Prospectus* and make its case.

In September, Grant McConnell wrote to Brower. He had heard from a friend who worked in Udall's office that the point of the public hearings was to discern public sentiment for a park, but the Washington, DC, office of the Interior Department believed such sentiment was "slight," and the trend appeared to be for continued Forest Service management. "This is the time to pull all stops," McConnell wrote, "many people + organizations appearing—both local and national."[30] As McCloskey and Goldsworthy worked feverishly to finish the *Prospectus*, the Joint Study

Team's hearings, set for October 1963 in Wenatchee, Seattle, and Mount Vernon, drew closer.[31]

❖

By the time of the hearings in October, the Joint Study Team had completed a significant amount of work. Although some conservationists wished the team had spent more time in the field, its five members were at least passingly familiar with the study area.[32]

With the winter season fast approaching, the team gathered on the crisp, clear morning of October 7 at the striking ten-story art deco Cascadian Hotel in Wenatchee. The choice of location was significant. The city was known as "The Buckle of the Power Belt of the Great Northwest," a reference to its location at the midpoint of the Columbia River's system of hydroelectric dams, and its economy was agriculture- and resource-dependent.[33]

Several dozen people testified. The arguments mirrored those espoused during the Glacier Peak controversy. Testimony opened with a written message from native son Rep. Walt Horan, a fruit grower and packer who argued Forest Service multiple-use management was crucial to the economic survival of resource-dependent communities adjacent to the North Cascades, such as Chelan and Wenatchee. Chambers of commerce, county commissioners, and resource and sportsmen groups vociferously opposed a park, which would "lock up" land for a single use, recreation. An Okanogan accountant grumbled the Sierra Club should "stay with California…Death Valley, preferably," and stay out of Washington's business.[34]

Those for a park, represented by McCloskey, N3C board member Chuck Hessey, and other recreation and conservation group members, argued population growth meant increased pressure on public lands, endangering what remained of the nation's unprotected scenic beauty. The multiple-use doctrine effectively prevented the Forest Service from providing permanent protection to the scenic lands it managed. The Park Service, on the other hand, was designed to manage such lands and would therefore be the best custodian. Moreover, tourist dollars from a national park would quickly exceed any benefits accrued from extractive industries.[35]

The *Prospectus* gave conservationists a credible base from which to argue for a park. *Seattle Times* columnist Byron Fish wrote, "Conservationists have been charged with supporting their views most on sentiment. This time, the tables appear to have been turned. The [*Prospectus*] is statistical and detailed, and apparently is the first genuine research on a subject that has been discussed on emotion, pro and con, for 57 years."[36] Unveiling the *Prospectus* at the hearings demonstrated that conservationists were ready to leverage political opportunities to publicize their position.

National forest or national park? Multiple-use or wilderness preservation? National or local interests paramount? Testimony boiled down to these basic questions throughout the hearings. Two days later at Mount Vernon, the hearing again opened with an anti-park statement, this one by Rep. Jack Westland. More than two hundred people crowded into the Elks Club to hear about sixty witnesses.[37] In Seattle, which also attracted large crowds, Goldsworthy dramatically hauled a foot-high stack of signed petitions to the witness table to demonstrate pro-park sentiment. These were N3C petitions supporting a park study bill from three years earlier, but the visual impact was undeniable.[38]

Almost unanimously, local newspapers opposed the park. The *Everett Herald* said the Forest Service was doing "an excellent job…There's no need to change." The *Skagit Valley Herald* agreed the Forest Service managed the area "fairly and wisely." It would be "very hard to justify any further restrictions or reduction in our economic resources." Writing in the *Seattle Times*, outdoor writer and fly fisherman Enos Bradner warned hunting and fishing would be severely curtailed if a national park were established, and argued Mount Rainier and Olympic national parks already provided the "same type of mountain grandeur." The *Wenatchee World* also favored the Forest Service, but presciently warned that despite anti-park testimony, the final decision was not "up to the people who live here," but would be made by "congressmen and senators from New York, California, Illinois, and the other states—not by our own representatives."[39] The *World's* editors recognized that retaining Forest Service management would keep local interests paramount, ensuring the continued flow of logging receipts and jobs to towns adjacent to the national forests. By definition, a national park privileged national interests.

By the end of the hearings, more than two hundred people had testified. When the dust settled, the Wenatchee and Mount Vernon hearings had been mostly pro-Forest Service, while Seattle had been mostly pro-park. The urban-rural divide was as evident as the local-national split. The team accepted written comments until mid-November, and when the final numbers were tallied, they had heard from more than 2,500 people, 90 percent via letter. The conservation groups effectively galvanized their supporters. Although oral testimony had been three-to-two in favor of continued Forest Service management, perhaps because two of the three hearings had been held in resource-dependent towns adjacent to the proposed park, more than three-fourths of the written statements supported a national park in the North Cascades. Nearly 80 percent of the people who wrote or spoke wanted a North Cascades National Park, but it would be months before anyone outside the Study Team would know that.[40]

Hearings over, conservationists used the *Prospectus* to publicize and build support for a North Cascades National Park, using a two-level strategy McCloskey developed. At the local level, the N3C issued press releases about the *Prospectus*, solicited radio and television contacts, created a speakers bureau to fulfill and pursue invitations, contacted local politicians to urge support, developed a portable exhibit for use at meetings and speeches, and instigated a letters-to-the-editor campaign for members. Nationally, press releases on the hearings and the *Prospectus* were sent to national conservation organizations and interested individuals, *The Wild Cascades* newsletter was sent upon request, and a new film, newsletter, and brochure about the park went into production.[41]

Less than a week after the Seattle hearing, the pro-park forces got a bit of potentially encouraging news: Study Team member George Hartzog Jr. would succeed Conrad Wirth as director of the National Park Service. Wirth's enthusiastic support of Mission 66 did not sit well with many conservationists, who viewed the director "at best as an obstructionist to their wilderness protection goals." Faced with dilapidated parks desperate for infrastructure improvements, Wirth pragmatically focused on accommodating tourists and providing recreation more than he did on wilderness preservation.[42] But the new administration, especially Udall, increasingly applied an ecological lens to land use, viewing the natural world as composed of interdependent parts. From this perspective, wilderness preservation was at least as important as public access to scenic places. In Hartzog, Udall found someone who shared this point of view and would manage the national parks accordingly.[43] If Hartzog supported a North Cascades national park—and given the Department of Interior's stated objective of expanding the park system plus Hartzog's position on the Joint Study Team, there was little reason to think he would not—Udall might be more inclined to back it as well.

At about the same time, Udall quietly reestablished a small National Park Service office in Seattle, telling Senator Jackson he planned to keep it permanently open henceforth.[44] Despite these positive developments, park proponents still awaited the Joint Study Team's report. Crafts warned the hearings record would take months to digest, and data gathered in the field during the summer had to be analyzed.[45] The waiting game was on again.

———————◆———————

President Kennedy's assassination in November 1963 stunned the nation, and likely temporarily stalled the Study Team's progress. Shaken, the N3C redoubled its resolve to fight for one of Kennedy's dearest conservation goals, expanding the national park system, by adding the North Cascades.[46] In April 1964, park supporters got a boost with the Mountaineers' publication of *The North Cascades*, a coffee-table book brimming with evocative black-and-white photos by mountaineer Tom Miller of some of the region's most spectacular scenery. Passionate essays by Harvey Manning enhanced the photos, making the case for a park: "Our group, and our generation, have only begun to discover the North Cascades. Our hope, now, is that the North Cascades will be there, essentially in the present condition, during years to come—for us to discover, and also for future generations of Americans to discover."[47] One reviewer termed the book "probably the loveliest and most expensive campaign tract ever printed."[48] Manning said, "Dave [Brower] used that book to introduce the North Cascades to America."[49]

In June, another promising development: the Study Team released reports on recreation, timber, water and power, minerals and geology, fish and wildlife, and forage (the socioeconomic report was not yet completed). Of these, park proponents most eagerly awaited the Park

Service's recreation study. The agency determined that 4.4 million acres of the 7-million-acre Study Area warranted management primarily for scenic values. Almost all the area proposed for a park in the N3C's *Prospectus* received the highest rating for meriting scenic protection.[50] North of Stevens Pass, the report concluded, the mountains were "so magnificent, so unspoiled and so uncommitted to other uses...highly suitable for dedication to inspirational purposes."[51] *The Wild Cascades* rejoiced, "Score One for Our Side."[52]

The recreation study was particularly heartening in light of another report, this one completed by a committee appointed by Albert Rosellini, governor of Washington. More than a year earlier, the Joint Study Team asked for the state's recommendations, but Rosellini declined, saying he wanted to study the area first.[53] With Bert Cole, the state's elected Lands Commissioner, Rosellini created the Washington Forest Area Use Council (WFAUC) in late 1962, directing its members to study the state's forested lands with an eye toward determining their highest use.[54] Also, Rosellini told WFAUC chair Scott Richards, a Skagit County commissioner, that members should expect to comment on the creation of a national park in the North Cascades and the reclassification of the North Cascade Primitive Area.[55]

A WFAUC subcommittee, which included representatives from mining, timber, railroads, and hunting groups—every major interest group except recreation—produced a report that favored continued Forest Service administration in the North Cascades, urged more logging, and warned against "permanent" land use classification, such as wilderness or national park.[56] The full WFAUC spent some time arguing about the subcommittee's report, and finally decided to send majority and minority reports to the governor. The minority presented the conservationist position favoring more wilderness areas and more national parks. The far more numerous foresters, game managers, geologists, and local officials on the council favored continued multiple-use administration.[57]

By April 1964, the Joint Study Team was politely but insistently asking for input from the state by June 9. Faced with a WFAUC at odds internally, Rosellini replied four days before the deadline, pleading the short timeline and simply forwarding both WFAUC reports to the Joint Study Team. The action left Washington State without a clear position.[58] Rosellini's slow response, perhaps prompted by a tough re-election campaign, meant the state would not have much say in the Joint Study Team's final report, a situation that would come back to haunt the next governor, Daniel J. Evans, after he took office the following January.

Days after sending the WFAUC reports to the Joint Study Team, Rosellini told the Washington State Sportsmen's Council, "It has yet to be demonstrated to me that there is any legitimate reason to lock up a large portion of the state's most scenic and beautiful hunting area...there is no reason why we should cede the management of these wildlife resources to a federal agency."[59] Rosellini's game management chief made a similar case a year earlier in a letter to the National Wildlife Federation.[60] These statements signaled that hunters would forcefully oppose a national park, as they had during the Study Team hearings.

Despite the discouraging report from the WFAUC, good news kept rolling in for park supporters. McCloskey's publicity strategies were working. *The North Cascades* book continued to garner favorable reviews around the country; Goldsworthy and others took the *Prospectus* on the road, showing their plans at meetings in Seattle, Wenatchee, Portland, and Olympia. The N3C distributed 50,000 copies of a new brochure, *The Last Chance for a Northern Cascades National Park*. In September Seattle's KING-TV aired *Wind in the Wilderness*, an hour-long documentary about the North Cascades controversy that featured Goldsworthy.[61]

—————◆—————

September 1964 brought more welcome, and long-awaited, news. President Lyndon B. Johnson signed the Wilderness Act, and Glacier Peak was now permanently protected as part of the newly established National Wilderness Preservation System. Enactment had taken eight years and the strain may have contributed to the early death of its primary proponent, Wilderness Society executive secretary Howard Zahniser, who passed away just four months before it was signed into law.[62]

Conservationists in the Pacific Northwest had long worked for the bill's passage, and it had special resonance for some. The final bill defined wilderness as "an area where the earth and its community of life are untrammeled by man."[63] Zahniser credited N3C founder Polly Dyer with suggesting the term "untrammeled," which she had used in 1956 to describe coastal beaches in Olympic National Park.[64] An untrammeled wilderness was one where "man is a visitor who does not remain."[65]

Although the Senate first passed the wilderness bill in 1961, the obstreperous chair of the House Interior and Insular Affairs Committee, Rep. Wayne Aspinall (D-CO), forced delay after delay. Aspinall disdained "preservationists who sought to establish 'mausoleum-like museums in which people can go to see resources which cannot be utilized.'"[66] His antipathy toward the wilderness bill was partially the result of "lingering bitterness" over the Echo Park dam controversy in 1955. Aspinall believed conservationists "had been misguided in their desire to save Echo Park, and he was now determined to stand fast against them."[67] His entrenched opposition to the idea of wilderness made him one of the biggest obstacles to its preservation and would nearly derail North Cascades national park legislation in a few years. But that was in the future.

In summer 1964, Aspinall forged a compromise requiring wilderness areas to be recommended by the president and created by an act of Congress, not by executive order as conservationists initially wanted. Ultimately, this requirement meant new wilderness areas had to have significant public support, and they therefore tended to be larger than proposed, an outcome Aspinall and opponents did not foresee.[68] It also meant the Forest Service and Park Service were now two of many "wilderness advisors" to Congress, which with passage of the Wilderness Act strengthened its own role in managing wilderness preservation and land use issues.[69] The act became law in September, marking a major victory for conservationists and a national shift in consciousness toward valuing wild places for noneconomic reasons.

Later in September, President Johnson signed legislation establishing Canyonlands National Park, a quarter-million acres of spectacular red rock country at the confluence of the Colorado and Green Rivers in southeastern Utah. This was the spot where, three years earlier, Udall and Freeman started the conversation that became the Peace of the Potomac.[70] The new crown jewel park, a labyrinth of sandstone arches, slickrock canyons, and mesas, represented a step forward in Udall's objective of expanding the national park system.

Also in September, McConnell attended a political science convention in Chicago, where he bumped into a friend who worked for Udall and had some inside information. First, the Study Team would recommend a park, not the N3C version but "good all the same." Second, Udall was solid in his support for the North Cascades. Third, Senator Jackson would publicly support the park after he was re-elected in November. Lastly,

Crafts also supported the park. McConnell wrote to Mike McCloskey, "For the first time, the National Park Service has somebody running interference for it and that is brother Crafts."[71] The path to a North Cascades National Park was getting brighter.

The 1964 elections brought more good news for conservationists. Reps. Jack Westland and Walt Horan, longtime opponents of wilderness and national parks in the North Cascades, were defeated in the landslide that swept Democrats into office nationwide and solidified their majorities in the House and Senate. Replacing Westland was Lloyd Meeds, a former Snohomish County prosecutor for whom Phil Zalesky and other conservationists campaigned. Replacing Horan was thirty-six-year-old Tom Foley, a former staff member in Senator Jackson's office who won in a surprise upset. Democrats Brock Adams and Floyd Hicks replaced Republicans in districts centered on Seattle and Tacoma respectively. One exception to the resounding Goldwater defeat was Daniel J. Evans, a Republican noted for his love of the outdoors who defeated Governor Rosellini in his bid for an unprecedented third term. In news that must have pleased founding members of the N3C, George Wall, the mill owner who in the mid-1950s wanted to log Forest Service land in the Stehekin Valley, lost his bid for a seat in the state legislature.[72] McCloskey concluded with characteristic understatement, "Politically speaking, the picture looks very good for conservation in the State of Washington."[73]

Yet in February 1965, a one-two punch of events surprised conservationists. First, McCloskey resigned as Pacific Northwest Conservation Representative to become assistant to the president of the Sierra Club.[74] Attorney Rodger Pegues took over in a smooth transition, but McCloskey's institutional memory was significant, and Pegues had a lot of catching up to do. He got his chance almost immediately, when conservationists were caught unawares by Wenatchee National Forest supervisor Ken Blair's announcement of a new recreation area between the statutorily protected Glacier Peak Wilderness and the Forest Service-designated North Cascade Primitive Area.[75]

The Eldorado Peaks Recreation Area was the latest moniker for most of the eight hundred thousand-acre Cascade Pass–Ruby Creek Area, which had been called out in the 1960 Glacier Peak Wilderness decision. At the time, the Secretary of Agriculture stipulated that the area be managed primarily for recreation and encouraged construction of new roads and campgrounds.[76] According to the Forest Service regional office, the new half-million-acre Eldorado Peaks Recreation Area was part of its ongoing management of Region 6 lands, well within its bailiwick, and fulfilled the secretary's 1960 directive.

The N3C was skeptical of the agency's motivation and timing.[77] Goldsworthy fired off letters to Senators Jackson and Magnuson and Regional Forester Herb Stone, charging a "formal area has been established without taking the steps necessary to do it," that is, drawing up plans and getting approval by the Agriculture Secretary.[78] Stone professed innocence, responding that the Regional Office was merely implementing the 1960 Glacier Peak decision requiring it to manage the Cascade Pass–Ruby Creek area for recreation. Further, he added, the Agriculture and Interior Secretaries had not issued any directive to suspend regular planning and management while the North Cascades Joint Study Team conducted its work.[79]

That was technically accurate, but the timing suggested that the appointment of the Study Team hastened the Forest Service's work. In May 1964, the agency circulated internally a draft proposal for a Cascade–Mt. Baker National Recreation Area that included the Cascade Pass–Ruby Creek area and Mt. Baker Recreation Area (originally set aside in the mid-1920s). These two areas would connect via the then-under-construction highway across the North Cascades.[80] In November 1964, Region 6 prepared yet another report about management of Forest Service lands, one that proposed renaming the Cascade Pass–Ruby Creek Area as the Eldorado Peaks High Country.[81]

Forest Service assistant chief and Study Team member Art Greeley hurriedly reassured Senator Jackson that the Study Team was unswayed and that the designation of the Eldorado Peaks Recreation Area was just part of normal, ongoing Forest Service work.[82] Study Team chair Ed Crafts chimed in, acknowledging that yes, the Mt. Baker and Wenatchee National Forest supervisors had been giving slide shows about the area, and yes, "timing and judgment in this matter might have been better." But, he countered, park supporters were obviously "making capital of Forest Service actions and have placed the Forest Service on the defensive."[83]

The flurry died down, but the conservationist response and the Forest Service's protestations illustrate persistent fundamental differences in their values. Even as the Forest Service tried to embrace recreation à la the National Park Service, proposing campgrounds, ski resorts, and scenic roads, the N3C held fast to its goal of preserving as much wilderness as possible by limiting recreational development.

━━━━━━━◆━━━━━━━

By June 1965, the North Cascades controversy could be described properly as a national issue. What had started as a local boundary dispute between the regional Forest Service office and a handful of conservationists shifted to the federal stage with the introduction of park study legislation, the Peace of the Potomac, and the appointment of the Joint Study Team. The efforts of the N3C, Sierra Club, and other conservation groups had paid off. *Sunset* magazine's June cover asked, "Does Washington Get the Next National Park?" Inside, a fourteen-page article extolled the virtues of "our wilderness Alps." As they waited for the study team to complete its work, pro-park forces savored the publicity. The North Cascades had gone national.

The same month, the Sierra Club published *The Wild Cascades: Forgotten Parkland*, the eleventh in its Exhibit Format series of "big, four-pound, creamily beautiful, living-room-furniture books."[84] At about twenty-five dollars a copy, it was designed to be prominently displayed on the coffee tables of conservation-minded people. Originally based on an exhibit of Ansel Adams photographs, books in the series interwove stunning photos and evocative text to "convey an initial experience of the beauty of the physical landscape."[85] The books "helped shape the environmental perception of the American landscape for millions of people" and were an important political tool to enlist public support for conservation causes.[86] *The Wild Cascades* book provided a compelling introduction both to the region and the issue.

Its objective was unmistakable. "The purpose of this book," Justice William O. Douglas wrote in the foreword, "is to assemble the reinforcements needed to complete the [North Cascades] campaign successfully." With text by Harvey Manning, poems by Theodore Roethke, and photos by Ansel Adams, Philip Hyde, Dave Simons, and others, *The Wild Cascades* was a lush blend of gorgeous color photos and forceful arguments for preserving the North Cascades. Douglas wrote,

"What wilderness we decide to save within the next critical decade or two of decision-making will be all we will ever have. Probably it will not be enough...The wilderness of the North Cascades is a national resource of the future, not merely a local commodity, and we need it all, as a nation."[87]

While the book and the magazine coverage were noteworthy for their national scope, the North Cascades had garnered to this point only sporadic local press coverage. To this point, local media covered major news stories such as the Glacier Peak decision and the Joint Study Team, but not in any contextualized way. That changed in summer 1965, when the North Cascades controversy landed squarely on the doorsteps of many Seattle-area readers. *Seattle Times* reporter Walt Woodward wrote a series of thirteen articles about the North Cascades exploring the controversy in depth. This unprecedented media exposure brought the issue home to many in the state who were not necessarily ardent conservationists.

"It is no cheap pun to say that 'the woods are full of controversy,'" Woodward began. He honed in on two major opposition groups, hunters and the timber industry, predicting the North Cascades were "a critical phase in the historic battle over resource utilization." Over the next three weeks, just about everyone involved had their say in Woodward's stories. Northwest Conservation Representative Rod Pegues said profits from resource extraction within the N3C's proposed park "do not begin to compare with the benefits derived from its recreation use." The Western Forestry and Conservation Association council responded, "The appetite of some recreationists for forest land is insatiable...Why do their open-space demands always have to contain productive forest land?" Fred Overly, the former superintendent of Olympic National Park and now BOR's Pacific Northwest regional director, called the issue "a question of economics. The wilderness concept, with no roads, overrides economic values and bars mass use."[88]

The definition of "national park" was debated in Woodward's stories. Some, including a University of Washington forestry professor who served on Governor Rosellini's state North Cascades committee, defined a national park an "outdoor living museum. Scenery is not necessarily its No. 1 criterion. It must be unique." Other park opponents agreed, arguing the North Cascades was too similar to other national parks in the state to be worthy of the title. These included two state officials, Department of Natural Resources (DNR) head Bert Cole and J. Burton Lauckhart, chief of the game management division in that agency. Lauckhart said "a museum-type management" would hurt hunters by locking up game in off-limits areas. Cole said park advocates were "preying on a misconception of what the word 'wilderness' means" because for most tourists wilderness meant driving or strolling a short trail to viewpoints, not backpacking for days in rugged country. Mount Rainier National Park superintendent John Rutter, the Park Service's liaison to the Joint Study Team, refuted these suggestions. "We are charged by the Congress with both preservation and use," he said. "They have equal status with us." Longtime wilderness preservation advocate John Osseward, known for his work at Olympic National Park, said the Park Service "places more national significance on its areas" and could successfully combine wilderness and recreational developments within the park.[89]

In another Woodward story, Mt. Baker National Forest supervisor Chris Chriswell outlined the Forest Service's plan for the North Cascades: retain the Glacier Peak Wilderness Area, reclassify the North Cascade Primitive Area as wilderness, and manage the Eldorado Peaks country primarily for recreation by creating the Recreation Area that had precipitated the flurry of accusations and letter-writing a few months earlier. Chriswell said as a Forest Service employee, he was bound to serve the public. Whatever the public decided it wanted for the North Cascades, the Forest Service would do to the best of its ability. Still, he said, if the entire North Cascades were wilderness, the "ordinary person" would never get to see it because access was too difficult, and that contradicted the Forest Service's "greatest good for the greatest number" philosophy.[90] The Forest Service still considered wilderness the domain of those who could afford to get there, which ran counter to the concept of multiple-use. By this time, though, there was widespread doubt the agency was equipped to handle competing demands on public lands. Its Eldorado Peaks plan and other proposals were clearly reactions to what the Forest Service saw as the distinct possibility of a Park Service takeover.[91]

Speaking as a board member of the Mountaineers, Harvey Manning told Woodward the "real battle" would begin when the Joint Study Team released its report. "The principal value of the North Cascades is that it is a large intact wilderness," he said. "America needs to save her big wildernesses." Gov. Daniel J. Evans, who had appointed yet another committee to develop the state's position on the North Cascades, said, "We cannot use up and enjoy everything in this generation…I always have thought that there is something of value in the single use of some lands—the setting aside of certain areas." While not exactly a ringing endorsement, this was a far cry from Rosellini's hemming and hawing, and implied the governor was open to preservation of some sort.[92]

Woodward ended his series in early July, outlining the process by which a decision on the North Cascades would be reached. First, the governor's committee would develop a recommendation. The governor would consider it and send his views to the Joint Study Team. The Study Team would release its report, and President Johnson would probably take a position. Depending on what that was, he might request legislation.[93] As things turned out, Woodward had it almost exactly right, but for now, everything was still on hold as the governor's committee and the Study Team did their work.

As 1965 waned, conservationists could point to continued media coverage of the North Cascades as evidence of its status as a national issue. In September, a CBS television program, *Bulldozed America*, featured the controversy. The next month, Goldsworthy appeared on *Public Pulse*, a Seattle radio program. In November, the N3C held its first annual banquet at the Edgewater Hotel, perched on a pier at Seattle's downtown waterfront. Opened in 1962 to house visitors during the World's Fair, the hotel famously hosted the Beatles during their 1964 tour of the United States. The banquet keynote speaker, appropriately, was Brower.[94] Four days before the year ended, an article by Grant McConnell lamenting the Forest Service's focus on multiple-use to the detriment of scenery appeared in *The Nation*.[95] Still, the one Christmas present conservationists wanted most, the Study Team report, was not forthcoming. It had been nearly a year since the report was originally expected, and the Study Team had announced no new release dates.[96] The Study Team's silence was nerve-wracking. The year ended with no news.

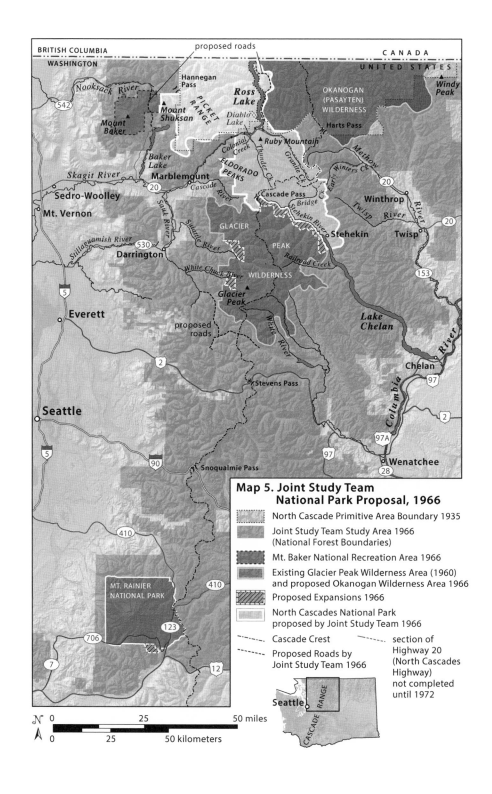

BRITISH COLUMBIA

WASHINGTON

proposed roads

CANADA

UNITED STATES

Nooksack River

Hannegan Pass

PICKET RANGE

Ross Lake

OKANOGAN (PASAYTEN) WILDERNESS

Windy Peak

542

Mount Shuksan

Diablo Lake

Mount Baker

Baker Lake

Colonial Creek

Ruby Mountain

Harts Pass

Methow

Skagit River

Marblemount

20

ELDORADO PEAKS

Thunder Ck.

Granite Ck.

Cascade Pass

Early Winters Ck.

20

Sedro-Woolley

Cascade River

Bridge Ck.

Stehekin River

Winthrop

Mt. Vernon

Sauk River

GLACIER

Stehekin

Twisp River

Twisp

Stillaguamish River

530

Darrington

Suiattle River

White Chuck River

PEAK

WILDERNESS

Railroad Creek

153

5

Everett

Glacier Peak

proposed roads

White River

Lake Chelan

Columbia River

2

Chelan

97

Seattle

Stevens Pass

97A

2

5

90

Snoqualmie Pass

97

Wenatchee

28

Map 5. Joint Study Team National Park Proposal, 1966

410

North Cascade Primitive Area Boundary 1935

Joint Study Team Study Area 1966 (National Forest Boundaries)

Mt. Baker National Recreation Area 1966

Existing Glacier Peak Wilderness Area (1960) and proposed Okanogan Wilderness Area 1966

MT. RAINIER NATIONAL PARK

410

Proposed Expansions 1966

North Cascades National Park proposed by Joint Study Team 1966

706

123

Cascade Crest

section of Highway 20 (North Cascades Highway) not completed until 1972

7

12

Proposed Roads by Joint Study Team 1966

Seattle

CASCADE RANGE

N

0   25   50 miles

0   25   50 kilometers

CHAPTER 7

The National Stage

Seattle awoke on January 6, 1966, to the roar of a ferocious winter storm that inundated downtown with nearly two-and-a-half inches of rain in two days. Houses squelched down hills, avalanches blocked mountain roads. It mattered little to the soggy crowd stuffed into a conference room at downtown's handsome, art deco Washington Athletic Club, because the Joint Study Team report was finally ready. Sen. Henry "Scoop" Jackson, Secretaries Orville Freeman and Stewart Udall, and Study Team chair Ed Crafts unveiled the results of the team's nearly three years of work. While the team members agreed on many of the twenty-one recommendations, the Departments of Agriculture and Interior continued to disagree about whether some portion of the North Cascades should get national park status. The team was divided. The two representatives from Agriculture said no; the two from Interior said yes.

As chair, Crafts had to break the stalemate. The former Forest Service official went for a park, recommending a 698,000-acre tract stretching from Lake Chelan northwestward over Cascade Pass, the Eldorado Peaks country, Ross Lake, and the Pickets to the Canadian border.[1] Nearly half of the area was already protected within the North Cascade Primitive Area. "One of the basic reasons for recommending a National Park," the report said, "is to give national recognition, National Park stature and special legislative protection to the unique and unparalleled mountain masses which occur so close to major metropolitan areas and in such grandeur and magnificence no place else in the United States." So far, so good. The entire team recognized the national significance of the North Cascades and a majority proposed to preserve an exceptionally scenic part of it in a national park.

But, Crafts wrote, a new park was feasible only with significant recreational development, including helicopters and tramways to transport people to scenic but remote areas, such as the Picket Range. A

Bureau of Outdoor Recreation chair Ed Crafts, chair of the Joint Study Team, speaks at the press conference announcing the team's recommendations, January 6, 1966, Seattle. Front row, left to right: Sen. Henry M. Jackson, Agriculture Secretary Orville Freeman, and Interior Secretary Stewart Udall. *North Cascades National Park Service Complex Museum Collection, NOCA 19632c*

primary reason for recommending a park was that "by means of access and development, the area can be made available to large numbers of people rather than retaining half the area in Wilderness area status, as would be done by the Forest Service."[2] The message was clear. Conservationists had pushed hard for a park and it appeared more likely than ever they would get one, but it would not be the purely wilderness park they hoped for. This park would be more along the lines of a traditional crown jewel park, with plenty of development to accommodate lots of people.

Crafts summarized other arguments for the park. It would have little effect on logging, mining, grazing, and fishing. It would remove less than one percent of the commercial timber within the study area. It would be a boon to state tourism. Timber receipts to the four affected counties— Chelan, Okanogan, Whatcom, and Skagit—would remain unchanged.

The Study Team made other recommendations, including reclassifying the eastern part of the North Cascade Primitive Area, which was not within the proposed park, as the Okanogan Wilderness, and expanding by some thirty-nine-thousand acres the Glacier Peak Wilderness to include more of the Suiattle and White Chuck River corridors and more land north to the Stehekin River. The road system should be improved and expanded by completing the North Cross-State (later North Cascades) Highway and constructing a road along Ross Lake from British Columbia to the new highway.

In sum, the result would have something for everyone. Tourism would grow, adding economic diversification to resource-dependent communities adjacent to the park. Timber would be virtually unaffected. The new national park would bring "great intangible benefits to the population of the State, the region, and the Nation through new opportunities for mass recreation."[3]

This optimistic prediction did not preclude the other team members from appending separate dissenting opinions. National Park Service members wanted Mount Baker included in the park. Forest Service members opposed a national park, instead proposing to enlarge and reclassify the North Cascade Primitive Area as wilderness and establish a 537,000-acre North Cascades National Recreation Area in the Eldorado Peaks country.[4]

Thus, while the entire Study Team agreed the highest use of the North Cascades was recreation, questions of what types of recreation, boundaries, and jurisdiction remained unresolved. The two departments and their respective agencies were, in the words of Senate Interior Committee member Sen. Alan Bible (D-NV), "still jousting to see who is the greatest empire builder."[5] And while a cooperative atmosphere prevailed at the January 6 press conference, Freeman remained opposed to the park plan, stalwart in his belief that the Forest Service could competently manage the area for wilderness and recreation, even as Udall called the North Cascades "the most superb unspoiled large area left in the United States."[6]

As expected, stakeholder reaction to the handsome, 190-page *Study Report* was mixed. Opponents, including Washington State Lands Commissioner Bert Cole and sportsmen's groups, were unpersuaded, vowing to fight the park proposal. Seattle's KIRO radio aired a three-part series on the *Study Report* and ultimately supported the Crafts proposal. One timber industry representative interviewed for the program allowed the recommendations were a "moderate approach to the problem."[7]

Disappointed Glacier Peak was not included in the proposed park, the North Cascades Conservation Council's Patrick Goldsworthy called the recommendations an expected compromise.[8] Mike McCloskey was "tempted to denounce" the proposal as "short-sighted and a letdown," but Dave Brower warned against it. The important thing, he reminded conservationists, was to gain credence for the idea of a national park in the North Cascades. "Let's get on a train that is going somewhere," Brower said. "Once we're on it we can get it to go further."[9] After an emergency board meeting, the N3C adjusted its position. While its *Prospectus for a North Cascades National Park* still offered the best solution, the N3C would back the Study Team's proposal with the addition of Mount Baker, the suggested additions to Glacier Peak Wilderness, and a recreation area around most of Glacier Peak Wilderness extending north to the proposed Okanogan Wilderness.[10] The tempered response demonstrated the N3C's political sophistication and Brower's continuing influence.

Everyone would get an opportunity to express their views, because at the press conference Senator Jackson announced the Senate Committee on Interior and Insular Affairs, which he chaired, would hold hearings on the *Study Report* and on a proposal to eliminate fifty-nine thousand acres of forest from Olympic National Park.[11] Within days, the hearings had been scheduled for February 11 and 12 in Seattle. With less than a month to prepare, those interested in the North Cascades scrambled to marshal their forces.[12]

———————◆———————

Bright and early on February 11, television cameras jostled for floor space with more than four hundred people crammed into a meeting room at Seattle's posh Olympic Hotel. Committee chair Jackson shared the head table with Sen. Warren Magnuson and fellow committee members Sens. Lee Metcalf (D-MT) and Paul Fannin (R-AZ). Reps. Brock Adams and Lloyd Meeds, whose districts would contain most of the park, waited attentively. Rep. Tom Foley, a former Jackson aide, would arrive later. Already, 260 people had signed up to testify.[13]

At 9:00 a.m. sharp, Jackson opened in typical statesman fashion, welcoming fellow dignitaries and reminding the audience the committee was there to hear opinions on the Joint Study Team's recommendations and on the Olympic National Park boundary proposal. The hearings would be transcribed, and a copy sent to the Bureau of the Budget, which would use it to help craft an administration bill that would embody the *Study Report* and public opinion. As Interior Committee chair, Jackson would introduce the bill, and more hearings would be held in Washington State and Washington, DC. Everyone would have a chance to be heard.

The February hearings were unprecedented, Jackson continued. Never before had a congressional committee held hearings on a report *before* legislation was introduced.[14] Jackson's comments underscored the contentiousness of the North Cascades issue, while subtly nudging attendees to finalize their positions, because there would definitely be a bill, and it would likely include a park. The pre-legislation hearings also indicate the shift in the balance of power on conservation issues. Along with the Study Team's recommendations, public opinion would be given substantial weight in the final say.

First up was Harold Pebbles, president of the Washington State Game Commission. The commission "unequivocally opposed" a national park, Pebbles said, and hunters across the state were prepared to fight it. The Joint Study Team had erred in saying the area contained in the planned park was not a major hunting ground, he added; in fact, nearly one-third of the high mountain deer hunting in the state took place there. The Washington State Sportsmen's Council echoed Pebbles, arguing fish and wildlife management throughout the North Cascades should remain in state control. Charles Graham, a former Game Commission chair, sounded a familiar note in natural resources debates, saying he was there as a "private citizen with a deep, devoted, dedicated, lifelong interest in our…God-given heritage of natural resources." That heritage was meant to be used, particularly by hunters. Sportsmen's clubs from Yakima to Bellingham spoke with one emphatic voice. They wanted no park.[15]

Goldsworthy was next, speaking for the North Cascades Conservation Council's 1,200 members. While the N3C generally supported the Crafts compromise, it wanted Mount Baker added to the park, plus wilderness protection for the Okanogan, Alpine Lakes, and Cougar Lakes areas. That, Goldsworthy said, represented a political compromise the N3C could live with. What was best for the North Cascades was a different story. Refer-ring to color maps, he showed the N3C's Plan A, consisting of the 1960 North Cascade Wilderness Area and the 1963 *Prospectus* proposals. This was the best solution, Goldsworthy said. Underneath was Plan B, which included the Crafts proposal plus Mount Baker. The N3C strenuously objected to the Park Service's proposals for tramways and helicopters, wanted "mass visitation" limited to the south end of Ross Lake and to the developed areas of Mount Baker, and supported the North Cross-State Highway, albeit hoping it would be a "proper scenic" road; that is, a parkway similar to those in other national parks with recreational development concentrated along its route.[16] As the group representing the viewpoint of local conservationists, the N3C's stated willingness to compromise signaled Jackson that the organization would work with him to pass a bill.

Goldsworthy concluded by talking about the highway, so it seemed appropriate that Charles Prahl, the director of the Washington State Highways Department, sat down next at the witness table. The North Cross-State Highway, under construction at the time of the hearings, sliced through land slated for the proposed park. The highway project was dear to the hearts of many in north-central Washington, where it had been under sporadic construction since 1893.

———————————◆———————————

Since the early days of Washington statehood, visions of a commercial corridor to transport mineral riches and cattle between north-central Washington and Puget Sound ports captured the imagination of legislators. Boosters proposed a road from the Nooksack River north of Mount Baker to the Columbia River at Marcus, in the far northeastern corner of the state.[17] The 1893 legislature appropriated $20,000 to begin surveys and construction of "State Road No. 17," popularly known as the Cascade Wagon Road. It was the first state highway, designated a dozen years before the state created a Highways Department and well before reliable information about the topography of the North Cascades was known, and the vaguely described route went through "260 miles of the wildest, most imposing real estate in North America."[18] The legislature provided more funds in 1894, and the western end of the road was relocated closer to Marblemount.[19] An 1896 survey explored three potential routes for the road. One followed that of the current highway, although at the time it was rejected as the longest and most expensive. Cascade Pass was the preferred passage.[20]

The legislature continued throwing money at the Cascade Wagon Road, spending about $100,000 by 1905 with little to show for it. Another $15,000 was appropriated over the next few years, but as the realities of constructing a road over such forbidding terrain became clear, legislators and the young Highways Department turned their attention to a route over Snoqualmie Pass (now Interstate 90), concluding there would never be need for more than one good road across the state.[21]

Some minor work was done on existing roads in the Methow Valley and at Marblemount during 1913 and 1915, but World War I ended further efforts. A postwar spurt of enthusiasm briefly revived interest in the northern road, and the legislature provided more than $100,000 between 1921 and 1925. Construction difficulties, the Depression, and the opening of the Stevens Pass Highway (Highway 2), which offered a new route for commercial transport north of Snoqualmie Pass, combined to halt progress by 1930.[22]

During the New Deal, a twenty-mile road along the Cascade River was improved almost to Cascade Pass but was not completed, and the legislature set aside some money for mine-to-market roads, hoping to spur mineral development throughout the Cascades. Road boosters favored a road across or tunnel underneath Cascade Pass that continued east through Horseshoe Basin's rich mineral deposits to Stehekin. As before, the topography of the northern mountains defeated most of these projects.[23]

Boosters of the northern road had not given up, though, and after World War II they formed the Northern Cross-State Highway Association (NCSHA) to promote the highway's completion. The legislature was still reluctant, and a 1947 report argued the low traffic volume and short season did not justify pursuing the road, which ended near Diablo Dam on the west and Mazama on the east.[24] But by 1960, powered by the state's population boom, the construction of Interstate 5 as the main north-south freeway, and Gov. Albert Rosellini's blessing, construction was again under way. The state relied on a combination of federal forest highway money and state appropriations to fund the road.[25] In 1959, the state had awarded a contract to extend the road five miles from Diablo Dam to Thunder Lake, and by early 1966, only about thirty miles remained unbuilt.[26]

And now the federal government might plunk a national park down directly atop the highway's route through the mountains. Highways director Prahl and the NCSHA worried the National Park Service would impose fees or limit commercial traffic on the highway. When open, the highway "will have great scenic value but…will also serve as an important transportation facility for commercial, business, and recreation travel," Prahl said. He wanted the State Highway Commission to retain administrative authority for the highway and a right-of-way along its corridor.

Signaling compromise would shape the final outcome in the North Cascades, Sen. Jackson, Sen. Magnuson, and Crafts assured Prahl the North Cascades highway would remain under state management regardless of land use decisions along its route.

By 1968, most of the North Cascades Highway had been built, although the road was rough and mostly unpaved. *Washington State Archives photo, July 1968*

And so the hearings continued. Most resource and some recreational interests echoed the sportsmen. Chambers of commerce, economic development councils, trail bike clubs, packers, guides, grazers, and granges opposed the park. Fishermen, worried fishing would be restricted, wanted continued state management. Ski groups felt the Forest Service was friendlier to their pastime. When Jackson asked one ski group representative whether he would support a national park if trams were installed that could be used by skiers, the reply was blunt: the Forest Service was "far more capable of handling the winter business."[27] The ski groups regarded as suspect the Park Service's proposal for intense recreational development in the North Cascades. Mining companies protested locking up the fabled mineral wealth of the Cascades. That few companies had ever pulled a profit from the mountains was irrelevant.

The timber industry was a partial exception to the opposition. The Western Forest Industries Association, implicitly conceding the paucity of commercial timber available in the area, agreed "the primary use of much of the North Cascades should be recreational."[28] The Western Council Lumber and Sawmill Workers, the International Woodworkers Association, and the Washington State Labor Council concurred: "We see nothing wrong with the proper use of the North Cascades area for recreational purposes. After all, our workers on their vacations and weekends are some of the greatest users of recreational facilities on our public lands."[29]

That at least some in the timber industry believed the best use of the North Cascades was recreational may have influenced the evolution of the Forest Service multiple-use concept to embrace wilderness and other recreational uses that did not have quantifiable economic benefits. Testimony like this facilitated the compromise strategy that would ultimately lead to the complex of land use designations enacted in 1968. Timber interests were remarkably moderate in their testimony about the North Cascades. But then, they had a much more attractive prospect in their sights.

At the January press conference announcing the recommendations, Jackson included a scheme to delete fifty-nine thousand acres of coastal rain forest along the Bogachiel River and the north shore of Lake

Quinault from Olympic National Park. The proposal came from Fred J. Overly, a former logging engineer and Olympic superintendent who was now the Pacific Northwest regional director of the Bureau of Outdoor Recreation. Overly had long desired to make Olympic timber available to the logging industry. As park superintendent in 1947, he had suggested reducing Olympic's boundaries and persuaded then-Representative Jackson to introduce a bill to that effect. But local timber companies had wanted much more of the park's timber, and conservationists responded forcefully to the threat, founding Olympic Park Associates in 1948 to fight such proposals (Polly Dyer was its president for thirty years). Jackson backed off, and the Park Service in 1958 transferred Overly to Great Smoky Mountains National Park, where presumably he would be less of a threat to Park Service standards.[30]

Now, twenty years later, it was plain the simultaneous release of the *Study Report* and the so-called Overly report was not coincidental. Crafts had agreed to broach the Olympic proposal if "it is not made to look like a quid pro quo for a North Cascades Park," but it was hard to interpret it as anything else.[31] Timber interests indicated they were willing to "give up" some timber in the remote, inaccessible, mostly rock-and-ice North Cascades in exchange for a huge parcel of lowland, old-growth rain forest on the Olympic peninsula. A number of timber groups testified that the two questions, Olympic boundaries and a North Cascades national park, should be jointly resolved. Business and political groups from the Olympic peninsula, and most timber groups, supported the Overly plan.

But many others did not. One critic suggested the "trade of the North Cascades timber for 59,000 acres of Olympic rain forest for the price of withheld opposition...by the lumber industry is...an outcome of the esoteric game of footie-footie played between the Forest Service and the timber industry." The *New York Times* editorialized, "The timber raiders are riding again...The national parks are not up for grabs." Olympic Park Associates charged the "integrity of all national parks" was at stake. Martin Litton, the influential travel editor of *Sunset* magazine, wired Crafts: "Amazed at what [Overly] got away with as Olympic National Park superintendent...and now will be even more amazed if he is not summarily dismissed. Sunset will publish major article defending Bogachiel [a pristine rain forest river valley in the Olympics] in spring issue."[32]

Dozens at the Seattle hearings derided the Overly report as a personal, ill-conceived attack on national parks. One might not agree with the *Study Report*, but at least it had the imprimatur of federal support. About 10 percent of the witnesses at the February hearings and 40 percent of the one thousand letters received afterward addressed only the proposed Olympic deletion. Writers were "amazed, saddened, and shocked into protest" by the "secret, one-man" "land steal" that would wreak "desecration" on one of America's treasures.[33] Crafts himself wrote Udall, "I am fearful that opposition to the Olympic change is going to torpedo the possibility of a North Cascades park."[34]

Jackson might have been trying to help timber companies on the Olympic peninsula, or doing a personal favor for Overly, or had another motivation. Whatever the reason for the Overly proposal, in the face of overwhelming and indignant opposition Jackson eventually dropped it.[35] Environmental historian Hal Rothman believed the failure of the Olympic deletion marked the beginning of the postindustrial economy in the West, because public opinion deemed timber "more valuable as scenery than as board-feet."[36] This shift worked in favor of those supporting a North Cascades national park.

The second day of the hearings began at 7:30 a.m. to squeeze in as many witnesses as possible, but many people were there to see just one, Gov. Daniel J. Evans. When the *Study Report* was released in January, Evans declined to comment, saying he had not had time to thoroughly read it.

Governor Evans had been in office less than a year when the report came out. A Seattle native, he grew up hiking the Olympics on Boy Scout trips. He loved the outdoors. First elected to the state legislature in 1956, he won the governorship in 1964, bucking the national Democratic sweep. Respected for his ability to work constructively with members of both parties, Evans said in his January 1965 inaugural address, "We must assure that our heritage of great mountains, extensive shorelines, inland lakes, rivers and game ranges is conserved and properly developed," verbiage that employed both preservationist and utilitarian elements.[37]

At the Interior Committee hearings a year later, he found himself the immediate focus of attention on the North Cascades, for his predecessor had effectively avoided the issue during his entire second term in office. Gov. Albert Rosellini had employed classic delay tactics, first appointing a committee to study it and then refusing to release the committee's conflicting reports (one favored multiple-use, the other more wilderness) to the Joint Study Team, pleading a lack of time. The federal team ultimately released its report without the benefit of any recommendations, opinions, or input from the state.

In February 1966, however, the stakes were considerably higher. Although all the land under consideration was federal, a new national park and additional wilderness areas had been recommended. These would impact local communities, industry, and citizens who used the area for recreation. Legislation addressing the issue was all but assured. At a minimum, the state had an economic interest in the outcome. Opinion in Washington State was split between pro-park and no-park advocates. Finding a happy medium for the two camps was going to be challenging, but the state could no longer avoid taking a stand.

It was in this context that Evans seated himself at the witness table at the Olympic Hotel on February 12 and got right to the point. The North Cascades, he said, "are a heritage not just of the people of this State but of the entire Nation. They are an area of natural beauty and grandeur of national significance which deserve national recognition and protection." Moreover, Evans continued, "There is no argument that the recreational use of the area is the predominant consideration. There is also little argument but that vast areas should be preserved in their present natural wilderness state with a minimum incursion of the works of man."[38]

The historic Forest Service-Park Service fight was a "foolish rivalry," Evans said. The focus should be on the "legitimate interests" Washington citizens had in the land-use decision that had not yet been addressed, including skiing, hunting and fishing, national forest receipts (a percentage of which was returned to local communities), and the North Cross-State Highway. He urged a "recreation corridor" be maintained along the highway and outside of any park and wilderness boundaries to permit intense development, such as ski areas.[39] Attuned to possibilities for compromise legislation, Sens. Jackson and Metcalf both praised the corridor idea as "very helpful" to the administration.

Finally, Evans broached the most delicate topic. The state believed the national interest should prevail in protecting the scenic wilderness of the North Cascades for recreation. What forms that recreation took, and who would administer the set-aside lands, was still to be decided. The country west of Ross Lake and north of the highway was of "national park caliber and should seriously be considered by Congress for inclusion in the national park system," he stated. However, he added, if "there is to be a national park, let it be a park in the true and traditional sense of the term and not be simply of the type that transfers administration for the area from one agency of Government to another." The state of Washington would conditionally support a third national park, one that exhibited the crown jewel quality and visitor access characteristic of the great scenic parks of the West.

Evans was not finished. He announced he was appointing a Governor's Study Committee of citizens and officials interested in the North Cascades that would develop its own recommendation for the area. This proposal would define the state's position. Jackson assured Evans the Governor's Study Committee report would also be sent to the Bureau of the Budget for consideration in developing an administration bill, thanked him graciously, and moved on. Evans had been the fortieth speaker that day. There were seventy-five more to go.

———————————◆———————————

When the hearing finally adjourned at 3:55 p.m. on Saturday, February 12, certain things were clear. First, Jackson was determined to get the North Cascades resolved one way or another. When some witnesses suggested the entire matter be referred to the Public Land Law Review Commission (PLLRC), then embroiled in its mission of examining federal land law and recommending a public land policy, Jackson somewhat impatiently demurred. He told one hapless witness if every contentious issue were referred to the PLLRC, of which he was a member, "we would close down the Senate Interior Committee for the next 5 years…This is a great American habit, you know, if we have a problem which you can't solve, we can appoint a committee and let them work on it."[40]

When others asked for more hearings or hearings outside Seattle, Jackson reminded them the Joint Study Team had held public hearings in Mount Vernon, Wenatchee, and Seattle. "Now what towns would you suggest we go out and hold hearings in?" he queried. One witness boldly responded, "Omak, Wenatchee, Bellingham, Sedro Woolley, and Everett." Jackson retorted, "Monte Cristo, Silverton," referring to an abandoned mining town and a tiny hamlet in his home county.[41]

Second, passions ran high on the national park proposal. The *Study Report* contained twenty-one separate recommendations, only one of which addressed a national park. All of the other recommendations would also influence land use in Washington. Nonetheless, the park issue energized people the most. The overwhelming majority of the 191 witnesses spoke about the North Cascades. Sixty percent of them favored some kind of national park, be it the *Study Report* plan, the N3C plan or something else. Forty percent supported continued Forest Service management and expressly opposed a park.

Finally, of the pro-park voices, two-thirds of those who came to Seattle to plead for a park were individuals not representing organizations. Through phone calls, letters, and notices in *The Wild Cascades*, the N3C succeeded in getting out the grassroots. The resource organizations responded quickly, considering the short notice given for the hearings. Nearly 75 percent of the anti-park advocates represented hunting, skiing, fishing, logging, and other organizations. It appeared serious opposition was just beginning to coalesce, although it was less clear whether the committee might be more persuaded by individuals or organizations.

Jackson extended the hearing record for two weeks to allow additional statements to be filed. When the comment period ended, the senator's office had received more than one thousand responses, of which more than nine hundred were from individuals.[42] Of those, more than half specifically supported a national park in the North Cascades. Fewer than one hundred rejected the park idea outright. Most of the rest addressed only the Olympic proposal. In contrast, organizations were more divided: 28 percent wanted a park, 44 percent did not, and 28 percent did not address the North Cascades park issue. As Jackson's staff totted up the letters, the pro-park advocates carried the day with nearly 50 percent. Park opponents amounted to barely 13 percent of the written statements. Judging by the hearings record, Washington citizens and those of thirty-two other states plus the District of Columbia enthusiastically supported a new national park in the North Cascades.

So, it seemed, did the notoriously close-mouthed Senator Jackson. At the end of the hearings, Ed Crafts approached Grant McConnell "with great friendliness and told me that the Senator was convinced… that public opinion was for the park and then added he thought 'we could push this thing through.'" McConnell continued, "Crafts really felt he had taken a good bit of a beating; I think we really must adopt this guy—from now on he is our man, I suspect."[43] Crafts indeed supported a national park, telling Udall that Jackson was "quite pleased" with the hearings, but "really teed off" at the Forest Service for what he perceived as underhanded attempts to derail the park.[44]

The record compiled, it was sent to the Bureau of the Budget, and the waiting began again. Closer to home, meanwhile, park advocates looked to Governor Evans to make the next move.

Although Evans waited until the February hearings to even hint at what position the state might take, he'd been aware of the North Cascades issue for several months. In November 1965, Game Department Director John Biggs submitted to Evans possible members for a North Cascades study committee, which suggests Evans was already thinking about how to approach the issue.[45] Just four days before the hearings, the governor met with nine leading conservationists at his Seattle office. There, Patrick Goldsworthy, Polly Dyer, and others talked about the differences between the N3C and Joint Study Team proposals, the role of the governor to date, and how the conservation community and the state might work together.[46]

It is fair to assume Evans was thoroughly informed on the conservationist position when he announced the sixteen members of the Governor's Study Committee shortly after the hearings. The Committee represented the full spectrum of those interested in the North Cascades. Weyerhaeuser executive Bernard Orell, who had also served on Gov. Rosellini's North Cascades study committee, and the dean of the University of Washington forestry school, James Bethel, represented timber interests and forestry. Counties affected by the proposed park were represented by *Wenatchee World* publisher Wilfred Woods (Chelan County) and *Omak Chronicle* publisher John Andrist (Okanogan County), as well as Bellingham Chamber of Commerce president Nicholas Lidstone (Whatcom County), Mount Vernon insurance agent Robert Hill (Skagit County), and attorney Lewis Bell (Snohomish County). State Highway Commission chair George Zahn, an ardent booster of the North Cross-State Highway, filled a slot. Emily Haig, longtime Audubon Society activist and N3C board member, Jonathan Whetzel, a state representative from West Seattle, and Bill Halliday, a noted caver and member of the Mountaineers and Seattle Physicians' Committee for a North Cascades National Park, represented conservation interests. Several state agency directors, including Charles H. Odegaard from State Parks (not to be confused with then-University of Washington president Charles E. Odegaard), Daniel Ward from Economic Development, H. Maurice Ahlquist from Conservation, and John Biggs from Game, plus State Lands Commissioner Bert Cole, rounded out the group.

In early March, Evans asked each member to send preliminary recommendations on the North Cascades. Most demurred, saying they needed to see more information, but a few key people responded at length. Cole sent a letter reaffirming his stand against a national park. And Biggs forwarded the detailed proposal of the Washington State Game Commission.[47]

Longtime state officials Cole and Biggs had followed the North Cascades controversy since Glacier Peak. Elected in 1956 as the state's first Commissioner of Public Lands to head the new Department of Natural Resources (DNR), Cole in 1960 penned a diatribe against "ultraconservationists" and "carpet-bagger" groups like the Sierra Club in the department's monthly newsletter, *The Totem*. Cole argued the state would end up paying if the proposed Glacier Peak Wilderness Area included large tracts of timber, since a portion of receipts from federal timber sales was returned to the counties in which the timber was cut and used to pay for roads and schools. Less timber equaled lower receipts to the counties, and Cole feared the state would have to make up the difference. Cole was adamant. He believed timber was a crop, there were plenty of recreation opportunities already, and elitist wilderness preservationists wanted to lock up huge pieces of land for their personal use.[48]

Biggs also had long opposed the national park idea. In an April 1960 article in the *Washington State Game Bulletin*, he listed several reasons why Washington could not afford another national park. For one, "valuable natural resources are going completely unused" within proposed park boundaries. Second, Washington was the smallest state west of Iowa and already had two national parks. If more parks were needed, he suggested, create them in one of the bigger Western states that had none or only one or two. In other words, just pick some pretty area in, say, Nevada, and make it a park.

Biggs' closing argument became a clarion call repeated throughout the park debate. He charged that a North Cascades park would remove important high mountain hunting country. The North Cascades were Washington's "most scenic and attractive deer hunting area," with more than four thousand deer taken each year within the proposed park. Eighty mountain goats and one thousand bear were also harvested annually. The newly instituted "high mountain" deer season, a chance for hunters to pursue the animals in alpine high country before winter set in, would cease if a park was created, and the North Cascades would be "restricted to the relatively few people who care to view the country as hikers or campers."[49]

In spring 1963, Biggs had expressed his concern about limiting hunting in the North Cascades to Sen. Jackson, who replied he was "keenly interested in the problems associated with managing game around the National Parks" but did not take a position.[50]

Biggs encouraged the Washington State Sportsmen's Council (WSSC) to oppose a North Cascades national park. The council's 150-plus member clubs comprised an important interest group, one that followed closely State Game Commission policy. Biggs's game management chief had presented arguments against a park at the September 1963 convention of the WSSC. That report was sent to all the member clubs, which were urged to develop their own positions.[51]

By 1966, Cole's and Biggs's views on the North Cascades had, if anything, hardened. The Washington State Game Commission, undoubtedly with Biggs' close guidance, created its own proposal for a congressionally established North Cascades National Recreation Area composed of wilderness, wilderness buffers, and multiple outdoor recreation zones. Wilderness would remain primitive and would be surrounded by buffer zones allowing camping, recreational roads, and otherwise minimal development. The buffers would border more heavily developed outdoor recreation lands to include RV parks, cabins, campgrounds, lodges, and ski areas. No mining or grazing would be allowed in any zone. Small-scale logging might be allowed where needed to allow recreational development, such as cutting down trees for campsites or roadways. The Forest Service should manage the entire area, except for the North Cross-State Highway corridor, which the state should administer. The Game Commission would manage the wildlife and determine where hunting would be permitted. A management board composed of the secretaries of Agriculture and Interior and the governor would have to approve any development within the national recreation area, a novel but highly unlikely scheme.[52]

The Game Commission proposal was, if perhaps overly focused on game and blue-sky management scenarios, quite detailed. It included a color map of the North Cascade National Recreation Area, and combined with the Joint Study Team report, could conceivably provide a starting point for the Governor's Study Committee.

Governor Evans had a slightly different idea, however. On March 31, 1966, he notified committee members he was creating two subcommittees. The first would focus on land use—not, he cautioned, the Park Service-Forest Service fight—while the second would develop a definition of recreation within the North Cascades. For example, he asked, could recreation include skiing, high density lodging, and hunting? Biggs was assigned to the land use committee, as were Halliday, Bethel, Ward, Ahlquist, Orell, Lidstone, and Andrist.

By May, it was clear the two subcommittees were too unwieldy and contentious to complete their tasks. Acting on a suggestion from Biggs, Evans interceded again, assigning the Game Department director, Halliday, and Weyerhaeuser executive Bernie Orell to develop boundaries.[53] The three quickly agreed on everything but a national park. Halliday argued a park was needed to satisfy conservationists but said it did not need to be as big as those groups had proposed, because the *Study Report* indicated most of the area would be protected. He suggested placing Mount Baker and the Picket Range into a 500,000-acre park, a position in line with that of the Seattle Physicians' Committee for a North Cascades National Park, a group with which he was closely affiliated. Orell said the Pickets alone would be acceptable managed as a national park, but not actually designated as such. Given Orell's long tenure in the timber industry and his experience in government relations, his idea was likely an attempt at a politically acceptable solution, even though it blatantly ignored the political realities of the Park and Forest services.

Finally, a compromise was reached: the Picket Range and part of Mount Shuksan (Mount Baker's imposing neighbor to the east) would be a 335,000-acre national park managed by the Park Service but left completely roadless and undeveloped. It would be a small, wilderness national park accessible only to the most determined visitors, hardly in line with the governor's call for a crown jewel at the *Study Report* hearings, but perhaps enough to satisfy conservationists.[54]

The compromise came tangled with conditions. Each member had to deliver the unequivocal support of his constituency. Orell had to bring along the timber industry, and Biggs had to win over the sportsmen. Halliday had to persuade local and national conservation groups not to overtly oppose the governor's plan and to voice support for it. Given the contrast between this proposal and both the *Study Report* and the N3C's *Prospectus*, Halliday's promise seems in retrospect woefully naïve.[55]

With the last piece of the puzzle in place, Evans released the Governor's Study Committee report in mid-June 1966. It proposed a 1.8 million-acre North Cascades National Recreation Area composed of three land use designations. About 430,000 acres would be set aside as Recreation Areas, including areas around Mount Baker, Ross Lake, Lake Chelan, the Cascade River, and the North Cross-State Highway. Their primary use would be recreation and preservation, but mining, grazing, logging, power development, hunting, fishing, camping, skiing, and so forth would be allowed where appropriate. Another 1.05 million acres would be Wilderness Areas, including the Eldorado Peaks, the Okanogan country east of Ross Lake, and Glacier Peak, which was already so designated. Fishing and hunting would be allowed in these areas. Finally, 320,000 acres in the Picket Range would be set aside as North Cascades National Park. The Forest Service would manage the recreation and wilderness areas, the Park Service would manage the park, and the state would oversee fishing, hunting, and the highway. A North Cascades Advisory Board composed of the governor and the Secretaries of Agriculture and Interior would administer the whole thing.[56]

For those in the know, the similarities to the Game Commission's earlier proposal were obvious, with the exception of the rather smaller national park added to mollify conservationists. Reaction to the governor's plan was generally favorable. Four hundred copies were sent to resource industry representatives, sportsmen's clubs, conservation groups, legislators, and media. At last, Washington State had a plan for the North Cascades.

Still, not everyone approved of it. Representative Whetzel wrote a dissenting minority report to Governor Evans, saying neither roads nor ski areas belonged in the North Cascades wilderness, and important areas omitted from the Governor's Study Committee park should be added under Park Service management, including the Eldorado Peaks, Thunder Creek, Cascade Pass, Granite Creek, and the Stehekin valley.

Whetzel's response was mild, however, compared to that of conservation groups, the same people Halliday had promised would not openly oppose the governor's plan. When the Governor's Study Committee report was released, Halliday sent copies to members of the Federation of Western Outdoor Clubs, regional and national conservation organizations, and individuals. He attached to each copy a four-page letter that argued the recommendations constituted a "wholly new concept of great significance" superior to anything else thus far proposed.

This did not sit well with many conservationists, some of whom had been working on the North Cascades issue for a decade or more. *Wild Cascades* editor Harvey Manning bluntly told Governor Evans, "I understand you labor under the misconception that many conservation organizations based in the State of Washington will support the recommendations of your committee. In my personal opinion, you have been badly misinformed…The conservation consensus has been many years in the development, and though it will surely evolve further…I find it beyond belief that any flip-flop will take place." Manning advised the governor not to "rely on second-hand reports" of what conservationists were willing to support.[57]

Perhaps sensing impending disaster, Governor Evans quickly scheduled a meeting with conservationists for July 1966. While the governor and conservationists agreed the area deserved protection, they differed on boundaries and land use designations. In the end, they agreed to disagree.[58] Nevertheless, Governor Evans warned Patrick Goldsworthy, "There's not going to be a North Cascades park up there unless I agree to it."[59] In the meantime, Halliday paid a price for his hubris, losing his position as chair of the Mountaineers' National Parks Committee when it was merged with another committee focused on national forests.[60]

The Interior Committee hearings and the release of the Governor's Study Committee report fixed the North Cascades as a major controversy in the Northwest and beyond, a status reflected in media coverage. For example, Pacific Northwest Bell customers could read about the North Cascades in the summer issue of the company's magazine, *Cascades*.[61] Regional newspapers covered the story in depth; among these the *Wenatchee World* was notably vigilant.

Nationally, *Field & Stream* published a major article on the North Cascades in November 1966. "The North Cascades is probably the greatest remaining unspoiled outdoor area in the continental United States, offering limitless opportunities to fishermen, hunters, campers, explorers, and every type of outdoorsman," the author enthused. But a national park, with its mandate to provide visitor access, could turn the region into a "virtual outdoor Disneyland, overrun by wrapper-scattering, bottle-tossing sightseers who would quickly change the wilderness atmosphere into that of a Christmas-tree sales lot."[62] *The Atlantic* offered a different perspective. The North Cascades were the loveliest mountains south of Alaska and the least known, it said: "Until recently, their inaccessibility has been their salvation. That time is past." The story placed the North Cascades in the context of a "larger conservation battle which is being waged…from Alaska to the Rio Grande, from California's Point Reyes to Massachusetts's Cape Cod." In their efforts to preserve wilderness, conservationists had become "organized, sophisticated, articulate." A May 1966 *Life* magazine profile of Dave Brower, the leader of the 38,000-member Sierra Club, confirmed the conservation movement's powerful stature.[63]

Increasing media coverage, plus the hearings and the governor's recommendations, portended legislation and still more publicity. Accordingly, prominent officials began to visit the area. In late August 1966, Governor Evans spent four days inspecting progress on the North Cross-State Highway. Accompanied by a posse of highway boosters, conservationists, and reporters, the governor and his young son rode horseback over the uncompleted route.[64]

Around the same time, Secretary of Agriculture Orville Freeman traveled to the North Cascades, but with much less fanfare. Two weeks before leaving, he wrote to the Bureau of the Budget, the agency that would draft an administration bill based on the Study Report, and asked that no further work be done on legislation until he returned.[65] In fact,

Freeman wanted "no publicity" for the air trip through what is now the heart of the park and refused Jackson's request for a joint tour. Accompanied by his wife, Forest Service chief Ed Cliff, and the Mt. Baker and Okanogan national forest supervisors, Freeman went to Mount Baker, then flew southeast over the Pickets to Diablo for lunch. After a short car tour to nearby Colonial Creek, the party boarded helicopters for a winding flight down Thunder, Granite, and Bridge Creeks to Stehekin.[66]

Although Freeman's ostensible reason for the trip was to compare the Governor's Study Report recommendations to current Forest Service plans, he told a *Wenatchee World* reporter, "I haven't yet found any reason… that would justify the additional investment, the additional cost, the additional personnel, or the duplication that would be involved by putting a park in where there has been for over 60 years a Forest Service administration."[67] Peace of the Potomac and Joint Study Team report aside, Freeman continued to support the Forest Service.

The Forest Service had been trying to make the same point for months.[68] As early as April 1966, Region 6 developed a public relations plan for the North Cascades, known in the agency as an "I & E" or Information & Education plan. Its goals were simple: promote public understanding of the Department of Agriculture's viewpoints in the *Study Report*, publicize the Forest Service's management plans for the North Cascades, and call into question whether a change in administration was in the best public interest. Each of the four forests involved—Mt. Baker, Okanogan, Wenatchee, and Snoqualmie—coordinated the I & E effort, which included conducting slide shows for local groups, show-me trips for local officials, free maps, news releases, and the like. Skiers, climbers, sportsmen, politicians, and businessmen were the Forest Service's key target audiences.[69]

At the same time, the Forest Service needed to demonstrate it had a comprehensive plan for managing the North Cascades, which meant finalizing what to do with the area between Glacier Peak Wilderness Area and North Cascade Primitive Area—the same region Bob Marshall urged the agency to protect several decades earlier. To this end, the Forest Service sent Dick "Bush" Buscher, a Cle Elum-based resource assistant, on a summer-long hiking and horseback tour to locate potential trails and recreation sites. The result was the Forest Service's proposal for a 560,000-acre North Cascades National Recreation Area, wedged north of Glacier Peak Wilderness Area and encompassing Ross Lake to the

Canadian border. The existing North Cascade Primitive Area would be split into two statutory wildernesses, the Picket (west of Ross Lake) and the Pasayten (east of the lake).[70]

The North Cascades National Recreation Area was to be divided into four management zones: untrammeled wilderness (no modifications, mostly alpine), backcountry (trails, shelters, planned primitive campsites, no roads), recreational (developed campgrounds, day use areas, and vehicle access, all designed to accommodate large numbers of visitors), and roadside (mass recreation development along the North Cross-State Highway, including visitor centers and year-round resorts). Buscher's ten-day trips into the North Cascades resulted in a number of potential recreational developments, including four resort sites, a tramway on Ruby Mountain, and backcountry hostels in the country above Granite Creek. The "enchanting Stehekin Valley will not be deteriorated by the construction of a road" via Bridge Creek, a possibility that worried conservationists and Stehekinites alike. Logging would only be allowed for recreational development.[71]

With the completion of the North Cascades National Recreation Area proposal in late 1966, the Forest Service's plans for the North Cascades were finished. As the Study Team recommended, the entire area would be managed for recreation. The differences between the Forest Service and Park Service plans remained the degree of development and, of course, the administering agency.

While Buscher was humping a 107-pound pack through the high country, Secretary Freeman returned to the North Cascades in September, this time at the request of President Lyndon B. Johnson and with Senator Jackson, Forest Service Chief Cliff, Secretary Udall, Study Team chair Crafts, Park Service director George Hartzog, and a Budget Bureau official.[72] Cloudy weather limited the trip to the west side of the Cascades, scrapping a planned helicopter flight to Stehekin. Nonetheless, the party flew from Seattle over the Glacier Peak region north to the Eldorado Peak area, to Diablo and Ross Lakes, over the Pickets and to Mts. Shuksan and Baker, seeing most of the area proposed for a park.[73] Again, Freeman saw nothing to change his mind about the best management option for the North Cascades: "Since last January, I have been looking for reasons why there should be a park...After this weekend, I'm still looking."[74] The Secretary was loyal to his employees.

The Agriculture Department had a "family atmosphere," according to Cliff, and Freeman "stood shoulder to shoulder…resisting the transfer."[75]

Udall recalled, "That evening we had sort of a fireside chat. We didn't come into agreement at that point. But I do not know that there has ever been a field study of this kind that was made where the principals, not their substitutes or deputies, actually saw a great area personally and sat around the table to discuss it in the most informal way possible. We saw the area by airplane, by helicopter, and on the ground, and I must say that it is to me one of the most magnificent scenic areas on the North American continent that I have seen."[76] Udall felt the North Cascades compared favorably to the great crown jewel national parks, the monumental scenery that defined America's natural heritage, and deserved the same protection as Yosemite, Yellowstone, and Grand Canyon. Freeman begged to differ, but both men agreed with Jackson the question was now down to who would manage the area, not its best use.

After days of hints, the question of which agency should manage the North Cascades was answered abruptly in late January 1967. In his annual budget message mid-month, President Johnson told Congress immediate action was needed to "preserve scenic areas of irreplaceable natural beauty," including the North Cascades.[77] Udall notified the Senate Interior Committee his department would submit proposals to make the North Cascades a national park.[78] A few days later, on January 30, the president asked specifically for a national park in the North Cascades during a special message to Congress on the environment. The bulk of the speech focused on water and air pollution and natural resource development, including geothermal power and mineral extraction from the oceans, but the president closed with a plea to "protect what remains of the natural beauty and tranquility that was here long before man…We must make significant additions to our present domain of land and water merely to keep pace with the need."[79]

To that end, he called for a Redwoods National Park in northern California, national scenic river and trail systems, and more funding for acquiring recreation lands. And the president wanted a North Cascades National Park, "provided that the wilderness and recreation areas are protected. This spectacular area of unparalleled mountain masses, glaciers, meadows, and timbered valleys is close to major metropolitan areas, and lies entirely within national forests."[80] Like the Study Team, President Johnson conflated wilderness with the scenic values of the North Cascades to justify its national park caliber. By implication, roads paving the way from Seattle and its suburbs to the wilderness were part of the equation. He somberly concluded, "There is much to be done. And we are losing ground…The domain of nature shrinks before the demands of commerce."[81]

Mt. Baker National Forest supervisor Chris Chriswell recalled when the president announced he wanted a park, the Forest Service fell into line. Forest Service Chief Ed Cliff recalled President Johnson had listened to Freeman's arguments against a park, then said, "I think we owe one to Scoop, so I'm going to go along with Interior." Proposals for new national recreation and wilderness areas were shelved. Going forward, the administration and Cabinet-level departments would speak with one voice.[82]

But what that voice would ask for by way of boundaries was still an open question. Sen. Jackson said the Interior Department was drafting a bill that he would introduce in the Senate, but gave no hint as to what the proposed park might look like. At this point, legislation could use any of the five proposals as its foundation: the Joint Study Team Report (usually called the Crafts compromise), either the National Park Service's or Forest Service's alternatives, the Governor's Study Committee Report, or the North Cascades Conservation Council's *Prospectus*. Any of the various options would permanently protect at least a million acres in the North Cascades.

In mid-February, Crafts told the *Wenatchee World* he expected a bill within a month, although he did not know what the park's boundaries would be. "My guess is that they will probably come fairly close to my recommendations in the Federal study report," he mused. He was right.

On March 20, 1967, the Department of the Interior submitted a bill to establish North Cascades National Park to Congress; Washington State Senators Jackson and Magnuson cosponsored it as S. 1321. The park covered most of the same territory as the Crafts proposal, but was smaller than Crafts had recommended, 570,000 acres instead of 698,000, because 100,000 acres along Ross Lake and the highway corridor were now proposed as a national recreation area. Granite Creek, along the highway route on the eastern slopes of the mountains, was excluded in the administration bill, an omission conservationists opposed.

The idea that portions of the North Cascades should be contained within a national recreation area had been broached before. The Forest Service had floated an Eldorado Peaks Recreation Area and North Cascades National Recreation Area, and the Governor's Study Committee had also suggested a national recreation area. However, national recreation areas were not consistently defined. This was partially because the concept of a national recreation area, while not new, was yet another land designation in a fast-growing list of such designations. By the mid-1960s, for example, the National Park Service alone managed public lands designated as national parks, national monuments, national historical parks, national cemeteries, national military parks, national historic sites, national battlefields, national memorials, national seashores, national lakeshores, and more. The definition of each type of site informed the uses allowed there.

Although not numerous, national recreation areas have been around since the 1930s, when they were conceived as recreation zones around manmade reservoirs created by dams. Generally speaking, national recreation areas prioritize recreation and allow more activities than do national parks, including hunting and fishing, and do not quite meet the scenic standards of national parks.[83]

In 1963, as a result of the Outdoor Recreation Resources Review Commission (ORRRC) report that recommended increasing the amount of federally managed recreation lands, the presidential Recreation Advisory Council developed policy for the creation of national recreation areas by Congress, promoting them as a way to provide more recreation lands for the public. The policy defined national recreation areas as "areas which have natural endowments that are well above the ordinary in quality and recreation appeal, being of lesser significance than the unique scenic and historic elements of the National Park System, but affording a quality of recreation experience which transcends" that of state or locally managed areas.[84]

Administered by any of several federal agencies, including the National Park and Forest services, national recreation areas are typically assigned to the agency that manages adjacent lands. The first congressionally authorized national recreation area under the new policy was Lake Mead in 1964, which had been administratively created in 1936 as Boulder Dam National Recreation Area under the Park Service. In 1965, the first Forest Service national recreation area, Spruce Knob-Seneca Rocks, was created in West Virginia, and a half-dozen others followed by 1968. While the designation gained popularity, it remained a catchall recreation lands label. National recreation areas were not national parks, wilderness, or multiple-use sites, but rather prioritized recreation sites for large numbers of people.[85]

Ross Lake National Recreation Area is a major recreational corridor in the North Cascades. The twenty-three-mile reservoir behind Ross Dam offers boat access to trailheads otherwise accessible only on foot. *North Cascades National Park Service Complex Museum Collection, NOCA 11931y-3*

Accordingly, Ross Lake National Recreation Area as proposed in the administration bill would surround the reservoirs created by Ross and Diablo dams and provide a buffer along the North Cascades Highway. As highway boosters desired, none of the highway would be in the national park. Hunting would be allowed in the national recreation area, though its boundaries did not contain land the state defined as major hunting areas. Heavy recreational development was planned, including campgrounds, resorts, fishing and motorized and non-motorized boating on Ross Lake, winter sports facilities, visitor centers, nature trails, and an aerial tram on Ruby Mountain that would afford visitors views of the lake and the southern part of the Picket Range.[86]

The insertion of Ross Lake National Recreation Area bisected the park. The northern unit included the Picket Range and Mount Shuksan. Two more trams were proposed, one at Arctic Creek overlooking the Pickets and the other at Price Lake offering views of Mount Shuksan. The southern section encompassed Cascade Pass, the Eldorado Peaks, and the Stehekin valley.

The small community of Stehekin would now be inside the national park. This caused immediate concern among its handful of residents, who wondered what would become of their property holdings. The bill allowed the Secretary of the Interior to acquire property by donation, purchase, or exchange, but some Stehekinites worried about what would happen when they died. "I don't want to develop my property and then kick the bucket and have the government take it over," one resident said.[87] Managing the Stehekin area would be a challenge.[88]

The prospect of a National Park Service takeover caused other concerns in Stehekin. Chelan Box Manufacturing Company, which a decade earlier strongly opposed the Glacier Peak Wilderness, complained that some 19,000 acres of commercial timber growing at the north end of Lake Chelan would now be unavailable for harvest. The Chelan Public Utility District had an application pending to build a hydroelectric plant in Stehekin to provide additional electricity to residents. Although the Forest Service had recommended approval, the plant would be located within the new national park, and seemed incompatible with park principles. Outflow from the power plant was supposed to supply a new trout spawning channel on Company Creek; its fate also now seemed uncertain. Finally, sportsmen were concerned about loss of hunting grounds. Although the Joint Study Team had not identified the Stehekin area as important for hunting, the Wenatchee Sportsmen's Association predicted the Park Service would end up slaughtering game in the Stehekin valley if it were made a park.[89]

In the eastern area of the proposed park complex, where the Study Team had recommended a 495,000-acre Okanogan Wilderness, the North Cascade Primitive Area would become designated wilderness and be renamed the Pasayten Wilderness after the river flowing through it. About ten thousand acres in the White Chuck and Suiattle River corridors were added to Glacier Peak Wilderness.[90]

The Park Service would manage the national park and national recreation area. The Forest Service would manage the Pasayten Wilderness and continue its administration of all other lands in the North Cascades, including Glacier Peak. It was a new concept for public lands: a complex whose management was to be shared by two agencies known for often-bitter rivalry.

As with the Study Team Report, pro- and anti-park advocates would have ample opportunity to be heard. The Washington State Legislature wasted no time, sending a joint memorial to President Johnson urging the Governor's Study Committee recommendations be adopted.[91] Senator Jackson scheduled hearings for Washington, DC, in April, and in Washington State in May. Conservationists finally had a viable bill for a national park. Now they had to decide whether to support the administration bill as written, or to continue pushing for the larger park they originally proposed.

CHAPTER 8

Hearings + Hearings + Politics = Park

Although Senator Jackson sponsored the administration's park bill, he had carefully stayed above the fray thus far. The North Cascades Conservation Council's Patrick Goldsworthy remembered a meeting with Jackson in the early 1960s during which the senator told him, "I can't give you a national park. But if you get up a big enough parade, I'll step out front and lead it on in."[1] Jackson's approach to the North Cascades issue is revealing in what it shows about his political instincts. This was vintage Scoop: canny, cautious, waiting to gauge public opinion before wielding his considerable influence for a park.[2]

Former Pacific Northwest Conservation Representative Mike McCloskey said it was Jackson who induced the Kennedy administration to set up the Joint Study Team in the first place.[3] Yet even after the *Study Report* recommended a park, Jackson preferred to wait for an administration bill rather than introduce his own because, as Study Team chair Ed Crafts noted, it meant Jackson was "off the hook while holding hearings."[4] Nonetheless, Jerry Verkler, former staff director of the Senate Interior and Insular Affairs Committee under Jackson, noted the senator vetted drafts of the bill to make sure "the President is sending up what [Jackson] would like to have him send."[5] Interior Secretary Stewart Udall recalled that Jackson brought "awareness and an enlightened approach" to conservation issues.[6]

To Jackson, the North Cascades were more than the focus of a political dispute over public lands management. "The North Cascades area has a special personal importance to me," Jackson wrote a friend on the first day of hearings. "Some of the most memorable experiences of my boyhood were gained tramping its trails. I find it hard to escape the feeling of proprietary interest in its fate."[7] Over five days of hearings, two in April in Washington, DC, and three in May in Seattle, Wenatchee, and Mount Vernon, Jackson had to balance his personal affection for the North Cascades with his responsibilities as Interior Committee chair and ensure those concerned about the park bill fully understood its provisions, a task he performed brilliantly again and again.

One group already on board, at least conditionally, was the conservationists. At last, they had a North Cascades National Park bill with a real chance of passing, imperfect though it may have seemed. The N3C and its allies were disappointed the bill did not include some of the forested valleys they had pushed so hard for. Brock Evans, who became Northwest Conservation Representative in early March 1967, recalled the administration park was "just a bare bone of the North Cascades, just the rock and ice, none of the great forests…We had a bitter internal debate among ourselves: should we go all the way for our own bill, or give qualified support to the Senator?"[8]

As the recognized local leader in the decade-long campaign to preserve the North Cascades, the N3C's position would set the tone for the conservation movement as a whole. The organization endorsed the bill with eleven proposed changes. Most of these added more land to the proposed national park and national recreation area, including in the Cascade River valley, the Granite Creek valley (the under-construction North Cross-State Highway ran along the creek), Mount Baker, and the Image Lake area of Glacier Peak. The group wanted to expand the boundaries of the existing Glacier Peak Wilderness to protect more of the White Chuck River and several of its tributaries, and expand the proposed Pasayten Wilderness to the east to include Windy Peak and to the west to include the Lightning Creek drainage. Another recreation area was needed from the middle of Lake Chelan uplake to the park boundary. The council opposed tramways in the park but reluctantly acceded to the one proposed for Ruby Mountain since it would lie entirely within the Ross Lake National Recreation Area. Finally, the N3C wanted wilderness areas inside the park defined in the bill and established within two years of the park's creation.[9] It supported the administration bill with amendments while still promoting its vision for a 1.3-million-acre wilderness national park outlined in the 1963 *Prospectus for a North Cascades National Park*.

The council's decision to support the bill rephrased the central question for conservationists, from "how much wilderness do we need" to "how much wilderness can we get."[10] In choosing to focus on the maximum politically attainable wilderness, conservation groups let Senator Jackson know he had their qualified support for a compromise, even as they wanted more land preserved, opposed mining at Glacier Peak, and raised concerns about recreational development within the proposed park. Now the senator had to deal with opponents.

By the end of the April and May 1967 hearings on the Senate bill, it was clear certain issues dominated the discussion. Hunters feared the park would limit access to game.[11] Skiers worried it would reduce the number of potential ski sites. Hydroelectric interests, particularly Seattle City Light, wanted assurances development would be allowed to proceed. Private property owners in Stehekin feared a government takeover of their land. The powerful timber lobby warned of regional economic devastation. And many were confused about the differences among the national park, national forest, wilderness, and national recreation area designations under consideration.

Despite these obstacles, Jackson was confident Washington State sentiment generally favored a park. The state's congressional delegation was largely supportive—Sen. Warren Magnuson had cosponsored the administration bill and the House members were generally in favor— which should ease the way to passing legislation. Buttressed by the *Study Report* and conservationists' continued efforts, Jackson was prepared to deal with naysayers. Polite but steadfast, he took them all on.

------◆------

The hearings opened on April 24, 1967, with Interior Secretary Udall, National Park Service director George Hartzog Jr., and Forest Service associate chief Arthur Greeley presenting the administration bill, S. 1321. The first witness, Washington State Game Department director John Biggs, read Gov. Daniel J. Evans's testimony into the record and submitted a memorial passed by the Washington State Legislature supporting the governor's plan for the North Cascades, a large national recreation area surrounding a smallish wilderness national park. Governor Evans would testify in person at a later hearing.

Then Biggs put on his other hat and spoke for the state's sportsmen in opposition to the bill. A national park would remove the "epitome of hunting in our State," Biggs warned. Each year, hunters bagged a thousand deer and forty mountain goats in the area of the North Cascades proposed for a national park. In doing so, they helped prevent overpopulation, disease, and the need for a slaughter program. The best way to ensure healthy game populations was no park, or at most the governor's proposed small park.[12] Former State Game Commission chair Harold Pebbles reiterated most of these points, noting if the Senate bill were enacted, the Game Department would probably eliminate its Cascade high mountain deer hunt and curtail the mountain goat hunt because of the loss of open hunting land.

In using the health of existing populations of deer and mountain goat as a reason against creating a national park, Biggs and Pebbles obliquely referenced the Park Service's difficulties with wildlife management. Predator control programs in parks like Yellowstone during the 1920s and 1930s had led to an overpopulation of big game harmful to ecosystems and other species. This eventually forced the agency to slaughter animals to bring herd sizes down to healthier levels, sparking public outcry. In 1963, a study known as the Leopold Report addressed wildlife in the national parks, calling out the need for active, science-based management to maintain natural balances within ecosystems. In Olympic National Park, Biggs said, "huge herds of elk are locked up and unused," endangering the animals' health and causing problems when they strayed outside park boundaries. Prohibiting hunting in national parks was an "outmoded, worn out, disproved policy of preservation" that "destroys the great national dignity of this wonderful specie of wildlife," he stated. The same could happen with deer and mountain goats in the North Cascades.[13]

Pebbles added that hunters favored wilderness preservation, because wilderness afforded the opportunity for primitive recreation in highly scenic areas. Hunters tested themselves in the wilderness, perpetuating a long and honorable American tradition. Intense visitor use such as that at Mount Rainier is "not the kind of wildlife and wild land experience we would like to offer in the North Cascades to the rest of the nation." In sum, Pebbles said, "The single, major, valid issue in this case seems to be that of land designation and the continuance of wilderness values, including hunting and fishing, and the vast majority on both sides do subscribe to continuance of these values." It was an accurate assessment.[14]

Biggs and Pebbles were longtime associates, and Jackson did not challenge them. But he did not have to. He knew the state would support a national park, and he had recruited the conservationists almost a year earlier to deal with the game question.[15] Testifying in the capital, Pacific Northwest Conservation Representative Brock Evans pointed out that according to the *Study Report*, no major hunting areas would be inside the proposed park. While he conceded there would be "some conflict" with the goat and deer hunt, Evans said the Game Department's own figures showed perhaps 12 percent of the goats bagged each year came from within the proposed park and deer figures were even lower. "We still believe that this is a minimum interference with hunting activity, and provides a needed refuge for those who wish to enjoy the high country in the autumn months free from fear of being shot," he said. Washington State had twenty-two million acres open for hunting. The park would make barely a dent.[16]

———————◆———————

While the hunters worried about losing game lands, the skiers wanted more ski areas. According to William Lenihan, speaking for the Pacific Northwest Ski Association, winter sports needs were ignored in the *Study Report* and the Senate bill. He intimated the state's 100,000-plus skiers, who participated in a growing form of outdoor recreation, were overlooked because the Joint Study Team had not evaluated potential winter sports sites. Since such studies took three to five years—"you have to evaluate snow depths, temperatures, wind, climate, avalanche factors," Lenihan said—establishing a "vast national park and vast wilderness areas [was] premature."[17]

Jackson turned to Bureau of Outdoor Recreation director Ed Crafts, chair of the Joint Study Team and author of the *Study Report*, for a response. Far from neglecting winter sports, Crafts said, the issue had been thoroughly studied. The Forest Service developed plans that included winter sports facilities at Snowy Lakes and Liberty Bell Mountain, both on slopes east of Granite Creek. In fact, he continued, the potential for ski resorts was one of the reasons the Study Team omitted Granite Creek from the proposed park.[18] Further, Park Service plans for a tram on Ruby Mountain, which could conceivably ferry skiers, had been a factor in proposing the Ross Lake National Recreation Area along the Skagit River corridor. If multi-year studies were required, Jackson summarized, "it would not be possible for us to act on anything in this bill until all studies had been completed for each and every mountain."[19]

The Pacific Northwest Ski Areas Association echoed everything Lenihan said and went one step further, asking for a congressional directive in the bill ordering Udall to "specifically develop adequate skiing in the North Cascades." For longtime skier Jackson, this was a bit much. While not opposed to sensitive ski developments within national parks—in fact, he had worked to expand skiing at both Mount Rainier and Olympic national parks—such a directive was beyond the scope of the Senate bill. In the end, Jackson simply sidestepped the issue, first bouncing it to Crafts, and then deflecting the idea for a directive.[20]

Another looming issue was how to integrate existing hydroelectric developments on the Skagit River with the proposed park. Seattle City Light operated three dams on the Skagit River that would be inside the proposed Ross Lake National Recreation Area and was keenly interested in how the area would be managed.

Created in 1910 to supply electricity to fast-growing Seattle, the public utility had a long history of operating hydroelectric dams on the Skagit, which drains 1.7 million acres of the northern Cascades. The power company's energetic superintendent, J. D. Ross, won federal approval for three dams on the Skagit in 1918, and Gorge Dam began operation in 1924. Diablo Dam followed in 1930, its reservoir known for its shimmering turquoise color produced by light reflecting off glacial silt suspended in the water. Ruby (now Ross) Dam was completed in 1940 and raised to its current height of 540 feet thirteen years later. The Skagit turns north above Ross Dam, and twenty-three-mile-long Ross Lake stretches about a mile into British Columbia when full. The dams were a popular tourist destination from their earliest days. For years, Seattle City Light operated a tour that included riding an incline railway to the top of the Diablo Dam followed by a homestyle chicken dinner.[21]

In 1967, Seattle City Light superintendent John Nelson testified early in the April hearings in Washington, DC. He wanted to ensure the proposed park would not interfere with three planned projects to provide more power to Seattle.

First, under a 1967 agreement with British Columbia, the utility planned to raise Ross Dam, elevating Ross Lake another 125 feet and flooding most of the river's valley in Canada.[22] Second, it wanted to dam Copper Creek, about eight miles downstream from Newhalem. Neither project was anticipated to cause conflict with whichever agency managed the land, and Nelson declined to take a position favoring the National Park Service or Forest Service. He asked for the Ross Lake National Recreation Area boundary to be changed to include the proposed Copper Creek dam and part of its reservoir to maximize recreational opportunities. The third project was potentially stickier. The proposed Thunder Creek dam would create a mile-long lake inside the park boundary, and called for a 6.5-mile tunnel to be built through Ruby Mountain to Ross Lake. Nelson wanted the park bill to guarantee Seattle City Light would be allowed to construct the project even though Thunder Creek was inside the proposed park.[23]

Jackson told him to submit an amendment to change the national recreation area boundaries at Copper Creek, but refrained from commenting on the Thunder Creek proposal. As with the hunting issue, he did not need to, because conservationists had plenty to say about it. They wanted this lowland valley stretching south from Diablo Lake to remain a wilderness recreation access route to Mount Logan and Park Creek Pass, a northern approach to the Stehekin valley. Goldsworthy and Brock Evans both argued damming Thunder Creek was unnecessary. When all of the utility's planned projects were completed, it would add less than 2 percent to Seattle City Light's total generating capacity. Furthermore, the current power output of existing Seattle City Light projects on the Skagit exceeded the city's peak demand.[24]

Stehekin presented a thornier problem. About 99 percent of the land proposed for the national park, and 98 percent of that slated for Ross Lake National Recreation Area, was already federally owned. Parks and Recreation Subcommittee chair Sen. Alan Bible (D-NV) wanted to know why it was necessary to acquire four thousand additional acres in Stehekin at a projected cost of $3.5 million. "The U.S. government owns plenty of land just as it is," Bible said.[25]

Udall and Hartzog replied the planned Stehekin acquisition served two purposes. First, it would protect unpatented mining claims in the area from development, and given the spectacular scenery there, this was most urgent. Second, a national park offered protection and sustainability for the community's way of life, in which tourism already played a big part. The Park Service planned to develop lodging, boat moorage, and a visitor center in Stehekin. A shuttle would take visitors upvalley to trailheads and campgrounds.[26] Bible wryly responded to Udall: "I am sure this area has great national park significance, but I also take off my hat and compliment you. You regularly, year after year, come in with more crown jewels than any man I have ever heard testify...I have no doubt that you will soon be down to the Appropriations Committee to get some money to put these crown jewels wherever you put a crown jewel."[27]

Regardless of whether they supported a park, Stehekinites were concerned about possible federal condemnation of their land. Fifty-five property owners signed a petition asking for Stehekin to be outside the national park and for continued Forest Service management, possibly in a recreation area. Resident Guy Imus, who opposed a park, argued property owners should be guaranteed perpetual ownership, estate rights, road access, and utilities rights-of-way. Pro-park resident Ray Courtney urged caution in private property acquisition. Jackson encouraged both to read the National Park Service's statement on the issue, which clarified that certain property types deemed compatible with the park could be acquired by mutual agreement, but owners would retain use and occupancy rights for their lifetime or for twenty-five years, whichever they chose.[28] Nonetheless, Stehekin remained a controversial issue that eventually changed the final park boundaries.

When timber industry representatives signed up to testify, it was not clear what stand they would take. In the hearings on the *Study Report* more than a year earlier, the timber industry's lack of vigorous opposition had been noteworthy. At the time, the proposed fifty-nine-thousand-acre deletion from Olympic National Park was perceived as a bargaining chip to ensure the industry would not oppose protecting the North Cascades. But when the Olympic plan was dropped, the industry refocused on the North Cascades.

Bill Hagenstein represented the Portland-based Industrial Forestry Association at the hearings. A Seattle native and graduate of the University of Washington School of Forestry, Hagenstein was a self-proclaimed passionate preacher of the forestry gospel. A protégé of William B. Greeley, the Forest Service's third chief, the tart-tongued Hagenstein had little tolerance for those who opposed logging. "We don't cut trees for the fun of it," he wrote. "We cut them because people want to build and live with wood...wood furniture, floors, windows, walls."[29] The Industrial Forestry Association opposed the park on economic grounds, he said. The Senate bill was a "serious threat to the economy of Washington," a claim he reinforced with a variety of tables and charts showing timber employment and production in Whatcom, Skagit, Snohomish, Chelan, and Okanogan Counties, all of which would be affected by the park. Combined with two other pending bills, one for a scenic rivers system and one for a scenic trails system, the legislation was a "blueprint for making forestry passé."[30]

Jackson launched into the first of what would be many ripostes on timber. He wanted to be clear: the Industrial Forestry Association was mostly interested in reducing the boundaries of the Glacier Peak Wilderness, correct? And the Picket Range was part of a primitive area created by the Forest Service long ago and so had always been off-limits to logging, correct? Hagenstein agreed.

"So," Jackson said, "the bulk of the park area is pretty well removed from commercial logging operations, isn't it, generally?" Hagenstein concurred.[31]

As for the economic impact, Jackson recalled employment in the timber industry was down over the past ten years, but output was up due to improved technology and efficiencies. Hagenstein again concurred. In fact, Jackson continued, economic diversification in most of the counties affected by the park meant timber employment was decreasing, while other industries such as aerospace and aluminum production were increasing. In Jackson's home Snohomish County, the Boeing 747 plant alone employed nineteen thousand people, while the entire timber industry accounted for only seven thousand jobs. "It will make us look pretty small by comparison, for sure," Hagenstein acknowledged.[32]

Jackson was courteous, but dogged. Having decided to back a park, he wanted to be crystal clear about the actual economic impact on the timber industry and timber communities. He hailed from Everett, historically a timber town, and the Sierra Club's Mike McCloskey believed Jackson remained sensitive to the timber industry even as he recognized economic diversification and technological advances had diminished its influence. "I think he had bet on the idea that Boeing and the employment built around it was where his political base and future was," McCloskey said. "But he still realized there were a lot of people in the rural areas and the timber industry wasn't dead yet and he remembered all of that and just wanted to be careful."[33] Ed Crafts, for one, believed Hagenstein's testimony was more about pleasing his own state's senator, Mark Hatfield (R-OR). Hatfield stayed at the hearing long enough to hear Hagenstein's testimony, and "they made some music for tomorrow's Oregon papers," Crafts wrote Udall. "It is pure politics and a love feast between Hatfield and the timber industry."[34]

Jackson also was not letting anyone get away with simply opposing a park, a point he made most plainly in an exchange with William Pearson, the mayor of Sedro-Woolley, a small town on the lower Skagit River. Pearson said the park would devastate the local timber economy by taking between one and three billion board feet of timber out of production. His community wanted continued Forest Service administration, although if there had to be a park, they supported the governor's plan.

When Jackson challenged Pearson on his familiarity with the plan, Pearson admitted he was "not fully informed." Jackson dryly replied that less timber would be available for harvest under the State proposal than the Senate bill: "I thought you should know what actually was recommended in the State proposal."[35]

Now Jackson turned to the supposed loss of billions of board feet of timber. "This figure comes as a surprise to me," he said. Pearson replied the number came partly from the Forest Service and partly from a forester who "traveled the area very closely." Jackson asked Crafts, who authored the *Study Report*, to comment.[36]

In the 670,000 acres proposed for a park and national recreation area, Crafts said, there was about five thousand acres of commercial timber, or less than 1 percent of the area. While the park contained a lot of forested area, that was "deceiving." The Forest Service had classified most of it as noncommercial for many years, because the trees were inaccessible, on unstable soil, or grew in sparse stringer stands. The Forest Service had never counted that timber when calculating the allowable annual cut. Pearson's statement was, Crafts concluded, "incorrect." Moreover, the bill stipulated that timber receipts to adjacent counties would not be affected by the creation of the new park. Jackson asked Crafts to supply a full statement on timber resources within the proposed park and national recreation area.[37]

As a politician weaned on the power of timber in Washington State, Jackson was careful to respect its position as a diminishing, but still important, industry. In a July 1967 meeting in Sedro-Woolley, accompanied by Forest Service associate chief Art Greeley, Mt. Baker National Forest supervisor Chris Chriswell, and two aides, he discussed the timber volume issue with local officials and timber industry representatives. After the group hashed out the differences in projected board feet available for logging, Greeley observed the timber interests modified their anti-park position. They now supported a national park in the Picket Range (à la Governor Evans's plan) and a Pasayten wilderness area. But they wanted the Forest Service to manage Ross Lake National Recreation Area and the Eldorado Peaks (the southern unit of the proposed park), and strongly opposed any additions to Glacier Peak Wilderness. Greeley cautioned, "Storm signals are waving that some segments of the forest industry want to fight" on this issue. After the meeting, Jackson asked the Forest and Park services to provide a report of how each would manage timber within Ross Lake National Recreation Area. Greeley got the feeling Jackson had decided to put something in the bill that guaranteed timber would be cut only when needed for recreational development.[38]

The timber industry made a lot of noise during the hearings, but in the end had little impact because both the Park and Forest Services planned to manage the North Cascades for recreation. There simply was not enough commercial timber inside the proposed park, national recreation area, and wilderness to formulate a credible case against it.

Testimony sometimes indicated a reflexive opposition to national parks without a corresponding understanding of the various land use designations under consideration. The testimony of Sam Binnian of the Seattle Chamber of Commerce is a good example. The chamber opposed a national park but supported a national recreation area, which it believed would allow more flexibility in development and access. Jackson wanted clarification, asking whether the chamber preferred national recreation areas over wilderness areas or only national parks. Binnian replied the chamber did not address parts of the legislation dealing with wilderness; it was concerned only with the prospect of a third national park.[39]

What uses would the chamber permit in a national recreation area? How about logging? Jackson asked. Whatever was ordinarily permitted, if it did not detract from the scenery, Binnian responded.

Did the chamber know, Jackson continued, the Forest Service already prohibited logging in most of what would become the northern unit of the park? "This is where the confusion comes in," he said. "A recreation area, sir, opens it to mining, and it opens it to timber cutting," Jackson retorted. "What is the chamber's stand on the mining business?"

Flustered, Binnian said he did not know.

Jackson drove his point home: "Yes; but you see we need your advice... We can't be vague and pass a vague law, you know."[40]

Capturing far more attention, both at the hearings and in the media, was the threat of a giant open-pit mine in one of the loveliest places in the North Cascades, the slopes of Glacier Peak near Image Lake. In 1954, Kennecott Copper had taken over existing claims on Miners Ridge. The next year, Phil and Laura Zalesky and Polly Dyer saw helicopters flying near Suiattle Pass. In 1958, Harvey Manning talked with friends at Kennecott who said while the company was enthusiastic about Glacier Peak's potential, there were no immediate plans to mine. In July 1966, about the same time rumors began circulating about a planned copper mine on Miners Ridge, hikers saw a thirty-five-person crew there. In November 1966, Kennecott representatives met with the Forest Service about developing the company's Glacier Peak patents. As part of the compromise that made its passage possible, the Wilderness Act of 1964 allowed development of existing mineral patents within wilderness areas until 1983, provided the mining company restored the affected area.[41]

In January 1967, Kennecott met with the N3C, Sierra Club, and other conservationists, explaining its vision for an open-pit mine between Image Lake and Suiattle Pass. One company vice president said Kennecott hoped the half-mile-wide, five-hundred-foot-deep mine would operate for thirty years.[42] For maximum efficiency, the company needed a mine plant, tailings dump, dump site, concentrator with a five thousand ton-per-day capacity, crushing plant, power right-of-way, water storage and supply, and a fifteen-mile-long access road to carry heavy equipment, trucks, and workers to and from the mine. Company officials estimated they would invest $15 million and employ two hundred people at the site.[43]

Kennecott was the second-largest copper company in the world in 1967. Only Montana's Anaconda was larger. Company officials dismissed concerns about the mine's impact, saying time would take care of the scars left by mining. "True enough," *The Wild Cascades* retorted. "After 1500 or 2000 years, you'll hardly know they were ever there."[44] Kennecott also tried to play to public sentiment, saying the Glacier Peak mine was urgently needed to supply copper for U.S. operations in Vietnam. Yet Miners Ridge would yield only one-half of one percent of the nation's annual copper consumption. Speaking at the Sierra Club's 10th Biennial Wilderness Conference in San Francisco three weeks before the hearings, Agriculture Secretary Orville Freeman said flatly, "Our present war effort will not suffer if Miners Ridge is left undeveloped."[45]

Image Lake and Glacier Peak. The threat of an open-pit mine operation in this area galvanized widespread opposition in the 1960s. *North Cascades National Park Service Complex Museum Collection, NOCA 16609*

When associate chief Art Greeley presented the Forest Service's plans for managing the North Cascades as outlined in the Senate bill, he noted Freeman's opposition to the mine and said the agency was working on a proposal to deal with the situation.[46] In fact, the Forest Service suggested to Freeman the administration should seek legislation to prevent Kennecott from proceeding.[47] McCloskey reminded the Interior Committee the N3C had long urged Glacier Peak be part of a national park, in which case the mining issue would be moot. Given the current legislation, though, "we hope public officials will be no less vigilant in using every available authority to protect" the Glacier Peak Wilderness Area.[48]

In June, the N3C ran a full-page ad in the *Seattle Times*, warning in enormous letters, "An Open Pit, Big Enough To Be Seen From The Moon." Showing a photo of a large open-pit mine in Utah of the type proposed for Miners Ridge, the ad urged readers to clip the form letter at the bottom of the page and send it to their elected officials.[49] The Sierra Club promised "all-out assistance" to stop Kennecott, the *New York Times* editorialized against the mine, and Justice William O. Douglas planned a summer camp-out to protest Kennecott's plan.[50] Even Herb Stone, the Forest Service's Region 6 director who had initially opposed including Miners Ridge and Image Lake in the Glacier Peak Wilderness, thought "the proposed Kennecott Copper open-pit mine isn't compatible" with wilderness."[51] Except for a few mining industry representatives, virtually no one wanted an open-pit mine at Glacier Peak.[52]

———————◆———————

A final area of concern was the prospect of substantial recreational development espoused in the Senate bill. Ross Lake National Recreation Area was proposed in part to accommodate such development, including lodging, campgrounds, boat docks, ferries, and tramways. The Park Service proposed a car ferry on Ross Lake that would travel more than twenty miles to Hozomeen, just shy of the Canadian border. It would build tramways at Arctic Creek to transport sightseers and hikers to a Picket Range viewpoint, at Ruby Mountain to afford views of the North Cascades, and at Price Lake on the flanks of Mount Shuksan.

Committee member Sen. Clifford Hansen (R-WY) expressed surprise at the tramway proposal, noting the Park Service usually opposed development that changed the profile of a park. Udall responded the tramways idea represented the latest in park planning. If Yosemite were made a park today, he said, the Park Service might propose a different transportation system than the road through the valley. It was necessary to update the agency's early thinking about public access, which advocated scenic roads into the heart of the national parks, often diminishing their wilderness character. Udall and Hartzog argued tramways could be camouflaged in the forest landscape, offered a viable substitute for cars, and would accommodate large numbers of visitors.

Hansen did not agree: "I think a national park is to preserve something else. It is not to try to get people access to every square foot of an area. It is to set aside an area of singular national significance."[53] Born and raised at the foot of the Grand Tetons, Hansen had been active in the battle over the now-iconic Grand Teton National Park. Initially opposed to expanding the park in the 1940s, by the 1960s he "freely admitted [the park] was an asset to the community and the state."[54] As Wyoming's governor in the mid-1960s, he had watched as an aerial tram was built at the Jackson Hole Mountain Resort just south of the park, and he knew there was no such thing as an unobtrusive tramway.

———————◆———————

When Jackson banged the gavel to close the last hearing on May 29 in Wenatchee, committee members had listened to more than two hundred people over five days. Opinion about a park was split. Park advocates held sway in urban Seattle but were outnumbered by opponents in Mount Vernon and Wenatchee, as might be expected given the rural towns' reliance on natural resource industries. When the field hearings began in Seattle on May 25, committee member Sen. Quentin Burdick (D-ND) commented, "We get more out of the oral presentations than we do the written presentations." But even he must have been impressed by the volume of mail about the Senate bill. The Interior Committee received more than nine hundred letters, four-fifths of which favored a North Cascades National Park.[55] Given the overwhelming support for a park, it seemed likely committee approval was forthcoming.

Goldsworthy later recalled that Jackson was cautiously optimistic about the bill. At one hearing, "Scoop said, 'Come on over to the corner,

I want to talk to you.' And he said, 'You know, we've got a lot of support for this park, and I'm for it. But we've got some opposition we've got to deal with…We can't get everything you'd like but I think I can manage it so we can come out ahead in the long run.'"[56] Jackson was signaling the conservationists should be prepared for a North Cascades compromise. The hearings over, the Subcommittee on Parks and Recreation marked up the bill through the summer and into autumn.[57]

In late October 1967, the subcommittee approved a revised version of the Senate bill that incorporated some changes suggested during the hearings. The Stehekin area was removed from the park and a Lake Chelan National Recreation Area was proposed instead. Private owners could continue to own their property as long as its use was deemed compatible with the national recreation area. About nine thousand acres were added to the east side of the Pasayten Wilderness to include Windy Peak. The Ross Lake National Recreation Area boundary dipped south to include the lower six miles of Thunder Creek, where Seattle City Light wanted to build a dam. Also at Seattle City Light's urging, the west end of the national recreation area boundary bumped out to include the mouth of Copper Creek to accommodate a proposed hydroelectric project. Finally, specific language protecting the state's interest in the North Cross-State Highway was added to the bill.[58] The two-unit national park, more than a half-million acres of wilderness, remained largely intact. Within a week, the full Senate Interior Committee approved the bill, and it went to the Senate floor.[59]

On November 2, 1967, the North Cascades National Park bill "whooshed" through the Senate so quickly Senator Jackson did not have a chance to make a floor speech supporting it before it passed by voice vote. A *Seattle Times* columnist chortled: Jackson "had the skids so well greased that his colleagues…left him speechless, speech in hand." With the exception of the timber industry, which sent Jackson a last-minute telegram opposing the bill, even opponents were grudgingly satisfied. The bill was praised as a "politically safe, non-controversial compromise with something in it for everybody."[60]

The bill still had to pass the House of Representatives, where House Interior Committee chair Rep. Wayne Aspinall (D-CO) had promised to give it priority in the following year, 1968. Sen. Jackson's counterpart in the House, Representative Aspinall was influential, irascible, and an outspoken proponent of multiple-use as interpreted by the Forest Service. He had singlehandedly delayed passage of the Wilderness Act for years, and made it clear he thought logging and mining more important than recreation as uses for public lands.[61] Aspinall had announced in September his committee would consider no further legislation in 1967, which effectively stalled the North Cascades bill as well as bills creating Redwoods National Park and the Wild and Scenic Rivers system.[62] This was precisely what Jackson feared, because it meant the House would now have an entire legislative session to modify, or possibly ignore, the politically acceptable North Cascades bill he worked so hard to construct. Park supporters realized they still had a long way to go.[63]

————————————◆————————————

Despite Rep. Aspinall's delay tactics, several of Washington State's House members had been busy on the park issue. When Aspinall finally scheduled House hearings on the North Cascades for April 1968, three bills were on the table. The first was H. R. 8970, the House companion to the Senate bill, sponsored by Rep. Lloyd Meeds (D-WA) in April 1967. Rep. Thomas Pelly (R-WA) had added H.R. 12139 to the mix in August 1967. It mirrored the N3C's 1963 proposal, providing for a park and mountain recreation area encompassing 1.3 million acres. For Northwest Conservation Representative Brock Evans, the Pelly bill had two functions. First, it showed Jackson "was by far not the most imaginative or bold in the North Cascades," and second, it "served the political purpose of getting Jackson more in the middle."[64] In other words, Jackson's bill looked moderate when compared with the N3C's proposal, which could help appease skeptical constituents. In March 1968, Rep. Catherine May (R-WA) introduced H.R. 16252, which contained the major elements of the Governor's Study Report: a North Cascades National Recreation Area consisting of 1.18 million acres of wilderness, about 400,000 acres of recreation area, and a 312,000-acre national park, all to be overseen by a federal-state advisory board.[65] All the bills advocated managing the North Cascades for recreation, but only the N3C bill explicitly promoted wilderness as the chief reason for protecting the region.

Table 2. North Cascades Legislation in the U.S. House of Representatives, 1967–1968		
Bill, Sponsor, Source	**Area Included**	**Acreage**
HR 8970, Meeds, administration plan	North Cascades NP	570,000
	Ross Lake NRA	100,000
	Pasayten WA	500,000
	Glacier Park WA additions	10,000
	Total	**1,180,000**
HR 16252, May, governor's plan	North Cascades NP	312,320
	Recreation Areas	398,852
	Wilderness Areas	1,179,681
	Total	**1,890,853**
HR 12139, Pelly, N3C plan	North Cascades NP	1,038,665
	Chelan Mountain NRA	269,521
	Total	**1,308,186**

On April 19 and 20, 1968, the House Interior Subcommittee on National Parks and Recreation held hearings on the proposed bills in Seattle. Nine members forewent their Easter recess to come to Seattle, prompting committee member Rep. Tom Foley (D-WA) to quip it was probably the largest Congressional contingent ever to appear in the state. He hoped, however, Aspinall would hold a hearing in Foley's district east of the mountains, a request Aspinall promised to grant before any action was taken on the bills.[66] In contrast to the Senate hearings, where about two hundred people spoke over five days, more than seven hundred people signed up to testify at the House hearings. To accommodate the unprecedented response, the subcommittee split into two simultaneous hearings and used a lottery system to determine the speaking order of witnesses.

From the start, it was clear these hearings would have a different tone. Representative Aspinall, visibly irritated by the huge turnout, set down strict ground rules, warning: "There will be no show of emotion. That means that there will be no applause. There will be no hissing, and there will be no clapping of hands. You would not do it in a courtroom. You will not do it in this room…We are here only for facts."[67] With that admonition, the committee proceeded to hear more than 450 witnesses.

Most spoke for less than a minute. To expedite the process and allow as many people as possible to speak, committee members generally refrained from asking questions.

Early in the proceedings, Representative Aspinall rather dramatically, if perhaps unintentionally, confirmed Washington State's official position on a national park in the North Cascades. Commissioner of Public Lands Bert Cole and Game Department director John Biggs appeared early in the hearing, and Aspinall asked each whether he opposed a park. Cole responded affirmatively, arguing for multiple-use management in the North Cascades. Biggs also opposed a park, fearing it would limit hunting and fishing. But Aspinall pressed Biggs, "Even if it could be limited to 100,000 or 200,000 acres? You would be opposed to it just the same?" Biggs reluctantly admitted, "Mr. Chairman, I think I understand the realities of this situation and I cannot deny that a park could be placed in the North Cascades of moderate size of a wilderness type and that the deprivation of fishing and hunting would not be great."[68] Biggs comprehended the political momentum behind a national park and hoped to minimize its impact by keeping the park as small as possible.

A few minutes later, Gov. Daniel J. Evans sat down at the witness table. Two weeks earlier, Pacific Northwest Conservation Representative Brock Evans had urged the governor to use the hearings to demonstrate that despite the differences among the various House bills, Washington State citizens were united behind the park concept and wanted to protect wilderness. Brock Evans worried that if the governor supported only his own proposal, Aspinall might infer opposition to the other options, providing a convenient reason to kill the legislation.[69]

Now, the moment of truth was at hand. Representative Aspinall asked the governor to spell out what the state would accept: "Are you all in agreement...with the 312,000 acres for a national park, with the rest of it to be left under the jurisdiction of the Department of Agriculture?" Yes, the governor responded, adding Cole was separately elected and an independent commission oversaw Biggs's agency. He couldn't force either of them to go along with a park, but they had served on the committee that produced the state recommendation and had agreed with it at the time.[70] Aspinall was satisfied that he could push for the smallest possible park.

But Rep. Morris Udall (D-AZ), brother of Interior Secretary Stewart Udall, wanted more clarification. He queried Governor Evans, "If it comes down to a question of the Senate-passed bill [S. 1321], a national park of that size [570,000 acres], or no national park at all, how do you advise me to vote?" Evans answered, "If I were in your place and had a vote, I would vote 'Yes.'"[71] The audience gasped. Washington State was now on record. It would support a large national park over no park in the North Cascades.[72]

Brock Evans understood the significance of the moment, writing to the governor, "You were there when it counted…you spoke your soul when it was most important of all that you do so…Conservation owes you a great debt and we will not forget it."[73] But Governor Evans's response was as much as an acknowledgement of his state's post-industrial economy, one no longer solely reliant on extractive industries, as it was a tribute to conservationists' effectiveness in garnering public support for protecting wilderness in the North Cascades.

Besides Governor Evans's stunning testimony, no new arguments pro or con were offered from the more than 450 witnesses who won the chance to testify. As at the Senate hearings a year earlier, about 80 percent favored a park. The N3C had done an outstanding job energizing the grassroots. More than three hundred attendees were individuals testifying as individual citizens. Nearly all of them supported a national park, most often citing population growth, open space needs, wilderness preservation, natural beauty, and demand for recreation as reasons for its creation. Park opponents spoke warningly of economic losses to adjacent communities, unnecessary bureaucratic duplication, loss of mineral wealth, reduced timber resources, and favoritism to the privileged few. The *New York Times* weighed in after the hearings, opining that a park along the lines of Pelly's bill, which mirrored the N3C proposal, would be "truly scaled to the heroic dimensions of America's Alps."[74]

True to his word, Representative Aspinall scheduled a hearing in Representative Foley's district for mid-July in Wenatchee. Only three committee members attended: Foley, Rep. Morris Udall, and Rep. James McClure (R-ID). National Park Service director George Hartzog Jr. came for part of the day. This time testimony was more evenly split, with just over half of the eighty witnesses, virtually all from east of the Cascades, opposing a park.

After three days of field hearings, pro-park sentiment seemed stronger than ever. More than five hundred people had testified in Wenatchee, and three-quarters of them favored a park. Curiously, relatively few people sent letters during the comment period after the House hearings. The committee received only fifty-eight letters (twenty-five for and thirty-three against a park), compared with the Senate Interior Committee's more than nine hundred. If Representative Aspinall had been waiting to get a feel for public opinion within Washington State before acting on the legislation, he certainly got an earful.

But Aspinall was less concerned with local opinion than with using the North Cascades as a device to achieve other political goals. At the end of May, National Parks and Recreation Subcommittee chair Rep. Roy Taylor (D-NC) announced he was prioritizing other park bills (including one to create Redwoods National Park) because he was getting so much mail opposing the North Cascades park plan.[75] Brock Evans found this implausible, and thought he knew what was really going on. "The reading of all this is plain to me: all the statements made about the reasons for not taking up the legislation have no weight," he wrote to a sympathetic reporter in June. "They are a smokescreen for the real reason."[76]

To understand the delay tactic, it is helpful to go back more than two years to February 14, 1966, two days after the hearings on the *Study Report* concluded. Readers of the *Wenatchee World* that day may have noticed a brief item on page two about water shortages forecast in the Colorado River basin states and a plan to pipe Columbia River water south to help make up the shortfall. The article warned that Northwest residents, who enjoyed abundant water from the Columbia and its tributaries, were likely to oppose such a scheme.[77] Now, two years later, the problem of Colorado River water apportionment was about to have major consequences for North Cascades national park legislation.

In 1968, Representative Aspinall championed a bill for the Colorado River Basin Project, which would determine water allocation in parts of the arid West. Aspinall's home state relied on Colorado River water and would directly benefit from the legislation. The bill included a provision that authorized a study about the potential of diverting Northwest water to the Southwest. Senator Jackson, protecting his constituents' interests, refused to let the bill out of his committee unless the study provision was removed. The Sierra Club's DC-based lobbyist, Lloyd Tupling, wired McCloskey that Jackson had confided he planned to "sit on" the Senate report about the Colorado River legislation until the "North Cascades clears [the] House."[78] But Aspinall refused to vote the North Cascades bill out of his committee until the Colorado Basin bill passed. It became a question of who would blink first.

After some behind-the-scenes negotiation, undoubtedly lubricated by the national election looming in the fall, Representative Aspinall dropped the Columbia River study provision from the water bill, and Jackson passed it out of committee. In return, Aspinall moved the North Cascades bill through, surprising many by scheduling hearings in Washington, DC, in July 1968.[79] Stewart Udall later called Aspinall the "most severe obstacle we had" on wilderness preservation.[80]

Representative Aspinall's announcement of July hearings was the death knell for any lingering Forest Service hopes of retaining its entire jurisdiction in the North Cascades. The agency closely tracked the bill's progress and, when it looked as though Aspinall might kill the legislation, was ready to revive its plans for the North Cascades. The Forest Service had developed management plans for more than two million acres of land in the North Cascades during the Study Team investigations, and was ready to resurrect them should the park bill fail. Reports from 1967 and 1968 describe Forest Service plans for proposed Glacier Peak, Picket, and Pasayten wilderness areas (1.28 million acres total) and North Cascades and Mount Baker recreation areas (783,600 acres total).[81] In a last-ditch attempt to keep all of the North Cascades under Forest Service management, former Study Team member George Selke had given the agency's plans to some county commissioners in north central Washington, who promptly passed them to the local media while decrying the "muzzling" of the Forest Service. In reality, these were simply the same plans developed by the agency in 1966 as an alternative to the Study Team recommendations.[82]

On July 25 and 26, 1968, the House Subcommittee on National Parks and Recreation held hearings in Washington, DC, just for congressional and departmental witnesses. Unlike the prior hearings in Washington State, which solicited public opinion, these were an opportunity for subcommittee members to question the House bills' sponsors, as well as Interior Secretary Udall, National Park Service director Hartzog, and Joint Study Team chair Crafts. Chair Roy Taylor wryly observed that after hearing from several hundred witnesses in Washington State, "we have listened, I guess, to more of the local people on this bill than any other bill that has ever been considered by this committee. Unfortunately, they are not in agreement as to what we should do about the matter."[83] Neither were the sponsors.

Rep. Morris Udall put the same question to Rep. Catherine May as he had to Governor Evans several months earlier. If the choice was between the Senate bill and no park, how would she vote? She sidestepped the issue, saying, "We all feel strongly that something should be done here, and we all sincerely hope…this would not be that kind of a do or die choice."[84] Representative Pelly, who did not attend the hearing, sent a straightforward written statement. He hoped the Committee would pass a bill for the largest possible park. But, he added, "I will vote for my bill, Mrs. May's bill or the Senate passed bill."[85]

Rep. Joe Skubitz (R-KS) asked Hartzog a variation on the same question. What would Hartzog do if asked to choose between the May bill, which represented the governor's recommendation for a 312,000-acre national park in the Picket Range, and no park? Hewing to the arguments for tramways he and Secretary Udall had made during the Senate bill hearings, Hartzog said he would rather have no park. On this matter, it appeared the National Park Service was less willing to compromise than the State of Washington. National parks, Hartzog said, must be "unique, superlative, scenic and scientific," an accurate description of the Pickets. But they also had to provide "reasonable and appropriate visitor access." The Picket Range was simply too rugged, too remote, and "only those who can walk in can get in."[86] A national park should be accessible to large numbers of visitors, and a larger park would provide more opportunities for recreational development and access.

In one succinct answer, Hartzog upheld the Park Service's proclivity for development and co-opted the one claim made most frequently by the Forest Service in opposition to the park idea. The Forest Service had applied its multiple-use philosophy to recreation in the North Cascades in what may be seen as an evolution of the concept during an era of growing sentiment for wilderness preservation. In the 1950s, the Forest Service had opposed a larger Glacier Peak Wilderness on the grounds that wilderness was available only to those with the physical and financial resources to access it. In the mid-1960s, it had argued intensive recreational development in the Eldorado Peaks country would serve the most people. The agency developed plan after plan showing how it would provide multiple recreation opportunities from backcountry camping to ski resorts. In contrast, Hartzog argued the Park Service had the expertise and experience to provide large-scale access to recreation in the rugged country of the North Cascades because it was part of its founding mission. From a political perspective, visitor access to the scenic North Cascades wilderness overshadowed any other considerations, and the Park Service was best equipped to provide it. In the battle over which agency was best able to manage the North Cascades for recreation, the Park Service prevailed.

＋

On September 4, 1968, the full House Interior Committee held a perfunctory hearing so the National Wildlife Federation could register its opposition to the legislation. Aspinall made a "gentleman's agreement" to allow this testimony, apparently because the organization had not taken a position at the earlier hearings. The bill passed out of committee that day, and the full House of Representatives passed it by voice vote on September 16. All that remained was for President Johnson to sign the bill.

"In conserving a great portion of this superb wilderness unspoiled forever," the *New York Times* gushed, "the Ninetieth Congress has performed a major service for this nation and its posterity."[87] Closer to home, the *Wenatchee World* termed the legislation a "masterpiece of political compromise. No special interest got exactly what it wanted. But all special interests won some concessions."[88]

The *World* had it right. The bill created a recreational and wilderness complex, the first of its kind, whose units would be managed by the National Park and Forest services. Its centerpiece was North Cascades National Park, 505,000 acres of wilderness that included the Picket Range in the northern unit and the Eldorado Peaks in the southern, but not Mount Baker or Glacier Peak, both of which conservationists had wanted in the park. Nearly all of the conservationists' amendments had been incorporated into the final legislation. The 62,000-acre Lake Chelan National Recreation Area appeased hunters and Stehekinites. Placing the yet-to-be-finished North Cross-State Highway and Ross Lake in the Ross Lake National Recreation Area (107,000 acres) pacified state officials, road boosters, dam builders, and recreationists. About ten thousand acres along the White Chuck and Suiattle Rivers were added to the Glacier Peak Wilderness, effectively protecting those lushly forested valleys from logging. And the Pasayten country, long part of the North Cascade Primitive Area, was statutorily preserved as the half-million-acre Pasayten Wilderness. Finally, the bill required the Forest and Park services to create a joint development plan for the entire area, and the Park Service to create a plan for wilderness preservation, within two years of enactment. Although the Forest Service felt it played defense in the North Cascades, in offering something for everyone, the legislation embodied multiple-use principles.[89]

October 2, 1968, was a beautiful autumn day in the nation's capital. Patrick Goldsworthy, Grant McConnell, Mike McCloskey, Brock Evans, Dave Brower, and Senator Jackson walked across the Pennsylvania Avenue portico and into the East Room of the White House. With the faint strains of a military band playing in the background, they watched

President Lyndon B. Johnson gives Sen. Henry "Scoop" Jackson a pen used to sign the North Cascades national park complex bill into law, October 2, 1968. Immediately surrounding the president, left to right: Lady Bird Johnson, Interior Secretary Stewart Udall, Bureau of Outdoor Recreation director Ed Crafts, Senator Jackson, unknown, Sen. Warren Magnuson, and National Park Service director George B. Hartzog Jr. *North Cascades National Park Service Complex Museum Collection, NOCA 16697*

President Lyndon Johnson sign the North Cascades National Park complex into law. The president also signed bills creating Redwoods National Park, the Wild and Scenic Rivers System, and the National Scenic Trails system that day, cementing the Ninetieth Congress's reputation as "one of the greatest in conservation history."[90]

It had been ten years since Goldsworthy helped found the North Cascades Conservation Council, thirteen since McConnell first warned of Forest Service logging plans in the Stehekin valley, fourteen since the beginning of the Glacier Peak wilderness boundary dispute. Including Glacier Peak, twenty federal hearings had been held about the fate of the North Cascades. The result, according to Jackson, was "the nation's showcase of natural beauty."[91] The park was far from perfect, conservationists agreed. More land needed stricter protection as wilderness, and they would have to closely monitor the National Park Service's plans for recreational development. Much work remained to be done. But on this day they could savor victory. They had saved America's Alps, the crown jewel wilderness of the North Cascades.

CHAPTER 9

Managing the Wilderness
Crown Jewel

On October 26, 1968, the North Cascades Conservation Council hosted a victory banquet at Seattle's University Tower hotel, a prominent art deco landmark near the University of Washington. Fittingly, the hotel was designed by Robert Reamer, an architect known for Yellowstone National Park's celebrated Old Faithful Inn and Olympic National Park's Lake Quinault Lodge. Mingling among the hundreds of attendees were David Brower, Rep. Lloyd Meeds (D-WA), and the superintendents of Washington's "Golden Triangle" of national parks, including Roger Contor, newly appointed to North Cascades National Park. The party took place almost thirty years to the day after a similar bash for Olympic National Park.[1]

"That park is your monument," *Seattle Times* reporter Walt Woodward congratulated Patrick Goldsworthy.[2] But for the affectionately nicknamed "Mr. North Cascades," the party was merely a brief intermission to celebrate the milestone. A number of issues pitting preservation against use remained unresolved. Kennecott Copper's proposed open pit mine seriously threatened the unsullied Miners Ridge area of Glacier Peak. The National Park and Forest services had two years to come up with a cooperative plan for recreational development and management that was likely to include tramways and trailside hostels. The Park Service was required to develop wilderness recommendations within the same time period. Seattle City Light wanted to raise Ross Dam and its reservoir and build more dams, one of which would flood part of the scenic Thunder Creek valley that provided access to Park Creek Pass and the Stehekin River basin. The future of remote Stehekin was unclear, its fifty permanent residents now living inside a national recreation area. The North Cross-State Highway was nearing completion, and no one knew for sure what its impact would be.[3]

The celebrations did not last long. North Cascades National Park was a reality on paper, but what the wilderness national park would look like going forward remained to be seen.

For many, Kennecott Copper's plan for a half-mile-wide open pit mine on the 350 acres it owned at Miners Ridge loomed most urgently. During his wilderness trip in 1939, Bob Marshall had camped with a small party of Forest Service colleagues at Miners Ridge, widely lauded as one of the most beautiful spots in the North Cascades. After a dinner ending with tart huckleberries picked from nearby bushes, Marshall "silently withdrew from the cheerful campfire to commune with his idolized back country," a companion recalled.[4]

While Marshall urged protection of what he deemed a superlative wilderness, on the trail the very next day he encountered a near-mythical prospector called Blue Mountain Ole, who had mined in the North Cascades since at least the 1920s. After chatting with Ole in his "haphazard, leanto" cabin with its "'million dollar' view," Marshall declared the miner and his gear "belonged" in the wilderness.[5] Ole lived about five miles east of Miners Ridge, in the shadow of Lyman Glacier.[6] The glacier drains into Lyman Lakes, the source of Railroad Creek, along which Howe Sound operated a profitable copper mine at Holden from 1938 to 1957.[7] Since the nineteenth century, mining had "cast a long human shadow over the North Cascades,"[8] and Glacier Peak was no exception.

Marshall's willingness to see Ole as part of the wilderness under-scores incongruities in the wilderness concept. Like his Forest Service colleague Aldo Leopold, Marshall saw wilderness as a place for humans to appreciate raw nature and recapture primitive America by testing themselves against the wild. Blue Mountain Ole had passed that test and thus should remain, part and parcel of the wilderness.

By the time the North Cascades National Park bill was enacted, wil-derness had been codified in legislation and its definition had evolved and expanded. In addition to its value for recreational use, wilderness also had intrinsic, noneconomic worth. Humans could ponder the meaning of their existence in wilderness, from whence the American character sprang. As ecological science gained prominence in the mid-twentieth century, many felt wilderness was essential to maintain the health of the planet. It was a laboratory in which ecological and biological processes could be observed, and a living record of the historic abundance of the nation's natural resources.[9] In this context, mining in the middle of a wilderness area, while temporarily allowed under the Wilderness Act, was an abomination.

In 1955, the sight of helicopters laden with mining equipment flying over Miners Ridge alarmed Polly Dyer and Phil and Laura Zalesky, an incident that contributed to the founding of the North Cascades Conservation Council two years later. Throughout the Glacier Peak controversy, conservationists repeatedly raised the prospect of a new mine to rally support for a large wilderness area and, later, a national park there.

When Glacier Peak Wilderness was created as part of the National Wilderness Preservation System with the passage of the Wilderness Act in 1964, the mining threat persisted. In order to pass the bill, the House had bowed to mining industry pressure and allowed twenty years for claims to be developed in wilderness areas, a concession granted by Rep. Wayne Aspinall. In 1967, as the park bill wended its way through the Senate and then the House, the N3C continued to press for Glacier Peak to be made part of the national park to exclude mining there permanently. Sen. Henry "Scoop" Jackson declined to amend the North Cascades legislation, saying the Kennecott issue was symptomatic of larger problems with the 1964 Wilderness Act and should be dealt with in that context.[10]

Virtually everyone agreed the mine threat was serious and many proffered ideas about how to handle the threat. Agriculture Secretary Orville Freeman publicly opposed the mine in a 1967 speech to the Sierra Club, suggesting Miners Ridge might be a "test [of] whether man could forego material riches for the fullness of the spirit." Freeman assured the club he would hold the company to "the highest standards of performance and restoration under the law," should Kennecott choose to develop its claims. But, he added, he did not "really believe that such an application will ever reach my desk." Kennecott's inholding in the wilderness was the flash point for "balancing a priceless, yet intangible, national treasure against ledger sheets and profits." Freeman bolstered his blunt message to Kennecott by urging the Sierra Club to take "every possible opportunity" to raise awareness of "the issues at stake on Miners Ridge."[11] For its part, the Forest Service told Freeman legislation specifically prohibiting the company from exploiting its Glacier Peak claims was necessary if the agency wanted to "to do more than snarl at Kennecott."[12]

One conservationist took an especially creative approach to the Kennecott issue. N3C member Fred Darvill, a physician from Mount Vernon, Washington, had purchased three shares of Kennecott stock and showed up at the May 1967 shareholders' meeting in New York City. Holding aloft an oil painting of Image Lake and Glacier Peak, Darvill and Sierra Club president George Marshall (brother of Bob) implored the company to leave Miners Ridge alone.[13]

Darvill urged Congress to purchase Kennecott's claims at Miners Ridge, pleading, "nothing more defacing to the primeval landscape can be imagined than the permanent scar of an open pit mine superimposed upon the previously pristine scenic heart land of America's wilderness alps."[14] He also funded bumper stickers jeering "Spit in Your Open Pit," which adorned many conservationists' cars during the controversy.[15]

In August 1967, Justice William O. Douglas led a protest camp-out along the Suiattle River, where he told 150 attendees "just because something's legal doesn't mean it's right."[16] The Sierra Club's Dave Brower also worked hard against Kennecott, famously hiking across the Glacier Peak Wilderness with writer John McPhee and pro-mine geologist Charles Park, a trip recounted in McPhee's 1971 acclaimed book *Encounters with the Archdruid.*

Despite mine opponents' efforts to protect Glacier Peak, the park bill signed into law in fall 1968 did not resolve the matter. Kennecott still threatened and some, such as residents of Darrington, about thirty miles from the mine site, greeted Douglas and his companions with signs reading "Welcome Kennecott." Many local residents saw the mine as a way to bring economic prosperity to local communities.[17]

In spring 1969, Ben Shaine, an Oberlin College student who the previous summer worked for Brock Evans in the office of the Pacific Northwest Conservation Representative, finagled a meeting with Kennecott's president to ask about plans for Miners Ridge. Dissatisfied with the company's response, Shaine circulated a petition against the mine, getting signatures from more than four hundred scientists across the country. It was another in a constant barrage of attacks against Kennecott that taken together demonstrated widespread interest in the issue of mining in a statutory wilderness.[18]

Sometime near the end of 1969, the N3C's Phil Zalesky asked Representative Meeds, a member of the House Interior Committee who had pushed hard to pass the park bill, "How are we going to stop Kennecott?" Without offering details, Meeds firmly told Zalesky he needn't worry.[19]

Zalesky later realized Meeds was signaling that Senator Jackson would take care of it. In his position as Interior Committee chair, Jackson had the power to make things difficult for Kennecott, perhaps by revisiting the Wilderness Act's mining exception. By early February 1970, Kennecott told Jackson it was abandoning its Glacier Peak plans, citing the "environmental restrictions the Forest Service had announced it would impose on the operations." A colleague wrote Goldsworthy that the N3C should be proud of its part in defeating Kennecott, and "feel grateful that we have a powerful Senator so strategically placed as Scoop Jackson."[20]

Kennecott's experience at Glacier Peak was a turning point for the mining exception to the Wilderness Act of 1964. Since Miners Ridge, "no other Mining Law controversy of such dramatic proportions has erupted in congressionally designated wilderness." Squeezed between public opinion in favor of wilderness and federal agencies willing to impose strict regulations on proposed mining in wilderness areas, the mining industry found itself working to minimize proposed new wilderness areas instead of developing existing mining claims in established ones.[21] Still, it took another four decades before the threat of mining inside Glacier Peak Wilderness was permanently erased.

In the mid-1980s, Kennecott sold its holdings at Miners Ridge to the Chelan County Public Utility District (PUD). Beginning in 1962, Chelan PUD had measured snowpack, knowledge critical for predicting hydroelectric capacity during the dry summer season, by landing helicopters at Lyman Lake. But in 1966 the Forest Service prohibited the practice under the tenets of the Wilderness Act. It took Chelan PUD two decades to find another site, but in 1986 it purchased Kennecott's Miners Ridge inholding and started measuring snowpack there instead. Dissatisfied with the accuracy of measurements taken at Miners Ridge, the PUD proposed exchanging its Miners Ridge property for permission to land at the Lyman Lake site several times each year. The final agreement granting the easement was written into the 2008 bill that created the nearby Wild Sky Wilderness, and took effect in 2010, finally ending the threat of mining on Glacier Peak.[22]

———————◆———————

When the official transfer of North Cascades management took place on January 1, 1969, the Park Service had already established temporary park headquarters at Sedro-Woolley, a small town of about 4,500 whose mayor, William O. Pearson, had vociferously opposed the park bill during the congressional hearings. Although the town sits about sixty miles west of the park proper, both Senator Jackson and Governor Evans supported the location to encourage economic development in the historically timber-dependent area. Superintendent Roger Contor, who had been working from the Park Service's Seattle field office during the run-up to the bill's passage, effectively signaled the agency's presence in the North Cascades when he moved to the Sedro-Woolley office shortly after the bill signing. Contor had been transferred from his post as assistant superintendent at Utah's Canyonlands National Park, established less than five years earlier and itself an example of Interior Secretary Stewart Udall's park system expansion program.[23]

To pacify residual resentment over the new park, in late 1968 and 1969 Senator Jackson, Representative Meeds, and officials from the Park and Forest services held public meetings in Bellingham, Sedro-Woolley, Wenatchee, and Chelan, communities near the new complex. Beyond visibly demonstrating the federal agencies' cooperative attitude toward managing the North Cascades, this public relations strategy brought people together to formulate plans for boosting tourism and local economic development. Governor Evans followed suit at the state level, creating the North Cascades Reconnaissance Task Force in December 1968. Charged with monitoring developments in the new park, particularly in the recreation areas and access corridors, the task force was "Washington State's version of the United Nations for the management of the North Cascades."[24]

By mid-1969, seven permanent and forty seasonal staff had been hired, a mix of Park Service, former Forest Service, and local residents. District offices were situated at Chelan and Marblemount, both outside the park boundary but logical points of entry to the complex. A third district office at Stehekin, inside the new Lake Chelan National Recreation Area, was strategically located to focus on the small community's conversion to national park gateway.[25]

With its three crown jewel parks, Washington became "national park central," a status recognized when the National Park Service upgraded the Seattle field office to a regional headquarters in early 1970; the nearest until then had been in San Francisco.[26] Former Mt. Baker National Forest supervisor Chris Chriswell remembered the transition as "very smooth." After the park was established, Chriswell and Patrick Goldsworthy met for coffee. Chriswell admitted he "never would have predicted that the Forest Service would lose that much land," but he did not feel bad about the change, because he "worked for the people, and this is what the people wanted."[27]

The North Cascades bill produced something unique in America's system of scenic and wilderness preservation: a complex, politically crafted to satisfy incompatible interests. In a sense, the complex embodied the principles of multiple-use. Different portions of the North Cascades had been deemed to have diverse recreational values, and land use designations (national park, wilderness, national forest, national recreation area) had been applied to address those. Managing these diverse units as an integrated whole presented challenges, which the legislation required the Park and Forest services to address within two years with coordinated management plans. The bill stipulated the Park Service also had to recommend wilderness areas within the new park.

The selfsame characteristics that had preserved *de facto* for decades the North Cascades wilderness—magnificently precipitous terrain that obstructed access to resources and impeded cross-country travel—meant the Park Service now had "the chance to begin anew, to plan before developing, and to implement ecological principles from the beginning." At the same time, management of the new complex had to take into account the two million people who lived within a two-hour drive and would use the North Cross-State Highway once completed, a fact that influenced planning.[28]

The two agencies got to work.[29] In June 1970, the Park Service held hearings in Mount Vernon and Wenatchee on its portion of the joint management plan and its wilderness recommendations. Despite having achieved the park, conservationists remained wary of the agency's engagement with wilderness preservation. The N3C's 1958 decision to push for a national park in the North Cascades had been made in spite of deep misgivings about the Park Service's emphasis on development

Table 3. Land-Use Designations in the North Cascades

National Park (*National Park Service)	Created to "to conserve the scenery and the natural and historic objects and the wild life therein and to provide for the enjoyment of the same in such manner and by such means as will leave them unimpaired for the enjoyment of future generations." Construction of appropriate visitor facilities (interpretive centers, roads, trails, lodging, etc.) allowed to provide access for public enjoyment. Commercial fishing, livestock grazing, mining, logging, and most hunting are prohibited.
National Recreation Area (*National Park Service, Forest Service, Bureau of Land Management)	Defined as "areas which have natural endowments that are well above the ordinary in quality and recreation appeal, being of lesser significance than the unique scenic and historic elements of the National Park System, but affording a quality of recreation experience which transcends" that of state or locally managed areas. Hunting and fishing permitted in certain areas and at certain times. Generally, livestock grazing, mining, and logging are prohibited except as they are deemed to enhance public enjoyment (removing trees to build a campground, for example).
Wilderness (*Forest Service, *National Park Service, Bureau of Land Management, Fish & Wildlife Service)	Defined as "an area where the earth and its community of life are untrammeled by man, where man himself is a visitor who does not remain." Wilderness retains its "primeval character" and is managed for the preservation of natural conditions, "has outstanding opportunities for solitude or a primitive and unconfined type of recreation," is at least 5,000 acres in size, "may also contain ecological, geological, or other features of scientific, educational, scenic, or historical value."
National Forest (*Forest Service)	Sustainably preserves federal land for the benefit of the public. Multiple-use management dictates that different uses, including logging, grazing, watershed protection, recreation, and wildlife, are balanced in the public interest.
* managing agency in the North Cascades	

and visitor access over wilderness. The agency's tepid response to the Wilderness Act of 1964 did little to allay these fears, as the Park Service initially opposed the legislation on the grounds that lands it managed were already wilderness. It did not want additional regulation.[30] But by the late 1950s, the Park Service had come around, in part because it was persuaded supporting the bill would help its image with conservationists, who were skeptical of the agency's commitment to wilderness preservation in light of its enthusiasm for Mission 66.[31] The maturation of the environmental movement in the late 1960s and early 1970s shifted the Park Service's thinking about wilderness toward maintaining the parks' ecological health together with their scenic wonders.[32] The vast, untouched landscape of the nation's "wildest national park"[33] was an ideal laboratory in which to carry out this approach.

Accordingly, the agency proposed three-quarters of the national park—more than a half-million acres centered on the Picket Range and Mount Shuksan in the northern unit and the Eldorado Peaks in the southern unit—be given statutory wilderness status. "Most of the park will remain what it has always been—wilderness," a *Seattle Times* article said. "The Park Service is determined to keep it that way."[34] The agency's plans illustrate its effort to balance wilderness in the heart of the park with visitor facilities at the periphery.[35] It proposed to concentrate development in the national recreation areas and especially along the not-yet-completed North Cross-State Highway, managing these areas as "wilderness thresholds" offering recreational options such as campgrounds, visitor centers, sightseeing boats on Ross Lake, and tramways at Price Lake and Ruby Mountain.[36]

Wilderness "enclaves" of up to thirty acres within designated wilderness would be reserved for hostels and chalets along the lines of those found in Glacier National Park; some would house scientific instruments such as snow-measuring devices.[37] Spaced at six-mile intervals, these would allow visitors to hike the backcountry without having to carry a heavy pack and supplies. The hostels would be staffed and provide meals and rustic overnight lodging, ostensibly making the scenery accessible to more people.[38]

Conservationists were generally pleased by the Park Service's plans. They continued to oppose tramways but grudgingly acceded to one at Ruby Mountain because it lay entirely within Ross Lake National

Recreation Area and would therefore not disfigure the national park sections. However, they wanted more designated wilderness and strongly opposed the idea of enclaves because building hostels in North Cascades backcountry would undermine the Wilderness Act. Park superintendent Contor, reprising the central paradox of preservation versus use in Park Service management, replied there "is not much point in having the park if you don't let people in to enjoy it."[39]

Even with limited facilities, people were coming. The Park Service recorded nearly 300,000 visits to the complex in 1970. From the time conservationists got behind a national park, it was clear that promising recreational development was a political selling point for the North Cascades, making the prospect of a national park there potentially easier to swallow. In fact, the Park Service proposals seemed fair to recreation groups such as hunters and skiers, and most supported the plans. The imminent completion of the North Cross-State Highway was also a factor. Its potential for bringing tourists to the area was widely touted by many, including Senator Jackson, who predicted a 500 percent increase in tourism by 1980.[40]

Nevertheless, written comments sent after the hearings were mostly opposed to development and the Park Service modified its plans, reducing the number of wilderness hostels, purportedly because of grizzly sightings in the park. A grizzly had been killed in the Fisher Creek basin (a tributary of Thunder Creek) the year before the park's creation, and the so-called "Night of the Grizzlies" in Glacier National Park in August 1967, which left two backcountry campers dead and others injured, still resonated. Eliminating hostels theoretically reduced the possibility of human-bear conflict, because presumably fewer people would want or be able to travel the backcountry if hostels were not available.[41]

The Park Service retained the Ruby Mountain tramway in the final plans, as well as a "conditional" tramway at Arctic Creek that was later dropped. Partly because of the proposed tramways, North Cascades National Park presented an opportunity for the National Park Service to approach cars in a different way. Booming national park visitation in the 1950s and 1960s resulted in long traffic jams and recognition that automobiles damaged the ecology of the scenic places through which park roads meandered. By the mid-1960s, Park Service officials and conservation groups both believed "parks and highways mixed poorly."

National Park Service director George Hartzog Jr. saw tramways as a feasible alternative to cars, one that would wreak far less damage on sensitive ecological zones, a point he repeatedly made during congressional hearings. "With the increasing population and the increasing visitation," he said, "I don't believe that we can continue to build roads to take care of the people who want to see these parks by automobile."[42]

Lack of funding and changing environmental values eventually killed a proposed tramway at Ruby Mountain that would have taken visitors to a viewpoint into the Picket Range. *North Cascades National Park Service Complex Museum Collection, NOCA 11931v*

Despite consistent, vocal support from Senator Jackson and especially Representative Meeds, who bird-dogged the National Park Service on recreational development in the North Cascades for the rest of his congressional career, some Park Service officials were not enthusiastic about tramways. Moreover, new environmental laws, like the National Environmental Policy Act of 1969 (known as NEPA, the law was sponsored by Senator Jackson), required impact studies. Damage from tramway construction would probably not pass NEPA's litmus test. Ultimately, though, the tramway's high cost hastened its undoing. When proposed in the 1970 Park Service plan, the tramway was projected to cost $8 million. When Meeds left Congress in 1979, the estimated cost had ballooned to $13 million. Without a champion and in the face of continuing opposition from most conservationists, the tramways proposal died.[43]

One month after the Park Service hearings, the Forest Service followed suit, holding hearings in July 1970 at Wenatchee and Mount Vernon on its portion of the cooperative management plan. Of the 2.5 million acres of wilderness and national forest areas surrounding the park complex, almost a million acres comprised the statutory Pasayten and Glacier Peak wildernesses. The agency proposed another 800,000 acres be designated roadless or scenic areas reserved for recreation. To accommodate the expected crowds of visitors, it recommended construction of more campgrounds, improved and extended roads and trails, and a tramway on Mount Baker. Although ski areas had been a contentious issue during the Study Team's work and in the congressional hearings, neither agency believed feasible sites could be developed and instead encouraged expansion of existing facilities, such as Heather Meadows at Mount Baker and cross-country ski trails in Stehekin.[44] About one-third of national forest land, 762,000 acres, would be retained for traditional multiple use.

Mt. Baker National Forest supervisor Chris Chriswell, who led the Forest Service planning team, correctly predicted the agency would "catch hell" at the hearings for its focus on wilderness and unmechanized recreation. Local communities and some recreational and resource interests accused the Forest Service of "drifting away from the long-established multiple-use principle" under which it was mandated to operate. A local lumber company official derided the plan as a "'raid by a vocal minority' of recreationists to the detriment of the public and [the timber] industry." Four-wheel-drive recreationists bitterly denounced the plan, saying it "removes land from recreational use by anyone except those who are willing and able to go in by foot or pack horse." Sedro-Woolley's outspoken mayor, William O. Pearson, tartly summarized the prevailing sentiment: "Stop acting like the Park Service...get back to [the] responsibility of providing wood and water for the community." Conservationists, in contrast, commended the Forest Service, and the *Seattle Times* declared the agency's plan made a "serious effort to do right by the matchless North Cascades."[45]

In the 1950s and early 1960s, the Forest Service tried to manage the North Cascades for multiple-use and had been pummeled by conservationists and rising pro-wilderness sentiment sparked in part by the agency's overly optimistic assessment of how much national forest timber could be sustainably cut. Now it tried to respond to that sentiment with more wilderness recreation-oriented management, only to be lambasted by its traditional constituents from the natural resource and motorized recreation industries. Like the National Park Service, dramatic changes in mid-century thinking about the environment thrust the agency into flux, emboldening Congress to assume more control over its operations, especially wilderness management.

In the end, the hubbub over the various plans mattered less than the lack of funds allocated to implement them. Despite repeated requests for more funding, both the National Park Service and the Forest Service saw their recreational building budgets slashed in the early 1970s.[46] In 1965, Washington's national parks had been allocated $4.5 million for construction of trails and campgrounds. Five years later, they were "limping through" on funding that had been cut to $1.1 million.[47] The recreational road- and trail-building budget for Washington State's national forests had been frozen at $2.6 million since 1966, despite a 10 to 15 percent yearly increase in recreational use from 1965 to 1970.[48]

By 1975, the park complex and surrounding national forests were suffering from the effects of their popularity. It was not uncommon to find several hundred people at one popular spot in Glacier Peak Wilderness, and the fragile subalpine environment at Cascade Pass suffered extreme damage from overuse.[49] Limiting visitor impact was a high priority, and both the Park Service and the Forest Service began requiring backcountry permits to try to mitigate the effects of use.[50]

From its creation in 1968, the Park Service "managed the complex's backcountry as if it were legalized wilderness," even though its wilderness recommendations "languished" in Congress for more than fifteen years after being forwarded to President Nixon in 1970. Finally, in 1988, then-Sen. Dan Evans co-sponsored legislation creating the Stephen Mather Wilderness inside North Cascades National Park, forever preserving 93 percent of the park untrammeled.[51]

Twenty years after Glacier Peak Wilderness was established in statute, the Washington State Wilderness Act of 1984 continued the wilderness preservation trend started in the North Cascades. Sponsored by Senator Jackson and Sen. Slade Gorton (R-WA), who had defeated Warren Magnuson in 1980, the act added more than a million acres of wilderness to national forests in the state, more than half of it in the North Cascades. When Jackson died suddenly in September 1983, former governor Daniel Evans was appointed to his Senate seat and won re-election in 1984, assuming Jackson's sponsorship of the bill. The Glacier Peak Wilderness grew by nearly 112,000 acres and the Pasayten Wilderness by more than 24,000 acres. Five new wilderness areas totaling more than 400,000 acres were established around the park complex: Noisy-Diobsud, Mount Baker, Henry M. Jackson, Boulder River, and Lake Chelan-Sawtooth.

It would take another quarter-century before any new national forest wilderness was created in Washington State, but in 2008, after years of effort by Sen. Patty Murray (D-WA) and Rep. Rick Larsen (D-WA), the 106,000-acre Wild Sky Wilderness was established adjacent to the Henry M. Jackson Wilderness, north of Highway 2 in the Mt. Baker-Snoqualmie National Forest (the Mt. Baker and Snoqualmie national forests were administratively combined in 1974).[52] As of early 2017, nearly half of the 1.75-million-acre Mt. Baker-Snoqualmie National Forest and just over one-third of the four-million-acre Okanogan-Wenatchee National Forest (combined in 2000) is statutory wilderness. Together, the two forests welcome nearly seven million visitors each year.[53]

———————◆———————

Beyond concentrating visitor facilities and use, Ross Lake National Recreation Area was designed to accommodate the potential expansion of the Skagit River Hydroelectric Project envisioned by Seattle City Light. The public utility, which has provided power to Seattle residents since 1910, sought to raise Ross Dam and build new dams on Thunder and Copper Creeks. The North Cascades park bill specified that the Federal Power Commission retained its authority to approve and regulate power projects within the recreation area. Now that the park was reality, Seattle City Light was ready to move forward.

The utility had operated on the Skagit since the early twentieth century, completing Gorge Dam in 1924 and Diablo Dam in 1936. Construction of Ross Dam, the largest in the eight-mile-long chain of dams impounding the river, began in 1937 with financing from the city of Seattle and the federal government, whose contribution targeted flood control downriver. Ross Dam was completed in 1949. Seattle City Light planned to raise it and earlier in the decade had reached a preliminary agreement with British Columbia to compensate for backing Ross Lake beyond the Canadian border. Behind the higher dam, the lake level would rise from 1,600 feet to 1,725 feet above sea level, flooding another twelve miles of the Skagit River valley in Canada. By the early 1950s, the province had changed its position, postponing the project. The park controversy added another layer of delay, as conservationists opposed raising both dam and lake. But Seattle City Light struck a deal with Canada in 1967, and the North Cascades bill ensured the utility's autonomy from Park Service interference.[54] It looked as if the High Ross Dam project would proceed.

In summer 1968, Patrick Goldsworthy, Harvey Manning, and two others backpacked in the Pickets, choosing Big Beaver Creek as their outlet to Ross Lake and a ride home. Manning recalled they chose Big Beaver randomly; none of them had ever been there before. Hiking down the creek valley, they were awed by the spectacular old-growth Western redcedar forest towering above their heads. On the downlake boat later that day, they spotted workers scaling rocks near Ross Dam. The hikers asked what the workers were doing. "Getting ready to raise Ross Dam," came the reply. Conservationists had viewed the High Ross plan as a "political birthmark in the park's creation, something it would grow out of later." But the encounter at Ross Lake confirmed the plan was serious, and constant vigilance would be needed to defeat it.[55]

After the park's creation in fall 1968, opponents on both sides of the border stepped up efforts to derail High Ross Dam. Canadian conservationists created Run Out Skagit Spoilers (ROSS), concentrating on the prospective loss of fishing streams and the low mitigation payments negotiated with Seattle City Light in compensation for allowing the encroachment of the lake into Canada.[56] The N3C and its allies focused on loss of tributary valleys like Big Beaver Creek, where N3C board members Joe and Margaret Miller conducted an "ecosystem survey" with approval from park superintendent Roger Contor, revealing a unique lowland old-growth Western redcedar forest that would drown if the lake were raised.[57]

In October 1969, Manning spoke at a Seattle City Light budget hearing about the damage raising Ross Lake would cause: "The flooding of the Big Beaver valley would be a recreational, scenic, and ecological tragedy of the highest magnitude…Our 2-day walk down the valley trail was one of the most exciting experiences I've ever had in the North Cascades—and we had just spent a week among the great walls and glaciers of the Pickets."[58]

Manning's comments underscored the different conceptions of national recreation areas versus national parks, a tension that played out in hydroelectric development and other controversies in the North Cascades. Conservationists believed Ross Lake's scenery merited national park protection. But the Park Service did not view national recreation areas as equal to national parks. Originally conceived as a recreation zone around reservoirs created by dams, national recreation areas were considered "slightly lower in status and open to a wider range of uses than national parks…a kind of supporting cast for parks."[59]

The concept of a North Cascades National Park complex envisioned a holistic approach to the management of its component units. Management decisions about Ross Lake National Recreation Area affect the national park units it bisects, and cannot be separated from management of the national park. The National Park Service managed Ross Lake National Recreation Area as a "wilderness threshold," an area where visitor facility development would be concentrated away from the wilderness core of the park. National Park Service director Hartzog had coined the term at a 1965 meeting of national park superintendents. A wilderness threshold was a "zone of orientation" to both place and experience that could provide "unequalled opportunity for interpretation of the meaning of wilderness." The North Cascades provided an attractive place to test the idea on the ground. Conservationists opposed much of this visitor development. Wilderness, they asserted, should be the primary function of the entire complex to the greatest extent possible.[60]

The Park Service was in a difficult position. Its founding mandate required providing visitor access to spectacular natural areas, which in the North Cascades it tried to fulfill through the wilderness threshold idea. At the same time, its traditional emphasis on recreation in national recreation areas meant it could not prioritize wilderness values at Ross Lake National Recreation Area, so the agency relied on the Millers and the N3C and its supporters to fight for the Big Beaver valley's "cathedral of trees."[61]

Further, the agency's history with dams in national parks was a troubled one. Many conservationists got their start in environmental activism protesting the plan to flood Dinosaur National Monument, a protest that is widely considered the catalyst of the modern environmental movement. Grant McConnell drew an ironic parallel between the proposal to raise Ross Lake and the Hetch Hetchy dam controversy of the early twentieth century, a debate of preservation versus use that ended when the spectacular valley in Yosemite National Park was dammed to provide San Franciscans with drinking water.[62] Hetch Hetchy is still a sore point for many modern environmentalists.

The High Ross Dam controversy dragged into the early 1980s. By that time, the central issue had become whether the "environmental impact caused by the further flooding of the Skagit Valley justified... the additional electric power received by Seattle,"[63] not whether Seattle residents needed the power in the first place. The Federal Energy Regulatory Commission (FERC), the successor to the Federal Power Commission, and its Canadian counterpart ruled the project could proceed, but urged British Columbia and Seattle to come to a settlement. Stricter environmental rules and energy conservation measures initiated during the 1970s created more challenges to the project, and scenes of protesters lining the north shore of Ross Lake, holding signs opposing "Yankee oppression," encouraged neither tourism nor friendly international relations. In 1984, the city and the province reached a settlement in which British Columbia agreed to sell its own power to the utility, effectively terminating the High Ross Dam project.[64]

Other dam proposals also attracted public attention. For example, Seattle City Light in 1979 began moving forward with plans to dam Copper Creek, a small stream the utility had successfully petitioned to be included inside the western boundary of Ross Lake National Recreation Area.[65] Skagit River tribes led a coalition of conservationists, recreation groups, fishing interests, and local governments in opposing the project on the grounds it would adversely impact an important salmon spawning site and the tourist-attracting bald eagles that came there each winter to feed on the fish. Moreover, the Skagit had been awarded Wild and Scenic River status in 1978, a designation that precluded changing the river's "free-flowing condition." Local residents also worried about the seismic instability of the proposed dam site. These concerns and the fierce opposition, along with a variety of new laws requiring environmental studies of one kind or another (e.g., the Endangered Species Act, National Environmental Policy Act, and Clean Water Act) persuaded the utility to shelve the project in 1981.[66]

At Thunder Creek, a tributary of the Skagit that empties into Diablo Lake, Seattle City Light wanted to build a diversion dam to provide more power. The dam would redirect the creek's water from Diablo Lake into Ross Lake via a 6.5-mile-long tunnel through Ruby Mountain. As at Copper Creek, the bill establishing North Cascades National Park changed the Ross Lake National Recreation Area boundary to accommodate the project, including the lower six miles of Thunder Creek. Conservationists worried this dam would require a road, which could in turn open access to mining claims.[67] The 1988 Washington Park Wilderness Act, sponsored by Sen. Dan Evans, designated 93 percent of North Cascades National Park complex as wilderness and included more than 3,500 acres of lower Thunder Creek as a "potential wilderness addition." This allowed it to be managed like designated wilderness and, once any nonconforming uses ended, be added officially to the park's statutory wilderness.[68] In September 2012, after Seattle City Light officially abandoned the Thunder Creek project and at the urging of the National Park Service, the potential wilderness was made official, ending the dam threat once and for all.[69]

North Cascades was an "instant" national park in that very little private land needed to be acquired to make the park whole. Of the 674,000 acres contained in the national park and national recreation areas, only one-half of one percent, 3,500 acres, was privately owned. Most of that was in the Stehekin area, and Lake Chelan National Recreation Area was crafted to appease Stehekin property owners worried about government regulation. The park bill authorized the National Park Service to acquire privately held lands, and within five years of the park's creation, the Park Service had spent two-thirds of its initial $3.5 million land acquisition appropriation on 986 acres in Stehekin.[70] But land acquisition was allowed only with owner consent and only if land use was "compatible" with the new park and recreation areas.[71]

The struggle to define "compatible," wrote Park Service historian David Louter, was a principal characteristic of Stehekin's "complex and contentious" history with the agency.[72] According to one resident who lived there in the late 1970s, "most of the arguments had to do with whether the valley's future should be decided by the National Park Service or the local residents." How to balance protecting a nationally significant scenic and wilderness resource, providing a national park experience for visitors (the valley is a primary gateway to the park's southern unit), and preserving the sense of independence and pioneer spirit valued by many in the community was an objective that some have deemed unattainable.[73] Fifty-five miles from Chelan and accessible only by boat, plane, or afoot, Stehekin's remoteness amplified the challenges.

Paradoxically, the establishment of the national park and recreation areas publicized Stehekin's charms in ways some longtime residents found unsettling. In the first decade of Park Service management, Stehekin's population tripled to more than ninety people, "an explosive mix of… Park Service employees, resort workers, middle-age hippies, property-rights activists, and the descendants of the original homesteaders."[74] The increased population stressed the valley's infrastructure and stimulated rapid residential development. Subdivisions of cookie-cutter, 1970s-vintage vacation homes clashed glaringly with the pastoral character of the place, and many felt the Park Service should move to stop such development because it ran counter to the national park ideal. On the other hand, some believed private property owners should retain their right to do as they pleased with their holdings.

That held true in land acquisition as well. Some residents felt that by "acquiring more land in the community, the Park Service was slowly eliminating the Stehekin community from existence." Yet without the agency's land purchases, unchecked development might result in the loss of the rustic ambiance residents treasured. This conflict made it doubly difficult for the agency to preserve the pioneer atmosphere that made the area so attractive, partly because it "believed that Congress intended to preserve the historic community of Stehekin but not to freeze it in time."[75]

Lake Chelan National Recreation Area, reachable only by boat, plane, or on foot, includes the Stehekin River valley and upper Lake Chelan. *North Cascades National Park Service Complex Museum Collection, NOCA 11931aa*

The Park Service labored for years to strike a reasonable balance between national and local interests and confront its own inability or unwillingness to take a firm stand. A 1989 lawsuit filed by the North Cascades Conservation Council against the federal government resulted in a consent decree under which the National Park Service agreed to conduct environmental impact studies of the effect of private and public land use in the valley. It was a "benchmark in the history of land protection in Stehekin" and eventually resulted in the agency adopting a case-by-case approach to determining compatibility.[76]

Other issues illustrated the complexities of managing a national recreation area with a permanent, though small, population. Some conservationists urged closing the Stehekin airstrip, built in 1960 by the Forest Service for firefighting but primarily serving private and tourist planes. The state Department of Transportation, which manages the airstrip, called it "one of the most difficult airports in the state." The Park Service decided to leave it open. Today it operates only during the summer months. The valley landfill closed in the early 1970s, and in an attempt to foster friendly community relations the Park Service began barging out garbage. It also tried to regulate use of renewable natural resources. Under Forest Service management, residents had been able to cut their own firewood. Worried about the long-term visual and ecological impact of the practice, the Park Service eventually initiated a firewood collecting permit and sales program.

A continuing source of tension is the Stehekin River road, the primary means of travel through the valley. Twenty-three miles long, the "one-lane bumpy road that goes nowhere" meanders from the boat landing to Cottonwood Camp, twelve miles inside the national park boundary.[77] As at Ross Lake National Recreation Area, the Park Service sought to manage Lake Chelan National Recreation Area as a wilderness threshold, a place to concentrate visitation and use in order to protect the park's wild core. Toward that end, the Park Service acquired the road from Chelan County in 1970, spending $1.4 million over the next few years on maintenance, repair, and bridge replacement.[78] It instituted a shuttle bus service to discourage car traffic, providing day hikers with more options for excursions in the valley.[79]

In 1973, the Park Service paved the road, infuriating conservationists and some residents, including Grant McConnell, who argued the asphalt surface contradicted the valley's rural nature and diminished its wilderness character. The Park Service argued paving would improve maintenance and access to the national park. More saliently from the Park Service perspective, the road "allowed park visitors to experience this new parkland in a familiar way," that is, through the windows of a car. The agency also opted to leave the entire length of the road open, a decision "rooted in tradition, to ensure that all people could see the park."

Conservationists opposed both actions, preferring the road be closed at Bridge Creek, about five miles inside the park boundary.[80]

In 2003, a major flood washed out the road at Car Wash Falls, so named because passing cars often got a quick rinse at the base of the waterfall, and rendered it impassable beyond mile 12.9. After studying several alternatives, the Park Service in 2006 decided to close the road permanently from that point. This has meant access to the upper valley, including popular Horseshoe Basin and Cascade Pass, now requires an additional twenty miles of hiking round-trip. The debate over whether to rebuild the upper Stehekin River road has divided conservationists, who disagree about how much wilderness access should be provided. Some park supporters, including former Gov. Dan Evans, opposed the Park Service's decision on the grounds it limits access to those who are physically able to make the trek. They support rebuilding the road, and Congress in 2015 passed legislation altering statutory wilderness boundaries there so the road could be rerouted. It remains to be seen how the issue will be resolved.[81]

North Cascades has fewer roads than almost all other crown jewel national parks in the lower forty-eight states. The only two roads in the park proper are the now-closed Stehekin River road and six miles of the seasonal Cascade River road, which provides access to Cascade Pass and Eldorado Peaks trailheads from the west. But because the park and recreation areas are administered as a single unit, the North Cascades Highway since its opening in 1972 has assumed the function of the traditional parkway.[82]

The highway, which winds through the Ross Lake National Recreation Area, was envisaged as a wilderness threshold providing "traditional national park services and accommodations for windshield tourists." Most people would see the North Cascades through the glass of their cars, so the road's design needed to make them feel as if they were in wilderness, even if technically they motored through a not-quite-park-quality national recreation area. As the possibility of tramways dimmed, the importance of the highway as a scenic corridor increased. Historian David Louter argued North Cascades represents a new era in the relationship between automobiles and the national parks. It gave tourists the "sense of driving through the park's wilderness setting." Since the new park was located within a two-hour drive of two million people, many motor tourists seeking natural scenery from the comfort of their vehicles were expected. "Americans may have become more ecologically savvy," he said, "but they were not abandoning their cars."[83]

That was true for conservationists, too, who, far from opposing the highway in the N3C's 1963 *Prospectus* for a national park, believed the road would "always be a way through wilderness" so long as it was inside the park.[84] Conservationists embraced, if cautiously, the idea of a traditional national parkway as a way to experience wilderness. After the park's creation they advocated for managing the highway as a scenic corridor.[85] To some, it is a mixed blessing. "The highway affords access to what it defaces," one observer noted. "This portal to the wilderness is also the single biggest scar and intrusion, bisecting wildlands, often traveled by more than a thousand vehicles a day."[86]

The dream of a commercial corridor across the northern part of the state began at almost the same moment as the first suggestion for a national park there. Although it took "eight decades of wasted funds, frustration and failure" before the highway finally opened to regular traffic, the prospective completion of Interstate 5 renewed enthusiasm for the road in the mid-1950s. Construction of the North Cross-State Highway resumed in earnest in 1959, just as activism to preserve North Cascades wilderness was gaining steam. That nearly three-quarters of the $33 million spent on the road was expended after 1959 signifies the state's determination to finish it.[87]

During the park controversy, fears of federal limits on commercial traffic on the highway prompted Senator Jackson to insert language in the park legislation to ensure the state's continued administration of the road, an outcome that assuaged state officials. Three days before President Lyndon Johnson signed North Cascades National Park into law, Gov. Dan Evans dedicated a "rough draft" of the unfinished highway. With Sen. Warren Magnuson, Evans led hundreds on a bone-jarring ceremonial jeep trip over the "crude pioneer road." Governor Evans made (and kept) a campaign promise to complete the road by the end of his second term if re-elected.[88] The day-long ceremony sent a transparent reminder of the state's role in the North Cascades.

Ceremonially reaffirming the state's investment in the North Cascades Highway, Gov. Daniel J. Evans dedicated the road on September 29, 1968. Jeep convoys left from each side of the Cascades and met at Rainy Pass after a jolting ride. The road was not completed until 1972. *Washington State Archives*

That role has been largely one of maintenance and coordination. A sinuous motorway that follows the Skagit River gorge before turning to follow Granite Creek, it crests first Rainy Pass (4,875 feet) then Washington Pass

(5,476 feet, about the same elevation as Paradise on Mount Rainier) before following Early Winters Creek into the Methow Valley. Mountain weather typically closes about forty miles of the road from late November until mid-April, and the Washington State Department of Transportation spends weeks clearing snow from winter avalanches before reopening for the summer season. The Park and Forest services have authority to limit commercial development along the highway as it runs through about sixty miles of lands they manage, and the agencies agreed early on to emphasize its scenic qualities.[89] The result is a "highway [that] weaves through majestic beauty but is separate from it. Beyond the glass is an extraordinary realm, understood best on foot."[90] Visitors can feel as though they have experienced wilderness without leaving the highway corridor, which has the happy effect of preserving the park's wilderness core.

———————————◆———————————

The carefully crafted political compromise that enabled the park bill to pass meant many issues would be figured out as the new park took shape. Mining, wilderness management and recreational development, dams, Stehekin, and the North Cascades Highway captured attention in the years immediately following the park's creation. All were influenced by the emphasis on wilderness preservation that characterized the North Cascades issue beginning in the 1950s and solidified by the Wilderness Act of 1964. Some of these issues continue into the present, and others have arisen as environmental attitudes have evolved. The National Park Service and Forest Service continued to try to balance wilderness preservation with public demand for various types of recreation and access to the spectacular scenery of the North Cascades, a struggle conservationists leveraged to achieve their own objectives. In the North Cascades, the Park Service moved away from its historic emphasis on public access and recreational development, and the Forest Service moved toward treating recreation and wilderness as national forest uses equal to timber, mining, and grazing. Public input and lack of funding swayed management toward more wilderness preservation, reflecting the dominant land use value applied in the North Cascades. These factors have allowed the wilderness character of this crown jewel national park to prevail.

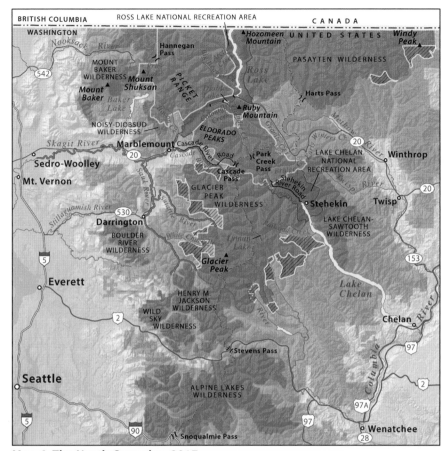

Map 6. The North Cascades, 2017

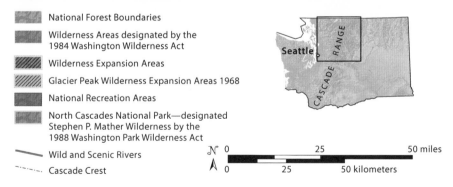

National Forest Boundaries

Wilderness Areas designated by the
1984 Washington Wilderness Act

Wilderness Expansion Areas

Glacier Peak Wilderness Expansion Areas 1968

National Recreation Areas

North Cascades National Park—designated
Stephen P. Mather Wilderness by the
1988 Washington Park Wilderness Act

Wild and Scenic Rivers

Cascade Crest

Afterword

"The Mountains Abide"

Look at a map today, and the North Cascades is a pastiche of labels and colors that embody different values applied to the land: wilderness, scenic beauty, recreation, access, and natural resources. As anticipated by the park legislation, visitation is concentrated mainly in Ross Lake National Recreation Area, which recorded more than 770,000 recreation visits in 2015. Far fewer people, about 32,000, made the long journey to Stehekin and Lake Chelan National Recreation Area. Barely 20,000 visitors crossed the invisible border into the national park during that year.[1] Labels notwithstanding, the North Cascades remain a wilderness, as Bob Marshall and many others believed it should.[2]

Nonetheless, some would like more people to visit Washington's third crown jewel national park. The relatively low visitation to North Cascades in 2015 (about 825,000 total for park and national recreation areas) stands in stark contrast to Olympic National Park, which recorded 3.26 million visitors that year, and Mount Rainier National Park, which saw 1.23 million.[3] The North Cascades is arguably the scenic equal of those parks, and equally handy to the greater Seattle metropolitan area.

To that end, the American Alps Legacy Project, a nonprofit that is a direct descendant of the North Cascades Conservation Council, has proposed converting most of the Ross Lake National Recreation Area and nearly 150,000 acres of national forest land adjacent to the park complex into a 238,000-acre North Cascades National Preserve.[4] The National Park Service defines national preserves as national park-quality sites where Congress may allow some uses prohibited in national parks, including hunting, mining, and gas and oil exploration.[5] Proponents of the project believe the national preserve label is more appealing and would raise the highway's status closer to that of a scenic national parkway, attracting more visitors and benefiting adjacent communities with an influx of tourist dollars. Right now, they say, Ross Lake is "only" a national recreation area. The wilderness core of the park would remain intact, while the highway corridor would be enhanced for recreation. New visitor and interpretive centers would be built, new trails would be added, ecotourism and cultural tourism sites would be highlighted, and camping opportunities would be expanded.[6] In a sense, the American Alps Legacy Project treads familiar ground in the North Cascades, trying to preserve maximum wilderness while providing recreational facilities that funnel visitors to specific areas of the park by using different land designations to signify allowed uses.

Studying a map of the North Cascades today is tantamount to viewing politics at work. Every boundary line, each turn up a valley or flow along a creek or jog around a ridge, represents a political decision. Many of the complex's borders are based on work done by forester Dick "Bush" Buscher, who spent weeks surveying the backcountry to develop the Forest Service's proposals. Senator Jackson used Bush's work to draw the boundaries in the Senate park bill. There may be no better indicator of the political nature of the park than this one fact: the Forest Service drew the boundaries of North Cascades National Park.[7] From the summit of McGregor Mountain in the southern unit of the park, one looks south down the beautiful Stehekin River valley or north toward Bridge Creek. The views in every direction are stunning, breathtaking. The scenery does not care about its land use designation. Nonetheless, standing on McGregor's summit, one perches on a carefully negotiated political line. One foot is in a national park, the other in a national recreation area. Climbers literally straddle a compromise.

While the park boundaries reflect meticulous political craftsmanship, the attainment of the park can be credited to savvy strategizing by conservationists during a time when the conservation movement was transforming into modern environmentalism. All across the country in the 1950s, people began to question the unchecked resource exploitation that characterized the postwar era. In the Pacific Northwest, that questioning focused on logging the national forests at a time when the roles of federal public lands agencies became increasingly complex. Where the Forest Service had been a mostly custodial agency, the 1950s brought increased demand for two conflicting uses, national forest timber and recreation. Where previously the National Park Service had been able to balance preserving scenery with providing access, the 1950s brought an onslaught of visitors that strained the parks in unanticipated ways, causing many to question the agency's commitment to preservation. Despite their distaste for the Park Service's orientation toward recreational development, wilderness advocates, an admittedly small group at the beginning of the controversy, knew they would have a better chance for protection with a national park, because they had tried to work with the Forest Service and gotten nowhere. The North Cascades became the "ultimate showdown that convinced citizen conservationists that the Forest Service could not be trusted to preserve wilderness."[8]

When Mike McCloskey was hired as Pacific Northwest Conservation Representative in 1961, the North Cascades was one of several wilderness preservation issues in the region. Logging in Three Sisters Wilderness, creating an Oregon Cascades national park, preserving Washington's Alpine Lakes region, and protecting the Oregon Dunes competed for attention. After consulting with David Brower, Patrick Goldsworthy, and others, McCloskey thought the North Cascades offered the best chance to achieve permanent protection, for several reasons.[9]

First, the North Cascades had a higher proportion of high mountain scenery to lowland forests. The ratio was flipped in Oregon, where there was a lot of forest compared to the amount of alpine scenery. Private timber concerns in Washington State were not as dependent on national forest lands as they were in Oregon and elsewhere in the West, because ownership was roughly equal among private industry, the state, and the Forest Service.[10] The timber industry cared intensely about the disposition of forests in Oregon and on the Olympic Peninsula because trees there were low-lying and easily accessible. Comparatively speaking, the rock and ice of the North Cascades, set off by its steep timbered valleys, gave the region the crown jewel quality that was politically more appealing.

Second, during and after World War II, Washington State's population boomed with people who came for good jobs and stayed for the beautiful natural environs, easily reachable by car. Seattle became the nexus of a powerful, sophisticated urban constituency who cared deeply about wilderness preservation.

Third, because the area's economy had diversified away from timber dominance, it was politically feasible for Senator Jackson to take a position that displeased the timber industry, although he was careful to address park opponents' concerns during the legislative process. The fact Jackson was one of the most powerful politicians in the country boded well for passing legislation, because he would only support a park effort if he was confident he could get a bill passed.[11]

For McCloskey, the campaign to create the park was like flying a plane. First it had to get off the ground by attracting support to achieve political plausibility, then remain airborne by maintaining interest and persuading politicians to get involved, and finally land safely by ceding control to those able to accomplish the final goal. The success of the North Cascades campaign, which attracted national media attention and led to political action by two presidents, cabinet secretaries, legislators, and state officials, meant its proponents had to relinquish control and accept a national park that did not fully satisfy their objectives.[12] With strong leadership by the N3C and Sierra Club, conservationists working to preserve the North Cascades handled each stage with professionalism. Their willingness to compromise, when it became clear that was the only route to getting a park, helped make the park a reality. The North Cascades controversy exemplifies conservationists' embrace of politics as an avenue for achieving environmental goals in midcentury America.

North Cascades National Park has been aptly described as one of the postwar environmental movement's "leading accomplishments" and "a flagship park for wilderness protection."[13] The Wilderness Act of 1964 influenced the design and intent of North Cascades National Park in novel ways. In addition to preserving monumental scenery, a baseline requirement for traditional national parks, this park would preserve vast swaths of wilderness. The alpine ruggedness that protected *de facto* the region from major inroads for resource development became the primary rationale for creating the park. Its scenery was unquestionably of national significance, and it had been left alone, thanks to its physical inaccessibility and mostly hands-off management by the Forest Service. The scenery was not going away. The question was how best to protect it. The answer was to create a crown jewel park that prioritized wilderness preservation.

The creation of North Cascades National Park was an important milestone in wilderness preservation that exemplified changing attitudes about the environment. Today, support for wilderness is ingrained in the Pacific Northwest, where 3.4 million acres of statutory wilderness lie within a one hundred-mile radius of Seattle's Space Needle, a higher proportion than any other major city in the United States.[14] But the region is not frozen in time. The North Cascades and those who live and work there today still face complicated, daunting issues, now more concerned with ecological integrity than recreational access. Two of the biggest are climate change and wildlife restoration.

The effects of climate change are already felt in the North Cascades. Glaciers are melting, snowmelt occurs earlier in the season, forest fires are more frequent and more devastating, and plant and animal communities are changing.[15] A 2014 study outlining the "largest climate change adaptation effort on federal lands to date" described the challenges and effects of climate change on six million acres between Snoqualmie Pass and the Canadian border as urgent and extensive.[16]

For example, the North Cascades is the most glaciated area in the lower forty-eight states. The park complex alone contains more than three hundred glaciers.[17] Glaciers are important indicators of climate change. As average temperatures rise, perhaps as much as three to four degrees Fahrenheit by the middle of the twenty-first century, glaciers retreat. Warmer temperatures result in lower snowpack levels and thinner glaciers. Higher runoff levels in winter and drier streams in summer change the timing of seasonal runoff in mountain watersheds, which in turn affects the ecology of plants and animals, as the conditions they have evolved to thrive in change. Recreationists will be affected as roads wash out more frequently, limiting access.[18]

Long-term monitoring of North Cascades glaciers has shown retreat to be "rapid and ubiquitous" since the current warming trend began in 1976.[19] Scientists estimate that from 1984 to 2007, the total volume of North Cascades glaciers decreased between 20 and 40 percent.[20]

The Lyman Glacier offers a grim snapshot of glacier loss. Using historic photographs and onsite measurements, the North Cascades Glacier Climate Project determined that the glacier, which feeds Lyman Lake and Railroad Creek, a tributary of Lake Chelan, retreated more than three-quarters of a mile and lost more than 90 percent of its volume between 1907 and 2008.[21] The glacier will disappear entirely within the next fifty years, along with many others in the North Cascades, if the warming trend continues.[22]

Even more immediately visible than glacial retreat is the increase in the frequency and severity of forest fires. Warmer, drier conditions have invited insect infestations that kill millions of trees, creating ideal fuel for forest fires. In 2014, the Carlton Complex Fire, the largest individual fire in Washington State history, burned more than a quarter-million acres, destroyed more than three hundred homes, and cost $60 million to fight. It was followed in 2015 by the Okanogan Complex Fire, which killed three firefighters and burned even more acreage.[23] Carbon dioxide released into the atmosphere from fires worsens global warming, creating an "insidious cycle with no end in sight."[24]

Overall, more than a million acres of Washington State burned during 2015, making it the state's worst and most expensive wildfire season. More than $347 million was spent fighting the fires, about half from the state, which was forced to dip into reserves to cover its share of the cost.[25] The state Department of Natural Resources, which has primary responsibility for fighting wildfires, received only $6.7 million of the $25 million it requested to expand its firefighting capacity in 2016, leading some to question the legislature's commitment to wildfire management.[26] Washington Gov. Jay Inslee ordered the state's National Guard to train several hundred members in firefighting techniques, and it is all but certain the state will need their services in the face of more fires and higher costs in years to come.[27]

At the federal level, the Forest Service is especially hard-hit by the cost of fighting wildfires because its budget is based on historical funding averages. In 1995, firefighting comprised 16 percent of the agency's annual budget. In 2015, it made up more than half, and by 2025 it will consume more than two-thirds of the Forest Service budget. The agency's budget is a zero-sum game, which means money used for fighting fires comes out of other programs, including those focused on fire suppression and forest health. Ironically, forest thinning programs could help prevent or reduce the severity of wildfires, but their funding is increasingly reassigned to firefighting. In the same vein, firefighting staff has more than doubled, while staff for other programs has been reduced by about 40 percent. The budget for recreation and wilderness management has suffered as well, cut by 15 percent since 2001.[28] In 2015, Sen. Maria Cantwell (D-WA) took the lead in a bipartisan effort to develop legislation addressing the funding issue and implementing measures to improve information sharing and firefighter safety.[29]

Climate change is one of many issues informing wildlife restoration efforts, such as that proposed for the grizzly bear.[30] The North Cascades is excellent habitat for grizzlies, which had been hunted to near-extinction in the area by the 1930s. In 1993 the U.S. Fish and Wildlife Service declared almost ten thousand square miles of the region an "official recovery zone" for the animals, creating a path for possible restoration.[31] Wildlife scientists believe the North Cascades is home to perhaps five or ten grizzlies, though they are rarely seen in the park complex and surrounding lands. Remote cameras captured images of individual grizzlies ten miles north of the Canadian border in 2010 and 2012.[32] At publication, the most recent verified sighting of a grizzly in the North Cascades was at Glacier Peak in 1996. A photo taken 2010 at Cascade Pass was thought to be a grizzly but may have been a black bear with a grizzly-like shoulder hump.[33] Previous confirmed sightings include 1991 in the Thunder Creek drainage and 1989 near Bacon Creek, a tributary of the Skagit River.[34] Grizzlies reproduce slowly, and there are not enough in the North Cascades for them to repopulate the region without human help.

Lack of political will and funding has hampered action on restoring the grizzly population in the North Cascades despite its status as the largest potential habitat in the lower forty-eight. Most of the small amount of federal funding for grizzly research is spent in the Rocky Mountains, where the species has rebounded.[35] It is generally thought about seven hundred grizzlies live in the greater Yellowstone ecosystem, where they are a major draw for the park's three million-plus visitors each year. Another three hundred live in the Northern Continental Divide ecosystem, which includes Glacier National Park.[36]

In 2014, the Park Service announced it would provide much of the funding for an Environmental Impact Statement on restoring grizzlies to the North Cascades.[37] A draft EIS was released in early 2017 that outlined four alternatives ranging from doing nothing to expedited restoration of perhaps five to seven bears per year.[38] Public hearings are an important part of the process, and unsurprisingly, the prospect of a viable grizzly population, which scientists suggest would eventually comprise about two hundred bears, has sparked fierce debate. Many are concerned about grizzlies' impact on livestock that range adjacent to the park complex. Others do not want recreation access restricted; some trails and roads could be closed during certain times of year.[39] And many are simply afraid of grizzlies, whose fearsome reputation dates at least to the Lewis and Clark Expedition. The explorers killed a grizzly in April 1805 in present-day Montana, and by the time they returned to St. Louis in 1806, expedition members had developed a healthy respect for the "furious and formidable" animals.[40]

For many, grizzly restoration would be the finishing touch on the wilderness of the North Cascades. *Seattle Times* writer Ron Judd noted, "Without the grizzly the land is still wild, yes. But not humbling."[41] Public opinion generally favors restoration, but the process must carefully consider all viewpoints.[42] In the end, humans will decide the fate of this magnificent creature. One social benefit of wilderness may be that it requires us to put other species' interests ahead of our own. The grizzly's "ultimate value and purpose may be to test our willingness to share part of Earth with a wild and fearsome creature that remains as intolerant of us as we have been of it."[43]

Nearly a half-century after the park's creation, concepts of wilderness, scenic preservation, and public access have shifted. As the national parks and forests try to accommodate record crowds without adequate funding, some have called for a modern-day Mission 66 to clear the multi-billion-dollar backlog of maintenance and repair that plagues the national park system. Others believe access to the crown jewel parks may eventually be rationed, with would-be visitors entering a lottery or purchasing entry tickets in advance.

Those who venture to the North Cascades do not typically have to deal with long lines at entry stations, crowded trails, campsite shortages, inadequate parking, uncollected garbage, or packed visitor facilities. At the time of this writing, nearly all of the 1.3 million acres of land proposed for a national park and mountain recreation area in the N3C's 1963 *Prospectus* are statutorily protected, preserving diverse environments that range from lushly forested river valleys to some of the most spectacular alpine scenery in the world. To the hiker standing on a high ridge in the Picket Range or auto tourist gazing at Diablo Lake's milky turquoise waters, the politics that raged around the fate of this alpine wonderland can feel very far away. But maps show the reality. The North Cascades are the beneficiaries of the efforts of thousands who believed them worth preserving. The jaw-droppingly magnificent North Cascades endure as one of the largest, wildest tracts in the continental United States, a crown jewel wilderness to treasure forever.

Acknowledgments

L ike millions of others, my love of national parks started early and runs deep. When I was a twelve-year-old in suburban New Jersey, my parents, Charlie and Eileen Schwartz, took me and my sister Ann on a three-week trip out West. We visited Yellowstone, Grand Teton, Zion, Bryce, and Yosemite National Parks, a stellar start for a lifelong passion. I am sure my folks did not anticipate the long-term effects the trip would have, including me making my home in the Pacific Northwest. This book is a direct result of that life-changing tour. Thank you, Mom and Dad, for introducing me to the magnificent landscapes that are our natural heritage.

Historian Richard Maxwell Brown, who served on my dissertation committee at the University of Oregon, encouraged me to expand my research on the North Cascades into a book. This project took a long time, and it saddens me that he did not live long enough to see its completion. I am grateful for his consistent support.

Teaching writing has made me a better writer. Many thanks to my students and colleagues at South Puget Sound Community College for their inspiration.

Librarians, archivists, and curators make the job of any researcher infinitely easier. I am grateful to the professionals at the University of Washington Manuscripts and Special Collections, Washington State Archives, Washington State Library, The Evergreen State College, North Cascades National Park, Mount Rainier National Park, National Archives Pacific Alaska Region, National Archives at College Park, National Archives Building, the Bancroft Library at University of California, Berkeley, University of Arizona Special Collections, and Denver Public Library. Craig Bartlett at the Washington Department of Fish & Wildlife pointed me to helpful resources. Samantha Richert at the North Cascades National Park Service Complex Museum Collection patiently waded through boxes of images to help me find many used in this book.

Working with Stacey Brewster at The Evergreen State College and Ben Helle at Washington State Archives was like having my own library specialist and archivist. I am deeply grateful for their cheerful assistance.

Al Ferrara and Robert Cromwell of Seattle City Light helped me understand the Skagit River Hydroelectric Project and the role of Ross and Diablo Lakes as recreation sites in the North Cascades.

The North Cascades Institute's Environmental Learning Center (ncascades.org) hosted me as a creative resident for three weeks in September 2016, an energizing experience thanks in large part to Katie Roloson, the terrific staff, and the C16 graduate student cohort there.

In January 2017, I was fortunate to be a Scholar-in-Residence at Grey Towers National Historic Site (greytowers.org), the ancestral home of Gifford Pinchot, first chief of the United States Forest Service. The Forest Service staff at Grey Towers and the board of the Grey Towers Heritage Association made me feel most welcome. The space and time to work on edits of this book was invaluable.

Photographer Andy Porter (andyporterimages.com), Phil Fenner of the North Cascades Conservation Council (northcascades.org), Michael McCloskey, author and longtime executive director of the Sierra Club, and photographer John Scurlock (www.jaggedridgeimaging.com) generously provided photographs for use in the book.

In 2003, I had the good fortune to interview a number of the people involved in the North Cascades controversy. Richard "Bush" Buscher's views on the role of the Forest Service and wilderness and his role in the North Cascades were insightful and illuminating. I first met Mike McCloskey at an environmental history conference, and his discussion of his role in the North Cascades controversy brought the political aspects of the issue into clearer focus.

Sadly, others I interviewed are no longer with us. Phil and Laura Zalesky talked with me at length, took me on a memorable tour of the Mountain Loop Highway, and provided introductions to other conservationists. Patrick Goldsworthy not only gave me an interview, but generously loaned me all of his records before donating them to the University of Washington. Harold "Chris" Chriswell provided a Forest Service perspective and gave me a copy of his fascinating memoirs as background. Interviewing Harvey Manning in his Issaquah kitchen was a singular treat.

Working with WSU Press has been a privilege and a pleasure. Editor-in-chief Bob Clark, manuscript editor Beth DeWeese, and the rest of the staff exemplify publishing professionalism. Dr. Chris Johnson of the National Park Service and Dr. Donna Sinclair of WSU Vancouver provided advice that improved and strengthened the manuscript. I am indebted to both for their close reading and guidance. Cartographer Chelsea Feeney (cmcfeeney.com) created wonderful maps that help bring the story to life. Any errors of fact are, of course, my own.

Heather Lockman, Annamary Fitzgerald, Maria DenOuden, Terry Danner, Gwen Schweitzer, Kathy Strauss, Rennie Kubik, and Steve and Kathryn Wang are stalwart friends who offered wise counsel and consistent encouragement through this long project. Heather, especially, talked me through moments of insecurity and not-so-gently pushed me to focus full-time on the book, excellent advice that I am glad I took.

Historian Barbara Kubik and wilderness advocate Bob DenOuden read the entire manuscript and offered detailed comments and edits. A signed copy of the final book is not sufficient reward for their hours of work, but that, plus my eternal gratitude and maybe a few beers, is what they are getting.

Sophie Danner has never known a time when her mom was not working on this book. She has cheerfully tolerated road trips, long hikes, some admittedly odd dinners, occasional distractedness, and my love of wilderness her whole life. As a native Pacific Northwesterner, she has an innate understanding of the necessity of special places like the North Cascades and applies her artistic talent to their preservation.

This project would not have happened without my husband, David Danner. He has read each chapter numerous times, applying his intellectual prowess, analytical acuity, and editing skill to the story's benefit. Through some pretty tough challenges, his unwavering belief in my ability to write this book has been my wellspring of strength and perseverance. Dave's steadfast love, support, good cheer, and encouragement made all the difference, and this book is gratefully and lovingly dedicated to him.

Notes

Introduction

"A stupendous, primitive wilderness," quote from Weldon F. Heald, "Cascade Holiday," in *The Cascades*, ed. Roderick Peattie (New York: Vanguard Press, 1949), 133.

1. James Glover, *A Wilderness Original: The Life of Bob Marshall* (Seattle: The Mountaineers, 1986), 116.

2. "Three Great Western Wildernesses: What Must be Done to Save Them?" *The Living Wilderness* 1:1 (September 1935), 9–11; Glover, *Wilderness Original*, 189.

3. Glover, *Wilderness Original*, 219, 248.

4. Fred Cleator, "Recollections of Bob Marshall" (unpublished manuscript), folder 3, box 28, CONS 130, Conservation Collection, Wilderness Society Records, Denver Public Library.

5. Ada Anderson Woodruff, "Lake Chelan and the American Alps," *Pacific Monthly* 11 (May 1904), 304; Robert Mierendorf, "Cultural History: Across Time and Terrain in the Skagit Valley," ncascades.org/discover/north-cascades-ecosystem/cultural-history; Bob Mierendorf, "Who Walks on the Ground," in *Impressions of the North Cascades*, ed. John C. Miles (Seattle: Mountaineers, 1996), 40; Steury, Tim, "Of Time and Wildness in the North Cascades," *Washington State University Magazine*, Spring 2010, wsm.wsu.edu/s/index.php?id=764.

6. Margaret Bundy Callahan, "The Last Frontier," in *The Cascades*, ed. Roderick Peattie (New York: Vanguard Press, 1949), 22.

7. Rowland Tabor and Ralph Haugerud, *Geology of the North Cascades: A Mountain Mosaic* (Seattle: Mountaineers, 1999); Grant McConnell, "The Cascade Range," in *The Cascades*, ed. Roderick Peattie (New York: Vanguard Press, 1949); quote from Richard L. Williams et al., *The Cascades* (New York: Time-Life Books, 1974), 32.

8. Tabor and Haugerud, *Geology*, 7.

9. Glover, *Wilderness Original*, 116.

10. F. W. Cleator, "Report on North Cascades Primitive Area," July 28, 1934, 2320 Wilderness & Primitive Areas, North Cascade Primitive Area, 1934–1962 (2320 Wilderness & Primitive Areas), Region 6 Records (Region 6), U.S. Forest Service (FS), Record Group 95 (RG 95), National Archives and Records Administration—Alaska Pacific Region (NARA-APR).

11. Marshall to Cleator, October 2, 1939, reprinted in Cleator, "Recollections of Bob Marshall," Wilderness Society Records.

12. Quote in Glover, *Wilderness Original*, 264.

13. John C. Miles, *Wilderness and National Parks: Playground or Preserve* (Seattle: University of Washington Press, 2009), 94–95.

14. Marshall to Buck, November 12, 1938, 2320 Wilderness & Primitive Areas, Region 6, FS, RG 95, NARA-APR. Marshall was pessimistic about the chances for a giant wilderness in the North Cascades. He knew why the Forest Service was reluctant, as he wrote to Seattle conservationist Irving M. Clark: "I have been trying to get [the North Cascades wilderness] area created, but [regional forester] C. J. Buck is scared that if we establish such an area it will be made into a national park." (Marshall to Clark, May 18, 1938, Irving M. Clark Papers [Clark Papers], box 1, University of Washington Manuscripts and Special Collections [UW]).

15. Marshall to Watts, November 6, 1939, 2320 Wilderness & Primitive Areas, Region 6, FS, RG 95, NARA-APR.

16. Forest Service recreation planner Fred Cleator, who accompanied Marshall on his North Cascades trip, recalled that when the party went to Wenatchee at the end of the trip, Marshall was "too ill to get out of bed" the next morning. By noon he was having convulsions and was taken to the local hospital. He died just a few weeks later in New York City (Cleator, "Recollections of Bob Marshall"). Shortly after Marshall's death, Seattle conservationist and Olympic National Park activist Irving M. Clark suggested to Forest Service Chief Ferdinand Silcox that a fitting tribute might be to name a wilderness area after Marshall, and that "the North Cascades was Bob's favorite." In 1940, the first piece of what would become the Bob Marshall Wilderness was created in Idaho (Clark to Silcox, December 13, 1939, box 3, Clark Papers, UW).

17. For consistency, the term "conservationists" is used throughout the book. By the time the park was created in 1968, a new word, "environmentalists," had arisen to describe people committed to protecting the natural environment. In the mid-1950s, when the North Cascades controversy heated up, "conservationist" was the accepted term, used self-referentially and by others to denote this group.

18. McConnell, "The Cascade Range," 87.

1. The Federal Government in the North Cascades, 1892–1940

1. Donald C. Swain, "The National Park Service and the New Deal, 1933–1940," *Pacific Historical Review* 41(3): 312–332 (August 1972), 314; Donald C. Swain, "Harold Ickes, Horace Albright, and the Hundred Days: A Study in Conservation Administration," *Pacific Historical Review* 34(4): 455–465 (November 1965).

2. Tomlinson to Cammerer, July 3, 1937, box IV, Patrick D. Goldsworthy Papers (Goldsworthy Papers).

3. Lawrence Rakestraw, *A History of Forest Conservation in the Pacific Northwest, 1891–1913* (New York: Arno Press, 1979), 1, 42–44; Harold K. Steen, *The U.S. Forest Service: A History* (Seattle: University of Washington Press, 1976), 26–28. Mount Rainier became the nation's fifth national park in 1899, and the forest reserves around it went through several iterations; today the park is surrounded by the Gifford Pinchot and Mt. Baker-Snoqualmie National Forests.

4. Rakestraw, *Forest Conservation*, 1, 42–44; Steen, *Forest Service*, 26–28.

5. The other two forest reserves in Washington State, created in 1898, were the Olympic and the Washington. Parts of the Washington Forest Reserve later became the Chelan, Mt. Baker, Okanogan, Snoqualmie, and Wenatchee national forests, which have since been recombined into the Mt. Baker-Snoqualmie and Okanogan-Wenatchee national forests.

6. Rakestraw, *Forest Conservation*, 60–68; Steen, *Forest Service*, 33, 67–70, 125–126.

7. Among many sources on mining history are Margaret Willis, ed., *Chechacos All: The Pioneering of Skagit* (Mount Vernon, WA: Skagit Valley Historical Society, 1973); Philip R. Woodhouse, *Monte Cristo* (Seattle: The Mountaineers, 1979); John C. Miles, *Koma Kulshan: The Story of Mount Baker* (Seattle: The Mountaineers, 1984); Alan C. Schmierer, *Northing Up the Nooksack* (Seattle: Pacific Northwest Parks and Forests Association, 1983); Gay Robertson, *Stehekin Remembered* (Seattle: Pacific Northwest Parks & Forests Association, 1987), 9; Nigel Bruce Adams, "The Holden Mine: From Discovery to Production, 1896–1938" (PhD diss., University of Washington, 1976).

8. Woodhouse, *Monte Cristo*; Adams, "The Holden Mine"; Miles, *Koma Kulshan*, 75–89. Rakestraw wrote that at the peak of the mining bubble in the late 1890s, more than forty thousand claims peppered the Washington Forest Reserve and seventy-six organizations had financial investments in stakes there (*Forest Conservation*, Ch. 2).

9. Schmierer, *Northing*, 28; Erwin N. Thompson, *North Cascades N.P., Ross Lake N.R.A. & Lake Chelan N.R.A. History Basic Data* (N.p.: Department of the Interior, NPS, Office of History and Historic Architecture, Eastern Service Center, 1970), 89, 97; Willis, *Chechacos All*, 22, 35, 40, 43.

10. Rakestraw, *Forest Conservation*, 70–71, 125–126.

11. Rakestraw, *Forest Conservation*, 136–145.

12. Robert Byrd, *Lake Chelan in the 1890s*, rev. ed. (Wenatchee, WA: Byrd-Song Publishing, 1992), 18. The earliest U.S. Census records for Chelan are from 1910 and show a population of 682.

13. "A Great National Park," *Chelan Falls Leader*, February 11, 1892.

14. Organic Administration Act of 1897, 16 U.S.C. § 473–478, 479–482 and 551 (1897).

15. Hal K. Rothman, "'A Regular Ding-Dong Fight': Agency Culture and Evolution in the NPS-USFS Dispute, 1916–1937," *Western Historical Quarterly* 20(2), 147; Muir description from T. H. Watkins, *Righteous Pilgrim: The Life and Times of Harold L. Ickes, 1874–1952* (New York: Henry Holt and Company, 1990), 456.

16. John Muir, "Selections from *Our National Parks*," 1901, in *The Great New Wilderness Debate*, eds. J. Callicott Baird and Michael P. Nelson. (Athens: University of Georgia Press, 1998), 48.

17. Char Miller, *Gifford Pinchot and the Making of Modern Environmentalism* (Washington, DC: Island Press, 2004), Kindle edition.

18. John Ise, *Our National Park Policy: A Critical History* (Baltimore, MD: Johns Hopkins University Press, 1961). See Richard West Sellars, *Preserving Nature in the National Parks: A History* (New Haven: Yale University Press, 1997), 10.

19. Sellars, *Preserving Nature*, 10. Alfred Runte points out that Yellowstone also helped a young nation establish its cultural identity by providing a unique kind of monument; instead of Europe's castle ruins, America had geologic antiquities unrivaled on the Continent (*National Parks: The American Experience*, 3rd ed. [Lincoln: University of Nebraska Press, 1997]).

20. Sellars, *Preserving Nature*, 23–27. "Natural conditions," the term used in many early parks' enabling legislation, including Yellowstone, would become the subject of intense debate in the 1960s.

21. Byrd cited accounts that estimate between seven hundred and five thousand men came to try their luck during 1892 (*Lake Chelan in the 1890's*, 23). Although they did not stay long, if even the lower number is accurate, the influx would have more than doubled the population around the lake.

22. L. H. Woodin, "A Park Not Wanted," *Spokane Review*, February 19, 1892; "A Very Vigorous Protest," *Chelan Falls Leader*, February 25, 1892; "Organize," *Chelan Falls Leader*, March 3, 1892.

23. *Chelan Falls Leader*, August 13, 1891; Tom Hackenmiller, *Ladies of the Lake: Transportation, Tragedy and Triumph on Lake Chelan* (Manson, WA: Point Publishing, 1998); "Lake Chelan is the Tourists' Elysium," *Chelan Falls Leader*, January 7, 1892.

24. Hackenmiller, *Ladies of the Lake;* Carol M. Stone, *Stehekin: Glimpses of the Past* (Friday Harbor, WA: Long House Printcrafters and Publishers, 1983), vii; Robertson, *Stehekin Remembered*, 14–15; W. M. Emerson, "History of Chelan Valley," in *A History of Central Washington*, ed. Hull, 469.

25. W. D. Lyman, "Lake Chelan," *Overland Monthly* 33(195): 195–201 (March 1899); W. G. Steel, "Lake Chelan and the Valley of the Stehekin," *Oregon Native Son* 1(3), 409, 414.

26. Henry Gannett, "Lake Chelan and Its Glacier," *Mazama* 3(1):185–189 (March 1907), 189; W. D. Lyman, "Beautiful Lake Chelan," *Walla Walla Union*, March 24, 1901.

27. See Jules Verne, *The Begum's Fortune* (1879; reprint, New York: Ace Books, 1958). Verne distinguished between the developed Swiss Alps and the Cascades, "just a crust of rocks, and earth and venerable pines." I am grateful to Patrick Goldsworthy for directing me to this source. The Alps were used as a metaphor for American mountains, particularly the Rockies, as early as 1868 (Marguerite S. Shaffer, *See America First: Tourism and National Identity, 1880–1940*, Washington, DC: Smithsonian Institution Press, 2001, 8–9).

28. Shaffer, *See America First*, 5.

29. Hal K. Rothman, *Devil's Bargains: Tourism in the Twentieth-Century American West* (Lawrence: University Press of Kansas, 1998), 23. The term "heritage tourism" is Rothman's. Steel, "Lake Chelan," 412; Shaffer, *See America First*, 25.

30. Shaffer, *See America First*, 26–29.
31. Seattle City Directory, 1903. Itter's reasons for coming to the Northwest are unclear; one newspaper account notes that health concerns brought him, but other articles note his hardy composition and love of the outdoors ("Mountains of Washington," *Everett Herald*, 21 May 1903); see also Francis Walker, "Julian Itter, Artist of Washington State, and His Work," *Spokesman-Review*, 7 April 1912. Quote from "For World's Fair," *Seattle Post-Intelligencer*, 17 May 1903; "For World's Fair"; "Mountains of Washington."
32. Dode Trip and Sherburne F. Cook Jr. *Washington State Art and Artists, 1850–1950* (Olympia, WA: Sherburne Antiques and Fine Art, 1992); William R. Halliday, "The Forgotten Father of North Cascades National Park," *Seattle Times Magazine*, March 16, 1969; *Seattle and its Hotel* [electronic record], 1904, Pamphlets and Textual Documents Collection, Pacific Northwest Collection, UW; "Perpetuating the Glories of Washington," *Seattle Times Magazine Section*, January 14, 1906.
33. "Want Lake Chelan Country Made Into a National Park," *Wenatchee Daily World*, March 8, 1906; "Make Chelan a National Park," *Chelan Leader*, March 9, 1906; "For a National Park"; "Beautiful Chelan—A National Park," *Seattle Times Magazine*, April 8, 1906; Mazamas, "Resolution: Lake Chelan, March 23, 1906, Portland, Oregon," box IV, Goldsworthy Papers; "A North Cascades National Park," *Conservation News Letter* 6(1):1 (May 1960); "Lake Chelan Region Beckons to Scenery Seeking Tourists," *Chelan Leader*, March 16, 1906; Shaffer, *See America First*, 29; "For a National Park," *Chelan Leader*, March 9, 1906; "Lake Chelan Region Beckons," *Chelan Leader*.
34. "Anent a National Park," *Chelan Leader*, March 16, 1906; "Unanimous Opposition," *Chelan Leader*, April 6, 1906; "Heavy Dose Already," *Chelan Leader*, April 20, 1906; "National Parks. What Are They and What Are They For," *Chelan Leader*, March 30, 1906; "We Cannot Afford It," *Chelan Leader*, April 6, 1906.
35. S. J. Gray, "Object to National Park," *Chelan Leader*, March 30, 1906; "National Parks. What Are They," *Chelan Leader*.
36. "Opposed to National Park," *Chelan Leader*, April 13, 1906; "Fancy or Fact, Which?" *Chelan Leader*, April 13, 1906; "No Park at Chelan," *Chelan Leader*, April 20, 1906; "Heavy Dose Already," *Chelan Leader*.
37. Runte, *National Parks*, 73.
38. "Gives It Up," *Chelan Leader*, April 27, 1906.
39. Shaffer, *See America First*, 79; Mary Roberts Rinehart, *Tenting To-Night* (Boston: Houghton Mifflin, 1918), 170–171.
40. Rakestraw, *Forest Conservation*, 76; Steen, *Forest Service*, 74, 96.
41. Rakestraw, *Forest Conservation*, 214–225. Quote from ch. 7.
42. Richard C. Davis, ed., *Encyclopedia of American Forest and Conservation History, Vol. II* (New York: Macmillan Publishing for the Forest History Society, 1983), www.foresthistory.org/ASPNET/Places/National%20Forests%20of%20the%20U.S.pdf; Thompson, *History Basic Data*, 193–194. The Mt. Baker and Snoqualmie National Forests were administratively combined in 1974. The Wenatchee and Okanogan National Forests followed suit in 2000.
43. Rakestraw, *Forest Conservation*, 220–236, 225.
44. Miles, *Koma Kulshan*, ch. 4.
45. Miles, *Koma Kulshan*, 60–89; Rakestraw, *Forest Conservation*, 1.
46. Michael P. Cohen, *The History of the Sierra Club, 1982–1970* (San Francisco: Sierra Club Books, 1988), 71.
47. Miles, *Koma Kulshan*, 90–111.
48. Steen, *Forest Service*, 113–116. Steen points out that Gifford Pinchot had been trying to get parks transferred to the Department of Agriculture (home of the Forest Service) since 1904, an effort continued by his successor, Henry Graves. See also Samuel P. Hays, *Con-*

servation and the Gospel of Efficiency: The Progressive Conservation Movement, 1890–1920 (Cambridge: Harvard University Press, 1959), 196–198; Miles, Koma Kulshan, 134–136.

49. Mount Olympus National Monument was an exception to the general rule of administration by the Interior Department. Designated by President Theodore Roosevelt in 1909 and carved out of the existing Olympic National Forest, the monument was administered by the Forest Service, likely because presidential confidante Gifford Pinchot requested it. When jurisdiction was transferred to the Park Service in 1933, the Forest Service fought the change (Lien, Olympic Battleground: The Power Politics of Timber Preservation, 2nd ed. [Seattle: The Mountaineers, 2000], 119–20).

50. E. E. Hale, "Baker National Park is Urged," Seattle Post-Intelligencer, December 15, 1915; Miles, Koma Kulshan, 114–139.

51. Club historian Charles Finley Easton drew a beautiful map of Mount Baker to help promote it; Hadley Peak is not labeled, but the legislator is remembered with a glacier in addition to the peak (C. F. Easton, A Map of Mt. Baker, Wash. (1912), Bellingham, WA: Engberg Pharmacy, 1912, Washington State University Libraries Map Collection, content.libraries.wsu.edu/cdm/singleitem/collection/maps/id/77/rec/4).

52. House Committee on Public Lands, Mount Baker National Park, Washington, 64th Cong., 2nd Sess., 1916, H. Rpt. 1372; Mount Baker National Park, 64th Cong., 1st Sess., H.R. 9805, Cong. Rec., 53, pt. 2, 1408; Mount Baker National Park, 64th Cong., 1st Sess., S. 3775, Cong. Rec., 53, pt. 2, 1424; Mount Baker National Park, 64th Cong., 1st. Sess., S. 3982, Cong. Rec., 53, pt. 2, 1549; Senate Joint Memorial No. 2, Washington State Legislature, 15th Sess., January 29, 1917; Miles, Koma Kulshan, 138–140.

53. U. S. Statutes at Large 39 (1917): 535–6.

54. Watkins, Righteous Pilgrim, 321.

55. Miller, Gifford Pinchot and the Making of Modern Environmentalism.

56. See Ise, National Park Policy; Sellars, Preserving Nature; Runte, National Parks.

57. Shaffer, See America First; Runte, National Parks.

58. Lassen Volcanic National Park in northern California was created just weeks before the Park Service Organic Act was signed into law.

59. Mather to Hadley, March 13, 1919, 5500–Land Classification, National Park 1916–1919 (5500–Land Classification), Region 6 Planning Records (Region 6), FS, RG 95, NARA-APR.

60. Mount Baker National Park, 65th Cong., 1st Sess.. S. 312, Cong. Rec., 55, pt. 1, 192; Mount Baker National Park, 65th Cong., 1st Sess., H.R. 6066, Cong. Rec., 55, pt. 1, 7168; Mount Baker National Park, 65th Cong., 2nd Sess., S. 3662, Cong. Rec., 56, pt. 2, 1498; Mount Baker National Park, 65th Cong., 2nd Sess.. S. 4014, Cong. Rec., 56, pt. 3, 3031; Mount Baker National Park, 66th Cong., 1st Sess., S. 371, Cong. Rec., 58, pt. 1, 59; Mount Baker National Park, 67th Cong., 1st Sess., S. 20, Cong. Rec., 61, pt. 1, 142; "Make Chelan National Park," Wenatchee Daily World, July 26, 1916; NPS, Summary of Proposals to Establish a National Park or Monument in the Glacier Peak–Northern Cascade Mountain Region of Washington, April 1957; rev. July 1958, L-58 North Cascades, Recreation Planning Records, NPS—Pacific Northwest Region, RG 79, NARA-APR.

61. Mather to Hadley, March 13, 1919, Region 6, FS, RG 95, NARA-APR.

62. Robert Shankland, Steve Mather of the National Parks, 3rd ed. (New York: Alfred A. Knopf, 1970), 185; "Mt. Baker is Greatest," Bellingham Sunday Reveille, July 16, 1922; Mather to Hadley, March 13, 1919, 5500–Land Classification, National Park 1916–1919 (5500–Land Classification), Region 6 Planning Records (Region 6), FS, RG 95, NARA-APR. Mather may have been mentally comparing Lake Chelan and Crater Lake; the latter was carved from national forest land in 1902.

63. Steen, Forest Service, 120.

64. Quoted in Robert W. Cermak, "'Plans Must be Big and Broad': The Beginning of Recreational Planning on the National Forests" January 19, 1973, www.foresthistory.org/ASPNET/policy/Recreation/documents/Cermak_Plans.pdf.

65. James P. Gilligan, "The Development of Policy and Administration of Forest Service Primitive and Wilderness Areas in the Western United States" (PhD diss., Univ. of Michigan, 1953), 82; Steen, *Forest Service*, 154–56.

66. Paul Sutter, *Driven Wild: How the Fight Against Automobiles Launched the Modern Wilderness Movement* (Seattle: University of Washington Press, 2002), 70.

67. Gilligan, "Policy and Administration," 83.

68. Sutter, *Driven Wild*, 72.

69. Gilligan, "Policy and Administration," 84.

70. Glover, *Wilderness Original*, 95–96; Robert Marshall, "Wilderness as a Minority Right" (1930), reprinted in Baird and Nelson, *The Great New Wilderness Debate*, 85–96.

71. Steen, *Forest Service*, 155.

72. Gilligan, "Policy and Administration," 86.

73. Rothman, "Ding-Dong Fight," discusses this conflict in detail.

74. Rothman, "Ding-Dong Fight," 142.

75. Gilligan, "Policy and Administration," 109; Sutter, *Driven Wild*, 85.

76. Gilligan, "Policy and Administration," 126–127, Appendix B.

77. Granger to Clark, March 1, 1929, folder 1, Office of the Executive Director, carton 13, BANC MSS 2002/230c, Sierra Club Records, BL.

78. Gilligan, "Policy and Administration," 114–116.

79. *Mt. Baker National Forest, Willamette Meridian (1931),* Washington State University Libraries Map Collection, content.libraries.wsu.edu/cdm/singleitem/collection/maps/id/1236.

80. Rothman, "Ding-Dong Fight," 143.

81. Steen, *Forest Service*, 152–62, Gilligan, "Policy and Administration," 98.

82. See Steen, *Forest Service*, 199–204.

83. Glover, *Wilderness Original*, 146–147.

84. At least one Forest Service employee warned about the consequences of Region 6's reluctance to create or expand primitive areas, writing that in the Whatcom Primitive Area, poorly designed boundaries leave out "every stick of second-grade sub-alpine timber, leaving nothing but the barren mountain-tops. . . [Region 6] has simply execluded [*sic*] everything that could ever be used for anything else, using the widest stretch of their imagination, and called what was left a 'Primitive Area.'" (Memo to Recreation file by "AMW," June 9, 1934, 2320 Wilderness & Primitive Areas, Region 6, FS, RG 95, NARA-APR.)

85. Denise M. Meringolo, *Museums, Monuments, and National Parks: Toward a New Genealogy of Public History* (Amherst: University of Massachusetts Press, 2012).

86. Gilligan, "Policy and Administration," 149–150, 176–183.

87. F. W. Cleator, "Report on North Cascade Primitive Area," July 28, 1934, 2320 Wilderness & Primitive Areas, Region 6, FS, RG 95, NARA-APR.

88. Gilligan, "Policy and Administration," 183, 200, quote from 189.

89. Executive Order No. 6166, *Organization of Executive Agencies,* June 10, 1933.

90. See Meringolo, *Museums, Monuments, and National Parks* for a fuller discussion of how the 1933 executive order transformed the Park Service.

91. Ise, *National Park Policy*, 352–53; Runte, *National Parks*, 195.

92. Lien (*Olympic Battleground*, 119–121) points out the Park Service was reluctant to take on management of Mount Olympus National Monument and delayed for two months before finally assuming control.

93. Gilligan, "Policy and Administration," 150.

94. Steen, *Forest Service*, 242–245.

95. National Resources Board, *A Report on National Planning and Public Works in Relation to Natural Resources and including Land Use and Water Resources with Findings and Recommendations* (Washington, DC: GPO, 1934); National Resources Board Land Planning Committee, *Part II: Report of the Land Planning Committee* (Washington, DC: GPO, 1934); National Park Service, *Recreational Use of Land in the United States, Part XI of the Report on Land Planning* (Washington, DC: GPO, 1938), 28, 225.
96. Tomlinson to Demaray, April 26, 1934, box IV, Goldsworthy Papers. The suggestion had been made as early as 1889 for a park that would reserve the crest of the range from Canada to California (Rakestraw, *Forest Conservation*, 31–34). Four decades later, a prominent East Coast conservationist recommended "at least two or three more national parks in the Cascade Mountains...saving some tracts of the marvelously beautiful fir and hemlock forests" (Willard van Name, *Vanishing Forest Reserves* [Boston: The Gorham Press, 1929], 170). But for the most part, these were wishful thinking.
97. NPS, *Summary of Proposals*, L-58, Recreation Planning, RG 79, NARA-APR; "Tomlinson Visits," *Bellingham Herald*, August 19, 1937; "Cascade Ice Peaks Park is Proposal for State," *Seattle Star*, June 15, 1937; "Cascade National Park Planned," *Seattle Post-Intelligencer*, June 15, 1937.
98. NPS, *Report of Committee, Northern Cascades Area Investigation*, 1937, n. p., 38.
99. Ibid.
100. Brian R. Wall, "Log Production in Washington and Oregon: An Historical Perspective" (Portland, OR: Pacific Northwest Forest and Range Experiment Station, USDA Forest Service, 1972), www.fs.fed.us/pnw/pubs/pnw_rb042.pdf.
101. Putnam to file, January 11, 1938, 5500–Land Classification, National Parks to 12/31/38, Region 6, FS, RG 95, NARA-APR. This suspicion was borne out in a later missive from the superintendent of Mount Rainier National Park in which he acknowledged the strategy (Tomlinson to Kittredge, May 3, 1941, folder 56: O. A. Tomlinson [I-K] [correspondence; procedure guide]; microfiche 49, MRNP).
102. Cleator to Putnam, July 29, 1937, 5500–Land Classification, Planning, Region 6, RG 95, NARA-APR.
103. Kniepp to Horton, September 30, 1939, 5500–Land Classification, Cascade National Park (Proposed), Region 6, FS, FS, RG 95, NARA-APR.
104. Sutter, *Driven Wild*.
105. Marshall to Clark, November 12, 1938, 2320 Wilderness & Primitive Areas, Recreation Planning, FS, RG 95, NARA-APR.
106. Glover, *A Wilderness Original*, 248; also see Gilligan, "Policy and Administration," for discussion of wilderness advocates within the Forest Service; Sutter, *Driven Wild*, 221–27, 234–37.
107. Quoted in Glover, *A Wilderness Original*, 264.
108. Clark, memo to file re: North Cascade Wilderness Area, June 17, 1939, box IV, NCCC Irving Clark, Goldsworthy Papers.
109. As noted in the introduction, Marshall died in November 1939, less than two months after his final North Cascades trip. Forest Service Chief Ferdinand Silcox was prepared to approve Marshall's proposal for a giant wilderness, but in a tragic coincidence was killed in a car accident before anything was finalized (Department of Agriculture, Forest Service, Region 6, *Management Plan for the Glacier Peak Wilderness, Mt. Baker and Wenatchee Forests*, 1965). Reclassification was delayed by their deaths, and then by the onset of World War II. Discussion of limited area vs. primitive area designation is found in Kevin R. Marsh, *Drawing Lines in the Forest: Creating Wilderness Areas in the Pacific Northwest* (Seattle: University of Washington Press, 2007), 27, 80.

110. Tomlinson to Hetherton, August 20, 1939, Cascade Mountains, Planning & Development, WSPC Records, WSA; Watts to Kizer, August 14, 1939, Cascade Mtns., Planning & Devt., WSPC records, WSA; *Summary of Proposals to Establish a National Park or Monument in the Glacier Peak–Northern Cascade Mountain Region*, February 20, 1957, L-58, Recreation Planning, RG 79, NARA-APR.

111. For more on the composition and history of the Washington State Planning Council and the planning movement, see National Resources Board, "State Planning—Review of Activities and Progress" (Washington, DC: GPO, 1935); National Resources Committee, "State Planning Programs and Accomplishments (supplementing State Planning Report of 1935)" (Washington, DC: GPO, 1936).

112. WSPC, Minutes, April 17, 1937, Cascades Committee, Planning and Development, WSPC Records, WSA.

113. Lien, *Olympic Battleground*, 129–131, 188.

114. The park also cost regional forester C.J. Buck, with whom Bob Marshall tangled over primitive area designations, his job. Buck and Mount Rainier National Park superintendent O.A. Tomlinson were assigned to accompany President Franklin D. Roosevelt on his tour of the Olympic peninsula in 1937. Taking turns riding in the president's car, each tried to convince Roosevelt of his position. In opposing an Olympic National Park, Buck antagonized the president, who later ordered the chief of the Forest Service to remove Buck from his position as regional forester. Buck was transferred to Washington, DC, in 1939 (Gerald W. Williams, "National Monuments and the Forest Service," November 2003, www.nps.gov/parkhistory/online_books/fs/monuments.htm).

115. For more on Ickes and his interaction with the Forest and Park Services, see Watkins, *Righteous Pilgrim*; Swain, "Harold Ickes, Horace Albright"; Swain, "National Park Service and the New Deal"; and Barry Mackintosh, "Harold L. Ickes and the National Park Service," *Journal of Forest History* 29(2): 78–84 (April 1985).

116. P. Hetherton, "Washington Cascade Ridge Area Study," *Pacific Northwest Regional Planning Commission News*, October 15, 1939, 12–13; WSPC, Minutes, August 5, 1939, Cascades Comm., Planning and Devt., WSPC Records, WSA.

117. Clark to Marshall, October 24, 1938, 2320 Wilderness & Primitive Areas, Region 6, FS, RG 95, NARA-APR.

118. WSPC, Minutes, July 10, 1939, Cascades Comm., Planning & Devt., WSPC Records, WSA; "Is Mrs. Edge Getting in your Hair too, Boys?" *Montesano Vidette*, September 28, 1939. The article quotes the *Sedro-Woolley Courier-Times* and the *Ferndale Record* in the same vein.

119. "New National Park," *Tacoma Journal*, October 13, 1939. The *Saturday Evening Post* covered the story in much the same vein (Richard L. Neuberger, "How Much Conservation?" *Saturday Evening Post*, June 15, 1940, 12–13, 89–96); "Make It a Park?— Nay Cries Swelling," *Wenatchee World*, October 20, 1939. The *World*'s opposition seemed slightly paradoxical in light of its caption touting the North Cascades as "the PREMIER SCENIC WONDERLAND OF WESTERN AMERICA—challenging in grandeur any and all national parks in the United States." See also "State Good Roads Association and Other Groups Oppose Proposal," *Seattle Post-Intelligencer*, November 1, 1939.

120. WSPC, Minutes, December 7, 1939, Cascades Comm., Planning & Devt., WSPC Records, WSA.

121. "Not Needed," *The Argus*, November 11, 1939.

122. "No Decision Made on Cascade Park," *Seattle Post-Intelligencer*, November 1, 1939; "Park Service Studies Plan for Cascades," *Olympian*, October 12, 1939; Everett G. Richards, "A Giant Cascade Park…?" *Oregonian* April 21, 1940.

123. NPS, Cascades Committee, *National Park Potentialities in the Cascade Mountains of Washington*, 1940, Cascade Mtns., Planning & Devt., WSPC Records, WSA.

124. USFS, *Preliminary Report of North Cascade National Park Study Area*, April 27, 1940, 5500–Land Classification, Planning, FS, RG 95, NARA-APR, 2–3, II-3–6, III-4–8; see also Richards, "A Giant Cascade Park…?"
125. WSPC, *Cascade Mountains Study, State of Washington* (Olympia: WSPC, 1940); WSPC, *Cascade Mountains Study* [pamphlet] (Olympia.: WSPC, 1940); "Planners Rap Cascade Park," *Seattle Sunday Times Magazine*, May 12, 1940; "Plan Council Raps Proposed National Park," *Seattle Post-Intelligencer*, May 12, 1940.
126. Clapp to Hetherton, June 29, 1940, Cascade Comm., Planning & Devt., WSPC Records, WSA.
127. Tomlinson to file, October 7, 1940, 10: Cascade National Park [Ickes vs. Freeman], Development & Maintenance, microfiche 10, MRNP; WSPC, *Cascade Mountains Study* [pamphlet].
128. Hetherton to Healy, May 15, 1940, Cascade Mtns., Planning & Devt., WSPC Records, WSA; Hetherton to WSPC, July 18, 1940, Cascade Mtns., Planning & Devt., WSPC Records, WSA.
129. Kittredge to Cammerer, June 4, 1940, 12: Report on Contemplated Primitive Area, Development & Maintenance, mf 13, MRNP; Kittredge to file, June 4, 1940, 12: Report, Devt. & Maint., mf 13, MRNP; Greider to file, June 17, 1940, 11: Cascade Mountain Study, Development & Maintenance, mf 11/12, MRNP; Burlew to Hetherton, June 29, 1940, 11: Cascade, mf 11/12, MRNP; Demaray to Kizer, August 5, 1940, 11: Cascade, Devt. & Maint., mf 11/12, MRNP; Greider to file, September 4, 1940, 11: Cascade, Devt. & Maint., mf 11/12, MRNP; "Roosevelt Backs Ickes in Cascades Study Fight but Council Stands Pat," *Bellingham Herald*, October 3, 1940.
130. "Ickes Blocks Formation of Cascade Summit Park," *Yakima Morning Herald*, March 5, 1940; "Ickes Declares Cascade Park is Unreasonable," *Port Angeles News*, March 5, 1940; "Thinks Cascade Park Idea Joke," *Olympian*, March 5, 1940; "Mr. Ickes on Parks," *Oregonian*, June 10, 1940; "Cascades Park Project Dead," *Spokane Spokesman-Review*, June 23, 1940; for example, Demaray to Ickes, December 28, 1938, box IV, Goldsworthy Papers; "A Bill to Establish the North Cascades National Park, in the State of Washington, and for other purposes," box IV, Goldsworthy Papers; Schulz to Ickes, February 23, 1940, box V, Goldsworthy Papers.
131. "Change of Heart," *Tacoma News-Tribune*, March 30, 1940; NPS, *Summary of Proposals*, February 20, 1957, L-58, Recreation Planning, RG 79, NARA-APR; "Peninsula Sacrificed to Halt Cascade Park Says Tucker," *Aberdeen Daily World*, January 3, 1940.
132. Tomlinson to Kittredge, May 3, 1941, folder 56: O. A. Tomlinson [I-K] [correspondence; procedure guide]; mf 49, MRNP. Probably unbeknownst to Tomlinson, Washington Gov. Clarence Martin had said much the same thing more than a year earlier: "You are apt to get a park there some day," Martin commented during a visit to Spokane. "It is hard to explain why these natural resources should not be conserved" ["Martin is not Worried by State Funds," *Spokane Spokesman-Review*, January 13, 1940].
133. John Miles points out the Park Service had no wilderness policy per se in the 1930s. Olympic and Kings Canyon were proposed as wilderness *landscapes*, maintaining the scenic element required of national parks, in part because wilderness was cheaper to maintain during the Depression (*Wilderness in National Parks*, 84–94).

2. Conservationists Coalesce around Glacier Peak
1. Edmond Meany, "Glacier Peak," *The Mountaineer* (vol. III, November 1910): 24.
2. U.S. Geological Survey, "Glacier Peak," volcanoes.usgs.gov/volcanoes/glacier_peak.
3. Harvey Manning, *The Wild Cascades: Forgotten Parkland* (San Francisco: Sierra Club, 1965), 69.

4. USGS, "Glacier Peak–History and Hazards of a Cascade Volcano," pubs.usgs.gov/fs/2000/fs058-00; Lukas Velush and Bill Sheets, "Our Volcano: Glacier Peak is the Hidden Threat in our Back Yard," *Everett Herald*, September 13, 2010, www.heraldnet.com/article/20100516/NEWS01/705169935; Fred Beckey, *Cascade Alpine Guide: Climbing and High Routes, Stevens Pass to Rainy Pass*, vol. 2, 3rd ed. (Seattle: The Mountaineers, 2003), 162.

5. Stephen L. Harris, *Fire and Ice: The Cascade Volcanoes*, rev. ed. (Seattle: The Mountaineers, 1980), 226.

6. Ibid.

7. "Step in Right Direction," *Wenatchee World*, 6 October 1926; "Glacier Peak Association Formed," *Wenatchee World*, December 10, 1926.

8. Department of Agriculture, Forest Service, "Glacier Peak Recreation Area Approved," June 10, 1931; C. J. Buck, "Report on Whitechuck Timber Reservation Proposals," 8 February 1932; L-Recreation and L[U]-Recreation, 1929-1938, Region 6, FS, RG 95, NARA-APR; "Timber in the Whitechuck Valley," Federation of Western Outdoor Clubs, Bulletin No. 1, March 1933. See also "Step in Right Direction," "Glacier Peak Association Formed," and Philip H. Zalesky, "The Mountaineers: A Story of Conservation" (1993), unpublished manuscript in the author's collection.

9. James P. Gilligan, "The Development of Policy and Administration of Forest Service Primitive and Wilderness Areas in the Western United States" (PhD diss., University of Michigan, 1953), vol. 2, appendix A, 1.

10. Gilligan, "Policy and Administration," 196-197, 220.

11. During his trip to Glacier Peak in September 1939, Marshall camped at Lyman Lake. Virginia Olmsted, Marshall's longtime friend and a companion on this outing, wrote that she had noticed Marshall's "grimace of real pain" during the ride up to the first campsite. [Olmsted to Clark, November 21, 1939, box 3, Clark Papers, UW.] Also see John Sieker, "Farewell to the Wilderness," *Living Wilderness* 5(5): 19 (July 1940); Lloyd E. Eighme, "Through the Heart of the Northern Cascades," *Living Wilderness* 13(26): 9-15 (Autumn 1948).

12. William G. Robbins, "The Western Lumber Industry," in *The Twentieth-Century West*, eds. Gerald D. Nash and Richard Etulain (Albuquerque: University of New Mexico Press, 1989), 226. Timber sales rose from 1.552 billion board feet in 1941 to 2.732 billion board feet in 1945, an increase of 76 percent (David Clary, *Timber and the Forest Service* [Lawrence: University Press of Kansas, 1986], 111).

13. Gerald Williams, *The U.S. Forest Service in the Pacific Northwest: A History* (Corvallis: Oregon State University Press, 2009), 174.

14. Williams, *Forest Service in the Pacific Northwest*, 180-181.

15. Clary, *Timber and the Forest Service*, 122. Technological advances such as the chain saw, caterpillar tractor (used for clearing brush and hauling logs from the woods), and more powerful logging trucks all facilitated faster logging. It was said that one logger using a chain saw could fell as much wood in one day as two loggers using a crosscut saw could fell in one week (Michael Williams, *Americans and Their Forests: A Historical Geography* [Cambridge: University of Cambridge Press, 1989], 315-230; Gerald W. Williams, *The Forest Service: Fighting for Public Lands* [Westport, CT: Greenwood Press, 2007], 28).

16. Paul Hirt, *A Conspiracy of Optimism: Management of the National Forests Since World War Two* (Lincoln: University of Nebraska Press, 1994), xxii.

17. Robert E. Ficken and Charles P. LeWarne, *Washington: A Centennial History* (Seattle: University of Washington Press, 1988), 130.

18. Robbins, "The Western Lumber Industry," 225.

19. Norman H. Clark, *Washington: A Bicentennial History* (New York: W. W. Norton & Co., Inc., 1976), 190.

20. A board foot, the standard measurement for commercial timber, is equivalent to a 12" x 12" x 1" piece of lumber.
21. Hirt, *Conspiracy of Optimism*, 150.
22. Samuel P. Hays, "From Conservation to Environment: Environmental Politics in the United States Since World War II," in *Out of the Woods: Essays in Environmental History*, eds. Char Miller and Hal Rothman (Pittsburgh: University of Pittsburgh Press, 1997), 106. Also Williams, *Forest Service in the Pacific Northwest*, 167.
23. Clark, *Bicentennial History*, 170.
24. James William Scott, *Washington: A Centennial Atlas* (Bellingham, WA: Center for Pacific Northwest Studies, Western Washington University, 1989), 18.
25. Washington State Office of Financial Management, "Historical Estimates of April 1 Population and Housing for the State, Counties, and Cities: Decennial Census Counts," ofm. wa.gov/pop/april1/hseries/default.asp; Ficken and LeWarne, *Centennial History*, 130.
26. Williams, *Forest Service in the Pacific Northwest*, 187, 188. Mountaineers annuals list membership during the period (www.mountaineers.org/about/history/the-mountaineer-annuals).
27. Hirt, *Conspiracy of Optimism*, 169–72.
28. Also in 1946, a 15,000-acre Limited Area was designated at Monte Cristo, the site of a major mining operation in the early twentieth century (North Cascades Study Team, *The North Cascades Study Report* [Washington, DC: GPO, October 1965], 184).
29. Department of Agriculture, Forest Service, Region 6, "Management Plan for the Glacier Peak Wilderness, Mt. Baker and Wenatchee Forests," 1965.
30. Folsom to Clark, October 2, 1951, box IV, Patrick D. Goldsworthy Papers (Goldsworthy Papers); Folsom to Clark, February 18, 1953.
31. Harvey Manning, "Conservation and Conflict: The U.S. Forest Service and the National Park Service in the North Cascades, 1892–1992" (unpublished draft), box 1, Harvey Manning Papers (Manning Papers), UW.
32. Dave Fluharty, "In Memoriam: Grant McConnell," *Stehekin Choice*, December 1993/ January 1994, 8.
33. Grant McConnell, *Stehekin: A Valley in Time* (Seattle: The Mountaineers, 1988), 197.
34. Phil and Laura Zalesky, interview by the author, tape recording, Everett, WA, January 27, 2003.
35. Irving Clark, Meeting Notes, Glacier Peak Wilderness, February 27, 1950; Folsom to Clark, October 2, 1951, Folsom to Clark, September 29, 1952, Folsom to Clark, February 18, 1953, box IV, Goldsworthy Papers; Clark to Andrews, February 6, 1951, Clark to Folsom, February 9, 1953, BANC MSS 2002/230c, folder 8, carton 13, Office of the Executive Director, Sierra Club Records, The Bancroft Library, Berkeley (BL); Clark to Andrews, October 6, 1948, BANC MSS 2002/230c, folder 12, carton 13, Office of the Executive Director, Sierra Club, BL.
36. Mountaineers Committee on Conservation and Public Affairs minutes, March 30, 1953, box 1, Mountaineers Conservation Committee Papers (Mountaineers Papers), UW.
37. "Proposed Glacier Peak Wilderness Area," *The Mountaineer* 46(7), July 1953. Other areas listed were the Sauk, Suiattle, Whitechuck, Wenatchee and White River valleys, the Sulphur and Buck Creek valleys, Illabot Lake, and Cascade Pass.
38. Zalesky, "The Mountaineers"; also 2903, box 1, Richard J. Brooks Papers (Brooks Papers), UW.
39. Mountaineers Committee on Conservation and Public Affairs minutes, April 26, 1954, September 27, 1954, box 1, Mountaineers Papers, UW. Phil Zalesky later noted, "No conservation meeting of the [Mountaineers] went by without Brooks pressuring the conservationists into action on Glacier Peak." [Zalesky, "The Mountaineers," 28.]

40. Kevin R. Marsh, "Drawing Lines in the Woods: Debating Wilderness Boundaries on National Forest Lands in the Cascade Mountains, 1950-1984," (PhD diss., Washington State University, 2002, quote from 60).
41. Many outdoor recreation groups created Conservation Committees to monitor political activities that affected natural areas. As the environmental movement grew in strength and activity, such committees became the locus for political activity within the organizations. See Hays, "From Conservation to Environment."
42. Manning, "Conservation and Conflict"; Dee Arntz, *Extraordinary Women Conservationists of Washington* (Charleston, SC: History Press, 2015), 30.
43. An account of the Darrington trip appeared in the December 1955 issue of *Mazama*. See Irston Barnes, "Glacier Peak—Wilderness Wonderland," *Mazama* 37(13): 40-43 (December 1955). Quote from "Glacier Peak Wonderland," *Western Outdoor Quarterly* 22(4): 7-10 (November 1955).
44. Bernard DeVoto, "Let's Close the National Parks," *Harper's* 207(1241):49-52 (October 1953).
45. Zalesky, interview.
46. Polly Dyer, "Whose Ice Axes?" *The Wild Cascades*, Spring 1998, 13; Phil Zalesky, "In Memoriam: Jane McConnell," *The Wild Cascades*, Spring 1998, 14.
47. Zalesky, "In Memoriam," 14.
48. See, for example, Roderick Frazier Nash, *The Rights of Nature: A History of Environmental Ethics*, Madison: University of Wisconsin Press, 1989, 63-64.
49. Grant McConnell, "The Conservation Movement—Past and Present," *Western Political Quarterly* 7(3): 463-478 (September 1954), quote at 463.
50. Grant McConnell, "The Struggle for the North Cascades: A Personal Memoir" (unpublished draft), box 1, Grant McConnell Papers (McConnell Papers), UW.
51. "David Brower (1912-2000): Timeline," *Sierra Club*, content.sierraclub.org/brower/timeline; "David Brower," *Wilderness.net*, www.wilderness.net/NWPS/Brower.
52. Michael P. Cohen, *The History of the Sierra Club, 1892-1970* (San Francisco: Sierra Club Books, 1988), 117-131.
53. Mark W. T. Harvey, *A Symbol of Wilderness: Echo Park and the American Conservation Movement* (Albuquerque: University of New Mexico Press, 1994); Cohen, *History of the Sierra Club*, 155-168.
54. Brower to McConnell, November 18, 1955, McConnell to Brower, November 22, 1955, BANC MSS 71/103c, Historic Conservation Files, Conservation Department, Sierra Club Records, BL; McConnell, "The Struggle for the North Cascades"; Manning, "Conservation and Conflict."
55. Cohen, *History of the Sierra Club*, 191, 252.
56. Manning, "Conservation and Conflict," 37.
57. Patrick Goldsworthy, "Protecting the North Cascades, 1954-1983," oral history by Ann Lage, *Pacific Northwest Conservationists* (Berkeley: Regional Oral History Office, The Bancroft Library, University of California, Berkeley, 1986), 20.
58. Cohen, *History of the Sierra Club*, 154.
59. Polly Dyer, "Preserving Washington Parklands and Wilderness," oral history by Susan Schrepfer, *Pacific Northwest Conservationists* (Berkeley: Regional Oral History Office, The Bancroft Library, University of California, Berkeley, 1986).
60. Manning, "Conservation and Conflict."
61. McConnell, "The Struggle for the North Cascades"; Manning, "Conservation and Conflict."
62. Grant McConnell, "Conservation and Politics in the North Cascades," oral history by Rod Holmgren (Berkeley, CA: Sierra Club, 1983), 9; Manning, "Conservation and Conflict."

63. McConnell to Blair, October 24, 1955, Blair to McConnell, October 27, 1955, Blair to McConnell, March 7, 1956, acc. 4325-003, box 1, McConnell Papers, UW.
64. McConnell to Powell, June 22, 1956, "Glacier Peak Wilderness Area, 1956-1958," 2320, Region 6 Regional Forester Records, 95-73A898, box 25219, FS, RG 95, NARA-APR.
65. Blair to McConnell, June 27, 1956, box 1, McConnell Papers, UW.
66. McConnell, *Stehekin*, 197.
67. McConnell to Brower, June 30, 1956, box 1, McConnell Papers, UW.
68. McArdle to Jackson, July 31, 1956, box 1, McConnell Papers, UW. The letter was in response to a constituent query, and it seems likely that the original question came from McConnell himself. McArdle sent a similar letter to Jackson on July 27, 1956 (Office of the Executive Director, BANC MSS 2002/230c, Sierra Club Records, BL).
69. McConnell, *Stehekin*, 197.
70. Dyer, "Preserving Washington Parklands and Wilderness," 34, emphasis in original.
71. Mountaineers Committee on Conservation and Public Affairs minutes, June 18, 1955, box 1, Mountaineers Papers, UW.
72. "Proposed Glacier Peak Wilderness Area Mountaineer Recommendations," *The Mountaineer* 49(6): 11 (June 1956).
73. "Proposed Glacier Peak," 13, 9, 11.
74. Ibid.
75. Donald Worster, "John Muir and the Roots of Modern Environmentalism," in *The Wealth of Nature: Environmental History and the Ecological Imagination* (New York: Oxford University Press, 1993), 199.
76. "Proposed Glacier Peak," 9. That mechanization made it possible for people to derive benefits from wilderness was an irony not fully acknowledged at the time.
77. Marsh, "Drawing Lines in the Woods," 55.
78. Cohen, *History of the Sierra Club,* 216.
79. Washington State Sportsmen's Council resolution (no number), 1956, box 2, Philip H. Zalesky Papers (Zalesky Papers), UW.
80. Barnes, "Glacier Peak—Wilderness Wonderland," 40-43; Irston Barnes, "A Bounty to Claim: The Wilderness Area," *Washington Post*, 4 September 1955; "Lullaby of the River, Challenge of the Peak," *Washington Post*, August 21, 1955.
81. Wayburn to Conservation Cooperators, December 3, 1956, box III, Goldsworthy Papers.
82. Misch to Wayburn, November 9, 1956, box III, Goldsworthy Papers, is a letter about the mineral wealth potential of Glacier Peak.
83. Minutes, Sierra Club Pacific Northwest Chapter Executive Committee Meeting, August 4, 1956, box XIV, Goldsworthy Papers.
84. McConnell to Zahniser, November 26, 1955, box 1, McConnell Papers, UW.
85. Marsh, "Drawing Lines in the Woods," 63-64.
86. Howard Zahniser, "Wilderness in the Cascades," *Living Wilderness* 21(58): inside front cover (Fall-Winter 1956-57).
87. John F. Warth, "The Glacier Peak Wilderness," *National Parks* 30(127): 173-176, 193-194 (October-December 1956).
88. The map overlay method was pioneered in Region 6, apparently by Wenatchee National Forest supervisor Ken Blair (McConnell to Goldsworthy et al.; July 10, 1956, box III, Goldsworthy Papers).
89. Grant McConnell, "The Cascades Wilderness," *Sierra Club Bulletin* 41(10):24-31 (December 1956).
90. Wayburn to Conservation Cooperators, December 3, 1956, box III, Goldsworthy Papers; Brower to McArdle, May 2, 1957, box XVII, Goldsworthy Papers.

3. The Forest Service Stumbles, and Conservationists Debate

1. Department of Agriculture, Forest Service, Pacific Northwest Region, "Glacier Peak Land Management Study, Mount Baker and Wenatchee National Forests, Washington," February 7, 1957, 2–3.
2. Marshall, "The Problem of the Wilderness (1930)," in Baird and Nelson, *Great New Wilderness Debate*, 85.
3. Forest Service, "Glacier Peak Land Management Study," 2–3.
4. Ibid, 4, 9.
5. Whether the Forest Service envisioned a private resort operating under a special use permit or an agency-run facility, it may have overstated the area's potential for mass recreation. The hot springs could comfortably accommodate perhaps four people, six or seven if they were close friends. Buried by flood debris in 2003, the springs are no longer accessible.
6. Forest Service, "Glacier Peak Land Management Study," 9–10.
7. Ibid, 6. Since the area around Glacier Peak had been closed to logging since the 1930s, conservationists saw this argument as specious; the Forest Service was subtracting income from Darrington's economy that had not been available for decades.
8. Forest Service, "Glacier Peak Land Management Study," 9–10.
9. Gerald W. Williams, *The U.S. Forest Service in the Pacific Northwest: A History* (Corvallis: Oregon State University Press, 2009), 184.
10. Forest Service, "Glacier Peak Land Management Study," 2–3.
11. Forest Service, "Glacier Peak Land Management Study," 10.
12. Craig W. Allin, *The Politics of Wilderness Preservation* (Fairbanks: University of Alaska Press, 2008), 111.
13. Marsh, "Drawing Lines in the Woods."
14. James P. Gilligan, "The Development of Policy and Administration of Forest Service Primitive and Wilderness Areas in the Western United States" (Ph.D. diss., Univ. of Michigan, 1953), 222.
15. Simons to Stone, April 6, 1957, box 9, John Osseward Papers (Osseward Papers), UW.
16. Dennis M. Roth, *The Wilderness Movement and the National Forests* (College Station, TX: Intaglio Press, 1995), 5.
17. McConnell to Wayburn, November 17, 1956, box 9, Osseward Papers, UW.
18. Dyer to Osseward, December 15, 1956, box 9, Osseward Papers, UW.
19. Goldsworthy to Wayburn, January 25, 1957, box 1, McConnell Papers, UW.
20. Powell to Brooks et al., March 1, 1957, box B, Goldsworthy Papers.
21. USDA Forest Service, "Operation Outdoors," 1957, www.foresthistory.org/ASPNET/policy/Recreation/documents/Operation_Outdoors_1957.pdf.
22. See Paul Hirt, *A Conspiracy of Optimism: Management of the National Forests Since World War Two* (Lincoln: University of Nebraska Press, 1994).
23. Hirt, *Conspiracy of Optimism*, 157, 159; Williams, *The Forest Service in the Pacific Northwest*, 182.
24. "Rough Transcript, Meeting, Mazamas Clubroom, Portland, Oregon, March 23, 1957," box B, Goldsworthy Papers.
25. For notes on the name change, see "Preliminary Proposed By-Laws," March 20, 1957, box 27, Emily Haig Papers (Haig Papers), UW.
26. "Preliminary Proposed By-Laws," March 20, 1957, box 27, Haig Papers, UW.
27. Zalesky to McConnell, March 26, 1957, box 1, McConnell Papers, UW.
28. "List of Officers, Board of Directors and Members," *NCCC* 1(1): 5 (August 1957).
29. The three-member county commission included Benton M. Bangs, Homer J. Trefry, and W. Robert Murray (Chelan County Commissioners to Blair, March 4, 1957, Regional

Forester, 95-73A898, box 25219, Folder 2320 Glacier Peak Wilderness Area 1956–1958), Region 6 Records, RG 95, NARA-APR.

30. "New Mill and Box Factory to Rise in Chelan Region," *Portland 4-L Lumber News,* January 1, 1931, Washington State University Libraries Digital Collections, kaga.wsulibs.wsu.edu/cdm4/item_viewer.php?CISOROOT=/clipping& CISOPTR=27374&CISOBOX=1&REC=1; "Mill Starts Season," *Spokesman-Review,* April 26, 1937, WSU Libraries Digital Collections, kaga.wsulibs.wsu.edu/cdm4/item_ viewer.php?CISOROOT=/clipping&CISOPTR=27248&CISOBOX=1&REC=1.

31. Wall, "Log Production in Washington and Oregon," 54. www.fs.fed.us/pnw/pubs/pnw_ rb042.pdf.

32. "Protests Mounting Against Proposed Wilderness Area," *Chelan Valley Mirror,* February 28, 1957; Gretchen Luxenberg, "Marketing the Wilderness: Development of Commercial Enterprises," *North Cascades Historic Resource Study,* 1999, www.nps.gov/parkhistory/ online_books/noca/hrs/sec3.htm.

33. Chelan County Commissioners to Blair, March 4, 1957, Glacier Peak Wilderness Area 1956–1958, folder 2320, 95-73A898, box 25219, Region 6 Regional Forester Records, FS, RG 95, NARA-APR.

34. "Chelan Chamber Opposes Wilderness Boundaries," *Wenatchee Daily World,* March 5, 1957.

35. "Omak Chamber Also Opposes Recreation Area," *Wenatchee Daily World,* September 24, 1957; Glaze to Blair, September 27, 1957, Glacier Peak Wilderness Area 1956–1958, folder 2320, 95-73A898, box 25219, Region 6 Regional Forester Records, USFS, RG 95, NARA-APR; Manson Grange No. 796, "A Resolution: Proposed Wilderness Area," December 10, 1957; "Development Group Takes Anti-Wilderness Position," *Wenatchee Daily World,* November 22, 1957.

36. "Glacier Peak Wilderness Area," *Your Congressman Reports,* March 15, 1957.

37. Gallagher to Zalesky, June 11, 1957, box 6, Osseward Papers, UW.

38. Forest Service, "Glacier Peak Land Management Study," 12.

39. Kenneth B. Pomeroy, "Glacier Peak Wilderness," *American Forests* 63(7), 26–27, 63–64 (July 1957).

40. National Park Service, "National Register of Historic Places, Continuation Sheet: St. Andrews Episcopal Church," 1992. npgallery.nps.gov/GetAsset/602afc52-e7b9-4041-bbf1-75da5497ca03.

41. "Wilderness Area Status Reviewed," *Western Forester* 3(4), January 1958; Matthias Olshausen, "From Company Town to Company Town: Holden and Holden Village, Washington, 1937–1980 & Today" (2013), *Dissertations and Theses,* Paper 717, 2, 63–64, 71. See also "Shall We Lock it up?" *Western Conservation Journal* 15(1): 4–7 (January-February 1958).

42. Dick Larsen, "Foresters Group Hears Wilderness Area Debate," *Wenatchee World,* December 9, 1957, 2.

43. Riley Johnson, *Have You Been Told? Do You Know the Facts? on the Proposed Glacier Peak Wilderness Area* (pamphlet), January 1958, National Forest Multiple Use Association.

44. Johnson, *Have You Been Told?* (emphasis added).

45. North Cascades Conservation Council, *Are You Aware? Comments Concerning the Glacier Peak Wilderness Area* (pamphlet), March 1958.

46. North Cascades Conservation Council, *Are You Aware?*

47. Ibid.

48. Michael Cohen, *The History of the Sierra Club, 1892–1970* (San Francisco: Sierra Club Books, 1988), 155.

49. Abigail Avery first visited the North Cascades in 1940. In addition to donating money to complete the film, she provided the impetus for Wilderness Society executive director

Olaus Murie to schedule the group's board of directors meeting for Stehekin in 1958, giving NPS director Conrad Wirth the opportunity to see the area firsthand. (Abigail Avery, "Nurturing the Earth: North Cascades, Alaska, New England, and Issues of War and Peace," oral history, 1988 by Polly Kaufman in Sierra Club Nationwide IV, Sierra Club Oral History Project, Sierra Club, 1996, 9–10). Also Brower to Avery, May 10, 1957, BANC MSS 2002/230c, Office of the Executive Director, Sierra Club Records, BL; Grant McConnell, "The Struggle for the North Cascades: A Personal Memoir"; (unpublished draft), box 1, McConnell Papers, UW; Harvey Manning, *Conservation and Conflict: The U.S. Forest Service and the National Park Service in the North Cascades, 1892–1992* (Seattle: North Cascades Conservation Council, 1992 [preliminary unpublished edition]).

50. Philip and Laura Zalesky, interview. This was not the first time "west siders" had clashed with "east siders" and Brower over Glacier Peak. Some felt that McConnell and Brower were too focused on the Stehekin valley, to the detriment of the western river approaches. [See Brower, "North Cascades—Thoughts," February 22, 1958, box X, Goldsworthy Papers; Goldsworthy to Brower, June 17, 1958, box III, Goldsworthy Papers.]

51. David Brower, "Wilderness Alps of Stehekin," *Living Wilderness* 23(66):18–24 (Autumn 1958), reprints the film's narration.

52. Zalesky, interview.

53. For a detailed account of the making of the film and its impact on the park controversy, see Nicolas Timothy Bergmann, "Preserving Nature through Film: Wilderness Alps of Stehekin and the North Cascades, 1956–1968" (2013), *Dissertations and Theses*, paper 973.

54. Douglas H. Strong, *Dreamers and Defenders: American Conservationists* (Lincoln: University of Nebraska Press, 1988), 205.

55. Clark to Yard, October 5, 1940, box IV, Goldsworthy Papers.

56. Brower to McConnell, November 18, 1955, box III, Goldsworthy Papers.

57. McConnell to Brower, November 22, 1955, BANC MSS 71/103c, folder 19, carton 72, Conservation Department Records, Sierra Club Records, BL.

58. McConnell, "The Struggle for the North Cascades." See also Zalesky to McConnell, April 5, 1957, reel 1 (microfilm), John Warth Papers (Warth Papers), UW. In April 1957, writer Weldon Heald wrote to McConnell, "I think it's a national park or not very much of anything" [April 26, 1957, BANC MSS 2002/230c, Office of the Executive Director, Sierra Club Records, BL]. The following month, *New York Times* conservation writer John Oakes (a friend of McConnell's) suggested that "what this incomparable region really needs is permanent protection in its entirety as a national park" [John R. Oakes, "Conservation: Program to Save the Wilds," *New York Times*, May 5, 1957, 46].

59. Ronald A. Foresta, *America's National Parks and their Keepers* (Washington: Resources for the Future, 1984), 50; John Ise, *Our National Park Policy: A Critical History* (Baltimore: Johns Hopkins University Press, 1961), 534. "Park visits" indicates the number of times a park was visited in a given year, not the number of individuals who visited the park. If one person visits Mount Rainier National Park four times in a year, it is tallied as four park visits.

60. Bernard DeVoto, "Let's Close the National Parks," *Harper's*, October 1953, 49–52, reprinted in *America's National Park System: The Critical Documents*, "Chapter 4: The Poverty Years, 1942–1956," www.nps.gov/parkhistory/online_books/anps/anps_4d.htm. As of this writing, the deferred maintenance backlog in the national parks stands at $12 billion ("NPS Deferred Maintenance Reports, Planning, Design, and Construction Management,: *National Park Service*, www.nps.gov/subjects/plandesignconstruct/defermain. htm); Josh Hicks, "National Park Service Delayed $11 Billion in Maintenance Last Year Because of Budget Challenges," *Washington Post*, March 25, 2015, www.washingtonpost.

com/news/federal-eye/wp/2015/03/25/national-park-service-delayed-11-billion-in-maintenance-last-year.
61. Alfred Runte, *National Parks: The American Experience*, 4th ed. (Lanham, MD: Taylor Trade Publishing, 2010), 156.
62. Richard West Sellars, *Preserving Nature in the National Parks: A History* (New Haven: Yale University Press, 1997), 181.
63. Foresta, *America's National Parks*, 53–54.
64. See Marguerite S. Shaffer, *See America First: Tourism and National Identity, 1880–1940* (Washington, DC: Smithsonian Institution Press, 2001), esp. ch. 4; William C. Everhart, *The National Park Service* (Boulder, CO: Westview Press, 1983), 9.
65. Runte, *National Parks*, 76–82.
66. Runte, *National Parks*, 143.
67. Paul Sutter's *Driven Wild: How the Fight Against Automobiles Launched the Modern Wilderness Movement* (Seattle: University of Washington Press, 2002) is a compelling account of this development.
68. Runte, *National Parks*, 143.
69. Miles, *Wilderness and the National Parks*, 35, 48.
70. Foresta, *America's National Parks*, 53.
71. Sellars, *Preserving Nature*, 202.
72. Cohen, *History of the Sierra Club*, 120, 138.
73. Sellars, *Preserving Nature*, 202.
74. McConnell to Brower, May 15, 1958, box 7, Osseward Papers, UW.
75. Ibid.
76. Harvey Manning, "You Don't Have to be Old to be an Elder," *Backpacker* (Spring 1975), 56–59, 84–89; Marsh, "Drawing Lines in the Woods," 111–112.
77. David R. Simons, *The Need for Scenic Resource Conservation in the Northern Cascades of Washington* (San Francisco: Sierra Club Conservation Committee, Northern Cascades Subcommittee, 1958), quotes from 12, 21.
78. Cohen, *History of the Sierra Club*, 224–225.
79. Patrick Goldsworthy, interview by the author, tape recording, Seattle, WA, February 6, 2003.
80. Brower to Goldsworthy, December 26, 1958, box IV-AR, Goldsworthy Papers, exemplifies this attitude (emphasis in original).
81. David Brower, "North Cascades—Thoughts," February 22, 1958, box X, Goldsworthy Papers.
82. Zalesky, interview. Zalesky had taken a position as a seasonal ranger at Mount Rainier National Park the previous summer, which led to an internal discussion about how it looked if the N3C's primary spokesperson worked for the service. Although he remained as president at the time, he declined to run again when his one-year term ended, and Goldsworthy took over. See: Goldsworthy to Zalesky, July 2, 1957; Zalesky to Goldsworthy, July 6, 1957; Brower to Zalesky, July 9, 1957, box B, Goldsworthy Papers.
83. J. Michael McCloskey, interview by the author, tape recording, Portland, OR, May 2, 2003.
84. Goldsworthy to Brower, January 13, 1958, box IV-AR, Goldsworthy Papers.
85. Goldsworthy, interview.
86. Zalesky, interview.
87. Zalesky to McConnell, July 14, 1958, box 1, McConnell Papers, UW.
88. Brower to McConnell, July 11, 1958, box 7, Osseward Papers, UW.
89. See Michael McCloskey, "Wilderness Movement at the Crossroads, 1945–1970," *Pacific Historical Review* 41(3):346–361 (August 1972).
90. Neva Karrick, the N3C's recording secretary.
91. Brower to North Cascades Conservation Council directors, etc., July 16, 1958, acc. 3818, box 7, Osseward Papers, UW; *NCCC News*, September 1958.

92. Foresta, *America's National Parks*, 62–65; Sellars, *Preserving Nature*, 194–195; Hirt, *Conspiracy of Optimism*, 159.
93. Minutes, Mountaineers Conservation Committee, March 16, April 20, July 20, August 17, September 21, and October 19, 1959, box 1, Mountaineers Papers, UW. The Mountaineers were keenly aware of the national groups' interest in a national park: the minutes of the Conservation Committee's April 1957 meeting note, "California people [i.e., the Sierra Club] are particularly desirous of the [national park] approach."
94. Philip Hyde, "The Wilderness World of the Cascades," *Living Wilderness* 22(6):5–16 (Spring 1957); "Wilderness Society Council," *Living Wilderness* 22(62):35 (Autumn 1957); "North of Glacier Peak Limited Area," *Living Wilderness* 22(63):35 (Winter-Spring 1958); David Brower, "Wilderness Alps of Stehekin," *Living Wilderness* 23(66):18–24 (Autumn 1958).
95. Manning, "Conservation and Conflict."
96. "Wilderness Society Council Meets," *Living Wilderness* 23(66):39–42 (Autumn 1958), 40.
97. Ise, *Our National Park Policy*, 525.
98. Murie to Brower, August 14, 1958, folder 1, carton 13, BANC MSS 2002/230c, Office of the Executive Director, Sierra Club Records, BL.
99. Marshall to Dyer, September 7, 1958, box 1, Polly Dyer Papers (Dyer Papers), UW.
100. Marshall to Clark, November 12, 1938, 2320 Wilderness & Primitive Areas, Recreation Planning, FS, RG 95, NARA-APR.
101. "Skyscraper Country," *Sunset*, August 1958, 42–48.
102. C. Edward Graves, "Washington's Stehekin Valley," *National Parks* 31(130):140–141 (July–September 1957). See also Paul R. Tschirley and Oliver H. Heintzelman, "The Case for Recreation in the Stehekin Watershed," *National Parks* 32(135):147–152 (October–December 1958).
103. Wayburn to McConnell, August 6, 1958, Conservation Department, folder 16, Historic Conservation Files, carton 78, BANC MSS 71/103c, Sierra Club Records, BL.
104. Sierra Club and North Cascades Conservation Council, *Our Greatest National Park?* (pamphlet), January 1959 (ellipses in original).

4. Glacier Peak Redux

1. Department of Agriculture, Forest Service, Pacific Northwest Region, *Glacier Peak Land Management Study, Mt. Baker and Wenatchee National Forests, Washington*, February 7, 1957, rev. March 10, 1958, 2320 Glacier Peak Wilderness Area 1956-1958, Region 6, FS, RG 95, NARA-APR.
2. Department of Agriculture, Forest Service, Pacific Northwest Region, *Glacier Peak Wilderness Area Proposal*, February 1959, 2320 Glacier Peak Wilderness Area 1956-1958, Region 6, FS, RG 95, NARA-APR.
3. Forest Service, *Glacier Peak Land Management Study*, rev. March 10, 1958.
4. Ibid.
5. Forest Service, *Glacier Peak Wilderness Area Proposal*, February 1959.
6. Ibid.
7. David Brower credited Simons with inventing these descriptive phrases (see David Ross Brower, *Environmental Activist, Publicist, and Prophet: Oral History Transcript* [Reprint, London: Forgotten Books, 2013], 94-5).
8. Forest Service, *Glacier Peak Wilderness Area Proposal*, February 1959.
9. Forest Service, *Glacier Peak Wilderness Area Proposal*, February 1959; Paul Brooks, "Kennecott Copper and Glacier Peak," in *The Pursuit of Wilderness* (New York: Houghton Mifflin, 1971), 45-56.

10. Forest Service, *Glacier Peak Wilderness Area Proposal*, February 1959, 2; Forest Service, *Glacier Peak Land Management Study*, rev. March 10, 1958, 10.
11. James P. Gilligan, "The Development of Policy and Administration of Forest Service Primitive and Wilderness Areas in the Western United States" (PhD diss., University of Michigan, 1953), 224.
12. Grant McConnell, *Stehekin: A Valley in Time* (Seattle: The Mountaineers, 1988), 203.
13. Gilligan, "Policy and Administration," 222.
14. Quoted in Gilligan, "Development of Policy and Administration," 195-6.
15. *NCCC News*, February 1959.
16. Grant McConnell, "Struggle for the North Cascades: A Personal Memoir," (unpublished draft), McConnell Papers, UW.
17. *NCCC News*, April 1959.
18. David Brower, "The Missing Million," *Sierra Club Bulletin* 44(2):10-15 (February 1959).
19. See back cover, *Sierra Club Bulletin* 44(3), March 1959.
20. Margaret Oberteuffer, "A Northern Cascades Wilderness Trek," *Living Wilderness* 24(70):1-9 (Autumn 1959), quote at 7; J. Herbert Stone, "Glacier Peak Wilderness Proposal (1959)," *Living Wilderness* 24(70):10-13 (Autumn 1959).
21. Weldon F. Heald, "The Undiscovered Cascades," *National Parks* 33(145):8-11 (October 1959). The magazine had printed the full Forest Service proposal in April 1959 ("A Wilderness Starfish," *National Parks* 33(139):6-7).
22. The Mountaineers, "Wilderness Status Recommendations for the Glacier Peak Area," May 1959.
23. Simons to Brower, August 27, 1959, folder 3, carton 13, BANC MSS 2002/230c, Office of the Executive Director, Sierra Club Records, BL.
24. Platt to Goldsworthy, July 1, 1958, box 2, Zalesky Papers, UW; Jolley to Region 6 Forest Supervisors, July 15, 1959, Glacier Peak Wilderness Area 1959-1967, Region 6, FS, RG 95, NARA-APR. For Platt's involvement in the wilderness bill, see *National Wilderness Preservation Act, Hearings Before the Committee on Interior and Insular Affairs*, U.S. Senate, 85th Cong., 1st Sess., June 19-20, 1957, 62-69.
25. Chriswell to Stone, June 10, 1959, Alpha Files: U-Recreation & Lands, 1905-57, Mt. Baker-Snoqualmie National Forest Records, FS, RG 95, NARA-APR.
26. As of 1953, only five areas with Forest Service primitive or wilderness area status contained more than five hundred thousand acres. North Cascade Primitive Area was one (see Gilligan, "The Development of Policy and Administration," 211). Quotes from F.W. Cleator, "Report on North Cascade Primitive Area," July 28, 1934, Wilderness & Primitive Areas, folder #3, Maps–Reports–Photos–Releases, box 75835, folder 2320, Region 6, FS, RG 95, NARA-APR.
27. Fred Beckey noted the "remarkably linear" range's "extreme compactness," which added to its isolation. (Fred Beckey, *Cascade Alpine Guide: Climbing & High Routes, Vol. 3: Rainy Pass to Fraser River* [Seattle: Mountaineers, 1995]), 94.
28. John Suiter, *Poets on the Peaks: Gary Snyder, Philip Whalen & Jack Kerouac in the North Cascades* (Washington, DC: Counterpoint, 2002), 32.
29. Manning, *Conservation and Conflict: The U.S. Forest Service and the National Park Service in the North Cascades, 1892-1992*. Seattle: North Cascades Conservation Council, 1992 (preliminary unpublished edition).
30. Cleator, "Report on North Cascade Primitive Area."
31. "North Cascades Wilderness Area," n.d. (probably early 1961), Wilderness & Primitive Areas, North Cascade Primitive Area, 1934-1962, box 75835, folder 2320, Region 6 Records, Recreation Planning, FS, RG 95, NARA-APR. In 1955, the primitive area

had logged only half as many visits, suggesting that increased publicity about the North Cascades in general and regional population growth had an impact.

32. Chriswell to Stone, June 10, 1959, Alpha Files: U-Recreation & Lands, 1905-57, Mt. Baker-Snoqualmie National Forest Records, FS, RG 95, NARA-APR, emphasis added.

33. Stone to Chriswell, June 13, 1959, Alpha Files: U-Recreation & Lands, 1905-57, Mt. Baker-Snoqualmie National Forest Records, FS, RG 95, NARA-APR.

34. Harold C. "Chris" Chriswell, "Memoirs, 1933-1971" (unpublished manuscript, collection of the author).

35. Stone to division chiefs, August 4, 1959, Glacier Peak Wilderness Area 1959-1967, Region 6, FS, RG 95, NARA-APR.

36. The Mountaineers, North Cascades Conservation Council, and the Sierra Club, *An Urgent Request that You Help Conserve the Northern Cascades* (pamphlet), October 1959.

37. For example, see "Glacier Peak Wilderness Hearings October 13, 16," *The Mountaineer* 52(11): 4-5 (October 1959).

38. Hazle to McArdle, 6 July 1959, box 14, Thomas M. Pelly Papers (Pelly Papers), UW.

39. McArdle to Hazle, 18 August 1959, box 14, Pelly Papers, UW.

40. *Official Report of Proceedings before the United States Department of Agriculture Forest Service In the Matter of: The Proposed Establishment of Glacier Peak Wilderness Area, Wenatchee, Washington, October 16, 1959*, 472-3, 485.

41. Ibid, 70.

42. "Glacier Peak Wilderness Hearings," *Living Wilderness* 24(71):35-37 (Winter 1959-60).

43. *Official Report...Glacier Peak Wilderness Area*, 169.

44. "Glacier Peak Wilderness Hearings," *Living Wilderness*. Washington Gov. Albert Rosellini had expressed a similar sentiment to the Mountaineers a year earlier; he favored high-elevation wilderness areas only, because timber was too important (Rosellini to Wiseman, June 12, 1958, box 2, Mountaineers Papers, UW).

45. "Glacier Peak Wilderness Hearings," *Living Wilderness*.

46. Ibid.

47. "Three Positions Emerge from Wilderness Area Testimony," *Wenatchee World*, October 18, 1959.

48. Both the N3C and the Mountaineers kept tallies at the hearings. See *NCCC News* 3(11): 1 (November 1959), and "The Line-Up at Glacier Peak Hearings," *The Mountaineer* 53(1):4-5 (January 1960). For other media coverage, see "Wilderness Area Plan Debated Before Hearing," *Bellingham Herald*, October 13, 1959; "Arguments Heard on Wilderness," *Seattle Times*, October 13, 1959; "Conflicting Views on Glacier Peak," *Seattle Times*, October 13, 1959; "Wilderness Area Hearing Stormy," *Wenatchee World*, October 16, 1959; "Glacier Peak Plan Hit by Mountaineers," *Seattle Times*, October 16, 1959; "Friends, Foes of Wilderness Area Heard," *Seattle Times*, October 17, 1959; "Wilderness Area Testimony Taken in Wenatchee," *Bellingham Herald*, October 18, 1959.

49. Conservationists got a little boost when an Interior Department advisory committee recommended conducting a joint study of the North Cascades to determine the region's best use. The recommendation, released simultaneously with the hearings in Bellingham and Wenatchee, was reported adjacent to the coverage of the hearings in a few papers. See "Lake Chelan National Park Recommended," *Wenatchee World*, October 16, 1959; "Park Proposed," *Seattle Times*, October 16, 1959.

50. Magnuson to Goldsworthy, July 24, 1958, box 17, Donald H. Magnuson Papers (D. Magnuson Papers), UW; Goldsworthy to Pelly, December 7, 1958, box 14, Pelly Papers.

51. Goldsworthy to McArdle, December 3, 1958, box 14, Pelly Papers, UW; McArdle to Goldsworthy, December 17, 1958, box 14, Pelly Papers, UW.

52. Goldsworthy to Pelly, February 12, 1959, box 2, Zalesky Papers, UW.

53. Pelly to Brady, December 18, 1959, box 16, Pelly Papers, UW; quote from Pelly to Mountaineers, September 24, 1959, box 14, Pelly Papers, UW.

54. Pelly to Goldsworthy, February 23, 1959, box 14, Pelly Papers, UW.

55. Brower to Pelly, March 7, 1959, box 14, Pelly Papers, UW; also in folder 2, carton 13, BANC MSS 2002/230c, Office of the Executive Director, Sierra Club Records, BL.

56. Pelly to Wirth, March 9, 1959, box 1, McConnell Papers, UW.

57. Ibid.

58. Ernst to Pelly, March 25, 1959, box 14, Pelly Papers, UW.

59. Diederich to Goldsworthy, June 22, 1959, box 2, Zalesky Papers, UW; Scoyen to Pelly, June 22, 1959, box 14, Pelly Papers, UW.

60. Pelly to McArdle, July 15, 1959, box 14, Pelly Papers, UW.

61. McArdle to Pelly, August 24, 1959, box 14, Pelly Papers, UW.

62. Wirth to Seaton, August 31, 1959, Seaton to Benson, September 22, 1959, Investigative Projects, box 175; Central Classified Files, 1959 1963; Records of the Office of the Secretary of the Interior (Interior Records), Record Group 48 (RG 48), National Archives at College Park, College Park, MD (NACP).

63. Magnuson to Goldsworthy, April 6, 1959, box 17, D. Magnuson Papers, UW.

64. Goldsworthy to May, November 26, 1959, Ernst to Pelly, November 3, 1959, box 14, Pelly Papers, UW.

65. Pelly to Goldsworthy, December 31, 1959, box 14, Pelly Papers, UW. Rep. Pelly sent copies of the draft bill to the N3C, asking for edits (Pelly and D. Magnuson to Goldsworthy, December 15, 1959, box 2, Zalesky Papers, UW).

66. H.R. 9342, 86th Cong., 2nd Sess., *Congressional Record*, 106, pt. 1 (January 6, 1960); H.R. 9360, 86th Cong., 2nd Sess., *Congressional Record*, 106, pt. 1 (January 6, 1960). It's not clear why two identical bills were introduced. Both congressmen had asked the N3C for input on the bills' text; see Pelly and D. Magnuson to Goldsworthy, December 15, 1959, box 2, Zalesky Papers, UW.

67. "Champion and Candidate," *Life*, September 8, 1952, 47.

68. S. 2980, 86th Cong., 2nd Sess., *Congressional Record*, 106, pt. 2 (February 4, 1960). The current iteration of the Interior and Insular Affairs Committee is the Energy & Natural Resources Committee, which deals with public lands issues.

69. "North Cascades Park Study Bills Introduced," *The Mountaineer* 53(2):3 (February 1960).

70. See *NCCC News*, 4(2) (February 1960), 4(3) (March 1960), 4(5) (May 1960).

71. Magnuson to Goldsworthy, July 7, 1960, box 17, D. Magnuson Papers, UW.

72. Goldsworthy to Brower, June 17, 1958, box III, Goldsworthy Papers.

73. Goldsworthy to Brower, December 22, 1958 (two letters), box IV-AR, Goldsworthy Papers.

74. Ibid.

75. Brower to Pelly, March 7, 1959; Brower to Wirth, March 7, 1959, Office of the Executive Director, BANC MSS 2002/230c, Sierra Club Records, Bancroft Library, Berkeley.

76. Jackson to Goldsworthy, April 24, 1959, BANC MSS 71/103c, Conservation Department, Historic Conservation Files, Sierra Club Records, BL.

77. Mark W. T. Harvey, *A Symbol of Wilderness: Echo Park and the American Conservation Movement* (Albuquerque: University of New Mexico Press, 1994).

78. Echo Park taught conservationists the importance of on-the-ground knowledge. Instead of an Echo Park dam, they agreed to one at Glen Canyon, realizing too late it was even more spectacular. (See Harvey, *A Symbol of Wilderness*, 222-234; Michael Cohen, *The History of the Sierra Club, 1892-1970* [San Francisco: Sierra Club Books, 1988]).

79. Mark T. Harvey, *Wilderness Forever: Howard Zahniser and the Path to the Wilderness Act* (Seattle: University of Washington Press, 2005), esp. ch. 13.

80. One co-sponsor was Oregon Sen. Richard Neuberger, whose fury about the Forest Service's Three Sisters Wilderness decision led him to become one of the bill's most ardent supporters until his death in 1960.

81. Harvey, *Wilderness Forever*, 198.

82. *Multiple-Use and Sustained Yield Act of 1960*, Public Law 86-517, 86th Congress (June 12, 1960), section 4(a). See also Forest History Society, "The Fully Managed, Multiple-Use Forest Era, 1960-1970," *The USDA Forest Service: The First Century*, accessed March 10, 2016, http://www.foresthistory.org/ASPNET/Publications/first_century/sec7.htm.

83. Quoted in Delbert V. Mercure Jr., and William M. Ross, "The Wilderness Act: A Product of Congressional Compromise," in *Congress and the Environment*, Richard A. Cooley and Geoffrey Wandesforde-Smith, eds. (Seattle: University of Washington Press, 1970), 54.

84. *Multiple-Use and Sustained Yield Act of 1960*, section 2.

85. McArdle to Stone, July 29, 1960, 2320 Glacier Peak Wilderness Area, 1959-1967, Region 6, FS, RG 95, NARA-APR.

86. "Decision of the Secretary of Agriculture Establishing the Glacier Peak Wilderness Area, Mt. Baker and Wenatchee National Forests, Washington," September 6, 1960, "Glacier Peak Wilderness Area Decision 9-6-60," Region 6, FS, RG 95, NARA-APR.

87. "Decision of the Secretary of Agriculture Establishing the Glacier Peak Wilderness Area."

88. "A Job One-Fourth Done," *NCCC News* 4(10): 1 (October 1960).

89. Ibid.

90. Grant McConnell, "The North Cascades Wilderness—Almost Half Safe," *Sierra Club Bulletin* 45(7) (October 1960).

91. Kevin R. Marsh, "Drawing Lines in the Woods," 85.

92. Michael Frome, *Battle for the Wilderness*, rev. ed. (Salt Lake City: University of Utah Press, 1997), 135.

93. Halliday to Stone, March 27, 1959, US Forest Service, Mt. Baker-Snoqualmie National Forest, Alpha Files: U-Recreation & Lands, 1905-57, RG 95, box 3, NARA-APR.

5. A Freshening Political Wind

1. Samuel P. Hays, *Beauty, Health, and Permanence: Environmental Politics in the United States, 1955–1985* (Cambridge: Cambridge University Press, 1987), 53.

2. See Elmo Richardson, *Dams, Parks & Politics: Resource Development & Preservation in the Truman-Eisenhower Era* (Lexington: University Press of Kentucky, 1973); Harvey, *Wilderness Forever*; and Hays, *Beauty, Health, and Permanence*.

3. Harvey, *A Symbol of Wilderness*, 221.

4. Harvey, *Wilderness Forever*, 219, 214.

5. Michael P. Cohen, *The History of the Sierra Club, 1892–1970*, San Francisco: Sierra Club Books, 1988), 243. In fact, Brower wrote a long letter to Udall a week before Kennedy's inauguration in January 1961, suggesting several names for key Interior Department positions—including his own (Brower to Udall, January 13, 1961, AZ 372, Series V: Personal Files, 1950–1977, folder 4, box 190, "'Personal: Special Correspondents, Brower, David R., 1961–1966," Stewart L. Udall Papers [Udall Papers], University of Arizona Library [UA]).

6. "The Golden Year for the Golden Triangle," *NCCC News* 5(5) (May 1961).

7. Becker, Paula, "Pelly, Thomas M. (1902–1973)," *HistoryLink*, January 4, 2005, www.historylink.org/index.cfm?DisplayPage=output.cfm&file_id=7199.

8. Roger Sale, *Seattle Past to Present* (Seattle: University of Washington Press, 1976), especially Chapter 6, "The Boeing Years." Quote from 180.

9. Sale, *Seattle Past to Present*, 180, 186, 190, quoted at 196, 194. All statistics in this and previous paragraph are from this source.

10. Williams, *U.S. Forest Service in the Pacific Northwest*, 235.
11. John Steinbeck, *Travels with Charley*, excerpt reprinted in Bruce Barcott, ed., *Northwest Passages* (Seattle: Sasquatch Books, 1994), 221.
12. H.R. 2056, 87th Cong., 1st Sess., *Congressional Record*, vol. 107, pt. 1 (January 6, 1961).
13. Edwards Park, "Washington Wilderness, the North Cascades," *National Geographic*, March 1961, 334–367. Only Mississippi had no signatories on the petitions.
14. "Grassroots Support of North Cascade Park Study," 87th Cong., 1st Sess., *Congressional Record*, vol. 107, pt. 1 (June 7, 1961).
15. In fact, the Waldo Lake issue was brought to Morse's attention by Mike McCloskey, who had organized Students for Morse in 1956 and, as president of Young Democrats of Oregon, became acquainted with Scoop Jackson and Warren Magnuson. By the time the High Mountain Policy came along, he "had no trouble moving in and out of those offices" (McCloskey, interview); J. Michael McCloskey, "The Product of an Appeal: The New High Mountain Policy," *NCCC News* 6(6): 6–7 (June 1962).
16. William O. Douglas, *My Wilderness: The Pacific West* (Garden City, NY: Doubleday & Co., Inc., 1960), includes a chapter on Glacier Peak that argues for its importance as wilderness.
17. Morse and Jackson to Freeman, May 4, 1961, 2320 Glacier Peak Wilderness Area 1959–1967, Region 6, FS, RG 95, NARA-APR. Douglas's involvement likely was prompted by the proposal to develop national forest around Copper City, an abandoned mining town near his cabin at Goose Prairie, about forty miles northwest of Yakima. The Minam River in northeastern Oregon drains the Wallowa Mountains; its source is now protected in Eagle Cap Wilderness.
18. Paul Hirt, *A Conspiracy of Optimism: Management of the National Forests Since World War Two* (Lincoln: University of Nebraska Press, 1994), 226.
19. Freeman to Morse et al., June 7, 1961, 2320 Glacier Peak Wilderness Area 1959–1967.
20. McNeil to Linstedt, July 5, 1961, 2150 Special Planning Areas, High Mountain Task Force 1961–1962, Region 6, FS, RG 95, USFS, NARA-APR.
21. "Orville Freeman, 84, Dies; 60's Agriculture Secretary," *New York Times*, February 22, 2003, www.nytimes.com/2003/02/22/us/orville-freeman-84-dies-60-s-agriculture-secretary.html?pagewanted=1.
22. Thomas G. Smith, "John Kennedy, Stewart Udall, and New Frontier Conservation," *The Pacific Historical Quarterly* 64:3 (August 1995): 329–362.
23. "The Saddest, Least Necessary Feud of All," *Desert*, November 1961, reprinted in *Wild Cascades* 6(2): 5 (February 1962). See also Julius Duscha, "The Undercover Fight Over the Wilderness," *Harper's* 224 (1343):55–59 (April 1962).
24. John B. Oakes, "Conservation: Fight for Parks," *New York Times*, October 2, 1960.
25. John B. Oakes, "Conservation: The Parks Issue," *New York Times*, November 13, 1960.
26. "Multiple Use," *New York Times*, June 27, 1960.
27. "Text of President Kennedy's Special Message to Congress on Natural Resources," *New York Times*, February 24, 1961.
28. "Kennedy on Natural Resources," *New York Times*, February 24, 1961.
29. "Crisis in Natural Resources," *New York Times*, February 26, 1961.
30. Nona B. Brown, "Park Plan for Tomorrow," *New York Times*, July 30, 1961.
31. Tiny Virgin Islands National Park was added to the system in 1956.
32. Heald to Goldsworthy, July 10, 1961, box X, Goldsworthy Papers.
33. Heald to Douglas, October 26, 1961, reel 1 (microfilm), Warth Papers, UW.
34. Goldsworthy to Heald, October 27, 1961, Heald to Goldsworthy, November 1, 1961, box 62, Brock Evans Papers (B. Evans Papers), UW.
35. Spring to Udall, June 14, 1961; Udall to Spring, July 12, 1961, L-58 North Cascades, Recreation Planning, Pacific Northwest Region Records, NPS, RG 79, NARA-APR.

36. Smith, "John Kennedy, Stewart Udall, and New Frontier Conservation," 340.
37. David Brower, "The Sierra Club and the North Cascades," February 16, 1961, box X, Goldsworthy Papers.
38. McConnell to Brower, October 1, 1960; October 2, 1960, box 1, McConnell Papers, UW.
39. Brower to Gallagher, October 9, 1961, box 62, B. Evans Papers, UW.
40. "Northwest Conservation Representative Appointed," *Sierra Club Bulletin* 46(9):3 (November 1961).
41. Cohen, *History of the Sierra Club*, 310, 269.
42. J. Michael McCloskey, Northern Cascades National Park bill (first draft), November 16, 1961, box 2, B. Evans Papers, UW.
43. Brower to Dickey et al., November 30, 1961, box 1, McConnell Papers, UW.
44. Brower to Udall, 12/7/61 (typed version of handwritten note, emphasis in original), box 62, B. Evans Papers, UW. The other two priorities were the California redwoods and Rainbow Bridge, Arizona. Handwritten note, Brower to Udall, December 7, 1961, folder 4, "Personal: Special Correspondents, Brower, David R., 1961–1966,"AZ 372, Box 190, Series V: Personal Files, 1950–1977, Udall Papers, UA.
45. North Cascades Conservation Council, report on meeting with Sen.Warren Magnuson, November 27, 1961, box 62, B. Evans Papers, UW.
46. Brower to Udall, December 15, 1961, folder 4, "Personal: Special Correspondents, Brower, David R., 1961–1966," Udall Papers, UA.
47. Douglas to Brower, December 12, 1961, box 2 (pre-processing), B. Evans Papers, UW.
48. Brower to Udall, December 7, 1961, folder 4,"Personal: Special Correspondents, Brower, David R., 1961–1966,"Udall Papers, UA; Brower to Feldman, December 8, 1961, box 62, B. Evans Papers, UW; Brower to Udall, December 15, 1961, folder 4, "Personal: Special Correspondents, Brower, David R., 1961–1966," Udall Papers, UA.
49. Heald to Warth, November 29, 1961, box 1 (pre-processing), B. Evans Papers, UW.
50. The tactic of having a national monument created by a sympathetic president, often with the goal of eventual national park status, was not new. Since enactment in 1906 of the Antiquities Act, presidents sometimes expanded the definition of protecting "objects of historic and scientific interest" to include places that were arguably not intended in the original law. For example, the Olympic Peninsula's endemic Roosevelt elk were protected by President Theodore Roosevelt in the Mount Olympus National Monument, which was expanded three decades later into Olympic National Park. Grand Canyon National Monument, also created by Roosevelt, was challenged in court but upheld, and the national park was created about ten years later. President Jimmy Carter proclaimed fifteen national monuments comprising fifty-six million acres in Alaska in anticipation of 1980's Alaska National Interest Lands Conservation Act; several have since been made national parks.
51. "Needed: New National Parks—I," *New York Times*, January 2, 1962; "Needed: New National Parks—II," *New York Times*, January 3, 1962.
52. Duscha, "The Undercover Fight Over the Wilderness."
53. Outdoor Recreation Resources Review Commission, "Outdoor Recreation in America: A Report to the President and to the Congress by the Outdoor Recreation Resources Review Commission" (Washington, DC: GPO, January 1962).
54. "Text of Kennedy's Conservation Message Asking an Expanded 8-Year Program," *New York Times*, March 2, 1962.
55. "Udall Urges Aid on Conservation," *New York Times*, May 25, 1962.
56. "Census Linked to Sharing of National Forest," *New York Times*, May 17, 1962.
57. For example, see Donald Whisenhunt, *The Environment and the American Experience* (Port Washington, NY: Kennikat Press, 1974).

58. Roderick Nash, *Wilderness and the American Mind,* rev. ed. (New Haven: Yale University Press, 1973), 237.

59. Cohen, *History of the Sierra Club.* Much of this growth can be attributed to the club's leadership and activism on the Echo Park dam issue, which it successfully transformed into a national referendum on development versus preservation.

60. AMW to Recreation File, June 9, 1934, 2320 Wilderness & Primitive Areas, North Cascade Primitive Area, 1934–1962, in-service correspondence, Recreation Planning, Region 6, FS, RG 95, NARA-APR; Fred W. Cleator, "Report on North Cascade Primitive Area," U.S. Department of Agriculture, Forest Service, July 28, 1934, 2320 Wilderness & Primitive Areas, North Cascade Primitive Area, Recreation Planning.

61. Writing anonymously in the inaugural issue of *The Living Wilderness,* Bob Marshall noted the new primitive area was the "second largest potential forest wilderness remaining in the United States"—and then urged that the area south of the North Cascade Primitive Area, from Ruby Creek to Glacier Peak, be designated wilderness as well. It was not, of course, and the Glacier Peak controversy was a direct result ["Three Great Western Wildernesses—What Must be Done to Save Them?" *The Living Wilderness* 1(1): 9–11 (September 1935)].

62. An undated Forest Service report shows visitation at 502 in 1942, 1,385 in 1950, and 3,960 in 1960 ["North Cascade Wilderness Area," n.d. {probably early 1961}, 2320 Wilderness & Primitive Areas, North Cascade Primitive Area, 1934–1962, in-service correspondence, Recreation Planning].

63. Fred Beckey, *Cascade Alpine Guide: Climbing & High Routes, Vol. 3: Rainy Pass to Fraser River,* 2nd ed. (Seattle: Mountaineers, 1995), 94.

64. Cleator, "Report on North Cascade Primitive Area."

65. William N. Parke, "Report on the Reclassification of the North Cascade Primitive Area," January 26, 1950, 2320 Wilderness & Primitive Areas, North Cascade Primitive Area, 1934–1962, in-service correspondence, Recreation Planning.

66. John Suiter, *Poets on the Peaks: Gary Snyder, Philip Whalen & Jack Kerouac in the North Cascades* (Washington, DC: Counterpoint, 2002). Quote from Jack Kerouac, *The Dharma Bums,* 1958, in Bruce Barcott, ed., *Northwest Passages,* 207.

67. Charles D. Hessey Jr., "Across the North Cascade Primitive Area," *Living Wilderness* 25(74):5–9 (Fall-Winter 1960–1961).

68. J. B. Hogan and J. R. Mitchell, "North Cascade Wilderness Area," *Living Wilderness* 18(46):14–15 (Autumn 1953).

69. Stone to Mt. Baker, Okanogan, Snoqualmie and Wenatchee National Forest Supervisors, June 7, 1960; Stone to forest supervisors, June 14, 1960; 2320 Wilderness & Primitive Areas, North Cascade Primitive Area, 1934–1962, in-service correspondence, Recreation Planning.

70. U. S. Department of Agriculture, Forest Service, Pacific Northwest Region, *Study and Reclassification of the North Cascades [sic] Primitive Area,* 1960. 2320 Wilderness & Primitive Areas, North Cascade Primitive Area 1934–1962, Maps-Reports-Photos-Releases, Recreation Planning.

71. Mailing list in 2320 North Cascades Study 1960–1965, Historical Collection, ca. 1902–1985, Portland, OR, Region 6, FS, RG 95, NARA-APR.

72. Chriswell to Goldsworthy, June 27, 1960, 2320 Wilderness & Primitive Areas, North Cascade Primitive Area, 1934–1962, in-service correspondence, Recreation Planning; "North Cascades Primitive Area Under Study," *The Mountaineer* 53(12):3 (November 1960).

73. A. E. Spaulding, "Summary of Observations at Annual Meeting of the Wilderness Society, Winthrop, Washington, August 6–11, 1961," 2320 Wilderness & Primitive

Areas, North Cascade Primitive Area, 1934–1962, in-service correspondence, Recreation Planning.

74. See "The Wilderness in the North Cascades" and "North Cascades Wilderness Area Proposal," *Wild Cascades* June–July 1964, 11–19.

75. "Another Battle?" *The Mountaineer* 53(10):6 (September 1960).

76. "Mountaineers' Recommendations on North Cascades Primitive Area," *The Mountaineer* 54(2):6–7 (February 1961); Department of Agriculture, Forest Service, Pacific Northwest Region, "Report on Proposed North Cascade Wilderness Area, Mt. Baker and Okanogan National Forests, Washington," February 6, 1962, 2320 Wilderness & Primitive Areas, North Cascade Primitive Area, folder #3, Maps-Reports-Photos-Releases, Recreation Planning.

77. Forest Service, "Report on Proposed North Cascade Wilderness Area."

78. Ibid.

79. Department of Agriculture, Forest Service, Pacific Northwest Region, "North Cascade Wilderness Area," n.d. (probably early 1961), 2320 Wilderness & Primitive Areas, North Cascade Primitive Area, folder 1, in-service correspondence.

80. Aspinall to Freeman, April 9, 1962; Welch to Aspinall, April 17, 1962, 2320 Wilderness & Primitive Areas, North Cascade Primitive Area, 1934–1962, Recreation Planning, Region 6, FS, RG 95, NARA-APR; *A Bill to Establish a National Wilderness Preservation System*, S. 174, 87th Cong., 1st sess., *Congressional Record*, January 5, 1961.

81. Department of Agriculture, Forest Service, *Management Objectives and Policies for the High Mountain Areas of the National Forests of the Pacific Northwest Region*, April 1962, Region 6 Historical Collection ca. 1905–1985, FS, RG 95, NARA-APR.

82. Forest Service, *Management Objectives and Policies*, 3.

83. Forest Service, *Management Objectives and Policies*.

84. Pelly to Freeman, June 19, 1962, and Freeman to Pelly, June 27, 1962, 2100–2310 Special Planning Areas 1927–1973 North Cascades, Mt. Baker-Snoqualmie National Forest Supervisor's Office, FS, RG 95, NARA-APR.

85. Stone to Cliff, June 28, 1962, 2100-2310 Special Planning Areas 1927-1973.

86. Magnuson to Freeman, August 14, 1962, folder 15 Ag-FS-NC Logging Moratorium, box 122, Warren G. Magnuson Papers (W. Magnuson Papers), UW.

87. Baker to Pelly, September 13, 1962, 2100–2310 Special Planning Areas 1927–1973.

6. The Peace of the Potomac

1. "Don Magnuson, ex-congressman, dead at 68," *Lewiston Morning Tribune*, October 8, 1979, news.google.com/newspapers?id=WcpeAAAAIBAJ&sjid=YjIMAAAAIBAJ&pg=1987,2973493&hl=en.

2. Kit Oldham, "Jackson, Henry M. 'Scoop' (1912–1983)," August 19, 2003, *HistoryLink*, historylink.org/File/5516.

3. Kit Oldham, "Magnuson, Warren G. (1905–1989), October 14, 2003, *HistoryLink*, historylink.org/File/5569.

4. Freeman and Udall to Kennedy, January 28, 1963; and Kennedy to Freeman and Udall, January 31, 1963, reprinted in North Cascades Study Team, *The North Cascades Study Report* (Washington, DC: GPO, October 1965). See also "Federal Feud Ends on Recreation Land," *New York Times*, February 2, 1963.

5. J. Michael McCloskey, *In the Thick of It: My Life in the Sierra Club* (Washington, DC: Island Press, 2005), 43.

6. Udall and Freeman to Crafts, March 5, 1963, reprinted in Study Team, *Study Report*.

7. Charles F. Hessey Jr., "Report on Trip with Forests Subcommittee, House Agriculture Committee, October 2 & 3, 1961," a report to the North Cascades Conservation Council, box 9, Osseward Papers, UW.

8. Harold K. Steen, *The Chiefs Remember: The Forest Service, 1952–2001* (Durham, NC: Forest History Society, 2004), 13–17, quote at 16.

9. For more on McArdle's retirement and replacement, see Paul Hirt, *A Conspiracy of Optimism: Management of the National Forests Since World War Two* (Lincoln: University of Nebraska Press, 1994), 220–221, and Steen, *The Chiefs Remember*, 27–28.

10. "The ORRRC Doom Fulfilled," *Wild Cascades* 6(5): 3 (May 1962).

11. Udall and Freeman to Crafts, March 5, 1963, reprinted in Study Team, *Study Report*.

12. Udall and Freeman to Crafts, March 5, 1963, North Cascades, Interior and Insular Affairs Committee, U.S. Senate Records 89A-F11, National Archives Building, Washington, DC.

13. Crafts to Cole, May 20, 1963, 2150 Special Planning Areas (North Cascades Study Team), FY 1963, Region 6–North Cascades Records, FS, RG 95, NARA-APR.

14. David Brower rued the inability of conservationists to successfully assign economic value to wilderness, because if wilderness could be considered a resource with economic value, it would be easier to argue for its preservation (see Douglas H. Strong, *Dreamers and Defenders: American Conservationists* [Lincoln: University of Nebraska Press, 1988], 206).

15. Department of the Interior, "Stratton Named Member of North Cascades Study Team; Succeeds Caulfield" (press release), September 27, 1963.

16. Selke to Greeley, August 7, 1963, 2150 Special Planning Areas, July–September 1963, Joint Study of North Cascades, Region 6 North Cascades Study Records, FS, RG 95, NARA-APR.

17. Greeley to Selke, August 13, 1963, 2150 Special Planning Areas, North Cascades Study folder no. 2., Region 6 North Cascades Records, FS, RG 95, NARA-APR.

18. Greeley to Stone, August 14, 1963, 2320 North Cascades Study, 1960–1965, Region 6 Historical Collection ca. 1902–1985, FS, RG 95, NARA-APR.

19. Selke to Greeley, August 7, 1963, 2150 Special Planning Areas, July–September 1963, Joint Study of North Cascades, Region 6.

20. Greeley to Selke, August 13, 1963, 2150 Special Planning Areas, North Cascades Study folder no. 2., Region 6 North Cascades Records, FS, RG 95, NARA-APR.

21. Alan J. Stein, "Century 21–The Seattle World's Fair, Part 1," April 18, 2000, *HistoryLink*, historylink.org/File/2290; Alan J. Stein, "Century 21–The Seattle World's Fair, Part II," April 19, 2000, *HistoryLink*, historylink.org/File/2291; "Boeing Spacearium Interior Model, Seattle World's Fair, January, 1962," Alden B. Couch Photographs of the Seattle World's Fair, PH Coll 1021, Seattle Photograph Collection, UW.

22. See "The New Strategy: Summer 1963," *Wild Cascades* May-June-July 1963, 2.

23. Joel Connelly, "Patrick Goldsworthy: An Appreciation," *Strange Bedfellows*, October 7, 2013, blog.seattlepi.com/seattlepolitics/2013/10/07/patrick-goldsworthy-an-appreciation/.

24. Goldsworthy, interview.

25. J. Michael McCloskey, interview.

26. J. Michael McCloskey, ed., *Prospectus for a North Cascades National Park* (Seattle: North Cascades Conservation Council, 1963).

27. McCloskey, *Prospectus*, S-4, S-5.

28. McCloskey, interview.

29. "The New Strategy: Summer 1963," *Wild Cascades* May-June-July 1963, 2.

30. McConnell to Brower, September 7, 1963, box 2 (pre-processing), B. Evans Papers, UW.

31. Mount Vernon was added at the request of Rep. Jack Westland (R-WA), whose opposition to the park proposal had become more entrenched (*Congressional Record*, 88th Cong., 1st Sess., 1963, pt. 5: 6724). Westland argued communities potentially affected by

a national park deserved a fair chance to make their views known. He wanted hearings at Bellingham, Everett, and Sedro Woolley, but the Study Team declined, adding only Mount Vernon to the schedule. Westland to Crafts, August 14, 1963; "Announcement of Field Meetings by North Cascades Mountains Study Team" (press release), September 20, 1963; 2320 North Cascades Study, 1960–1965, Historical Collection ca. 1902–1985, Region 6, FS, RG 95, NARA-APR.

32. See J. Michael McCloskey, "North Cascades Study Team: Progress in the Study of the North Cascades," *The Wild Cascades*, August–September 1963, 3–4.

33. Patrick Goldsworthy, "The Northern Cascades on the Witness Stand," *Sierra Club Bulletin* 48(8): 2, 18 (November 1963); "North Cascades Recreation Study, Revised July 24, 1963," folder 2150 Special Planning Areas, North Cascades Study, file 2 of 4, Decimal Files 2100-2310, Special Planning Areas, 1927–1973, North Cascades, Mount Baker-Snoqualmie National Forest Supervisor's Office records, FS, RG 95, NARA-APR.

34. "People Speak; Team Listens," *Wenatchee World*, October 7, 1963; "Opinion Split on Park Idea," *Wenatchee World*, October 8, 1963.

35. "People Speak," *Wenatchee World*; "Opinion Split on Park Idea," *Wenatchee World*; "Recreationists Testify for Cascades Park," *Seattle Times*, October 8, 1963.

36. Byron Fish, "'Organizations' End 'Testimony' for National-Park Study in State," *Seattle Times*, November 12, 1963.

37. "61 Testify at Hearing on N. Cascades Park Proposal," *Skagit Valley Herald*, October 10, 1963; Ned Carrick, "Cascades Park Proposal is Opposed by Speakers," *Everett Herald*, October 9, 1963; "Opponents Rap Plan for Park in North Cascades," *Skagit Valley Herald*, October 9, 1963; "Debate Centers on Use of North Cascades for Park," *Skagit Valley Herald*, October 10, 1963.

38. "Petitions with 22,000 Names Favor North Cascades Park," *Seattle Times*, October 10, 1963; "Chamber Speaker: Creation of Park in Cascades Fought," *Seattle Times*, October 11, 1963; "Park in Cascades Urged at Hearing," *New York Times*, October 20, 1963.

39. "We're Against National Park in North Cascades," *Everett Herald*, October 8, 1963; "No Park, Says Majority," *Skagit Valley Herald*, October 10, 1963; Enos Bradner, "A New National Park—Who Needs It?" *Seattle Times*, October 10, 1963; "Local Opinion had it's [sic] Say; How Well will it be Heard?" *Wenatchee World*, October 9, 1963.

40. Study Team, *Study*, 79–84.

41. J. M. McCloskey, "Schedule for Developing National and Statewide Support for a North Cascades National Park," October 27, 1963, box 3 (pre-processing), B. Evans Papers, UW.

42. Miles, *Wilderness and National Parks: Playground or Preserve* (Seattle: University of Washington Press, 2009), 163, 129.

43. William M. Blair, "Park Service Due for Big Changes," *New York Times*, October 17, 1963; Thomas G. Smith, "John Kennedy, Stewart Udall, and New Frontier Conservation," *The Pacific Historical Review* 64:3 (August 1995), 329–362.

44. Udall to Jackson, September 13, 1963, Investigative Projects, Box 175; Central Classified Files, 1959 1963; Records of the Office of the Secretary of the Interior, RG 48, NACP.

45. "Opinion Split on Park Idea," *Wenatchee World*.

46. Patrick Goldsworthy, "Crisis, Sorrow and Horizons," *The Wild Cascades*, December 1963 January 1964, 2.

47. Harvey Manning, *The North Cascades* (Seattle: The Mountaineers, 1964), 92.

48. Murray Morgan, "New Books," *Seattle Argus*, October 2, 1964.

49. Harvey Manning, personal interview by the author, tape recording, Issaquah, WA, September 30, 2003.

50. J. Michael McCloskey, "Resource Reports," *The Wild Cascades*, April–May 1964, 4–5.

51. Department of Agriculture and Department of the Interior, "Outdoor Recreation in the North Cascades Today and Tomorrow: A Recreation Sub-Study for the North Cascade Mountains Study Team," 1963, Region 6 Publications, FS, RG 95, NARA-APR.

52. Harvey Manning, "Strike Up the Band," *The Wild Cascades*, April–May 1964, 11–18.

53. Crafts to Rosellini, April 9, 1964, 2150 Special Planning Areas, Joint Study of North Cascades, Feb 64–June 65, FS, RG 95, NARA-APR.

54. "News Release," Governor's Office, 1962, Box 4, Preston Macy Papers (Macy Papers), UW; Rosellini to Locke, May 20, 1963, folder Conservation Dept., Subject Files "Commerce & Economic Development, Tourism–Conservation Department, Water Resources, 1963," box 281, Albert D. Rosellini Papers, (Rosellini Papers), Washington State Archives (WSA). Members of the Council included State Parks director Charles H. Odegaard, Mount Rainier National Park superintendent Preston Macy, Weyerhaeuser executive Bernard Orell, J. Burton Lauckhart of the state Game Department, and N3C representative Emily Haig, among others. The Technical Committee included timber industry representatives from Crown Zellerbach, Boise Cascade, and Scott Paper, two forestry professors, one each from UW and WSU, a UW professor of mineral engineering, Lauckhart, Department of Natural Resources representative Mike Bigley, and representatives from State Parks and the railroad industry. It did not include anyone representing recreation interests.

55. Rosellini to Richards, February 1, 1963, box 4, Macy Papers, UW.

56. Technical Committee, Washington Forest Area Use Council, "North Cascades Report," May 8, 1964, box 4, Macy Papers, UW.

57. See Washington Forest Area Use Council, *North Cascades Report*, 1964; and "State Committee Reacts to Federal Study," *The Wild Cascades*, June–July 1964, 6–7.

58. Crafts to Rosellini, April 9, 1964, box 4, Macy Papers, UW; Rosellini to Crafts, June 5, 1964, 2150 Special Planning Areas, North Cascades Study, folder No. 3, Region 6–North Cascades, FS, RG 95, NARA-APR.

59. "Remarks of Governor Albert D. Rosellini, Annual Convention, Washington State Sportsmen's Council, Wenatchee, June 14, 1964," copy attached to letter, Stone to Greeley, June 30, 1964, 2150 Special Planning Areas, North Cascades Study, FY 1964 1st half, Region 6 North Cascades, FS, RG 95, NARA-APR.

60. Lauckhart to Kimball, April 12, 1963, 2150 Special Planning Areas (North Cascades Study Team), FY 1963, Region 6 North Cascades, FS, RG 95, NARA-APR.

61. *The Wild Cascades*, August–September 1964, 4.

62. Mark W. T. Harvey, *Wilderness Forever: Howard Zahniser and the Path to the Wilderness Act* (Seattle: University of Washington Press, 2005).

63. *The Wilderness Act*, Public Law 88-577, U.S. Code 16 (1964), §2(c).

64. Harvey, *Wilderness Forever*, 202.

65. *The Wilderness Act*, Public Law 88-577.

66. Thomas G. Smith, "John Kennedy, Stewart Udall, and New Frontier Conservation," *The Pacific Historical Review* 64:3 (August 1995): 329–62, quote at 341.

67. Harvey, *Wilderness Forever*, 229.

68. Dennis Roth, *The Wilderness Movement and the National Forests* (College Station, TX: Intaglio Press, 1995), 11.

69. Roth, *Wilderness Movement and the National Forests*, 12; Miles, *Wilderness and the National Parks*, 156.

70. "The Saddest, Least Necessary Feud of All," *Desert*, November 1961, reprinted in *Wild Cascades* 6(2): 5 (February 1962).

71. McConnell to McCloskey, September 19, 1964, Office of the Executive Director, folder 2, carton 13, BANC MSS 2002/230c, Sierra Club Records, BL.

72. Wall apparently had no compunction about playing hardball on wilderness issues. At the end of 1959, when the Glacier Peak hearings had ended, he sent a memo to his employees asking them not to patronize the medical clinic of Don Fager, a Wenatchee physician and N3C member who spoke in support of a large Glacier Peak Wilderness. [Prater to Brower, December 14, 1959, Office of the Executive Director, folder 9, carton 13, BANC MSS 2002/230c, Sierra Club Records, BL.]

73. J. Michael McCloskey, "News Notes on North Cascades," *The Wild Cascades*, October–November 1964, 2–3.

74. McCloskey moved up in the Sierra Club, becoming executive director after Brower left in 1969, a position he held for sixteen years.

75. "Recreation Area Formed," *Wenatchee World*, February 23, 1965.

76. "Decision of the Secretary of Agriculture Establishing the Glacier Peak Wilderness Area, Mt. Baker and Wenatchee National Forests, Washington," September 6, 1960, "Glacier Peak Wilderness Area Decision 9-6-60," Region 6 Regional Forester Records, FS, RG 95, NARA-APR.

77. See Michael McCloskey, "A New Phase in the Cascades Campaign," *Sierra Club Bulletin* 50(6): 22 (June 1965).

78. Goldsworthy to Jackson, March 13, 1965, 2150 Special Planning Areas Moratorium Areas (20 Tracts in Northern Cascades), Decimal Files 2100-2310 Special Planning Areas 1927–1973, Mt. Baker-Snoqualmie National Forest Supervisor's Office, FS, RG 95, NARA-APR.

79. Stone to Goldsworthy, March 19, 1965, 2150 Special Planning Areas Moratorium Areas (20 Tracts in Northern Cascades), Decimal Files 2100-2310 Special Planning Areas 1927–1973, Mt. Baker-Snoqualmie National Forest Supervisor's Office, FS, RG 95, NARA-APR.

80. "A proposal to Create a Cascade–Mt. Baker National Recreation Area on the Mt. Baker & Okanogan National Forests of the Pacific Northwest Region, May 1964," Region 6 Publications, FS, RG, NARA-APR.

81. "A Summary Report on how the National Forest Lands in the North Cascades Study Area will be Managed by the U.S. Forest Service," November 1964, 2150 Special Planning Areas, North Cascades Study, FY 1965, 1st half, Region 6 Regional Forester Records, FS, RG 95, NARA-APR.

82. Greeley to Jackson, April 16, 1965, 2150 Special Planning Areas Moratorium Areas (20 Tracts in Northern Cascades), Decimal Files 2100-2310 Special Planning Areas 1927–1973, Mt. Baker-Snoqualmie National Forest Supervisor's Office, FS, RG 95, NARA-APR.

83. Crafts to Jackson, April 27, 1965, 2150 Special Planning Areas, North Cascades Study, FY 1965, 2nd half, Region 6 Regional Forest Records, FS, RG 95, NARA-APR. See also Rodger Pegues, "Outdoor Recreation Congress for the Pacific Northwest, Wenatchee, Wash.," *The Wild Cascades*, April–May 1965, 19–20.

84. John McPhee, *Encounters with the Archdruid* (New York: Farrar, Straus and Giroux, 1971), 15.

85. For more on the role of Exhibit Format books, see Cohen, *History of the Sierra Club*, 254–260; McPhee, *Encounters with the Archdruid*, 15.

86. Samuel Hays, *Beauty, Health, and Permanence*, 37.

87. Brower had been trying to get the book written for several years. He called Harvey Manning in March 1965 and by Memorial Day, Manning was finished, including the Foreword, which appeared under Douglas's signature. [Manning, interview; McCloskey, interview; Brower to Sierra Club Board and Publications Committee, June 18, 1963, box XV, Goldsworthy Papers; "Harvey Manning," *North Cascades Conservation Council*, www. northcascades.org/wordpress/in-memoriam/about-2.] Quotes from *The Wild Cascades* (San Francisco: Sierra Club Books, 1965), 17, 18.

88. Walt Woodward, "Woods are Full of Controversy," *Seattle Times*, June 13, 1965; "Park Proposal Pushed by Outdoor Clubs Official," *Seattle Times*, June 14, 1965; "Timber Interests Eye Park Proposal," Seattle Times, June 30, 1965; "N. Cascade Studied in '37," Seattle Times, June 29, 1965.
89. Walt Woodward, "National-Park Misconception Hit," *Seattle Times*, July 1, 1965; "9 Points Cited Against Park," *Seattle Times*, July 2, 1965; "Cole Favors 'Multiple Use' in North Cascades," *Seattle Times*, June 15, 1965; "Park Could be Wild and Mild," Seattle Times, June 23, 1965 "Park Advocate Replies," Seattle Times, July 4, 1965.
90. Walt Woodward, "Forest Service has Plan for North Cascades," *Seattle Times*, June 20, 1965.
91. Chriswell repeated this sentiment in an interview nearly forty years later, although he acknowledged that the Forest Service was trying to propose management plans that the Joint Study Team might find appealing. Chris Chriswell, personal interview by author, tape recording, Bellingham, WA, February 26, 2003.
92. Walt Woodward, "Mountaineers Push for Park in North Cascades," *Seattle Times*, June 25, 1965; "Evans Avoids Prejudging Land Decision," *Seattle Times*, June 27, 1965.
93. Walt Woodward, "Time Due for Action on Park," *Seattle Times*, July 5, 1965.
94. "First Banquet a Success," *The Wild Cascades*, August–September 1964, 26–27; Casey McNerthney, "Beatles' Stay at Edgewater Helped Mark its Place in History," n.d., *SeattlePI*, www.seattlepi.com/local/seattle-history/article/Beatles-stay-at-Edgewater-helped-mark-its-place-1433804.php.
95. Grant McConnell, "P.R. in the Forests," *The Nation* 201(22): 522–524 (December 27, 1965).
96. "Mongering Rumors," *The Wild Cascades*, October–November 1964, 2–3.

7. The National Stage
1. North Cascades Study Team, *The North Cascades: A Report to the Secretary of the Interior and the Secretary of Agriculture* (Washington, DC: GPO, 1965).
2. Study Team, *The North Cascades*, 15.
3. Study Team, *The North Cascades*, 17.
4. Study Team, *The North Cascades*, 76–79, 126–150.
5. Senate Committee on Interior and Insular Affairs, *The North Cascades*, 8.
6. "Adequate Access One Condition for Park," *Seattle Times*, January 6, 1966.
7. *National Park*, nos. 1–3, KIRO, week of January 17, 1966, box VIII, Goldsworthy Papers.
8. Lyle Burt, "North Cascade-Park Proposal Greeted by Mixed Reactions," *Seattle Times*, January 7, 1966.
9. McCloskey, interview.
10. NCCC Board of Directors Meeting, January 8, 1966, Motions, Goldsworthy Papers, Box II; "N. Cascades Council Offers New Park Plan," *Seattle Times*, January 10, 1966.
11. In fact, Jackson's chief of staff had recommended that the Subcommittee on Parks and Recreation host the hearings, so Jackson could "sit in objective participation" (Verkler to Jackson, January 11, 1966, North Cascades, Interior and Insular Affairs Committee files, U.S. Senate Records, NAB).
12. Northwest Conservation Representative Rod Pegues sent notice of the hearings to every member of the Federation of Western Outdoor Clubs (Pegues to Member Clubs, FWOC, January 25, 1966, box 1, B. Evans Papers, UW).
13. "Sen. Jackson Says North Cascades Legislation may be Introduced by April," *Wenatchee World*, February 11, 1966; Walt Woodward, "National Parks Hearing: State Authority on State Roads Urged," *Seattle Times*, February 11, 1966.
14. In fact, Jackson had formally requested the Bureau of the Budget draft a park bill several weeks earlier (Jackson to Schultze, January 20, 1966, folder 5, "Department of Interior: Issues and Achievements, National Parks—North Cascades, Washington, 1962–1967," box

156, Series II, Dept. of Interior, 1961–1972, AZ 372, Udall Papers, UA). Senate Committee on Interior and Insular Affairs, *North Cascades–Olympic National Park: Hearings Before the Committee on Interior and Insular Affairs*, 89th Cong., 2nd Sess., February 11–12, 1966, 5. Of course, now this tactic is commonplace. At the time, it was unusual enough that Jackson kept reminding witnesses of it when they pleaded for more study or other delays.

15. Senate Committee, *North Cascades–Olympic*, 59, 102.
16. Senate Committee, *North Cascades–Olympic*, 61–63, quote at 63.
17. Keith A. Murray, "Building a Wagon Road through the Northern Cascade Mountains," *Pacific Northwest Quarterly* 56(2): 49–56 (April 1965).
18. "Building the North Cascades Highway," *Washington Highways*, September 1972, 18.
19. *Guide to the Records of the Washington State Highways Department, 1923–1985* (Olympia: Office of Secretary of State, Division of Archives and Records Management, July 1999); Hoover to Finn, February 3, 1926, PSH #2-22, 1926, box B-23, Highways and Roads, Transportation Records, WSA.
20. Gretchen A. Luxenberg, *Historic Resource Study: North Cascades National Park Service Complex, Washington* (Seattle: National Park Service, Pacific Northwest Region, Cultural Resources Division, 1986), 43–50.
21. Hoover to Finn, February 3, 1926, Transportation Records, WSA; Murray, "Building a Wagon Road," 55.
22. Murray, "Building a Wagon Road," 55–56; Hoover to Finn, February 3, 1926, Transportation Records, WSA; Humes to Allmond, March 11, 1930, PSH #2-22, Cities and Towns, 1930, box B-41, Highways and Roads, Transportation Records, WSA.
23. Murray, "Building a Wagon Road," 56; *Guide to the Records of the Washington State Highways Department*, vii.
24. State of Washington, Department of Highways, *Highway Across Cascade Mountains, Skagit and Okanogan Counties, Report to the 1947 Legislature* (Olympia: January 1947); Richard Carroll, "A Personal Recollection," *Washington Highways*, September 1972, 10.
25. Prahl to Evans, September 22, 1966, Agency Files, Highway Department, 1966, box 2S-2-102, D. Evans Papers, WSA.
26. "Building the North Cascades Highway," 22.
27. Senate Committee, *North Cascades–Olympic*, 81–83.
28. Senate Committee, *North Cascades–Olympic*, 79.
29. Senate Committee, *North Cascades–Olympic*, 130.
30. See Carsten Lien, *Olympic Battleground: The Power Politics of Timber Preservation*, 2d. ed. (Seattle: Mountaineers Books, 2000); Olympic Park Associates, *Voice of the Wild Olympics 50th Anniversary Edition* (Seattle: OPA, 1998); and Senate Committee, *North Cascades–Olympic*, 299–305 (Statement of Irving Brant), for a complete treatment of the Olympic boundary dispute. Lien's is the most exhaustive.
31. Crafts to Udall, December 31, 1965, box 4, Fred Overly Papers (Overly Papers), UW.
32. Senate Committee, *North Cascades–Olympic*, 587; "Timber Raid," *New York Times*, February 10, 1966; Senate Committee, *North Cascades–Olympic*, 117; Litton to Crafts, January 12, 1966 (telegram), box 4, Overly Papers, UW. Two weeks later, Crafts warned Udall, "I am fearful that the opposition to the Olympic change is going to torpedo the possibility of a North Cascades park" (Crafts to Udall, January 29, 1966, folder 5, "Department of Interior: Issues and Achievements, National Parks—North Cascades, Washington, 1962–1967," box 156, Series II, Dept. of Interior, 1961–1972, AZ 372, Udall Papers, UA).
33. Senate Committee, *North Cascades–Olympic*, 945, 985, 1021, 986. A few dozen writers addressed other parts of the Joint Study Team report, most notably the proposed elimination of the Cougar Lakes Wilderness Area, which many viewed as another sop to the timber industry in exchange for the North Cascades.

34. Crafts to Udall, January 29, 1966, Udall Papers, UA.
35. Jackson asked Udall and Freeman to set up a joint study team for the Olympics, noting that the "question of boundary adjustments is timely" (Jackson to Udall, March 3, 1966, box 4, Overly Papers, UW). Eventually a joint study team did look at the Olympic question, but its recommendations were not acted upon. See Lien, "Senator Jackson and Fred Overly Team Up," in *Olympic Battleground*, 2nd ed., 321–337.
36. Mark Cioc and Char Miller, "Interview with Hal K. Rothman," *Environmental History* 12 (January 2007): 141–52, quote at 143.
37. "Inaugural Address of Daniel Evans, January 13, 1965," Governor Dan Evans Speech Collection, Washington State Library (WSL).
38. Senate Committee, *North Cascades–Olympic*, 347.
39. Senate Committee, *North Cascades–Olympic*, 348–352.
40. Senate Committee, *North Cascades–Olympic*, 482.
41. Senate Committee, *North Cascades–Olympic*, 483.
42. Most letters were written by individuals, with the notable exception of more than 700 form letters received from trail machine riders who opposed a national park. In the final tally, however, Senator Jackson's office counted those as one group in opposition (Senate Committee, *North Cascades–Olympic*).
43. McConnell to McCloskey, February 15, 1966, box 2, B. Evans Papers, UW.
44. Crafts to Udall, February 24, 1966, folder 5, "Department of Interior: Issues and Achievements, National Parks—North Cascades, Washington, 1962–1967," box 156, Series II, Dept. of Interior, 1961–1972, AZ 372, Udall Papers, UA.
45. Biggs to Evans, November 1, 1965, General Files, "New Employees, letter to–O", 1966, Box 2S-2-166, D. Evans Papers, WSA.
46. "Conservationists Meeting with Governor Daniel J. Evans, 312 1st Avenue North, Seattle, Monday, February 7, 1966," box VI, Goldsworthy Papers.
47. Cole to Evans, February 8, 1966, General Files, "North Cascades Study," Box 2S-2-265, D. Evans Papers, WSA; Biggs to Evans, March 10, 1966, General Files, "North Cascades Study," Box 2S-2-265, D. Evans Papers, WSA.
48. Bert Cole, "Wilderness at What Cost?" *The Totem* 2(10): 6 (February-March 1960).
49. John A. Biggs, "North Cascades National Park?" *Washington State Game Bulletin*, April 1960.
50. Biggs to Jackson, April 19, 1963, and Jackson to Biggs, April 29, 1963, box 93, Henry M. Jackson Papers (Jackson Papers), UW.
51. J. Burton Lauckhart, "North Cascades—A National Park?", Johnson to Lauckhart, September 20, 1963, Administration, Correspondence Series, box 6, Game Department Records, WSA; Lauckhart, "North Cascades Issue," Director, General Files Series, box 14, Wildlife Records, WSA.
52. Biggs to Evans, March 10, 1966, "Proposal of the Washington State Game Commission for the Preservation of the North Cascades Area," box II, Goldsworthy Papers.
53. Biggs to Evans, May 9, 1966, quoted in Allan Sommarstrom, "Wild Land Preservation Crisis: The North Cascades Controversy" (PhD diss., University of Washington, 1970), 114.
54. Biggs to Evans, June 3, 1966, General Files, "New Employees, letter to–O, 1966," Box 2S-2-166, D. Evans Papers, WSA.
55. Ibid.
56. "Governor Daniel J. Evans' North Cascades National Recreation Area Report and Recommendations" (Olympia: June 1966).
57. Manning to Evans, June 23, 1966, General Files, "New Employees, letter to–O," 1966, box 2S-2-166, D. Evans Papers, WSA.
58. Evans to Manning, July 5, 1966, General Files, "New Employees, letter to–O," 1966, box 2S-2-166, D. Evans Papers, WSA; "Confidential Briefing for Meeting July 20, 1966 with

Conservationists," General Files, "North Cascades Correspondence–North Cascades Study," box 2S-2-264; D. Evans Papers, WSA; Evans to Manning, July 29, 1966, box VI, Goldsworthy Papers.

59. Goldsworthy, interview.
60. "Board Business Briefs," *The Mountaineer* 59(13):2 (December 1966); Manning, interview.
61. "The American Alps," *Cascades*, Summer 1966, 18–21, 31.
62. Steve Raymond, "The Great Cascades Debate," *Field & Stream* 71(7):10–15, 42 (November 1966).
63. Paul Brooks, "The Fight for America's Alps, *The Atlantic* 219(2):87–90, 97–99 (February 1967); Hal Wingo, "Knight Errant to Nation's Rescue," *Life* 60(21):37–40 (May 27, 1966). Brooks was a director of the Sierra Club.
64. JoAnn Roe, *North Cascades Highway: Washington's Popular and Scenic Pass* (Seattle: The Mountaineers, 1997), 68.
65. Freeman to Schultze, August 2, 1966, 2150 North Cascades Study Area, FY 1967, FY 1968, Region 6 Regional Forester's Office, FS, RG 95, NARA-APR.
66. Chriswell to district rangers, August 16, 1966, North Cascades, Mt. Baker-Snoqualmie National Forest Supervisor's Office, Decimal Files 2100-2130 Special Planning Areas, 1927–1973, FS, RG 95, NARA-APR; Crafts to Udall, August 8, 1966, folder 5, "Department of Interior: Issues and Achievements, National Parks—North Cascades, Washington, 1962-1967," Series II, Dept. of Interior, 1961-1972, box 156, AZ 372, Udall Papers, UA.
67. Hu Blonk, "Freeman Still Against Park," *Wenatchee World*, August 24, 1966.
68. In February 1966, Crafts wrote Forest Service deputy chief A. W. Greeley that he thought Forest Service field staff was not letting "public opinion largely crystallize on the basis of the Report," but instead seemed to "aggressively oppose the recommendations in its public relations work." Greeley replied, "I do not see how the Forest Service could gag its people on this issue…" Crafts was frustrated by the lack of unity from the Study Team agencies, but given the Forest Service's decentralized organization, he could not have been surprised. [Crafts to Greeley, February 5, 1966, Greeley to Crafts, February 14, 1966, Crafts to Udall, February 23, 1966, folder 5, "Department of Interior: Issues and Achievements, National Parks—North Cascades, Washington, 1962–1967," Series II, Dept. of Interior, 1961–1972, box 156, AZ 372, Udall Papers, UA].
69. "I&E Plan North Cascades," April 1966, and Wood to Forest Supervisors, December 14, 1966, Joint Study of North Cascades #6 April 1966 thru April 1967, Region 6—North Cascades Study Plan, FS, RG 95, NARA-APR.
70. Richard Buscher, personal interview by the author, tape recording, Tigard, OR, October 18, 2003; U.S. Forest Service, *(Proposed) North Cascades National Recreation Area Management Plan, 1966* (Dick Buscher collection).
71. U.S. Forest Service, *(Proposed) North Cascades National Recreation Area Management Plan*.
72. "Jackson, Udall, Freeman to Tour North Cascades," *Wenatchee World*, September 14, 1966.
73. "Tour of North Cascades, September 17–18, 1966," August 31, 1966, Folder 4–National Parks (North Cascades, Wash., 1962–1967), box 134, AZ 372, Udall Papers, UA; Don Hannula, "Udall Takes First Look at North Cascades," *Seattle Times*, September 18, 1966; Bob Lane, "Officials Embark on Cascades Tour," *Seattle Times*, September 18, 1966; "Officials Laud Cascades as Scenic Masterpieces," *Sunday Oregonian*, September 18, 1966.
74. "Udall, Freeman Differ on N. Cascades Park Issue," *Wenatchee World*, September 19, 1966.
75. Harold K. Steen, *The Chiefs Remember: The Forest Service, 1952–2001* (Durham, NC: Forest History Society, 2004), 31, 33.
76. Senate Committee, *The North Cascades*, 11.
77. "Park Backers See Action in Johnson Talk," *Seattle Times*, January 24, 1967.

78. Cliff to Freeman, 27 January 1967, Joint Study of the North Cascades #6 April 1966 thru April 1967, Region 6-North Cascades Study Plan, FS, RG 95, NARA-APR.

79. "Text of President Johnson's Message to Congress on Pollution and Resources," *New York Times*, January 31, 1967.

80. "Text of President Johnson's Message"; William M. Blair, "Johnson Asks Redwoods Park as 'Last-Chance' Opportunity," *New York Times*, January 31, 1967.

81. "Message to Congress: Johnson on Pollution, Resources, Road Safety," In *CQ Almanac 1967*, 23rd ed., 20-36-A-20-40-A. Washington, DC: Congressional Quarterly, 1968, library.cqpress.com/cqalmanac/cqal67-1311900.

82. Chriswell, interview; Steen, *The Chiefs Remember*, 33.

83. Dwight F. Rettie, *Our National Park System* (Urbana: University of Illinois Press, 1995), 49–50; Neal Christensen, "Designated National Recreation Areas: Their History, Purpose, Management, and Influence on Local Communities," April 2012, www.yakimaforever. org/wp-content/uploads/2012/06/TWS-National-Recreation-Area-Report.pdf.

84. Recreation Advisory Council, *Policy of the Establishment and Administration of Recreation Areas, Circular No. 1* (Washington, DC: GPO, 1963), 32, www.nps.gov/parkhistory/ online_books/anps/anps_5g.htm.

85. Rettie, *Our National Park System*, 49-50.

86. *An Act to establish the North Cascades National Park and Ross Lake and Lake Chelan National Recreation Areas, to designate the Pasayten Wilderness and to modify the Glacier Peak Wilderness, in the State of Washington, and for other purposes*, 90th Cong., 1st Sess., S. 1321, October 2, 1968.

87. "Stehekin Ponders Fate Under Park," *Wenatchee World*, March 22, 1967.

88. David Louter, *Contested Terrain: North Cascades National Park Service Complex, An Administrative History* (Seattle: National Park Service, 1998).

89. "Stehekin Ponders Fate Under Park," *Wenatchee World*.

90. *An Act to establish the North Cascades National Park*, 90th Cong., 1st Sess., S. 1321.

91. Senate Joint Memorial No. 21, March 29, 1967.

8. Hearings + Hearings + Politics = Park

1. Manning, *Conservation and Conflict*, 59; Goldsworthy, interview. Polly Dyer said that Jackson declined to get involved until "all the legwork had been done" by Goldsworthy, the N3C, and especially Rep. Thomas Pelly (Dyer, oral history, 46).

2. McCloskey, interview.

3. Ibid.

4. After the Joint Study Team Report hearings in February 1966, Crafts warned Udall, "If Jackson has to surface his own bill in the event the Administration cannot or will not make up its mind, my guess is that he will put in a Park bill, but he would be unhappy about this." (Crafts to Udall, February 24, 1966, folder 5, "Department of Interior: Issues and Achievements, National Parks–North Cascades, Washington, 1962–1967," Series II, Dept. of Interior, 1961–1972, box 156, AZ 372, Udall Papers, UA; quote from same.)

5. Verkler to Jackson, January 11, 1966, North Cascades, Interior and Insular Affairs Committee files, U.S. Senate Records, NAB.

6. Transcript, Stewart L. Udall Oral History Interview V, December 16, 1969, by Joe B. Frantz, Internet Copy, LBJ Library, 5.

7. Jackson to Brooks, April 24, 1967, box 209, Jackson Papers, UW.

8. Brock Evans, Memo to North Cascades file 1967, January 12, 1973, box 26, B. Evans Papers, UW.

9. Patrick Donovan Goldsworthy, "North Cascades Proposal Before Congress," *Sierra Club Bulletin* 52(5):3–13 (June 1967).

10. Allan Sommarstrom, "Wild Land Preservation Crisis: The North Cascades Controversy," PhD diss., University of Washington, 1970, 141.

11. In March 1967, the Yakima Valley Sportsmen's Association tried a new tactic to elicit opposition to the park. Members visited area schools, warning that a national park would preclude hunting and fishing, and then asked students to sign a petition opposing the legislation (Maxwell to Magnuson, March 14, 1967, box 19, General Files "Minerals—North Cascades," Interior and Insular Affairs Committee, 90th Cong., U.S. Senate Records, NAB).

12. Senate Committee on Interior and Insular Affairs, *The North Cascades*, 90th Cong., 1st Sess., April 24, 1967, 43–56.

13. Senate Committee, *The North Cascades*, 51; A. Starker Leopold, S. A. Cain, C. M. Cottam, I. N. Gabrielson, T. L. Kimball, "Wildlife Management in the National Parks" (1963) (or, The Leopold Report), reprinted in *The Great New Wilderness Debate*, J. Michael Callicott and Michael P. Nelson, eds. (Athens: University of Georgia Press, 1998), 103–119; see also Richard West Sellars, *Preserving Nature in the National Parks: A History* (New Haven: Yale University Press, 1997), 214–216. Aldo Leopold's oldest son, naturalist A. Starker Leopold worked on many conservation issues and was best known for his work on the Leopold Report. A trained zoologist and forester, he taught at the University of California, Berkeley for more than three decades ("A. Starker Leopold, 69, Naturalist at Berkeley," *New York Times*, August 25, 1983, www.nytimes.com/1983/08/25/obituaries/a-starker-leopold-69-naturalist-at-berkeley.html).

14. Senate Committee, *The North Cascades*, 287–288.

15. As early as summer 1966, aware that hunters would be a problem, Jackson asked for and received conservationists' help on the issue (Goldsworthy to McCloskey, August 14, 1966, box VIII, Goldsworthy Papers).

16. Senate Committee, *The North Cascades*, 96; North Cascades Study Team, *The North Cascades Study Report* (Washington, DC: GPO, October 1965), 63.

17. Senate Committee, *The North Cascades*, 133–148, quote at 135.

18. Another reason, probably more pertinent, was that Granite Creek ran alongside the route of the unfinished North Cross-State Highway. Highway boosters and Governor Daniel J. Evans did not want the road inside the park.

19. Senate Committee, *The North Cascades*, 140–141, quote at 141; 258–261.

20. Senate Committee, *The North Cascades*, 243–247, quote at 245.

21. David Wilma, "Upper Skagit River Hydroelectric Project," March 3, 2003, *HistoryLink*, www.historylink.org/index.cfm?DisplayPage=output.cfm&file_id=5347; "A Brief History of Seattle City Light," *Seattle City Light*, n.dwww.seattle.gov/light/history/brief.asp. Although the incline railway no longer operates, as of 2016 Seattle City Light offered several tours of the Skagit Hydroelectric Project, including one with a chicken dinner.

22. Louter, *Contested Terrain*, 123–125.

23. Senate Committee, *The North Cascades*, 57–61.

24. Senate Committee, *The North Cascades*, 223, 483. In fact, as discussed in chapter 9, none of those facilities were ever built.

25. Senate Committee, *The North Cascades*, 17.

26. National Park Service, *North Cascades National Park and Ross Lake National Recreation Area: A Proposal* (N.p.: Parkscape USA, 1967), 6.

27. Senate Committee, *The North Cascades*, 17–18.

28. Senate Committee, *The North Cascades*, 626, 818, 971.

29. William D. Hagenstein, *Corks and Suspenders: Memoirs of an Early Forester* (N.p.: Giustina, 2010), quoted at *corksandsuspenders.com*, www.corksandsuspenders.com/billsbiography.

html; "William D. 'Bill' Hagenstein obituary," *OregonLive*, September 12, 2014, obits. oregonlive.com/obituaries/oregon/obituary.aspx?pid=172448251.

30. Senate Committee, *The North Cascades*, 83.
31. Senate Committee, *The North Cascades*, 83–84.
32. Senate Committee, *The North Cascades*, 84–85.
33. McCloskey, interview.
34. Crafts to Udall, April 24, 1967, folder 5, "Department of Interior: Issues and Achievements, National Parks–North Cascades, Washington, 1962–1967," Series II, Dept. of Interior, 1961–1972, box 156, AZ 372, Udall Papers, UA.
35. Senate Committee, *The North Cascades*, conversation condensed from 127–129.
36. Senate Committee, *The North Cascades*, 129.
37. Senate Committee, *The North Cascades*, 129–130, 225, 551.
38. Greeley to file, August 8, 1967, 2150 Joint Study of the North Cascades #6, April 1966–April 1967, Region 6–North Cascades Study Plan, FS, RG 95, NARA-APR.
39. Senate Committee, *The North Cascades*, 214–217.
40. Senate Committee, *The North Cascades*, 214–217, conversation from 216–217.
41. Albright to Brower, August 5, 1958, folder 8, Office of the Executive Director, carton 13, BANC MSS 2002/230c, Sierra Club Records, BL; Don Davis, "Tending to Business," *Everett Herald*, November 5, 1966; "About the Mine: Fact Sheet," *Wild Cascades*, December 1966–January 1967, 8–9.
42. Patrick Goldsworthy, "Kennecott Meets with Conservation Leaders," *Wild Cascades*, December 1966–January 1967, 4, 21; Rodger Pegues, "Mining the Glacier Peak Wilderness Area," *Wild Cascades*, December 1966–January 1967, 5–7; Paul Brooks, "A Copper Company in the North Cascades," *Harper's* 235(1408): 48–50 (September 1967).
43. "About the Mine," *Wild Cascades*, 8–9.
44. "Showdown at Miner's Ridge," *Wild Cascades*, December 1966–January 1967, 2–3.
45. Orville L. Freeman, "Address by Secretary of Agriculture" (10th Biennial Wilderness Conference of the Sierra Club, San Francisco, Calif., April 7, 1967).
46. Senate Committee, *The North Cascades*, 35–41; Crafts to Udall, April 24, 1967, folder 5, "Department of Interior: Issues and Achievements, National Parks–North Cascades, Washington, 1962–1967," Series II, Dept. of Interior, 1961–1972, box 156, AZ 372, Udall Papers, UA.
47. William M. Blair, "Kennecott Claim in Forest Fought," *New York Times*, May 12, 1967.
48. Senate Committee, *The North Cascades*, 171.
49. "An Open Pit, Big Enough To Be Seen From The Moon" (advertisement), *Seattle Times*, June 9, 1967.
50. Goldsworthy, "Kennecott Meets"; "News of Conservation and the Club," *Sierra Club Bulletin* 52(5): 3 (June 1967); William G. Wing, "Is this Mine Necessary?" *New York Times*, April 30, 1967; "Topics: A Precious Part of America's Northwest," *New York Times*, August 12, 1967.
51. "About the Mine," *Wild Cascades*.
52. Senate Committee, *The North Cascades*, 369, 411, 785, 44, 68, 171, 196; Walt Woodward, "One Step at a Time Necessary in Copper-Mine Controversy," *Seattle Times*, June 11, 1967.
53. Senate Committee, *The North Cascades*, 19–25, quote from 25. David Louter explores the notion of tramways as an alternative to cars in *Windshield Wilderness: Cars, Roads, and Nature in Washington's National Parks* (Seattle: University of Washington Press, 2006), 123–130.
54. Robert W. Righter, *Crucible for Conservation: The Struggle for Grand Teton National Park* (Moose, WY: Grand Teton Natural History Association, 1982), 143.
55. Senate Committee, *The North Cascades*, 210.
56. Goldsworthy, interview.

57. Jackson told subcommittee chair Alan Bible that he wanted action on the North Cascades before Labor Day; Bible almost made the deadline (Jackson to Bible, July 31, 1967, Reading File–1967 "A" to "D", Interior and Insular Affairs Committee, U.S. Senate records 90A-F11, NAB).

58. Senate Committee on Interior and Insular Affairs, *Authorizing the Establishment of the North Cascades National Park, the Ross Lake National Recreation Area, the Lake Chelan National Recreation Area, Designating the Pasayten Wilderness, and Modifying the Glacier Peak Wilderness, in the State of Washington, and for other Purposes,* 90th Cong., 1st Sess., 1967, S. Rept. 700, 2–3, 14; "Stehekin Excluded from Park Bill," *Wenatchee World,* October 24, 1967; William W. Prochnau, "Senate Group Approves New North Cascades National Park," *Seattle Times,* October 24, 1967.

59. "Full Senate Committee OK's Cascades Park," *Seattle Times,* October 25, 1967; "Cascades Park Bill Viewed Favorably," *Wenatchee World,* October 25, 1967.

60. William W. Prochnau, "Cascades Park Bill Whooshes Through Senate," *Seattle Times,* November 2, 1967; Ross Cunningham, "Jackson 'Robbed' of Fine Speech," *Seattle Times,* November 13, 1967; North Cascades Conservation Council, "Conservationists React to Senate Park," October 25, 1967, box G, Goldsworthy Papers; "Cascades Park Bill Viewed Favorably," *Wenatchee World,* October 27, 1967; "Cascades Park Plan Opposed," *Seattle Times,* November 2, 1967; Walt Woodward, "Bill Moved Too Fast for Timbermen," *Seattle Times,* November 6, 1967; Walt Woodward, "Dilemma for Timber Firms," *Seattle Times,* November 7, 1967.

61. Robert Browning, "Uphill Battle Looms over Cascades Park," *Seattle Times,* September 2, 1967; for Aspinall and the Wilderness Act, see Harvey, *Wilderness Forever.*

62. "Mr. Aspinall Marks Time," *New York Times,* September 8, 1967.

63. Goldsworthy to McCloskey, August 14, 1966, box VIII, Goldsworthy Papers.

64. Brock Evans, memo to North Cascades Legislation file, January 12, 1973, box 25, B. Evans Papers, UW.

65. House Subcommittee on National Parks and Recreation, Committee on Interior and Insular Affairs, *The North Cascades, Part I: Hearings Before the Subcommittee on National Parks and Recreation of the Committee on Interior and Insular Affairs, House of Representatives,* 90th Cong., 2nd Sess., 1968, 32–39, 76.

66. At the time, the 5th district included Chelan and Okanogan counties, which would be affected by the park. The district has since been redrawn.

67. "Aspinall's Snit," *Seattle Post-Intelligencer,* April 23, 1968; House Committee, *The North Cascades, Part I,* 58.

68. House Committee, *The North Cascades, Part I,* 63, 71.

69. B. Evans to D. Evans, 12 April 1968, "N–North Cascades," D. Evans Papers, WSA.

70. House Committee, *The North Cascades, Part I,* 78.

71. House Committee, *The North Cascades, Part I,* 80.

72. Brock Evans, "Field Hearings on North Cascades," *Sierra Club Bulletin* 53(6):17–18 (June 1968).

73. B. Evans to D. Evans, 23 April 1968, "N–North Cascades," D. Evans Papers, WSA.

74. "The American Alps," *New York Times,* April 21, 1968.

75. "Chance of Cascades Park Action Fades," *Seattle Times,* May 29, 1968.

76. Evans to Woodward, 16 June 1968, box 25, B. Evans Papers, UW.

77. "Colorado Covets Northwest Water," *Wenatchee World,* February 14, 1966; Wilfred Woods, "Talking it Over," *Wenatchee World,* April 22, 1968, also mentions the Colorado River legislation as a potential sticking point.

78. Tupling to McCloskey, n.d. [likely spring 1968], box 1 (pre-processing), B. Evans Papers, UW.

79. Sommarstrom, "Wild Land Preservation Crisis," 137; "House Panel Takes up Cascades Park Measure," *Seattle Times*, July 25, 1968; Transcript, Stewart L. Udall Oral History Interview II, 5/19/69, by Joe B. Frantz, Internet Copy, LBJ Library.
80. Transcript, Udall Oral History Interview V, 8.
81. George A. Selke, "A Review of U.S. Forest Service Management and Management Planning in the North Cascades," February 26, 1968, "New Employees, letter to–O," General Files, D. Evans Papers, WSA; Mt. Baker National Forest, "North Cascades National Recreation Area–A Preliminary Report," May 31, 1968, 2150 North Cascades Recreation Area/Picket Wilderness; Decimal Files 2100-2130 Special Planning Areas 1927–1973, North Cascades; Mt. Baker-Snoqualmie National Forest, Supervisor's Office; FS, RG 95, NARA-APR; Heaton to Forest Supervisors, July 29, 1968, 2150 Special Planning Areas Northern Cascades (Proposed Winter Sports Sites); 2100-2130 Special Planning Areas; Supervisor's Office; FS RG 95, NARA-APR.
82. "Forest Service Plan Revealed," *Wenatchee World*, March 5, 1968.
83. House Committee, *The North Cascades, Part III*, 921.
84. House Committee, *The North Cascades, Part III*, 929.
85. House Committee, *The North Cascades, Part III*, 921.
86. House Committee, *The North Cascades, Part III*, 952, 954.
87. "Saving America's Alps," *New York Times*, September 23, 1968.
88. "North Cascades Park Bill a Masterpiece of Compromise," *Wenatchee World*, September 26, 1968.
89. Forest Service chief Edward Cliff later said, "We were trying to defend our turf, and didn't defend it successfully," a pessimistic outlook on legislation that kept all but 674,000 acres of the North Cascades in Forest Service jurisdiction (Steen, *The Chiefs Remember*, 33).
90. David Louter, *Contested Terrain*, 57.
91. "President Signs Cascades Park, Scenic-River Bills," *Seattle Times*, October 2, 1968.

9. Managing the Wilderness Crown Jewel

1. "Cascade Park's New Head Hails Potential," *Seattle Times*, October 6, 1968; Thompson to Goldsworthy, October 15, 1968, box VII, Goldsworthy Papers; Harvey Manning, *Conservation and Conflict: The U.S. Forest Service and the National Park Service in the North Cascades, 1892–1992* (Seattle: North Cascades Conservation Council, 1992, preliminary unpublished edition), 77.
2. Woodward to Goldsworthy, October 18, 1968, box VII, Goldsworthy Papers.
3. "Who Gets Credit? Many Helped Obtain Park," *Seattle Times*, October 27, 1968; "Tramway to Park Site, *Seattle Times*, October 27, 1968; "Conservationists Not Satisfied," *Seattle Times*, October 27, 1968.
4. Fred W. Cleator, "Recollections of Bob Marshall," folder 3, Conservation Collection, box 28, CONS130, Wilderness Society Records, Denver Public Library.
5. Ibid., 10.
6. Grant McConnell, "The Cascade Range," in *The Cascades*, Roderick Peattie, ed. (New York, Vanguard Press, 1949), 90.
7. Matthias Olshausen, "From Company Town to Company Town: Holden and Holden Village, Washington, 1937-1980 & Today" (master's thesis, Portland State University, 2013). More than a decade after the mine shut down, visitors saw the old mill, "a macabre skeleton of bent, twisted, rusted beams," rusted iron equipment, and huge piles of tailings upon which no plants grew (McPhee, *Encounters with the Archdruid*, 24, 26). Holden today is the home of a Lutheran spiritual retreat center. The mine, now a Superfund site, is undergoing cleanup.
8. Louter, *Contested Terrain*, 106.

9. Early definitions can be found in Aldo Leopold, "Wilderness as a Form of Land Use" (1925) and Bob Marshall, "The Problem of the Wilderness" (1930).

10. See, for example, Senate Committee on Interior and Insular Affairs, *The North Cascades*, 90th Cong., 1st Sess., 39–40. Jackson made this point several times during the hearings.

11. Orville Freeman, 10th Biennial Wilderness Conference of the Sierra Club Address.

12. William M. Blair, "Kennecott Claim in Forest Fought," *New York Times*, May 12, 1967.

13. "Kennecott Copper Hears Conservationists' Plea," *Spokane Daily Chronicle*, May 3, 1967; "Scorecard," *Sports Illustrated*, April 24, 1967.

14. Senate Committee, *The North Cascades*, 419.

15. Joel Connelly, "Dr. Fred Darvill," *The Wild Cascades* (Spring 2008), 7.

16. "News of Conservation and the Club," *Sierra Club Bulletin* 52(5): 3 (June 1967); Adam Sowards, "Protecting American Lands with Justice William O. Douglas," *The George Wright Forum* 32(2): 165–173 (2015).

17. Walt Woodward, "Kennecott Adamant on Glacier Peak Mining," *Seattle Times*, May 16, 1969.

18. Woodward, "Kennecott Adamant"; Adam Sowards, "Confronting Kennecott in the Cascades" (poster presented at the annual meeting of the American Society for Environmental History, Seattle, WA, April 2016).

19. Zalesky, interview.

20. Enthoven to Goldsworthy, February 2, 1970, box VII, Goldsworthy Papers; John D. Leshy, *The Mining Law: A Study in Perpetual Motion* (Washington, DC: Resources for the Future, 1987), 235.

21. Leshy, *The Mining Law*, 235, 236.

22. Agriculture Department, United States Forest Service, Okanogan-Wenatchee National Forest, "Chelan County PUD and Forest Service Complete Land Exchange" (press release), May 3, 2010, www.fs.usda.gov/detail/okawen/news-events?cid=FSBDEV3_053721; Bill Sheets, "Swap Adds Miner's Ridge to Glacier Peak Wilderness," *Everett Herald*, May 7, 2010, www.heraldnet.com/article/20100507/NEWS01/705079879; Joel Connelly, "The Open Pit is Finally Put Away," Strange Bedfellows, *Seattle P-I*, May 5, 2010, blog. seattlepi.com/seattlepolitics/2010/05/05/the-open-pit-is-finally-put-away.

23. "Chief's Goal: 'One of World's Great Parks,'" *Seattle Times*, October 27, 1968; Louter, *Contested Terrain*, 63, 66 (see Chapter 8 for an account of the Jackson-Pearson exchange); Samuel J. Schmieding, *From Controversy to Compromise to Cooperation: The Administrative History of Canyonlands National Park* (National Park Service, 2008), www.nps.gov/cany/planyourvisit/upload/CanyAdminHistory_forweb.pdf.

24. "Federal, State Officials Discuss N. Cascades Park," *Seattle Times*, December 18, 1968; Louter, *Contested Terrain*, 64, 66.

25. Louter, *Contested Terrain*, 63, 65.

26. "Park Service Office Here Upgraded," *Seattle Times*, January 18, 1970.

27. Chriswell, interview; Goldsworthy, interview.

28. Louter, *Contested Terrain*, 59–60, 67, quote at 62.

29. "North Cascades Study Launched," *Wenatchee World*, October 5, 1969. N3C president Patrick Goldsworthy was a member of both the Park Service planning team and the Forest Service recreation planning team.

30. John C. Miles, *Wilderness in National Parks: Playground or Preserve* (Seattle: University of Washington Press, 2009); Sellars, *Preserving Nature*, 193.

31. Harvey, *Wilderness Forever*, 205; see also Sellars, *Preserving Nature*, 202.

32. See, for example, Ronald A. Foresta, *America's National Parks*, ch. 4; Alfred Runte, *National Parks: The American Experience*, 4th ed. (Lanham, MD; Taylor Trade Publishing, 2010); Sellars, *Preserving Nature*, 267; Miles, *Wilderness and National Parks*.

33. Contor, quoted in Louter, *Contested Terrain*, at 97.

34. Jack Hauptli, "Cascades Park Begins Year 2," *Seattle Times*, April 30, 1970.

35. Steve Raymond, "Cascades Plan Calls for 3 Wilderness Areas," *Seattle Times*, April 5, 1970; "North-Cascade Plan Hearings Scheduled," *Seattle Times*, May 31, 1970.

36. North Cascades National Park Service Complex, *Master Plan* (Washington: NPS, 1970). An alternative tramway site was Colonial Peak, about four miles southwest of Ruby Mountain.

37. Jack Hauptli, "North Cascades Park Chief Outlines Development Plans," *Seattle Times*, April 27, 1970; "Wilderness Prevails: Ferries, Hostels Included in N. Cascades Park Plan," *Seattle Times*, April 3, 1970; "514,000 Acres of Park Would be Left Wilderness in Plan," *Seattle Times*, April 3, 1970.

38. North Cascades National Park Service Complex, *Wilderness Recommendations* (Washington: NPS, 1970); "514,000 Acres of Park," Louter, *Contested Terrain*, 98.

39. Jerry Bergsman, "Cascades-Park Plan Modification Almost Sure," *Seattle Times*, June 5, 1970; Louter, *Contested Terrain*, 97–98; Jerry Bergsman, "Conservationists Want to Keep North Cascades 'Natural,'" *Seattle Times*, June 4, 1970; Ray Schrick, "Wilderness Fight Comes to a Head," *Wenatchee World*, June 7, 1970; Ray Schrick, "How Tough Should it be to Get Into Wilderness?" *Wenatchee World*, June 5, 1970.

40. Jack Hauptli, "Progress Report on North Cascades National Park," *Seattle Times*, June 3, 1971; "5-Fold Increase Predicted for North Cascade Tourism," *Seattle Times*, June 28, 1970.

41. Jerry Bergsman, "Mail Concerning Cascades Park Mostly Critical," *Seattle Times*, July 6, 1970 ; "Grizzly Bear History," *Western Wildlife Outreach*, n.d., westernwildlife.org/ grizzly-bear-outreach-project/history/; Nathan Rice, "The Forgotten North Cascades Grizzly Bear," *High Country News*, November 23, 2011, www.hcn.org/issues/43.19/ the-forgotten-north-cascades-grizzly-bear; "Glacier Park's Night of the Grizzlies," Montana Public Broadcasting System, aired May 17, 2010, www.montanapbs.org/ GlacierParksNightoftheGrizzlies; Louter, *Contested Terrain*, 99; "The Last Grizzly in the North Cascades," *WildernessWithinHer*, September 22, 2016, wildernesswithinher. com/2016/09/22/the-last-grizzly-in-the-north-cascades.

42. Louter, *Contested Terrain*, 99, 73-76; Louter, *Windshield Wilderness*, 124; Walt Woodward, "New Tramway Will Determine Future Course," *Seattle Times*, November 19, 1968; Foresta, *America's National Parks*, 107; Senate Interior Committee, *North Cascades* hearings record, 21–25, quote at 23.

43. Louter, *Contested Terrain*, 76–77; Louter, *Windshield Wilderness*, 145.

44. Bergsman, "Mail Concerning Cascades Park," *Seattle Times*; Jack Hauptli, "Forest Service Plan Does Right by North Cascades," *Seattle Times*, July 2, 1970; Louter, *Contested Terrain*, 69–70.

45. Jack Hauptli, "Forest Service Supervisors Leave Fire Lines to Face Heated Debate on N. Cascades," *Seattle Times*, July 19, 1970; "'Roadless' Plan for North Cascades Hit," *Seattle Times*, July 16, 1970; "Forest Plan Criticized at Session," *Wenatchee World*, July 15, 1970; Charles Kerr, "Forest Plans Get Critical Response," *Wenatchee World*, July 16, 1970; "Road Building Urged in Cascades Park," *Wenatchee World*, August 9, 1970; "Federal Agencies Review Proposals," *Seattle Times*, July 20, 1970, Hauptli, "Forest Service Plan," *Seattle Times*.

46. See, for example, "No Construction Funds For Cascades Park," *Seattle Times*, January 17, 1969; "Forest Plan Surprises Park Service," *Wenatchee World*, March 19, 1969; "Plan Would Spend $15 Million on N. Cascades Forests," *Seattle Times*, March 19, 1969; "Scenic Cross-State Highway will have 'No Place to Stop,'" *Seattle Times*, October 14, 1970.

47. "Budget Hobbles National Parks," *Seattle Times,* October 29, 1970.

48. Susan Schwartz, "Forest Recreation Stunted by Fund Shortage." *Seattle Times,* October 14, 1970. During the same period, funding for building roads to reach commercial timber in Washington and Oregon increased from $23 million to $40 million.

49. "Wise Wilderness Protectionism," *Seattle Times*, April 6, 1975.
50. Louter, *Contested Terrain*, 102–103.
51. See Miles, *Wilderness and National Parks*, 193–196; quote from Louter, *Contested Terrain*, 100; *Washington Park Wilderness Act of 1988*, Public Law 100-668, 100th Cong., 2nd sess., November 16, 1988.
52. *Washington State Wilderness Act of 1984*, Public Law 98-339, 98th Cong., 2nd sess., July 3, 1984 (the act also created the Mt. Baker National Recreation Area and designated the North Cascades Highway as a National Scenic Highway); "Wilderness: A Treasured Natural Resource" and "Ten Wild Years!" *North Cascades Challenger*, 1998 Visitor Information Guide (N.p.: North Cascades National Park and Mt. Baker Ranger District of the Mt. Baker-Snoqualmie National Forest, 1998), 1, 10, 11; *Consolidated Natural Resources Act of 2008*, Public Law 110-229, 110th Cong., 2nd sess., May 8, 2008.
53. U.S. Department of Agriculture, Forest Service, Region 6, "Pacific Northwest Regional Almanac 2017," 14, 17; U.S. Department of Agriculture, Forest Service Region 6, *Visitor Use Report: Wenatchee*, August 10, 2011, www.fs.usda.gov/Internet/FSE_DOCUMENTS/stelprdb5348736.pdf; U.S. Department of Agriculture, Forest Service Region 6, *Visitor Use Report: Okanogan*, August 10, 2011, www.fs.usda.gov/Internet/FSE_DOCUMENTS/stelprdb5348737.pdf.
54. Roe, *North Cascades Highway*, 103–106; JoAnn Roe, *The North Cascadians* (Seattle: Madrona Publishers, 1980), 116–139; Paul C. Pitzer, *Building the Skagit* (Portland, OR: The Galley Press, 1978); Dolly Connelly, "Indians, Miners, Stockmen Blazed the Way," *Seattle Times*, July 10, 1960; "North Cascades Dam Threat," *New York Times*, February 23, 1970; Louter, *Contested Terrain*, 123–124.
55. Manning, *Conservation and Conflict*, 122; Louter, *Contested Terrain*, 128; Walt Woodward, "First Skirmish Opens in Battle Over Hydroelectric Projects in Cascades Park," *Seattle Times*, May 6, 1969.
56. Jackie Krolopp Kirn and Marion E. Marts, "The Skagit-High Ross Dam Controversy: Negotiation and Settlement," *Natural Resources Journal* 26 (Spring 1986): 261–289.
57. The Kerosene Kid [Joe Miller], "North Cascades Under Attack: Battle Lines Drawn," *The Wild Cascades*, December 1969–January 1970, 2–21, quote at 8; Joseph W. and Margaret M. Miller, "Big Beaver, Valley," *The Mountaineer 1970–1971* (June 1972), 11–18. Miller wrote under the pseudonyms "The Kerosene Kid" and "The Kaopectate Kid" for *The Wild Cascades*, the N3C's newsletter ("Advocacy: Who Was 'The Kaopectate Kid?'" *From the Archives*, North Cascades Conservation Council, www.northcascades.org/wordpress/from-the-archives).
58. The Kerosene Kid, "North Cascades Under Attack," quote at 5.
59. Louter, *Contested Terrain*, 127; Dwight F. Rettie, *Our National Park System* (Urbana: University of Illinois Press, 1995), 49–50; Stephen R. Mark, "What Price Expansion? Dams Versus the National Park Concept," *George Wright Forum* 9(2): 53–61 (1992); Neal Christensen, "Designated National Recreation Areas: Their History, Purpose, Management, and Influence on Local Communities," April 2012, www.yakimaforever.org/wp-content/uploads/2012/06/TWS-National-Recreation-Area-Report.pdf; Louter, *Windshield Wilderness*, 106.
60. Louter, *Contested Terrain*, 126, 130; John C. Miles, *Wilderness and National Parks*, 172, 180; Louter, *Windshield Wilderness*, ch. 5.
61. Louter, *Contested Terrain*, 129.
62. Louter, *Contested Terrain*, 125–134; See, for example, Harvey, *Symbol of Wilderness: Echo Park and the American Conservation Movement*; Grant McConnell, "Threat to Cascades" (letter to the editor), *New York Times*, August 10, 1969.
63. Terry Allan Simmons, "The Damnation of a Dam: The High Ross Dam Controversy" (master's thesis, Simon Fraser University, May 1974), quote at iii. See also Jacqueline Krolopp

Kirn, "The Skagit River-High Ross Dam Controversy: A Case Study of a Canadian-U.S. Transboundary Conflict and Negotiated Resolution" (master's thesis, University of Washington, Seattle, WA, 1987).

64. "North Cascades Dam Threat," *New York Times*, February 23, 1970; Simmons, "Damnation of a Dam"; Kirn, "The Skagit River-High Ross Dam Controversy."

65. Senate Committee, *The North Cascades*, 57–61.

66. Louter, *Contested Terrain*, 215–216; *Wild and Scenic Rivers Act*, Public Law 90-542, 90th Cong., 2nd sess., October 2, 1968; "Dam Delay Urged," *Ellensburg Daily Record*, January 27, 1981; "Coal at Creston Preferred Over Dam," *Ellensburg Daily Record*, February 21, 1981.

67. The Kerosene Kid, "North Cascades Under Attack," 3.

68. *Washington Park Wilderness Act of 1988*.

69. "Conservation Groups Applaud New Wilderness Designation," *Washington Wild*, Newsroom, September 14, 2012, www.wawild.org/newsroom/press-releases/668-9142012-conservation-groups-applaud-new-wilderness-designation.

70. Louter, *Contested Terrain*, 145–146. One noteworthy acquisition was 300 acres owned by the Chelan Box Manufacturing Company, whose desire to log the Stehekin valley in the 1950s had motivated Grant McConnell's involvement in what became the campaign to preserve the North Cascades.

71. Public Law 90-544, 90th Cong., 2nd sess., October 2, 1968.

72. Louter, *Contested Terrain*, 136.

73. Wendy Walker, "Finding My Way Home," in *Impressions of the North Cascades: Essays about a Northwest Landscape*, John C. Miles, ed. (Seattle: The Mountaineers, 1996), 120; Louter, *Contested Terrain*, 135–136, 194.

74. Walker, "Finding My Way Home," 120.

75. Louter, *Contested Terrain*, 186, 194.

76. Louter, *Contested Terrain*, 137, 205-208; North Cascades Conservation Council v. Manuel Lujan, et al. (Civil Case No. C-89-1342D), April 22, 1991.

77. Walker, "Finding My Way Home," 110.

78. Louter, *Contested Terrain*, 84–86, 140; National Park Service, "Background Information Upper Stehekin Valley Road," August 2009, parkplanning.nps.gov/document.cfm?parkID=327&projectID=15383&documentID=36378.

79. Louter, *Contested Terrain*, 288; Louter, *Windshield Wilderness*, 153. The shuttle continues to operate as a private enterprise.

80. Louter, *Contested Terrain*, 148, 84, 285–288.

81. Joel Connelly, "National Park Service Refuses to Repair, Reopen Upper Stehekin River Road," Strange Bedfellows, *Seattle P-I*, May 13, 2015, blog.seattlepi.com/seattlepolitics/2015/05/13/national-park-service-refuses-to-repair-reopen-stehekin-river-road; Ron Judd, "Wilderness Advocates Battling Over Whether to Save the Ways In," *Seattle Times*, August 9, 2013, www.seattletimes.com/pacific-nw-magazine/wilderness-advocates-battling-over-whether-to-save-the-ways-in. Judd points out the argument is not unique to Stehekin's situation. Weather has destroyed other popular access roads over the last several decades, including Mount Rainier's Carbon River Road (2006) and Olympic's Dosewallips River Road (2002). At the time of publication, neither has reopened.

82. Louter, *Windshield Wilderness*, 160.

83. Louter, *Windshield Wilderness*, 133-34, 150; Louter, *Contested Terrain*, 139-140.

84. North Cascades Conservation Council, *Prospectus for a North Cascades National Park* (Seattle: N3C, 1963), 3–15.

85. Roe, *North Cascades Highway*, 68.

86. Jack McLeod, *The North Cascades Highway: A Roadside Guide to America's Alps* (Seattle: University of Washington Press, 2013), 7.

87. Solveig Torvik, "North Cascades Highway 40th Anniversary (part two)," *Methow Grist*, August 29, 2012, www.methownet.com/grist/features/highway_history.html; and Roe, *North Cascades Highway*, 77.
88. Phil Dougherty, "A Rough Draft of the North Cascades Highway is Dedicated on September 29, 1968," March 20, 2015, *HistoryLink*, www.historylink.org/File/11043; Phil Dougherty, "North Cascades Highway Opens on September 2, 1972," March 20, 2015, *HistoryLink*, www.historylink.org/File/11044. It was not Evans' first time over the highway route. In 1966, he and his son Danny traveled it on horseback to see the final route (Roe, *North Cascades Highway*, 68).
89. Louter, *Windshield Wilderness*, 157, 159.
90. McLeod, *The North Cascades Highway*, 7.

Afterword

"The mountains abide" quote from William Dietrich, *The North Cascades: Finding Beauty and Renewal in the Wild Nearby* (Seattle: Braided River, 2014), 26.
1. U.S. Department of the Interior, National Park Service (NPS), *Recreation Visitation by State and by Park for Year: 2015*, "NPS Stats: National Park Service Visitor Use Statistics," irma.nps.gov/Stats/SSRSReports/National Reports/Recreation Visitation By State and By Park (1979 - Last Calendar Year). The only national park in the lower 48 with fewer visitors was Michigan's Isle Royale, where access can require a several-hour boat ride or half-hour seaplane flight across Lake Superior. It is similar to Lake Chelan National Recreation Area in this regard.
2. National forest recreation visits are harder to tally, but the Mt. Baker-Snoqualmie National Forest estimates it receives about five million visits per year, 700,000 of which are to designated wilderness areas. The Okanogan-Wenatchee National Forest recorded 1.3 million recreation visits in 2010, with 92,000 of those in designated wilderness areas (U.S. Department of Agriculture (USDA), Forest Service Region 6, *National Visitor Use Monitoring Results, Mount Baker-Snoqualmie National Forest*, February 8, 2002, www.fs.fed.us/recreation/programs/nvum/reports/year1/R6_MBS_final.htm; USDA, Forest Service Region 6, *Visitor Use Report: Wenatchee*, August 10, 2011, www.fs.usda. gov/Internet/FSE_DOCUMENTS/stelprdb5348736.pdf; USDA, Forest Service Region 6, *Visitor Use Report: Okanogan*, August 10, 2011, www.fs.usda.gov/Internet/ FSE_DOCUMENTS/stelprdb5348737.pdf; Frances Chiem, "Reports Show Roads Maintenance, Funding Challenges for National Forest," *Signpost* (blog), *Washington Trails Association*, January 11, 2016, www.wta.org/signpost/sustainable-roads-report-mt-baker-snoqualmie-national-forest.
3. National Park Service, "Annual Park Ranking Report for Recreation Visitors in: 2015," *NPS Stats, National Park Service Visitor Use Statistics*.
4. American Alps Legacy Project, *American Alps Legacy Proposal: Completing the Conservation Vision for the North Cascades National Park, Part 1*, July 2014, www.americanalps. org/American%20Alps%20Legacy%20Proposal%207-21-14%20Revision%20-%20 Part%201.pdf. The single-purpose nonprofit American Alps is a collaboration of organizations including the N3C, Federation of Western Outdoor Clubs, Skagit and Seattle Audubon chapters, and Environment Washington. The Mountaineers Foundation is one of several funders. The project's list of advisors is a who's who of North Cascades luminaries, including Gov. Dan Evans, Mike McCloskey, Brock Evans, and before her death in 2016, Polly Dyer.
5. National Park Service, "Designations of National Park System Units," *Golden Gate National Recreation Area*, www.nps.gov/goga/planyourvisit/designations.htm.

6. American Alps Legacy Project, *American Alps Legacy Proposal: Completing the Conservation Vision for the North Cascades National Park, Part 3*, July 2014, www.americanalps.org/Am%20 Alps%20Proposal%207-21-14%20Revised%20-%20Part%203.pdf. Land proposed for the national preserve includes the Mount Baker rainforest, Nooksack River headwaters, Cascade River drainage, Skagit River valley, Liberty Bell Mountain, and much of the eastern portion of the North Cascades Highway, among other areas. Much of the additions are in the Mt. Baker-Snoqualmie and Okanogan-Wenatchee national forests, and placing them under the Park Service would preclude logging and mining there, although hunting, fishing, cross-country skiing, and horseback riding would still be allowed (Bill Sheets, "Plan Would Expand North Cascades Park by One-Half," *Everett Herald*, August 5, 2012, www. heraldnet.com/article/20120805/news01/708059967; American Alps, *The American Alps Legacy Project*, www.americanalps.org. Proponents suggest the protections offered by the preserve would protect wildlife connectivity corridors between the North Cascades, the Rockies, and the Coast Range in British Columbia, and "assure long-term ecological health and biodiversity conservation" in the North Cascades." American Alps Legacy Project, *American Alps Legacy Proposal, Part 3.*

7. Buscher, interview; Manning, interview.
8. Frome, *Battle for the Wilderness*, 135.
9. McCloskey, interview.
10. Grace Herndon, *Cut and Run: Saying Goodbye to the Last Great Forests in the West* (Telluride, CO: Western Eye Press, 1991), 176.
11. McCloskey, interview.
12. Ibid.
13. David Louter, *Contested Terrain*, 320.
14. Gary Paull, Mt. Baker-Snoqualmie National Forest, email message to author, February 22, 2017.
15. National Park Service, "Communicating Climate Change," *North Cascades National Park*, www.nps.gov/noca/blogs/communicating-climate-change.htm.
16. USDA, Forest Service, *Climate Change Vulnerability and Adaptation in the North Cascades Region, Washington*, Portland, OR: Pacific Northwest Research Station, September 2014, www.fs.fed.us/pnw/pubs/pnw_gtr892.pdf; Hannah Hickey, "Fires and Floods: North Cascades Federal Lands Prepare for Climate Change," *UW Today*, October 29, 2014, www.washington.edu/news/2014/10/29/fires-and-floods-north-cascades-federal-lands-prepare-for-climate-change/. The study was conducted by the North Cascadia Adaptation Partnership (NCAP), a collaboration that includes North Cascades and Mount Rainier national parks, Mt. Baker-Snoqualmie and Okanogan-Wenatchee national forests and Pacific Northwest Research Station, and the University of Washington Climate Impacts Group.
17. National Park Service, "Glaciers/Glacial Features," *North Cascades National Park*, www. nps.gov/noca/learn/nature/glaciers.htm.
18. Forest Service, *Climate Change Vulnerability and Adaptation.*
19. Mauri S. Pelto, "Impact of Climate Change on North Cascade Alpine Glaciers, and Alpine Runoff," *Northwest Science* 82(1): 65–75 (2008), www.nichols.edu/departments/ glacier/06%20Pelto%20hi-res.pdf.
20. Mauri S. Pelto, *North Cascade Response to Global Warming*, June 15, 2009, www.nichols. edu/departments/glacier/globalwarming.html.
21. Mauri S. Pelto, "Lyman Glacier a Century of Change–Years Numbered," *From a Glaciers Perspective*, June 26, 2009, glacierchange.wordpress.com/2009/06/26/lyman-glacier-a-century-of-change-years-numbered; M. S. Pelto, "Lyman Glacier: A Century of Change,"

Proceedings of the 66th Eastern Snow Conference, Niagara-on-the-Lake, Ontario, Canada, 2009, www.easternsnow.org/proceedings/2009/pelto.pdf.

22. *Lyman Glacier Continues to Melt Away*, www.nichols.edu/departments/glacier/lyman. htm; Pelto, *North Cascade Response to Global Warming.*

23. Michelle McNiel, "Cost of Fighting Carlton Complex Hits $60 Million; 322 Homes Destroyed," *Wenatchee World*, August 7, 2014, www.wenatcheeworld.com/news/2014/ aug/07/carlton-complex-now-cost-60-million-and-destroyed-nearly-500-structures; Glenn Nelson, "What We've Lost in the Methow Valley Wildfires," *High Country News*, August 21, 2015, www.hcn.org/articles/twisp-wildfire-washington-firefighter-deaths-methow-valley; Dee Riggs, "Carlton Complex is Still the Largest, Single Fire in State History," *Wenatchee World*, August 25, 2015, www.wenatcheeworld.com/news/2015/ aug/25/carlton-complex-is-still-the-largest-single-fire-in-state-history.

24. Nelson, "What We've Lost."

25. Washington State Department of Natural Resources, *2015 Wildland Fire Summary*, file. dnr.wa.gov/publications/em_wildfire_summary_2015.pdf; Jim Brunner, "Legislature Takes Heat for Squeezed Fire Budgets," *Seattle Times*, August 23, 2015, www.seattletimes. com/seattle-news/politics/legislature-takes-heat-for-squeezed-fire-budgets.

26. "Risking a Summer of Smoke," *Everett Herald*, May 17, 2016, www.heraldnet.com/ article/20160517/OPINION01/160519291.

27. "Inslee Orders Wildfire Training for National Guard Personnel," *Everett Herald*, May 9, 2016, www.heraldnet.com/article/20160509/NEWS03/160509004/1048.

28. USDA, Forest Service, *The Rising Cost of Wildfire Operations: Effects on the Forest Service's Non-Fire Work*, August 4, 2015, www.fs.fed.us/sites/default/files/2015-Rising-Cost-Wildfire-Operations.pdf.

29. U.S. Senate Committee on Energy and Natural Resources, *The Wildfire Management Act of 2015: A White Paper*, June 15, 2015, www.energy.senate.gov/public/index.cfm/files/ serve?File_id=0ab5f328-f73a-49da-b1b4-814d31b215bd; Bill Gabbert, "Congress Takes Another Tentative Step Toward Developing a Wildland Fire Bill," *Wildfire Today*, May 27, 2016, wildfiretoday.com/tag/legislation.

30. David Knibb's book, *Grizzly Wars: The Public Fight Over the Great Bear*, is a compelling account of the effort to restore grizzlies in the North Cascades (Cheney: Eastern Washington University Press, 2008) that informs much of this discussion.

31. U.S. Fish & Wildlife Service, Christopher Servheen, "Grizzly Bear Recovery Plan, Supplement: North Cascades Ecosystem Recovery Plan Chapter," June 23, 1997, www.nps. gov/noca/upload/NorthCascadesSupplement1997.pdf; Christian Martin, "The Rewilding of the North Cascades: A Tale of Gray Wolves and Grizzly Bears," *AdventuresNW*, February 19, 2014, www.adventuresnw.com/the-rewilding-of-the-north-cascades-a-tale-of-gray-wolves-and-grizzly-bears.

32. Servheen, "Grizzly Bear Recovery Plan, Supplement"; Chris Morgan, *Wanted: Grizzly Bears?*, Chris Morgan Wildlife, www.grizzlybearproject.org, 2016.

33. Kurt Repanshek, "Officials Propose Grizzly Bear Recovery Plan for North Cascades National Park," *National Parks Traveler*, January 12, 2017, www.nationalparkstraveler. com/2017/01/officials-propose-grizzly-bear-recovery-plan-north-cascades-national-park; U.S. Fish and Wildlife Service, "North Cascades Grizzly Bear Sighting," July 1, 2011, westernwildlife.org/wp-content/uploads/2011/07/NR_NCGB_sighting7_1_11.pdf.

34. "Grizzly Sightings," *Western Wildlife Outreach*, westernwildlife.org/grizzly-bear-outreach-project/grizzly-sightings.

35. Nathan Rice, "The Forgotten North Cascades Grizzly Bear," *High Country News*, November 23, 2011, www.hcn.org/issues/43.19/the-forgotten-north-cascades-grizzly-bear.

36. National Park Service, "Grizzly Bears," *Yellowstone National Park*, www.nps.gov/yell/ learn/nature/grizzlybear.htm; National Park Service, "Bears," *Glacier National Park*, www. nps.gov/glac/learn/nature/bears.htm.

37. U.S. Fish & Wildlife Service and National Park Service, "North Cascades Ecosystem: Grizzly Bear Restoration Plan/Environmental Impact Statement," February 2016, www.nps.gov/noca/upload/final-newsletter_Feb16_.pdf. Canada completed a grizzly bear recovery plan for its portion of the North Cascades ecosystem in 2004. See also "Update: North Cascades Grizzly Bear Restoration EIS," *Western Wildlife*, westernwildlife.org/update-north-cascades-grizzly-bear-restoration-eis-public-process-from-nps-and-usfws/.

38. National Park Service and U.S. Fish and Wildlife Service, "Draft Grizzly Bear Restoration Plan and Environmental Impact Statement January 2017," January 12, 2017, *PEPC Planning, Environment & Public Comment*, parkplanning.nps.gov/projectHome.cfm?projectId=44144.

39. Warren Cornwall, "Should Grizzlies be Restored to the North Cascades?" *National Geographic*, November 29, 2014, news.nationalgeographic.com/news/2014/11/141130-grizzly-reintroduction-cascades-national-park-environment.

40. Meriwether Lewis, William Clark, et al., April 29, 1805, entry in *The Journals of the Lewis and Clark Expedition*, ed. Gary Moulton (Lincoln, NE: University of Nebraska Press / University of Nebraska-Lincoln Libraries-Electronic Text Center, 2005), lewisandclarkjournals.unl.edu/journals.php?id=1806-09-04.

41. Ron Judd, "Why Returning Grizzlies to the North Cascades is the Right Thing to Do," *Seattle Times Pacific NW Magazine*, November 23, 2015, www.seattletimes.com/pacific-nw-magazine/returning-grizzlies-to-the-north-cascades-is-the-right-thing-to-do/?utm_source=RSS&utm_medium=Referral&utm_campaign=RSS_all.

42. Rich Landers, "Poll: Majority Favors Restoring Grizzly Bear in North Cascades," *The Spokesman-Review Outdoors Blog*, 6 June 6, 2016, www.spokesman.com/blogs/outdoors/2016/jun/06/poll-majority-favors-restoring-grizzly-bears-north-cascades; Kie Relyea, "Bring Grizzly Bears Back to the North Cascades, Survey Finds," *Bellingham Herald*, June 7, 2016, www.bellinghamherald.com/news/local/article82131452.html; "North Cascades Grizzly Bear," *Conservation Northwest*, www.conservationnw.org/what-we-do/northcascades/north-cascades-grizzly-bear.

43. Knibb, *Grizzly Wars*, 41. Gray wolves differ from grizzlies because they have moved into the North Cascades on their own from Idaho and Montana. Wolves have been sighted in the Glacier Peak and Pasayten wilderness areas, and three known packs live north and east of the park complex. Many ranchers oppose wolf reintroduction and protection, although the state offers compensation for livestock lost to wolves (and cougars and bears). See National Park Service, "Wolf Sightings and Distribution," *North Cascades*, www.nps.gov/noca/learn/nature/wolves2.htm, Lynda Mapes, "New Wolf Pack in Washington," *Seattle Times*, November 25, 2015, www.seattletimes.com/seattle-news/environment/wolf-pack; Martin, "The Rewilding of the North Cascades"; Washington State Department of Fish & Wildlife, "Compensation Rules for Depredation Incidents," *Gray Wolf Conservation and Management*, wdfw.wa.gov/conservation/gray_wolf/livestock/compensation.html, "Washington Wolf Population Continues to Grow," *About WDFW*, March 14, 2016, wdfw.wa.gov/news/mar1416b.

Bibliography

Abbreviations

BL   The Bancroft Library, Berkeley
FS   United States Forest Service
MRNP   Mount Rainier National Park Archives
NACP   National Archives and Records Administration–College Park,
              Maryland
NARA-APR   National Archives and Records Administration–Alaska Pacific
              Region, Seattle
NPS   National Park Service
UA   University of Arizona Library, Tucson
UW   University of Washington Manuscripts and Special Collections
WSA   Washington State Archives, Olympia
WSL   Washington State Library, Tumwater
WSPC   Washington State Planning Council

Sources

"About the Mine: Fact Sheet." *Wild Cascades*, December 1966–January 1967.

"A Brief History of Seattle City Light." *Seattle City Light*, n.d. www.seattle.gov/light/history/brief.asp.

Adams, Nigel Bruce. "The Holden Mine: From Discovery to Production, 1896–1938." PhD diss., University of Washington, 1976.

"A Job One-Fourth Done." *NCCC News* 4(10): 1 (October 1960).

Allen, Howard. "Outings at Lake Chelan." *Smalley's Magazine* 22(1): 24–29 (July 1903).

Allin, Craig. *The Politics of Wilderness Preservation*. Fairbanks: University of Alaska Press, 2008.

"The American Alps." *Cascades*, Summer 1966.

American Alps Legacy Project. *The American Alps Legacy Project*. www.americanalps.org.

An Act to establish the North Cascades National Park and Ross Lake and Lake Chelan National Recreation Areas, to designate the Pasayten Wilderness and to modify the Glacier Peak Wilderness, in the State of Washington, and for other purposes. 90th Cong., 1st Sess., S. 1321. October 2, 1968.

Anderson, Ada Woodruff. "Lake Chelan and the American Alps." *Pacific Monthly* 11(5): 300–30 (May 1904).

"A North Cascades National Park." *Conservation News Letter* 6(1): 1 (May 1960).

"Another Battle?" *The Mountaineer* 53(10): 6 (September 1960).

Arntz, Dee. *Extraordinary Women Conservationists of Washington*. Charleston, SC: History Press, 2015.

"A Wilderness Starfish." *National Parks* 33(139): 6–7 (April 1959).

Avery, Abigail. "Nurturing the Earth: North Cascades, Alaska, New England, and Issues of War and Peace." Oral history conducted in 1988 by Polly Kaufman. Sierra Club Nationwide IV, Sierra Club Oral History Project, Sierra Club, 1996.

Barcott, Bruce, ed. *Northwest Passages*. Seattle: Sasquatch Books, 1994.

Barnes, Irston. "Glacier Peak—Wilderness Wonderland." *Mazama* 37(13): 40–43 (December 1955).

Becker, Paula. "Pelly, Thomas M. (1902–1973)." *HistoryLink*, January 4, 2005. www.historylink.org/File/7199.

Beckey, Fred. *Cascade Alpine Guide: Climbing and High Routes, Stevens Pass to Rainy Pass, Vol. 2*, 3rd ed. Seattle: The Mountaineers, 2003.

———. *Cascade Alpine Guide: Climbing & High Routes, Vol. 3, Rainy Pass to Fraser River*. Seattle: Mountaineers, 1995.

———. *Range of Glaciers: The Exploration and Survey of the Northern Cascade Range*. Portland: Oregon Historical Society Press, 2003.

Bergmann, Nicolas Timothy. "Preserving Nature through Film: Wilderness Alps of Stehekin and the North Cascades, 1956–1968." Master's thesis, Portland State University, 2013. *Dissertations and Theses*, paper 973.

Biggs, John A. "North Cascades National Park?" *Washington State Game Bulletin*, April 1960.

"Board Business Briefs." *The Mountaineer* 59(13): 2 (December 1966).

Brock, Emily K. *Money Trees: The Douglas Fir and American Forestry, 1900–1944*. Corvallis: Oregon State University Press, 2015.

Brooks, Paul. "A Copper Company in the North Cascades." *Harper's* 235(1408): 48–50 (September 1967).

———. "The Fight for America's Alps," *The Atlantic* 219(2): 87–90, 97–99 (February 1967).

———. "Kennecott Copper and Glacier Peak." In *The Pursuit of Wilderness*. New York: Houghton Mifflin, 1971.

Brower, David. "The Missing Million." *Sierra Club Bulletin* 44(2): 10–15 (February 1959).

———. "Wilderness Alps of Stehekin." *Living Wilderness* 23(66): 18–24 (Autumn 1958).

Brower, David Ross. *Environmental Activist, Publicist, and Prophet: Oral History Transcript*. Reprint, London: Forgotten Books, 2013.

"Building the North Cascades Highway." *Washington Highways*, September 1972, 17–23.

Byrd, Robert. *Lake Chelan in the 1890s*. Rev. ed. Wenatchee, WA: Byrd-Song Publishing, 1992.

Callahan, Margaret Bundy. "The Last Frontier." In *The Cascades*, edited by Roderick Peattie. New York: Vanguard Press, 1949.

Callicott, J. Baird, and Michael P. Nelson, eds. *The Great New Wilderness Debate*. Athens: University of Georgia Press, 1998.

Carroll, Richard. "A Personal Recollection." *Washington Highways*, September 1972, 10.

Carson, Rachel. *Silent Spring*. Boston: Houghton Mifflin Co., 1962.

Catton, Theodore. *National Park, City Playground: Mount Rainier in the Twentieth Century*. Seattle: University of Washington Press, 2006.

"Champion and Candidate." *Life*, September 8, 1952, 47. Accessed through Google Books at books.google.com/books?id=flYEAAAAMBAJ.

"Chelan County, Washington." *Wilhelm's Magazine The Coast* 12(4): 193–201 (October 1906).

Christensen, Neal. "Designated National Recreation Areas: Their History, Purpose, Management, and Influence on Local Communities." April 2012. www.yakimaforever. org/wp-content/uploads/2012/06/TWS-National-Recreation-Area-Report.pdf.

Cioc, Mark, and Char Miller. "Interview with Hal K. Rothman." *Environmental History* 12 (January 2007): 141–52.

Clark, Norman H. *Washington: A Bicentennial History.* New York: W. W. Norton, 1976.

Clary, David A. *Timber and the Forest Service.* Lawrence: University Press of Kansas, 1986.

Cleator, Fred. "Recollections of Bob Marshall" (unpublished manuscript). Wilderness Society Records, Denver Public Library. N.d.

Cohen, Michael P. *The History of the Sierra Club, 1982–1970.* San Francisco: Sierra Club Books, 1988.

Congressional Record, 86th Cong., 2nd sess., 1960. Vol. 106, pt. 1.

Congressional Record, 86th Cong., 2nd sess., 1960. Vol. 106, pt. 2.

Congressional Record, 87th Cong., 1st Sess., 1961. Vol. 107, pt. 1.

Congressional Record, 88th Cong., 1st Sess., 1963. Vol. 109, pt. 5.

Connelly, Joel. "Dr. Fred Darvill." *Wild Cascades* (Spring 2008), 7.

———. *Strange Bedfellows* (blog). blog.seattlepi.com/seattlepolitics.

Consolidated Natural Resources Act of 2008. Public Law 110-229, 110th Cong., 2nd sess. May 8, 2008.

Cornwall, Warren. "Should Grizzlies be Restored to the North Cascades?" *National Geographic,* November 29, 2014. news.nationalgeographic.com/news/2014/11/141130-grizzly-reintroduction-cascades-national-park-environment.

Dant Ewert, Sara E. "Peak Park Politics: The Struggle Over the Sawtooths, From Borah to Church." *Pacific Northwest Quarterly* 91(3): 138–49 (Summer 2000).

"David Brower (1912–2000): Timeline." *Sierra Club.* content.sierraclub.org/brower/timeline.

"David Brower." *Wilderness.net.* www.wilderness.net/NWPS/Brower.

Denny, E.I. "Chelan: A Wonderful Lake of the Cascade Range." *Northwest Magazine,* June 1896, 5–10.

Department of Agriculture, Forest Service, Pacific Northwest Region. "Glacier Peak Land Management Study, Mount Baker and Wenatchee National Forests, Washington." Forest Service. February 7, 1957.

———. "Glacier Peak Land Management Study, Mt. Baker and Wenatchee National Forests, Washington." Forest Service. February 7, 1957, rev. March 10, 1958.

DeVoto, Bernard. "Let's Close the National Parks." *Harper's* 207(1241): 49–52 (October 1953).

Dietrich, William. *The North Cascades: Finding Beauty and Renewal in the Wild Nearby.* Seattle: Braided River, 2014.

Dougherty, Phil. "A Rough Draft of the North Cascades Highway is Dedicated on September 29, 1968." *HistoryLink,* March 20, 2015. www.historylink.org/File/11043.

———. "North Cascades Highway Opens on September 2, 1972." *HistoryLink,* March 20, 2015. www.historylink.org/File/11044.

Douglas, William O. *My Wilderness: The Pacific West*. Garden City, NY: Doubleday & Co., 1960.

Downing, Alfred. "The Pictured Rock of Lake Chelan." *Northwest Magazine*, October 1889, 3–4.

Dwelley, Charles M. *So They Called the Town 'Concrete.'* Concrete, WA: The Concrete *Herald*, 1980.

Duscha, Julius. "The Undercover Fight Over the Wilderness." *Harper's* 224 (1343): 55–59 (April 1962).

Dyer, Polly. "Preserving Washington Parklands and Wilderness." By Susan Schrepfer. In *Pacific Northwest Conservationists*. Berkeley: Regional Oral History Office, The Bancroft Library, University of California, Berkeley, 1986.

———. "Whose Ice Axes?" *Wild Cascades* (Spring 1998): 13.

Eighme, Lloyd E. "Through the Heart of the Northern Cascades." *Living Wilderness* 13(26): 9–15 (Autumn 1948).

Emerson, W. M. "History of Chelan Valley." In *A History of Central Washington*. Edited by Lindley M. Hull. Spokane: Shaw & Borden Company, 1929.

Evans, Brock. "Field Hearings on North Cascades." *Sierra Club Bulletin* 53(6): 17–18 (June 1968).

Everhart, William C. *The National Park Service*. Boulder, CO: Westview Press, 1983.

Ficken, Robert E., and Charles P. LeWarne. *Washington: A Centennial History*. Seattle: University of Washington Press, 1988.

"First Banquet a Success." *Wild Cascades*, August–September 1964.

Fish and Wildlife Service. "Grizzly Bear Recovery Plan, Supplement: North Cascades Ecosystem Recovery Plan Chapter," by Christopher Servheen. June 23, 1997. www.nps.gov/noca/upload/NorthCascadesSupplement1997.pdf.

———. "North Cascades Grizzly Bear Sighting," July 1, 2011. westernwildlife.org/wp-content/uploads/2011/07/NR_NCGB_sighting7_1_11.pdf.

Fish & Wildlife Service and National Park Service. "North Cascades Ecosystem: Grizzly Bear Restoration Plan/Environmental Impact Statement," February 2016. www.nps.gov/noca/upload/final-newsletter_Feb16_.pdf.

Fluharty, Dave. "In Memoriam: Grant McConnell." *Stehekin Choice*, December 1993/January 1994.

Forest History Society. "The Fully Managed, Multiple-Use Forest Era, 1960–1970." In *The USDA Forest Service: The First Century*. www.foresthistory.org/ASPNET/Publications/first_century/sec7.htm.

Forest Service. *Climate Change Vulnerability and Adaptation in the North Cascades Region, Washington*. Portland, OR: Pacific Northwest Research Station, September 2014. www.fs.fed.us/pnw/pubs/pnw_gtr892.pdf.

———. "Operation Outdoors," 1957. www.foresthistory.org/ASPNET/policy/Recreation/documents/Operation_Outdoors_1957.pdf.

———. *The Rising Cost of Wildfire Operations: Effects on the Forest Service's Non-Fire Work*, August 4, 2015. www.fs.fed.us/sites/default/files/2015-Rising-Cost-Wildfire-Operations.pdf.

Forest Service, Okanogan-Wenatchee National Forest. "Chelan County PUD and Forest Service Complete Land Exchange," Press Release, May 3, 2010.

Forest Service Region 6. *National Visitor Use Monitoring Results, Mount Baker-Snoqualmie National Forest*, February 8, 2002. www.fs.fed.us/recreation/programs/nvum/reports/year1/R6_MBS_final.htm.

———. *Visitor Use Report: Okanogan*, August 10, 2011. www.fs.usda.gov/Internet/FSE_DOCUMENTS/stelprdb5348737.pdf.

———. *Visitor Use Report: Wenatchee*, August 10, 2011. www.fs.usda.gov/Internet/FSE_DOCUMENTS/stelprdb5348736.pdf.

Foresta, Ronald A. *America's National Parks and Their Keepers*. Washington: Resources for the Future, 1984.

Freeman, Orville L. "Address by Secretary Orville L. Freeman." Speech to the Sierra Club 10th Biennial Wilderness Conference, San Francisco, April 7, 1967.

Frome, Michael. *Battle for the Wilderness*, rev. ed. Salt Lake City: University of Utah Press, 1997.

Gabbert, Bill. "Congress Takes Another Tentative Step Toward Developing a Wildland Fire Bill." *Wildfire Today*, May 27, 2016. wildfiretoday.com/2016/05/27/congress-takes-another-tentative-step-toward-developing-a-wildland-fire-bill.

Gannett, Henry. "Lake Chelan and its Glacier." *Mazama* 3(1): 185–89 (March 1907).

Georgette, Susan, and Ann Harvey. *Local Influence and the National Interest: Ten Years of National Park Service Administration in the Stehekin Valley, Washington: A Case Study*, Publication No. 4, Environmental Field Program. Santa Cruz: University of California, 1980.

Gilligan, James P. "The Development of Policy and Administration of Forest Service Primitive and Wilderness Areas in the Western United States." Ph.D. diss., University of Michigan, 1953.

"Glacier Park's Night of the Grizzlies." Montana Public Broadcasting System, aired May 17, 2010. www.montanapbs.org/GlacierParksNightoftheGrizzlies.

"Glacier Peak Wilderness Hearings." *Living Wilderness* 24(71): 35–37 (Winter 1959–60).

"Glacier Peak Wilderness Hearings, October 13, 16." *The Mountaineer* 52(11): 4–5 (October 1959).

"Glacier Peak Wonderland." *Western Outdoor Quarterly* 22(4): 7–10 (November 1955).

Glover, James. *A Wilderness Original: The Life of Bob Marshall*. Seattle: The Mountaineers, 1986.

"The Golden Year for the Golden Triangle." *NCCC News* 5(5) (May 1961).

Goldsworthy, Patrick. "Crisis, Sorrow and Horizons." *Wild Cascades*, December 1963–January 1964.

———. "Kennecott Meets with Conservation Leaders." *Wild Cascades*, December 1966–January 1967.

———. "The Northern Cascades on the Witness Stand." *Sierra Club Bulletin* 48(8): 2, 18 (November 1963).

———. "Protecting the North Cascades, 1954–1983." By Ann Lage. In *Pacific Northwest Conservationists*. Berkeley: Regional Oral History Office, The Bancroft Library, University of California, Berkeley, 1986.

"Governor Daniel J. Evans' North Cascades National Recreation Area Report and Recommendations." Olympia: June 1966.

Graves, C. Edward. "The Glacier Peak Wilderness." *National Parks* 30(125): 70 (April–June 1956).

———. "Washington's Stehekin Valley." *National Parks* 31(130): 140–41 (July–September 1957).

"Grizzly Bear History." *Western Wildlife Outreach.* westernwildlife.org/grizzly-bear-outreach-project/history.

"Grizzly Sightings." *Western Wildlife Outreach.* westernwildlife.org/grizzly-bear-outreach-project/grizzly-sightings.

Guide to the Records of the Washington State Highways Department, 1923–1985. Olympia: Office of Secretary of State, Division of Archives and Records Management, July 1999.

Hackenmiller, Tom. *Ladies of the Lake: Transportation, Tragedy and Triumph on Lake Chelan.* Manson, WA: Point Publishing, 1998.

Hagenstein, William D. *Corks and Suspenders: Memoirs of an Early Forester.* N.p.: Giustina, 2010.

Harris, Stephen L. *Fire & Ice: The Cascades Volcanoes,* rev. ed. Seattle: The Mountaineers, 1980.

Hartzog, George B., Jr. *Battling for the National Parks.* Mt. Kisco, NY: Moyer Bell, 1988.

Harvey, Mark W. T. *A Symbol of Wilderness: Echo Park and the American Conservation Movement.* Albuquerque: University of New Mexico Press, 1994.

———. *Wilderness Forever: Howard Zahniser and the Path to the Wilderness Act.* Seattle: University of Washington Press, 2005.

Hays, Samuel P. *Beauty, Health, and Permanence: Environmental Politics in the United States, 1955–1985.* Cambridge: Cambridge University Press, 1987.

———. *Conservation and the Gospel of Efficiency: The Progressive Conservation Movement, 1890–1920.* Cambridge: Harvard University Press, 1959.

———. "From Conservation to Environment: Environmental Politics in the United States Since World War II." In *Out of the Woods: Essays in Environmental History,* edited by Char Miller and Hal Rothman. Pittsburgh: University of Pittsburgh Press, 1997.

Heald, Weldon F. "Cascade Holiday." In *The Cascades,* edited by Roderick Peattie. New York: Vanguard Press, 1949, 97–138.

———. "The Undiscovered Cascades." *National Parks* 33(145): 8–11 (October 1959).

Herndon, Grace. *Cut and Run: Saying Goodbye to the Last Great Forests in the West.* Telluride, CO: Western Eye Press, 1991.

Hessey, Charles D., Jr. "Across the North Cascade Primitive Area." *Living Wilderness* 25(74): 5–9 (Fall–Winter 1960–1961).

Hetherton, P. "Washington Cascade Ridge Area Study." *Pacific Northwest Regional Planning Commission News,* October 15, 1939, 12–13.

Hickey, Hannah. "Fires and Floods: North Cascades Federal Lands Prepare for Climate Change." *UW Today,* October 29, 2014. www.washington.edu/news/2014/10/29/fires-and-floods-north-cascades-federal-lands-prepare-for-climate-change.

Hirt, Paul. *A Conspiracy of Optimism: Management of the National Forests Since World War Two.* Lincoln: University of Nebraska Press, 1994.

Hogan, J. B., and J. R. Mitchell, "North Cascade Wilderness Area." *Living Wilderness* 18(46): 14–15 (Autumn 1953).

House Subcommittee on National Parks and Recreation, Committee on Interior and Insular Affairs. *The North Cascades, Part I: Hearings Before the Subcommittee on National Parks and Recreation of the Committee on Interior and Insular Affairs, House of Representatives*. 90th Cong., 2nd Sess., 1968.

Huth, Hans. *Nature and the American: Three Centuries of Changing Attitudes*. New ed. Lincoln: University of Nebraska Press, 1990.

Hyde, Philip. "The Wilderness World of the Cascades." *Living Wilderness* 22(6): 5–16 (Spring 1957).

Ise, John. *Our National Park Policy: A Critical History*. Baltimore: Johns Hopkins Press, 1961.

Johnson, Riley. *Have You Been Told? Do You Know the Facts? On the Proposed Glacier Peak Wilderness Area* (pamphlet). National Forest Multiple Use Association: January 1958.

The Kerosene Kid [Joe Miller]. "North Cascades Under Attack: Battle Lines Drawn." *Wild Cascades*, December 1969–January 1970.

Kingman, W. Kenneth. "Mines and Mining of Chelan Valley." In *A History of Central Washington*, ed. Lindley M. Hull. Spokane: Shaw & Borden Company, 1929.

Kirn, Jacqueline Krolopp. "The Skagit River-High Ross Dam Controversy: A Case Study of a Canadian-U.S. Transboundary Conflict and Negotiated Resolution." Master's thesis, University of Washington, 1987.

Kirn, Jackie Krolopp, and Marion E. Marts. "The Skagit-High Ross Dam Controversy: Negotiation and Settlement." *Natural Resources Journal* 26 (Spring 1986): 261–89.

Knibb, David. *Backyard Wilderness: The Alpine Lakes Story*. Seattle: The Mountaineers, 1982.

———. *Grizzly Wars: The Public Fight Over the Great Bear*. Cheney: Eastern Washington University Press, 2008.

Lakes, Arthur. "Lake Chelan District: An Account of an Undeveloped Mining District in the State of Washington." *Mines and Minerals* 22 (January 1900): 268–70.

Landers, Rich. *Outdoors Blog*. www.spokesman.com/blogs/outdoors.

Leopold, A. Starker, S. A. Cain, C. M. Cottam, I. N. Gabrielson, and T. L. Kimball. "Wildlife Management in the National Parks (1963)." Reprinted in *The Great New Wilderness Debate*, edited by J. Baird Callicott and Michael P. Nelson. Athens: University of Georgia Press, 1998, 103–19.

Leopold, Aldo. "Conserving the Covered Wagon." *Sunset*, March 1925.

———. "Wilderness as a Form of Land Use." Reprinted in *The Great New Wilderness Debate*, edited by J. Baird Callicott and Michael P. Nelson. Athens: University of Georgia Press, 1998, 75–84.

Leshy, John D. *The Mining Law: A Study in Perpetual Motion*. Washington, DC: Resources for the Future, 1987.

Lewis, Meriwether, William Clark, et al., April 29, 1805, entry in *The Journals of the Lewis and Clark Expedition*, edited by Gary Moulton. Lincoln: University of Nebraska Press / University of Nebraska-Lincoln Libraries-Electronic Text Center, 2005. lewisandclarkjournals.unl.edu.

Lien, Carsten. *Olympic Battleground: The Power Politics of Timber Preservation*. 2nd ed. Seattle: Mountaineers Books, 2000.

"The Line-Up at Glacier Peak Hearings." *The Mountaineer* 53(1): 4–5 (January 1960).

Linsley, Daniel Chapman. "Lake Chelan and Agnes Creek in 1870." *Northwest Discovery* 2(6): 382 (June 1981).

"List of Officers, Board of Directors and Members." *NCCC* 1(1): 5 (August 1957).

Louter, David. *Contested Terrain: North Cascades National Park Service Complex; An Administrative History.* Seattle: National Park Service, 1998.

———. *Windshield Wilderness: Cars, Roads, and Nature in Washington's National Parks.* Seattle: University of Washington Press, 2006.

Luxenberg, Gretchen A. *Historic Resource Study: North Cascades National Park Service Complex, Washington.* Seattle: National Park Service, Pacific Northwest Region, Cultural Resources Division, 1986.

Lyman Glacier Continues to Melt Away. www.nichols.edu/departments/glacier/lyman.htm.

Lyman, W.D. "Lake Chelan." *Overland Monthly* 33(195): 195–201 (March 1899).

Mackintosh, Barry. "Harold L. Ickes and the National Park Service." *Journal of Forest History* 29(2): 78–84 (April 1985).

Majors, Harry, ed. "The First Crossing of the North Cascades." *Northwest Discovery* 1(3): 128 (August 1980).

Manning, Harvey. *Conservation and Conflict: The U.S. Forest Service and the National Park Service in the North Cascades, 1892–1992.* Seattle: North Cascades Conservation Council, 1992 (preliminary unpublished edition).

———. "Strike Up the Band." *Wild Cascades*, April–May 1964.

———. *The North Cascades.* Seattle: The Mountaineers, 1964.

———. "You Don't Have to be Old to be an Elder." *Backpacker*, Spring 1975, 56–59, 84–89.

Mark, Stephen R. "What Price Expansion? Dams Versus the National Park Concept." *George Wright Forum* 9(2): 53–61 (1992).

Marsh, Kevin R. *Drawing Lines in the Forest: Creating Wilderness Areas in the Pacific Northwest.* Seattle: University of Washington Press, 2007.

———. "Drawing Lines in the Woods: Debating Wilderness Boundaries on National Forest Lands in the Cascade Mountains, 1950–1984." PhD diss., Washington State University, 2002.

Marshall, Bob. "The Problem of the Wilderness." Reprinted in *The Great New Wilderness Debate*, edited by J. Baird Callicott and Michael P. Nelson. Athens: University of Georgia Press, 1998, 85–96.

———. "Three Great Western Wildernesses: What Must be Done to Save Them?" *The Living Wilderness* 1:1 (September 1935), 9–11.

Martin, Christian. "The Rewilding of the North Cascades: A Tale of Gray Wolves and Grizzly Bears." *AdventuresNW.* February 19, 2014. www.adventuresnw.com/the-rewilding-of-the-north-cascades-a-tale-of-gray-wolves-and-grizzly-bears.

McCloskey, J. Michael. *In the Thick of it: My Life in the Sierra Club.* Washington, DC: Island Press, 2005.

———. "News Notes on North Cascades." *Wild Cascades*, October–November 1964.

———. "North Cascades Study Team: Progress in the Study of the North Cascades." *Wild Cascades*, August–September 1963.

———. "The Product of an Appeal: The New High Mountain Policy." *NCCC News* 6(6): 6–7 (June 1962).

———, ed. *Prospectus for a North Cascades National Park*. Seattle: North Cascades Conservation Council, 1963.

———. "Resource Reports." *Wild Cascades*, April–May 1964.

McCloskey, Michael. "A New Phase in the Cascades Campaign." *Sierra Club Bulletin* 50(6): 22 (June 1965).

———. "Wilderness Movement at the Crossroads, 1945–1970." *Pacific Historical Review* 41(3): 346–61 (August 1972).

McConnell, Grant. "The Cascade Range." In *The Cascades*, edited by Roderick Peattie, New York: Vanguard Press, 1949.

———. "The Cascades Wilderness." *Sierra Club Bulletin* 41(10): 24–31 (December 1956).

———. "Conservation and Politics in the North Cascades." Oral history by Rod Holmgren. Berkeley, CA: Sierra Club, 1983.

———. "The Conservation Movement—Past and Present." *Western Political Quarterly* 7(3): 463–78.

———. "Five Years of National Park Service Administration in the North Cascades." *Wild Cascades* (December/January 1973–1974).

———. "The North Cascades Wilderness—Almost Half Safe." *Sierra Club Bulletin* 45(7) (October 1960).

———. "P.R. in the Forests." *The Nation* 201(22): 522–24 (December 27, 1965).

———. *Stehekin: A Valley in Time*. Seattle: The Mountaineers, 1988.

McLeod, Jack. *The North Cascades Highway: A Roadside Guide to America's Alps*. Seattle: University of Washington Press, 2013.

McPhee, John. *Encounters with the Archdruid*. New York: Farrar, Straus and Giroux, 1971.

Meany, Edmond. "Glacier Peak." *The Mountaineer* III (November 1910), 24.

Mercure, Delbert V., Jr., and William M. Ross. "The Wilderness Act: A Product of Congressional Compromise." In *Congress and the Environment*, edited by Richard A. Cooley and Geoffrey Wandesforde-Smith. Seattle: University of Washington Press, 1970.

Meringolo, Denise D. *Museums, Monuments, and National Parks: Toward a New Genealogy of Public History*. Amherst: University of Massachusetts Press, 2012.

"Message to Congress: Johnson on Pollution, Resources, Road Safety." *CQ Almanac 1967*, 23rd ed., 20-36-A-20-40-A. Washington, DC: Congressional Quarterly, 1968. library.cqpress.com/cqalmanac/cqal67-1311900.

Mierendorf, Bob. "Who Walks on the Ground," in *Impressions of the North Cascades*, edited by John Miles. Seattle: The Mountaineers, 1996, 39–53.

Mierendorf, Robert. "Cultural History: Across Time and Terrain in the Skagit Valley." ncascades.org/discover/north-cascades-ecosystem/cultural-history.

Mierendorf, Robert R. *People of the North Cascades*. Seattle: National Park Service, Pacific Northwest Region, 1986.

Miles, John, ed. *Impressions of the North Cascades: Essays About a Northwest Landscape*. Seattle: The Mountaineers, 1996.

Miles, John. *Koma Kulshan*. Seattle: The Mountaineers, 1984.

Miles, John C. *Wilderness in National Parks: Playground or Preserve*. Seattle: University of Washington Press, 2009.

Miller, Char, ed. *American Forests: Nature, Culture, and Politics*. Lawrence: University Press of Kansas, 1997.

———. *Gifford Pinchot and the Making of Modern Environmentalism.* Washington, DC: Island Press, 2004. Kindle edition.

———. *Public Lands, Public Debates: A Century of Controversy.* Corvallis: Oregon State University Press, 2012.

Miller, Jay. "Middle Columbia River Salishans." In *Handbook of North American Indians.* Vol. 12: *Plateau.* Vol. ed. Deward E. Walker Jr., series ed. William L. Sturtevant. Washington, DC: Smithsonian Institution, 1998.

Miller, Joseph W. and Margaret M. Miller. "Big Beaver Valley." *The Mountaineer 1970–1971* (June 1972).

Moen, Wayne S. *The Mineral Industry of Washington—Highlights of its Development, 1853–1980.* Information Circular No. 74. Olympia: Washington Department of Natural Resources, Division of Geology and Earth Resources, 1982.

"Mongering Rumors." *Wild Cascades*, October–November 1964.

Morgan, Chris. *Wanted: Grizzly Bears? Chris Morgan Wildlife*, www.grizzlybearfilm.org.

"Mountaineers' Recommendations on North Cascades Primitive Area." *Mountaineer Bulletin* 54(2): 6–7 (February 1961).

Mount Baker National Park. U.S. House. 64th Cong., 1st sess., H. R. 9805. *Cong. Rec.*, 53, pt. 2 (January 22, 1916): 1408; S. 3775. *Cong. Rec.*, 53, pt. 2 (January 24, 1916): 1424; S. 3982. *Cong. Rec.*, 53, pt. 2 (January 26, 1916): 1549.

Mount Baker National Park, 65th Cong., 1st sess., S. 312. *Cong. Rec.*, 55, pt. 1 (April 4, 1917}: 192; H. R. 6066. *Cong. Rec.*, 55, pt. 1 (September 15, 1917): 7168.

Mount Baker National Park, 65th Cong., 2nd sess., S. 3662. *Cong. Rec.*, 56, pt. 2 (July 31, 1918): 1498; S. 4014. *Cong. Rec.*, 56, pt. 3 (March 5, 1918): 3031.

Mount Baker National Park, 66th Cong., 1st Sess., S. 371. *Cong. Rec.*, 58, pt. 1 (May 20, 1919): 59.

Mount Baker National Park, 67th Cong., 1st Sess., S. 20. *Cong. Rec.*, 61, pt. 1 (April 12, 1921): 142.

Mountaineers, The, North Cascades Conservation Council, and the Sierra Club. *An Urgent Request that You Help Conserve the Northern Cascades* (pamphlet). N.p.: October 1959.

Mountaineers, The. "Wilderness Status Recommendations for the Glacier Peak Area." Seattle, May 1959.

Muir, John. "Selections from *Our National Parks* (1901)." Reprinted in *The Great New Wilderness Debate*, edited by J. Baird Callicott and Michael P. Nelson. Athens: University of Georgia Press, 1998, 48–62.

Multiple-Use and Sustained Yield Act of 1960. Public Law 86-517, 86th Congress, June 12, 1960.

Murray, Keith A. "Building a Wagon Road through the Northern Cascade Mountains." *Pacific Northwest Quarterly* 56(2): 49–56 (April 1965).

Nagle, John Copeland. "Wilderness Exceptions." *Environmental Law* 44(2): 373–414. law.lclark.edu/live/files/17164-44-2naglepdf.

Nash, Gerald D. *The American West Transformed: The Impact of the Second World War.* Lincoln: University of Nebraska Press, 1985.

Nash, Roderick. *Wilderness and the American Mind.* Rev. ed. New Haven: Yale University Press, 1973.

Nash, Roderick Frazier. *The Rights of Nature: A History of Environmental Ethics.* Madison: University of Wisconsin Press, 1989.

National Park Service. "Annual Park Ranking Report for Recreation Visitors in: 2015." *NPS Stats, National Park Service Visitor Use Statistics.* irma.nps.gov/Stats/Reports/ National.

———. "Background Information Upper Stehekin Valley Road." August 2009. *PEPC Planning, Environment, & Public Comment.* parkplanning.nps.gov/document. cfm?parkID=327&projectID=15383&documentID=36378.

———. "Bears." *Glacier National Park.* www.nps.gov/glac/learn/nature/bears.htm.

———. "Communicating Climate Change." *North Cascades National Park.* www.nps. gov/noca/blogs/communicating-climate-change.htm.

———. "Designations of National Park System Units." *Golden Gate National Recreation Area.* www.nps.gov/goga/planyourvisit/designations.htm.

———. *Final General Management Plan, Environmental Impact Statement, Vol. 1, Lake Chelan National Recreation Area, Chelan County, Washington.* June 1995. www.nps. gov/noca/learn/management/upload/1995-Lake-Chelan-NRA-Final-General-Management-Plan_vol1_figures.pdf.

———. "Glaciers/Glacial Features." *North Cascades National Park.* www.nps.gov/noca/ learn/nature/glaciers.htm.

———. "Grizzly Bears." *Yellowstone National Park.* www.nps.gov/yell/learn/nature/ grizzlybear.htm.

———. "National Register of Historic Places, Continuation Sheet: St. Andrews Episcopal Church." 1992. npgallery.nps.gov/GetAsset/602afc52-e7b9-4041-bbf1-75da5497ca03

———. *North Cascades National Park and Ross Lake National Recreation Area: A Proposal.* N.p.: Parkscape USA, 1967.

———. *Recreational Use of Land in the United States, Part XI of the Report on Land Planning.* Washington, DC: GPO, 1938.

———. "Recreation Visitation by State and by Park for Year: 2015." *NPS Stats: National Park Service Visitor Use Statistics.* irma.nps.gov/Stats/Reports/National.

———. *Report of Committee, Northern Cascades Area Investigation.* November 1937.

———. *Summary of Proposals to Establish a National Park or Monument in the Glacier Peak–Northern Cascade Mountain Region.* February 20, 1957; April 1957 (rev. July 1958).

———. "Wolf Sightings and Distribution." *North Cascades.* www.nps.gov/noca/learn/ nature/wolves2.htm.

National Park Service Cascades Committee. *National Park Potentialities in the Cascade Mountains of Washington.* 1940.

National Park Service and U.S. Fish and Wildlife Service. "Draft Grizzly Bear Restoration Plan and Environmental Impact Statement January 2017." January 12, 2017. *PEPC Planning, Environment & Public Comment.* parkplanning.nps.gov/projectHome. cfm?projectId=44144.

National Resources Board. *A Report on National Planning and Public Works in Relation to Natural Resources and including Land Use and Water Resources with Findings and Recommendations.* Washington, DC: GPO, 1934.

———. "State Planning—Review of Activities and Progress." Washington, DC: GPO, 1935.

National Resources Board Land Planning Committee. *Part II: Report of the Land Planning Committee.* Washington, DC: GPO, 1934.

National Resources Committee. "State Planning Programs and Accomplishments (supplementing State Planning Report of 1935)." Washington, DC: GPO, 1936.

Nelson, Glenn. "What We've Lost in the Methow Valley Wildfires." *High Country News,* August 21, 2015. www.hcn.org/articles/twisp-wildfire-washington-firefighter-deaths-methow-valley.

Nelson, Michael P. "An Amalgamation of Wilderness Preservation Arguments." In *The Great New Wilderness Debate,* edited by J. Baird Callicott and Michael P. Nelson. Athens: University of Georgia Press, 1998, 154–200.

"News of Conservation and the Club." *Sierra Club Bulletin* 52(5): 3 (June 1967).

"The New Strategy: Summer 1963," *Wild Cascades* May–June–July 1963, 2.

North Cascades Challenger, 1998 Visitor Information Guide. N.p.: North Cascades National Park and Mt. Baker Ranger District of the Mt. Baker-Snoqualmie National Forest, 1998.

North Cascades Conservation Council. *Are You Aware? Comments Concerning the Glacier Peak Wilderness Area* (pamphlet). March 1958.

North Cascades Conservation Council v. Manuel Lujan, et al. Civil Case No. C-89-1342D, April 22, 1991.

"North Cascades Grizzly Bear." *Conservation Northwest.* www.conservationnw.org/what-we-do/northcascades/north-cascades-grizzly-bear.

North Cascades National Park Service Complex. *Master Plan.* Washington: NPS, 1970.

———. *Wilderness Recommendations.* Washington: NPS, 1970.

"North Cascades Park Study Bills Introduced." *The Mountaineer* 53(2): 3 (February 1960).

"North Cascades Recreation Sites Planned by U.S." *Journal of Commerce,* November 23, 1964.

North Cascades Study Team. *The North Cascades Study Report.* Washington, DC: GPO, October 1965.

———. *The North Cascades: A Report to the Secretary of the Interior and the Secretary of Agriculture.* Washington, DC: GPO, 1965.

"North Cascades Wilderness Area Proposal." *Wild Cascades* June–July 1964, 11–19.

"North of Glacier Peak Limited Area." *Living Wilderness* 22(63): 35 (Winter–Spring 1958).

"Northwest Conservation Representative Appointed," *Sierra Club Bulletin* 46(9): 3 (November 1961).

Oberteuffer, Margaret. "A Northern Cascades Wilderness Trek." *Living Wilderness* 24(70): 1–9 (Autumn 1959).

Official Report of Proceedings before the United States Department of Agriculture Forest Service In the Matter of: The Proposed Establishment of Glacier Peak Wilderness Area, Wenatchee, Washington, October 16, 1959.

Oldham, Kit. "Jackson, Henry M. 'Scoop' (1912–1983)." *HistoryLink,* August 19, 2003. historylink.org/File/5516.

———. "Magnuson, Warren G. (1905–1989)." *HistoryLink,* October 14, 2003. historylink.org/File/5569.

Olshausen, Matthias. "From Company Town to Company Town: Holden and Holden Village, Washington, 1937–1980 & Today." Master's thesis, Portland State University, 2013. *Dissertations and Theses,* paper 717.

Olympic Park Associates. *Voice of the Wild Olympics 50th Anniversary Edition*. Seattle: OPA, 1998.

Organic Administration Act of 1897, 16 U.S.C. § 473-478, 479-482 and 551 (1897).

"The ORRRC Doom Fulfilled." *Wild Cascades* 6(5): 3 (May 1962).

Outdoor Recreation Resources Review Commission. "Outdoor Recreation in America: A Report to the President and to the Congress by the Outdoor Recreation Resources Review Commission." Washington, DC: GPO, January 1962.

Park, Edwards. "Washington Wilderness, the North Cascades." *National Geographic*, March 1961, 334–67.

Pattullo, A.S. "Lake Chelan and Mt. Sahale." *Mazama* 2(3): 138–42 (July 1903).

Peattie, Roderick, ed. *The Cascades*. New York: Vanguard Press, 1949.

Pegues, Rodger. "Mining the Glacier Peak Wilderness Area." *Wild Cascades*, December 1966–January 1967.

———. "Outdoor Recreation Congress for the Pacific Northwest, Wenatchee, Wash." *Wild Cascades*, April–May 1965.

Pelto, Mauri S. "Impact of Climate Change on North Cascade Alpine Glaciers, and Alpine Runoff." *Northwest Science* 82(1): 65–75 (2008). www.nichols.edu/departments/glacier/06%20Pelto%20hi-res.pdf.

———. "Lyman Glacier: A Century of Change." Proceedings of the 66th Eastern Snow Conference, Niagara-on-the-Lake, Ontario, Canada, 2009. www.easternsnow.org/proceedings/2009/pelto.pdf.

———. "Lyman Glacier a Century of Change–Years Numbered." *From a Glaciers Perspective*. June 26, 2009. glacierchange.wordpress.com/2009/06/26/lyman-glacier-a-century-of-change-years-numbered.

———. *North Cascade Response to Global Warming*. June 15, 2009. www.nichols.edu/departments/glacier/globalwarming.html.

Pierce, Henry H. *Report of an Expedition from Fort Colville to Puget Sound, Washington Territory, by way of Lake Chelan & Skagit River*. 1882. Reprint, Fairfield, WA: Ye Galleon Press, 1973.

Pitzer, Paul C. *Building the Skagit*. Portland, OR: The Galley Press, 1978.

Pomeroy, Earl. *In Search of the Golden West: The Tourist in Western America*. Lincoln: University of Nebraska Press, 1957.

Pomeroy, Kenneth B. "Glacier Peak Wilderness." *American Forests* 63(7): 26-27, 63-64 (July 1957).

"Proposed Glacier Peak Wilderness Area." *The Mountaineer* 46(7), July 1953.

"Proposed Glacier Peak Wilderness Area Mountaineer Recommendations." *The Mountaineer* 49(6): 11 (June 1956).

Rakestraw, Lawrence. *A History of Forest Conservation in the Pacific Northwest, 1891–1913*. New York: Arno Press, 1979.

Raymond, Steve. "The Great Cascades Debate." *Field & Stream* 71(7): 10–15, 42 (November 1966).

Recreation Advisory Council. *Policy of the Establishment and Administration of Recreation Areas, Circular No. 1*. Washington, DC: GPO, 1963. www.nps.gov/parkhistory/online_books/anps/anps_5g.htm.

Repanshek, Kurt. "Officials Propose Grizzly Bear Recovery Plan for North Cascades National Park." *National Parks Traveler*. January 12, 2017. www.nationalparkstraveler.com/2017/01/officials-propose-grizzly-bear-recovery-plan-north-cascades-national-park.

Rettie, Dwight F. *Our National Park System*. Urbana: University of Illinois Press, 1995.

Rice, Nathan. "The Forgotten North Cascades Grizzly Bear." *High Country News*, November 23, 2011. www.hcn.org/issues/43.19/the-forgotten-north-cascades-grizzly-bear.

Richardson, Elmo. *Dams, Parks & Politics: Resource Development and Preservation in the Truman-Eisenhower Era*. Lexington: University Press of Kentucky, 1973.

Righter, Robert W. *Crucible for Conservation: The Struggle for Grand Teton National Park*. Moose, WY: Grand Teton Natural History Association, 1982.

Rinehart, Mary Roberts. *Tenting To-Night*. Boston: Houghton Mifflin, 1918.

Robbins, William G. Introduction to *Adventures of the First Settlers on the Oregon or Columbia River, 1810–1813*, by Alexander Ross. Corvallis: Oregon State University Press, Northwest Reprints, 2000.

———. "The Western Lumber Industry: A Twentieth-Century Perspective." In *The Twentieth-Century West: Historical Interpretations*. Edited by Gerald D. Nash and Richard W. Etulain. Albuquerque: University of New Mexico Press, 1989.

Robertson, Gay. *Stehekin Remembered*. Seattle: Pacific Northwest Parks and Forests Association, 1987.

Roe, JoAnn. *North Cascades Highway: Washington's Popular and Scenic Pass*. Seattle: The Mountaineers, 1997.

———. *The North Cascadians*. Seattle: Madrona Publishers, 1980.

Roth, Dennis M. *The Wilderness Movement and the National Forests*. College Station, TX: Intaglio Press, 1995.

Rothman, Hal K. *America's National Monuments: The Politics of Preservation*. Lawrence: University Press of Kansas, 1994.

———. *Devil's Bargains: Tourism in the Twentieth-Century American West*. Lawrence: University Press of Kansas, 1998.

———. *The Greening of a Nation? Environmentalism in the United States Since 1945*. Fort Worth, TX: Harcourt Brace College Publishers, 1998.

———. "'A Regular Ding-Dong Fight': Agency Culture and Evolution in the NPS-USFS Dispute, 1916–1937." *Western Historical Quarterly* 20(2): 141–61.

Runte, Alfred. *National Parks: The American Experience*. 4th ed. Lanham, MD: Taylor Trade Publishing, 2010.

"The Saddest, Least Necessary Feud of All." *Desert*, November 1961, reprinted in *Wild Cascades* 6(2): 5 (February 1962).

Sale, Roger. *Seattle Past to Present*. Seattle: University of Washington Press, 1978.

Sax, Joseph L. *Mountains Without Handrails: Reflections on the National Parks*. Ann Arbor: University of Michigan Press, 1980.

Schmieding, Samuel J. *From Controversy to Compromise to Cooperation: The Administrative History of Canyonlands National Park*. National Park Service, 2008. www.nps.gov/cany/planyourvisit.

Schmierer, Alan C. *Northing Up the Nooksack*. Seattle: Pacific Northwest Parks and Forests Association, 1983.

Schrepfer, Susan R. *The Fight to Save the Redwoods: A History of Environmental Reform, 1917–1978*. Madison: University of Wisconsin Press, 1983.

Schwantes, Carlos Arnaldo. *Railroad Signatures Across the Pacific Northwest*. Seattle: University of Washington Press, 1993.

"Scorecard." *Sports Illustrated*, April 24, 1967.

Scott, James W. *Washington, A Centennial Atlas.* Bellingham, WA: Center for Pacific Northwest Studies, Western Washington University, 1989.

Seattle City Directory, 1903.

Sellars, Richard West. *Preserving Nature in the National Parks: A History.* New Haven: Yale University Press, 1997.

Senate Committee on Energy and Natural Resources. *The Wildfire Management Act of 2015: A White Paper.* June 15, 2015. www.energy.senate.gov/public/index.cfm/files/serve?File_id=0ab5f328-f73a-49da-b1b4-814d31b215bd.

Senate Committee on Interior and Insular Affairs. *Authorizing the Establishment of the North Cascades National Park, the Ross Lake National Recreation Area, the Lake Chelan National Recreation Area, Designating the Pasayten Wilderness, and Modifying the Glacier Peak Wilderness, in the State of Washington, and for other Purposes.* 90th Cong., 1st Sess., 1967, S. Rept. 700.

————. *North Cascades–Olympic National Park: Hearings Before the Committee on Interior and Insular Affairs.* 89th Cong., 2nd Sess., 1966.

————. *The North Cascades.* 90th Cong., 1st Sess., 1967.

Shaffer, Marguerite S. *See America First: Tourism and National Identity, 1880–1940.* Washington, DC: Smithsonian Institution Press, 2001.

"Shall We Lock it up?" *Western Conservation Journal* 15(1): 4–7 (January–February 1958).

Shankland, Robert. *Steve Mather of the National Parks.* 3rd ed. New York: Alfred A. Knopf, 1970.

"Showdown at Miner's Ridge." *Wild Cascades*, December 1966–January 1967.

Sieker, John. "Farewell to the Wilderness." *Living Wilderness* 5(5): 19.

Sierra Club and North Cascades Conservation Council. *Our Greatest National Park?* (pamphlet). January 1959.

Simmons, Terry Allan. "The Damnation of a Dam: The High Ross Dam Controversy." Master's thesis, Simon Fraser University, May 1974.

Simons, David R. *The Need for Scenic Resource Conservation in the Northern Cascades of Washington.* San Francisco: Sierra Club Conservation Committee, Northern Cascades Subcommittee, 1958.

"Skyscraper Country." *Sunset*, August 1958.

Smith, Allan H. *Ethnography of the North Cascades.* Center for Anthropology, Project Report No. 7. Pullman: Washington State University, 1988.

Smith, George Otis. "The Mount Baker Mining District." *Engineering and Mining Journal* 73 (March 15, 1902), 379–80.

Smith, Thomas G. "John Kennedy, Stewart Udall, and New Frontier Conservation." *The Pacific Historical Quarterly* 64:3 (August 1995): 329–62.

Sommarstrom, Allan. "Wild Land Preservation Crisis: The North Cascades Controversy." PhD diss., University of Washington, 1970.

Sowards, Adam. "Confronting Kennecott in the Cascades." Poster presented at the annual meeting of the American Society for Environmental History, Seattle, WA, April 2016.

————. "Protecting American Lands with Justice William O. Douglas." *The George Wright Forum* 32(2): 165–73 (2015).

State of Washington, Department of Highways. *Highway Across Cascade Mountains, Skagit and Okanogan Counties, Report to the 1947 Legislature.* Olympia, WA: January 1947.

Steel, W.G. "Lake Chelan and the Valley of the Stehekin." *Oregon Native Son* 1(3): 407–15 (January 1900).

Steele, Richard F. *An Illustrated History of Stevens, Ferry, Okanogan and Chelan Counties, State of Washington.* Spokane: Western Historical Publishing Company, 1904.

Steen, Harold K. *The Chiefs Remember: The Forest Service, 1952–2001.* Durham, NC: Forest History Society, 2004.

———. *The U.S. Forest Service: A History.* Seattle: University of Washington Press, 1976.

Stein, Alan J. "Century 21–The Seattle World's Fair, Part I." *HistoryLink*, April 18, 2000. historylink.org/File/2290.

———. "Century 21–The Seattle World's Fair, Part II." *HistoryLink*, April 19, 2000, historylink.org/File/2291.

Steury, Tim. "Of Time and Wildness in the North Cascades." *Washington State University Magazine.* wsm.wsu.edu/s/index.php?id=764.

Stone, Carol M. *Stehekin: Glimpses of the Past.* Friday Harbor, WA: Long House Printcrafters and Publishers, 1983.

Stone, J. Herbert. "Glacier Peak Wilderness Proposal (1959)." *Living Wilderness* 24(70): 10–13 (Autumn 1959).

Strong, Douglas H. *Dreamers and Defenders: American Conservationists.* Rev. ed. Lincoln: University of Nebraska Press, 1988.

Suiter, John. *Poets on the Peaks: Gary Snyder, Philip Whalen & Jack Kerouac in the North Cascades.* Washington, DC: Counterpoint, 2002.

Sutter, Paul S. *Driven Wild: How the Fight Against Automobiles Launched the Modern Wilderness Movement.* Seattle: University of Washington Press, 2002.

Swain, Donald C. "Harold Ickes, Horace Albright, and the Hundred Days: A Study in Conservation Administration." *Pacific Historical Review* 34(4): 455–65 (November 1965).

———. "The National Park Service and the New Deal, 1933–1940." *Pacific Historical Review* 41(3): 312–32 (August 1972).

Tabor, Rowland, and Ralph Haugerud, *Geology of the North Cascades: A Mountain Mosaic.* Seattle: The Mountaineers, 1999.

Thompson, Erwin N. *North Cascades N. P., Ross Lake N.R.A. & Lake Chelan N.R.A. History Basic Data.* N.p.: Department of the Interior, National Park Service, Office of History and Historic Architecture, Eastern Service Center, 1970.

Thompson, Margaret. "For A National Park in the High Cascades." Speech delivered to the Washington State Federation of Women's Clubs District Convention, Yakima, WA, November 2, 1940.

———. "A National Park in the Cascades." *The Northwest Conservationist* 2(2): 20–23 (April–June 1939).

———. "Shall We Have a Cascade Icy Peaks Park?" *Puget Sounder*, February 1939.

"Three Great Western Wildernesses: What Must be Done to Save Them?" *Living Wilderness* 1(1): 9–11 (September 1935).

Tillinghast, Isaac F. "Camping on Lake Chelan." *Northwest Illustrated Monthly* 9(4): 5–8.

Trip, Dode, and Sherburne F. Cook Jr. *Washington State Art and Artists, 1850–1950.* Olympia, WA: Sherburne Antiques and Fine Art, 1992.

Tschirley, Paul R., and Oliver H. Heintzelman. "The Case for Recreation in the Stehekin Watershed." *National Parks* 32(135): 147–52 (October–December 1958).

Turner, James Morton. *The Promise of Wilderness: American Environmental Politics Since 1964.* Seattle: University of Washington Press, 2012.

Udall, Stewart L. *The Quiet Crisis.* New York: Holt, Rinehart, and Winston, 1963.

———. Transcript, Oral History Interview by Joe B. Frantz. Internet Copy. Austin: Lyndon B. Johnson Presidential Library, December 16, 1969.

"Update: North Cascades Grizzly Bear Restoration EIS." *Western Wildlife.* westernwildlife.org/update-north-cascades-grizzly-bear-restoration-eis-public-process-from-nps-and-usfws.

U.S. Geological Survey. "Glacier Peak." February 2, 2015. volcanoes.usgs.gov/volcanoes/glacier_peak.

———. "Glacier Peak–History and Hazards of a Cascade Volcano." May 24, 2005. pubs.usgs.gov/fs/2000/fs058-00.

U.S. House Committee on Public Lands. *Mount Baker National Park, Washington.* 64th Cong., 2nd sess., 1916. H. Rpt. 1372.

U.S. Senate Committee on Energy and Natural Resources. *The Wildfire Management Act of 2015: A White Paper.* June 15, 2015. www.energy.senate.gov/public/index.cfm/files/serve?File_id=0ab5f328-f73a-49da-b1b4-814d31b215bd.

U.S. Statutes at Large 39 (1917): 535–36. *National Park Service Organic Act.*

Van Name, Willard. *Vanishing Forest Reserves.* Boston: The Gorham Press, 1929.

Verne, Jules. *The Begum's Fortune.* 1879; reprint, New York: Ace Books, 1958.

Walker, Wendy. "Finding My Way Home." In *Impressions of the North Cascades: Essays About a Northwest Landscape,* edited by John Miles. Seattle: The Mountaineers, 1996, 108–22.

Wall, Brian R. "Log Production in Washington and Oregon: An Historical Perspective." Portland, OR: Pacific Northwest Forest and Range Experiment Station, USDA Forest Service 1972. www.fs.fed.us/pnw/pubs/pnw_rb042.pdf.

Warth, John F. "The Glacier Peak Wilderness." *National Parks* 30(127): 173–76, 193–94 (October–December 1956).

Washington Park Wilderness Act of 1988. Public Law 100-668, 100th Cong., 2nd sess. November 16, 1988.

Washington State Department of Fish & Wildlife. "Compensation Rules for Depredation Incidents." *Gray Wolf Conservation and Management.* wdfw.wa.gov/conservation/gray_wolf/livestock/compensation.html.

———. "Washington Wolf Population Continues to Grow." *About WDFW.* March 14, 2016. wdfw.wa.gov/news/mar1416b.

Washington State Department of Natural Resources. *2015 Wildland Fire Summary.* file.dnr.wa.gov/publications/em_wildfire_summary_2015.pdf.

Washington State Department of Transportation. Stehekin State Airport www.wsdot.wa.gov/aviation/AllStateAirports/Stehekin_StehekinState.htm.

Washington State Legislature. Joint Memorial No. 2. January 29, 1917.

———. Senate Joint Memorial No. 21. March 29, 1967.

Washington State Office of Financial Management. "Historical Estimates of April 1 Population and Housing for the State, Counties, and Cities: Decennial Census Counts." ofm.wa.gov/pop/april1/hseries/default.asp.

Washington State Planning Council. *Cascade Mountains Study* [pamphlet]. Olympia, WA: State Planning Council, 1940.

Washington State Wilderness Act of 1984. Public Law 98-339, 98th Cong., 2nd sess. 3 July 1984.

Washington Trails Association. *Signpost* (blog). www.wta.org/signpost.

Washington Wild. "Conservation Groups Applaud New Wilderness Designation." wawild.org/wp-content/uploads/Thunder-Creek-Potential-Wilderness-Release-091412-FINAL.pdf.

"Washington Wolf Population Continues to Grow." *About WDFW*, March 14, 2016. wdfw.wa.gov/news/mar1416b.

Watkins, T. H. *Righteous Pilgrim: The Life and Times of Harold L. Ickes, 1874-1952*. New York: Henry Holt and Company, 1990.

"What They're Saying About the North Cascades—the Book and the Park." *Wild Cascades*, August–September 1964.

Whisenhunt, Donald. *The Environment and the American Experience*. Port Washington, NY: Kennikat Press, 1974.

Who's Who Among Pacific Northwest Authors. Hazel E. Mills, ed. Pacific Northwest Library Association, Reference Section, 1957.

Wild and Scenic Rivers Act. Public Law 90-542, 90th Cong., 2nd sess. October 2, 1968.

The Wilderness Act. Public Law 88-577, U.S. Code 16 (1964).

"Wilderness Area Status Reviewed." *Western Forester* 3(4), January 1958.

"The Wilderness in the North Cascades." *Wild Cascades* June–July 1964, 11–19.

"Wilderness Society Council." *Living Wilderness* 22(62): 35 (Autumn 1957).

"Wilderness Society Council Meets." *Living Wilderness* 23(66): 39–42 (Autumn 1958).

Williams, Gerald W. "National Monuments and the Forest Service." November 2003. www.nps.gov/parkhistory/online_books/fs/monuments.htm.

———. *The U.S. Forest Service in the Pacific Northwest: A History*. Corvallis: Oregon State University Press, 2009.

———. *The Forest Service: Fighting for Public Lands*. Westport, CT: Greenwood Press, 2007.

Williams, Michael. *Americans and Their Forests: A Historical Geography*. Cambridge: University of Cambridge Press, 1989.

Willis, Margaret, ed. *Chechacos All: The Pioneering of Skagit*. Mount Vernon, WA: Skagit Valley Historical Society, 1973.

Wilma, David. "Upper Skagit River Hydroelectric Project." *HistoryLink*. March 3, 2003. www.historylink.org/File/5347.

Wingo, Hal. "Knight Errant to Nation's Rescue." *Life* 60(21): 37–40 (May 27, 1966).

Woodhouse, Philip R. *Monte Cristo*. Seattle: The Mountaineers, 1979.

Worster, Donald. *The Wealth of Nature: Environmental History and the Ecological Imagination*. New York: Oxford University Press, 1993.

Zahniser, Howard. "Wilderness in the Cascades." *Living Wilderness* 21(58): n.p.

Zalesky, Philip H. "In Memoriam: Jane McConnell." *Wild Cascades*, Spring 1998.

————. "The Mountaineers: A Story of Conservation" (unpublished manuscript, 1993). Collection of the author.

Archival Sources

Brooks, Richard J. Papers. Manuscripts and University Archives Division. University of Washington Libraries, Seattle.

Clark, Irving M. Papers. Manuscripts and University Archives Division. University of Washington Libraries, Seattle.

Development and Maintenance Subject Group Records. Mount Rainier National Park Archives, Ashford, WA.

Dyer, Polly. Papers. Manuscripts and University Archives Division. University of Washington Libraries, Seattle.

Early Washington Maps. Digital Collection. Washington State University Library, Pullman.

Evans, Brock. Papers. Manuscripts and University Archives Division. University of Washington Libraries, Seattle.

Evans, Daniel J. Papers. Washington State Archives, Olympia.

Game Department Records. Washington State Archives, Olympia.

Goldsworthy, Patrick D. Papers. Private Collection (now at University of Washington Manuscripts and Special Collections). Used by permission.

Haig, Emily. Papers. Manuscripts and University Archives Division. University of Washington Libraries, Seattle.

Jackson, Henry M. Papers. Manuscripts and University Archives Division. University of Washington Libraries, Seattle.

Macy, Preston. Papers. Manuscripts and University Archives Division. University of Washington Libraries, Seattle.

Magnuson, Donald H. Papers. Manuscripts and University Archives Division. University of Washington Libraries, Seattle.

Magnuson, Warren G. Papers. Manuscripts and University Archives Division. University of Washington Libraries, Seattle.

Manning, Harvey. Papers. Manuscripts and University Archives Division. University of Washington Libraries, Seattle.

McConnell, Grant. Papers. Manuscripts and University Archives Division. University of Washington Libraries, Seattle.

Mountaineers Conservation Committee. Papers. Manuscripts and University Archives Division. University of Washington Libraries, Seattle.

North Cascades National Park Service Complex Museum Collection, Marblemount.

Osseward, John. Papers. Manuscripts and University Archives Division. University of Washington Libraries, Seattle.

Overly, Fred. Papers. Manuscripts and University Archives Division. University of Washington Libraries, Seattle.

Pelly, Thomas M. Papers. Manuscripts and University Archives Division. University of Washington Libraries, Seattle.

Records of the National Park Service. Pacific Northwest Region. Recreation Planning Records. Record Group 79. National Archives and Records Administration—Alaska Pacific Region (Seattle).

Records of the Office of the Secretary of the Interior. Record Group 48. National Archives and Records at College Park, MD.

Records of the United States Forest Service. Record Group 95. National Archives and Records Administration—Alaska Pacific Region (Seattle).

Rosellini, Albert D. Papers. Washington State Archives, Olympia.

Seattle Photograph Collection. Manuscripts and University Archives Division. University of Washington Libraries, Seattle.

Sierra Club Records. Bancroft Library, Berkeley.

Transportation Records. Washington State Archives, Olympia.

Warth, John. Papers. Manuscripts and University Archives Division. University of Washington Libraries, Seattle.

Washington (State) Board of State Road Commissioners Reports. Washington State Library, Tumwater.

Washington State Highways Department Records. Washington State Archives, Olympia.

Washington State Planning Council Records. Washington State Archives, Olympia.

Wilderness Society Records. Denver Public Library.

Udall, Stewart L. Papers. Special Collections. University of Arizona Library, Tucson.

U.S. Senate Records, Senate Committee on Interior and Insular Affairs. National Archives Building, Washington, DC.

Zalesky, Philip. Papers. Manuscripts and University Archives Division. University of Washington Libraries, Seattle.

Personal Interviews

Buscher, Richard. Tigard, OR, October 18, 2003.

Chriswell, Harold "Chris." Bellingham, WA, February 26, 2003.

Goldsworthy, Patrick. Seattle, WA, February 6, 2003.

Manning, Harvey. Issaquah, WA, September 30, 2003.

McCloskey, J. Michael. Portland, OR, May 3, 2003.

Zalesky, Philip and Laura. Everett, WA, January 27, 2003.

Index